Communications
in Computer and Information Science   524

More information about this series at http://www.springer.com/series/7899

Javier Bajo · Kasper Hallenborg
Pawel Pawlewski · Vicente Botti
Nayat Sánchez-Pi · Néstor Darío Duque Méndez
Fernando Lopes · Vicente Julian (Eds.)

Highlights of Practical Applications of Agents, Multi-Agent Systems, and Sustainability

The PAAMS Collection

International Workshops of PAAMS 2015
Salamanca, Spain, June 3–4, 2015
Proceedings

 Springer

Editors

Javier Bajo
Departamento de Inteligencia Artificial
Universidad Politécnica de Madrid
Madrid
Spain

Kasper Hallenborg
University of Southern Denmark
Odense
Denmark

Pawel Pawlewski
Faculty of Engineering Management
Poznan University
Poznan
Poland

Vicente Botti
Departamento de Sistemas Informáticos
    y Computación
Polytechnic University of Valencia
Valencia
Spain

Nayat Sánchez-Pi
Fluminense Federal University
Rio de Janeiro
Brazil

Néstor Darío Duque Méndez
Universidad Nacional de Colombia
Manizales, Caldas
Colombia

Fernando Lopes
Lab. Nacional de Energia e Geologia
Lisbon
Portugal

Vicente Julian
Universidad Politécnica de Valencia
Valencia
Spain

ISSN 1865-0929   ISSN 1865-0937   (electronic)
Communications in Computer and Information Science
ISBN 978-3-319-19032-7   ISBN 978-3-319-19033-4   (eBook)
DOI 10.1007/978-3-319-19033-4

Library of Congress Control Number: 2015938740

Springer Cham Heidelberg New York Dordrecht London

Printed on acid-free paper

Springer International Publishing AG Switzerland is part of Springer Science+Business Media
(www.springer.com)

Preface

PAAMS 2015 Workshops complement the regular program with new or emerging trends of particular interest connected to multi-agent systems.

PAAMS, the International Conference on Practical Applications of Agents and Multi-Agent Systems, is an evolution of the International Workshop on Practical Applications of Agents and Multi-Agent Systems. PAAMS is an international yearly tribune to present, to discuss, and to disseminate the latest developments and the most important outcomes related to real-world applications. It provides a unique opportunity to bring multi-disciplinary experts, academics, and practitioners together to exchange their experience in the development of Agents and Multi-Agent Systems.

This volume presents the papers that have been accepted in the workshops during the 2015 edition of PAAMS: Workshop on Agents and multi-agent Systems for AAL and e-HEALTH; Workshop on Agent-Based Solutions for Manufacturing and Supply Chain; Workshop on MAS for Complex Networks and Social Computation; Workshop on Intelligent Systems for Context-based Information Fusion; Workshop on Multi-agent based Applications for Smart Grids and Sustainable Energy Systems; Workshop on Multiagent System Based Learning Environments; Workshop in Intelligent Human-Agent Societies. Each paper submitted to PAAMS workshops went through a stringent peer-review by three members of the International committee of each workshop. From the 91 submissions received, 36 were selected for presentation at the conference.

We would like to thank all the contributing authors, as well as the members of the Program Committees of the workshops and the Organizing Committee for their hard and highly valuable work. Their work has helped to contribute to the success of the PAAMS 2015 event. Thank you for your help, PAAMS 2015 wouldn't exist without your contribution.

June 2015   Javier Bajo

Organization

Workshops

W1 – Workshop on Agents and multi-agent Systems for AAL and e-HEALTH
W2 – Workshop on Agent-Based Solutions for Manufacturing and Supply Chain
W3 – Workshop on MAS for Complex Networks and Social Computation
W4 – Workshop on Intelligent Systems for Context-based Information Fusion
W5 – Workshop on Multi-agent based Applications for Smart Grids and Sustainable Energy Systems
W6 – Workshop on Multiagent System based Learning Environments
W7 – Workshop on Intelligent Human-Agent Societies

Workshop on Agents and Multi-agent Systems for AAL and e-HEALTH Committee

Program Committee Chairs

Kasper Hallenborg   University of Southern Denmark, Denmark
  (Co-chairman)
Sylvain Giroux   University of Sherbrooke, Canada
  (Co-chairman)

Program Committee

Juan M. Corchado	University of Salamanca, Spain
Javier Bajo	Technical University of Madrid, Spain
Juan F. De Paz	University of Salamanca, Spain
Sara Rodríguez	University of Salamanca, Spain
Valerie Camps	University Paul Sabatier of Toulouse, France
Cristian I. Pinzón	Technical University of Panama, Panama
Sigeru Omatu	Osaka Institute of Technology, Japan
Paulo Novais	University of Minho, Portugal
Luis F. Castillo	University of Caldas, Colombia
Florentino Fernández	University of Vigo, Spain
Belén Pérez Lancho	University of Salamanca, Spain
Jesús García Herrero	University Carlos III of Madrid, Spain
Helena Lindgren	Umeå University, Sweden
Goretti Marreiros	Instituto Superior de Engenharia do Porto, Portugal
Gaetano Carmelo La Delfa	University of Catania, Italy
Tiancheng Li	Northwestern Polytechnical University, China

Workshop on Agent-Based Solutions for Manufacturing and Supply Chain Committee

Program Committee Chairs

Pawel Pawlewski   Poznan University of Technology, Poland
Patrycja Hoffa   Poznan University of Technology, Poland

Program Committee

Zbigniew J. Pasek   IMSE/University of Windsor, Canada
Paul-Eric Dossou   ICAM Vendée, France
Grzegorz Bocewicz   Koszalin University of Technology, Poland
Paweł Sitek   Kielce University of Technology, Poland
Izabela E. Nielsen   Aalborg University, Denmark
Joanna Kolodziej   Cracow University of Technology, Poland
Peter Nielsen   Aalborg University, Denmark
Allen Greenwood   Mississippi State University, USA

Workshop on MAS for Complex Networks and Social Computation

Program Committee Chairs

Vicente Botti   Universitat Politècnica de València, Spain
Miguel Rebollo   Universitat Politècnica de València, Spain
Elena Del Val   Universitat Politècnica de València, Spain
Alberto Palomares Universitat Politècnica de València, Spain

Program Committee

Daniel Villatoro   BBVA Data & Analytics, Spain
Carlos Carrascosa   Universitat Politècnica de València, Spain
Vicente Julián Inglada   Universitat Politècnica de València, Spain
Guillem Martínez   Universitat de València, Spain
Francisco Grimaldo   Universitat de València, Spain
Didac Busquets   Imperial College London, UK
Giulia Andrighetto   CNR, Italy
Andrea Omicini   Alma Mater Studiorum-Università di Bologna,
                          Italy
Katarzyna Musial-Gabrys   King's College London, UK
Jordi Herrera   Universitat Autònoma de Barcelona, Spain
Juan José Ramasco   Institute for Cross-Disciplinary Physics and
                          Complex Systems (IFISC), Spain
Juan Miguel Alberola   Universitat Politècnica de València, Spain
Sascha Ossowski   Universidad Rey Juan Carlos, Spain

Workshop on Intelligent Systems for Context-Based Information Fusion Committee

Program Committee Chairs

José Manuel Molina	University Carlos III of Madrid, Spain
Juan M. Corchado	University of Salamanca, Spain
Nayat Sánchez Pi	Universidade Federal Fluminense, Brazil
Jesús García Herrero	University Carlos III of Madrid, Spain
Gabriel Villarrubia González	University of Salamanca, Spain
Javier Bajo	Technical University of Madrid, Spain
Ana Cristina Bicharra García	Universidade Federal Fluminense, Brazil
Luis Marti	Pontificia Universidade Católica, Brazil
James Llinas	State University of New York at Buffalo, USA

Program Committee

Jesús Garcia Herrero	University Carlos III of Madrid, Spain
James Llinas	State University of New York at Buffalo, USA
Javier Bajo	Technical University of Madrid, Spain
Juan F. De Paz	University of Salamanca, Spain
Sara Rodríguez	University of Salamanca, Spain
Fernando de la Prieta Pintado	University of Salamanca, Spain
Gabriel Villarrubia González	University of Salamanca, Spain
Antonio Juan Sánchez Martín	University of Salamanca, Spain
Miguel Angel Patricio	Universidad Carlos III de Madrid, Spain
Antonio Berlanga	Universidad Carlos III de Madrid, Spain
Lauro Snidaro	University of Udine, Italy
Éloi Bossé	Université Laval, Canada
Subrata Das	Machine Analytics, Inc., USA
Vicente Julian	Technical University of Valencia, Spain
Eugenio Oliveira	University of Porto, Portugal
Florentino Fdez-Riverola	University of Vigo, Spain
Masanori Akiyoshi	Osaka University, Japan
Luís Lima	Polytechnic Institute of Porto, Portugal
Andrew Campbell	Dartmouth College, USA
Carlos Carrascosa	Technical University of Valencia, Spain
Ana Cristina Bicharra Garcia	Universidade Federal Fluminense, Brazil
Nayat Sánchez Pi	Universidade Federal Fluminense, Brazil
Luis Marti	Pontificia Universidade Católica, Brazil
Eleni Mangina	University College Dublin, Ireland
Luís Correia	University of Lisbon, Portugal
Cristian Iván Pinzón Trejos	Universidad Tecnológica de Panamá, Panamá
Ana Cristina Bicharra García	Universidade Federal Fluminense, Brazil
Luiz André Paes Leme	Universidade Federal Fluminense, Brazil
José Viterbo Filho	Universidade Federal Fluminense, Brazil

Marley Velasco	Pontifícia Universidade Católica, Brazil
Lyudmila Mihaylova	Lancaster University, UK
Joachim Biermann	FKIE, Germany
Kellyn Rein	FKIE, Germany
Eric Little	Modus Operandi, USA

Workshop on Multi-agent Based Applications for Smart Grids and Sustainable Energy Systems Committee

Program Committee Chairs

Fernando Lopes	LNEG National Research Institute, Portugal
Rainer Unland	University of Duisburg-Essen, Germany

Steering Committee

Fernando Lopes	LNEG National Research Institute, Portugal
Giancarlo Fortino	Università della Calabria, Italy
Hugo Morais	Technical University of Denmark, Denmark
Rainer Unland	University of Duisburg-Essen, Germany
Ryszard Kowalczyk	Swinburne University of Technology, Australia
Zita Vale	Polytechnic Institute of Porto Portugal

Program Committee

Alberto Fernández	Universidad Rey Juan Carlos, Spain
Anke Weidlich	Hochschule Offenburg, Germany
Bo Nørregaard Jørgensen	Mærsk Mc-Kinney Møller Instituttet, Denmark
Carlos Ramos	Polytechnic Institute of Porto, Portugal
Christian Derksen	Universität Duisburg-Essen, Germany
David Sislak	Gerstner Laboratory, Czech Republic
Fernando Lopes	LNEG National Research Institute, Portugal
Georg Frey	Universität des Saarlandes, Germany
Giancarlo Fortino	Università della Calabria, Italy
Huib Aldewereld	Universiteit Utrecht, The Netherlands
Hugo Algarvio	National Research Institute, Portugal
Hugo Morais	Technical University of Denmark, Denmark
Jan Treur	Vrije Universiteit Amsterdam, The Netherlands
Lars Braubach	University of Hamburg, Germany
Lars Mönch	FernUniversität Hagen, Germany
Marcin Paprzycki	Polish Academy of Sciences, Poland
Massimiliano Giacomin	University of Brescia, Italy
Mathijs de Weerdt	TU Delft, The Netherlands
Matthias Klusch	DFKI, Germany
Miguel Ángel López Carmona	University of Alcalá de Henares, Spain
Nick Bassiliades	Aristotle University of Thessaloniki, Greece
Nir Oren	University of Aberdeen, UK
Olivier Boissier	École Nationale Supérieure des Mines de Saint-Étienne, France

Paulo Leitão   Polytechnic Institute of Bragança, Portugal
Paulo Novais   Universidade do Minho, Portugal
Peter Palensky   AIT Austrian Institute of Technology, Austria
Rainer Unland   University of Duisburg-Essen, Germany
Ryszard Kowalczyk   Swinburne University of Technology, Australia
Sascha Ossowski   Universidad Rey Juan Carlos, Spain
Sudip Bhattacharjee   University of Connecticut, USA
Tiago Pinto   Polytechnic Institute of Porto, Portugal
Zita Vale   Polytechnic Institute of Porto, Portugal

Workshop on Multiagent System Based Learning Environments

Program Committee Chairs

Ricardo Azambuja Silveira   Universidade Federal de Santa Catarina, Brazil
Rosa Vicari   Universidade Federal do Rio Grande do Sul, Brazil
Néstor Darío Duque Méndez   Universidad Nacional de Colombia, Colombia

Program Committee

Ricardo Azambuja Silveira   Universidade Federal de Santa Catarina, Brazil
Rosa Vicari   Universidade Federal do Rio Grande do Sul, Brazil
Néstor Darío Duque Méndez   Universidad Nacional de Colombia, Colombia
Carlos Vaz de Carvalho   Instituto Politécnico do Porto, Portugal
Cecília Dias Flores   Universidade Federal de Ciências da Saúde de
                                 Porto Alegre, Brazil
Cesar Alberto Collazos Ordoñez   Universidad del Cauca, Colombia
Demetrio Arturo Ovalle   Universidad Nacional de Colombia -
   Carranza   Sede Medellín, Colombia
João Carlos Gluz   Universidade dos Açores, Portugal
José Cascalho   Universidade dos Açores, Portugal
Julian Moreno Cadavid   Universidad Nacional de Colombia -
                                 Sede Medellín, Colombia
Martín Llamas Nistal   Universidade de Vigo, Spain
Néstor Darío Duque Méndez   Universidad Nacional de Colombia, Colombia
Patricia Jaques   Universidade do Vale do Rio dos Sinos, Brazil
Ramon Fabregat   Universidad de Girona, Spain
Ricardo Azambuja Silveira   Universidade Federal de Santa Catarina, Brazil
Rosa Vicari   Universidade Federal do Rio Grande do Sul, Brazil
Silvia Margarita Baldiris   Universitat de Girona, Spain
   Navarro

Workshop on Intelligent Human-Agent Societies Committee

Program Committee Chairs

Vicente Julian   Universitat Politècnica de València, Spain
Holguer Bilhart   University Rey Juan Carlos, Spain
Juan M. Corchado   University of Salamanca, Spain

Program Committee

Olivier Boissier	École Nationale Supérieure des Mines de Saint-Étienne, France
Reyhan Aydogan	Delft University of Technology, The Netherlands
Sara Rodriguez	Universidad de Salamanca, Spain
Juan Antonio Rodriguez-Aguilar	IIIA-CSIC, Spain
Carles Sierra	IIIA-CSIC, Spain
Michael Ignaz Schumacher	University of Applied Sciences Western Switzerland, Switzerland
David Robertson	University of Edinburgh, UK
Kuldar Taveter	Tallinn University of Technology, Estonia
Jurgen Dunkel	Hannover University of Applied Sciences and Arts, Germany
Ramon Hermoso	University of Essex, UK
Javier Palanca	Universitat Politècnica de València, Spain
Stella Heras	Universitat Politècnica de València, Spain
Roberto Centeno	Universidad de Educación a Distancia, Spain
Alberto Fernández	University Rey Juan Carlos, Spain
Carlos Carrascosa	Universitat Politècnica de València, Spain
Miguel Rebollo	Universitat Politècnica de València, Spain

PAAMS 2015 Workshops Organizing Committee

Javier Bajo (Chair)	Technical University of Madrid, Spain
Juan F. De Paz	University of Salamanca, Spain
Sara Rodríguez	University of Salamanca, Spain
Fernando de la Prieta Pintado	University of Salamanca, Spain
Gabriel Villarrubia González	University of Salamanca, Spain
Javier Prieto Tejedor	University of Salamanca, Spain
Pablo Chamoso	University of Salamanca, Spain
Alberto López Barriuso	University of Salamanca, Spain

PAAMS 2015 Sponsors

IEEE Systems, Man and Cybernetics Society
Spain

AfIA
Association française
pour l'Intelligence Artificielle

Contents

Workshop on MAS for Complex Networks and Social Computation

Workshop on Intelligent Systems for Context-Based Information Fusion

Workshop on Multi-agent Based Applications for Smart Grids and Sustainable Energy Systems

Workshop on Multiagent System Based Learning Environments

Workshop in Intelligent Human-Agent Societies

Workshop on Agents and Multi-agent Systems for AAL and e-HEALTH

An Ambient Assisted Living Mobile Application for Helping People with Alzheimer

David Griol$^{(\boxtimes)}$ and José Manuel Molina

Computer Science Department, Carlos III University of Madrid,
Avda. de la Universidad, 30, 28911 Leganés, Spain
{david.griol,josemanuel.molina}@uc3m.es

Abstract. Ambient Assisted Living (AAL) systems must provide adapted services easily accessible by a wide variety of users. This can only be possible if the communication between the user and the system is carried out through an interface that is simple, rapid, effective, and robust. Natural language interfaces such as mobile multimodal conversational agents fulfill these requisites, as they can emulate communication capabilities of a human being including several communication modalities, such as speech, tactile and visual interaction. In this paper, we present a multimodal application for Android mobile devices aimed to patients suffering from Alzheimer. This application helps them to enhance their memory and to stimulate their cognitive abilities.

Keywords: Multimodal applications · Mobile devices · Android · Alzheimer · Cognitive capacity · Ambient Assisted Living

1 Introduction

Mutimodal conversational agents [1,2] and mobile devices have been proven useful for providing the general public with access to telemedicine services, promoting patients' involvement in their own care, assisting in health care delivery, supporting the elderly, and improving patient outcome [3]. Bickmore and Giorgino defined these systems as being "those automated systems whose primary goal is to provide health communication with patients or consumers primarily using natural language dialog" [3].

During the last two decades, these interfaces have been increasingly used in Ambient Assisted Living (AAL) providing services such as interviews [4], counseling [5,6], chronic symptoms monitoring [7], medication prescription assistance and adherence [8], changing dietary behavior [9], promoting physical activity [10], helping cigarette smokers quit [11], or speech therapy [12].

The remarkable rise in life expectancy during the last century has made Alzheimer's disease (AD) among the most common disorders of late life. An insidious loss of memory, cognition, reasoning, and behavioral stability leads inexorably to global dementia and premature death of the patient. The disease also implies an increasingly significant public health issue, with the number

© Springer International Publishing Switzerland 2015
J. Bajo et al. (Eds.): PAAMS 2015 Workshops, CCIS 524, pp. 3–14, 2015.
DOI: 10.1007/978-3-319-19033-4_1

of people living with AD projected to increase dramatically over the next few decades. Every year 4.6 million new cases of Alzheimer are detected.

Alzheimer's is characterized by the presence of cognitive disorders (memory disorders, aphasia, attention and concentration deficit disorders), physical problems (incontinence, weakness, slow down, and motor disabilities) and emotional and/or behavioral disorders (depression, anxiety, aggression, apathy, etc.). These disorders are treated by both non-pharmacological and pharmacological methods. Although no treatments stop or reverse its progression, exercise and cognitive programs are beneficial and potentially improve outcome.

In this paper, we describe a mobile application created for helping patients suffering from Alzheimer. Mobile devices programming has emerged as a new trend in software development. The main developers of operating systems for such devices have provided APIs for developers to implement their own applications, including different solutions for developing voice control. Currently the 75 % of smartphones and tablets operate with the Android OS [2].

Also, there is an active community of developers who use the Android Open Source Project and have made possible to have more than one million applications currently available at the official Play Store, many of them completely free. For these reasons, our framework makes use of different facilities integrated in Android-based devices. Android also offers libraries that can be employed to build more natural interaction with mobile devices particularly useful for the elderly and people with visual or motor disabilities, such as automatic speech recognition and text-to-speech synthesis.

The application allows accessing a wide range of exercises 24 h a day to try to preserve cognitive abilities as long as possible, slow the rapid course of the disease, and enhance patient relationship with its environment, trying to make it easier and bearable the long road that involves suffering from Alzheimer. Despite the increased use of mobile devices for personal and professional use, there are few rehabilitative purpose mobile applications designed for Alzheimer's patients. Most of them are only focused on specific functionalities, such as geolocation and tracking functionalities to locate patients who get lost, medication management and reminder, Alzheimers information and resources, memory and focus, relaxation, or enjoyment[1]. One of the main objectives of the developed application is to compile exercises with different complexity and main objectives specifically adapted to AD's patients, also ensuring an easy interaction with the application, the automatic correction, and the provision of an adequate feedback.

2   Developed Application

The developed application is mainly based on a detailed study of a large number of guides that collect exercises and activities carried out by AD's patients and caregivers to stimulate cognitive abilities [13–15]. In this respect, the main characteristic symptom is the loss of memory for recent events, preserving longer

---

[1] http://www.alzheimersblog.org.

Table 1. Summary of exercises collected from the bibliography

MEMORY	LANGUAGE
Immediate memory	**Oral language**
Repeat a word list.	Say the months, the seasons, or days of
Repeat words after hearing them.	the week.
Short-term memory	Complete numerical series.
Find pairs of images.	Say the name of the objects in different
Read a story and answer questions about it.	pictures.
Show a set pictures and try to remember as	Define words.
many as them as possible.	Say words that start with a letter or syllable.
Remember everyday events.	Complete word categories.
Long-term memory	Provide synonyms and antonyms.
Ask for personal information.	Use word association.
Ask for biographical memories.	Talk about topics of interest.
Remember places or people in the past life using	Try to describe photographs.
photographs or videos.	Repeat words, sentences, syllables, letters,
Talk about the previous profession, places	or numbers.
visited, school, children's games, etc.	Use simple commands to try to complete them.
Remember the past using objects.	Use body language to understand commands.
ORIENTATION	**Reading and writing**
Time orientation	Reading exercises.
Use a calendar to select the current day, month,	Reading comprehension.
and year.	Writing exercises (writing, dictation, copy
Decorate the environment according to the	sentences, etc.).
current season.	**PRAXIAS**
Perform parties, meetings or meals related to	**Ideomotor**
the current season.	Perform simple movements, such as brushing
Spatial orientation	teeth, combing hair, fastening up shirt, saying
Locate the city, address, etc.	hello.
Locate the different rooms of the house.	Imitate simple gestures.
Personal Guidance	**Ideational**
Complete a diary.	Perform a complete sequence of movements.
Make a family tree.	**Constructive**
ATTENTION	Complete a puzzle.
Search for specific elements among a group of	Copy drawings or figures.
varied elements.	Complete incomplete figures.
Search a specific element in a photograph.	Draw simple figures.
Find the differences between two images.	Copy symmetries.
Solve mazes.	**Calculation**
GNOSIA	Solve mathematical problems.
Sight	Simulate purchase calculations.
Recognize graphic or images.	Perform simple accounts.
Recognize images by looking at its shadow	Sort numbers.
or outline.	Recognize odd and even numbers.
Recognize letters and numbers.	Count in twos, threes or subtract.
Discriminate figure-ground.	Count from 1 to 10 or vice versa.
Recognize colors from a list of them.	Use games like bingo or Parcheesi.
Say the name of the color that is described.	**Body schema**
Classify objects depending on their color, shape	Touch different parts of the body.
or size.	Use instructions to do with the different parts
Recognize faces.	of the body.
Recognize facial expressions.	Select the different parts of the body using
Hearing	images.
Recognize sounds.	Identify where every garment is placed.
Remember and imitate different sounds.	
Recognize songs.	

memories, such as the youth and childhood memories. As the disease progresses, different disorders are related to language, attention, recognition, understanding and implementation of actions. Table 1 summarizes the different categories and types of exercises defined for the developed application after the study of the related bibliography and studies.

The developed application, which is accessible using desktop and mobile devices, provides multimodal interaction instead of usually mediated simple text-based forms interaction, including spoken access and a visual and tactile representation. Automatic Speech recognition (ASR) has been implemented by means of the Google Speech API (package *android.speech*). Using this package, spoken interaction can be carried out by means on a *RecognizerIntent*, or by creating an instance of *SpeechRecognizer*. The former starts the intent and process its results to complete the recognition, providing feedback to the user to inform that the ASR is ready or there were errors during the recognition process. The latter provides developers with different notifications of recognition related events, thus allowing a more fine-grained processing of the speech recognition process. Natural Language Understanding (NLU) to obtain the semantic interpretation of the user inputs is carried using very easy grammars that provides the sentences that are required in the corresponding exercises. The *android.speech.tts* package includes the classes and interfaces required to integrate Text-To-Speech synthesis (TTS) in an Android application. They allow the initialization of the TTS engine, a callback to return speech data synthesized by a TTS engine, and control the events related to completing and starting the synthesis of an utterance, among other functionalities.

The visual arrangement of the contents uses dynamically created and filled graphical layout elements (such as buttons, text fields, checkboxes, radio buttons, toggle buttons, spinners, and pickers). Since many objects can be shown at the same time on the display, the system re-arranges the objects on the screen and removes objects, if necessary. The visual structure of the user interface (UI) is defined in an Android-based multimodal application by means of layouts. Layouts can be defined by declaring UI elements in XML or instantiating layouts elements at runtime. Both alternatives can be combined in order to declare the application's default layouts in XML and add code that would modify the state of the screen objects at run time. Declaring the UI allows to better separate the presentation of the application from the code that controls its behavior.

The proposals for the development of the different modules of the application eases the construction of the application by isolating rehabilitation from the technical detail, so that caregivers and parents can add, delete, or modify new contents and exercises in the different folders of the categories without having a technical background at the same time as the software includes these new data for the interaction with the patients. The following subsections describe the main modules and types of practical exercises provided by the application.

2.1 Memory Module

Memory loss is the main symptom of this disease. Several types of memory are affected during the course of this disease (immediate memory, short-term memory, long-term memory, working memory, episodic memory, semantic memory, and procedural memory). The first type of exercise in this module is divided into two parts, the first part proposes reading a text (Fig. 1, first) and the second part requires to answer several questions about it (Fig. 1, second).

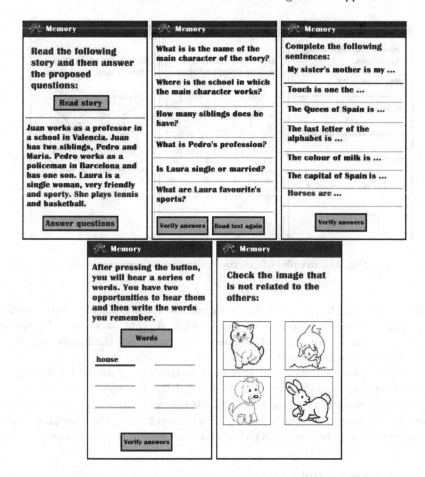

Fig. 1. Examples of exercises in the memory module

The second type of exercise (Fig. 1, third) is based on a series of unfinished sentences that must be correctly completed. The objective of this exercise is to develop long-term memory, given that the sentences try to recall distant events, situations that comes everyday but the patient learned many years ago, etc. The third type of exercise is based on a series of words reproduced by the text-to-speech synthesizer, which must be correctly written below (Fig. 1, fourth). This exercise is related to the immediate memory. The last exercise of this category is related to long-term memory. The exercise shows four images, one of which is not related to the other (Fig. 1, fifth).

2.2 Orientation Module

Another main symptom of Alzheimer's disease is the disorientation at three main levels. In the first stage of the disease (disorientation), the patient begins

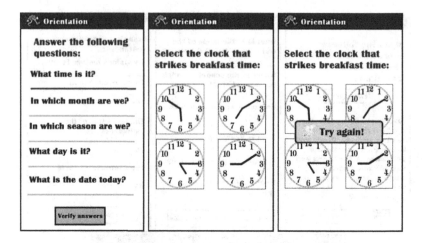

Fig. 2. Examples of exercises in the orientation module

to not recognizing the current date. In the second stage (spatial disorientation), the patient begins to become disoriented while driving or walking by spaces that are not familiar. In moderate stages, the patient loses the knowledge about themselves (personal disorientation).

The first type of exercise in this module consists of answering five questions related to temporal disorientation (Fig. 2, left). The second type of exercise (Fig. 2, center and right) is also related to the temporal orientation. The exercise presents four images showing a clock with a different time. The user must select the image showing the time in which a described action is usually carried on.

2.3 Attention Module

Attention, which can be defined as the ability to voluntarily apply understanding to a target and refer to, is also impaired by the disease. The first type of exercise in this module requires ordering a set of 12 images (Fig. 3, left and center). The images can be dragged to place them in the correct position. In the second type of exercises three different types of images are shown (Fig. 3, right). Images with the features required by the exercise must be chosen.

2.4 Gnosia Module

Gnosia can be defined as the ability to recognize the world around us through different senses. The disease causes the non-recognition of faces, colors, shapes, perspectives, sounds, smells, tastes, objects and associated functions.

In the first type of exercise of this module (Fig. 4, left), the objective is to first select the required specific color and then write the color corresponding to daily objects. In the second type of exercise, the objective is to select the mood of the person depicted in the image (Fig. 4, center). The last type of exercise

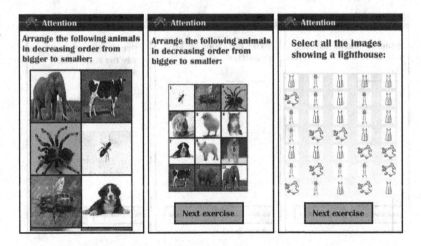

Fig. 3. Examples of exercises in the attention module

Fig. 4. Examples of exercises in the gnosia module

requires selecting the group of images corresponding to the category described in the exercise (Fig. 4, right).

2.5 Language Module

The alteration of language, increasingly less rich and fluid, is another characteristic symptoms of Alzheimer's disease. This affects oral and written language (troubles finding the right words in a conversation, difficulties to repeat words, change the words from other similarly sounding, etc.). The patient not only has problems with expressive language, but also with its understanding.

The main objective of the first exercise in this module is to write 10 different words starting with the given letter (Fig. 5, left). The second exercise requires

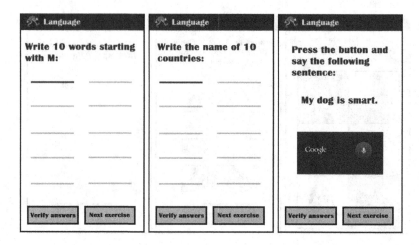

Fig. 5. Examples of exercises in the language module

writing 10 words fulfilling the given condition (Fig. 5, center). The last type of exercise uses the Automatic Speech Recognizer to require reading the sentence that is shown at the screen (Fig. 5, right).

2.6   Executive Functions Module

The decreased ability of praxia (ideomotor, ideational, and constructive) makes impossible to perform simple gestures, to make an appropriate use of everyday objects, and reduce writing and drawing skills, the capabilities for completing puzzles, etc. The capacity calculation or conception of the body, position and its parts also deteriorates.

In the first type of exercise in this module (Fig. 6, left) a series of dominoes has to be continued with the correct option. The second type of exercise consists of dragging coins required for the amount described in the exercise (Fig. 6, center). The third type of exercise (Fig. 6, right) consists of arranging 6 jumbled images that form a story.

3   Preliminary Evaluation

A preliminary evaluation of the developed application has been already completed with the participation of 6 caregivers, who rated the naturalness and rehabilitative potential of the system. The questionnaire shown in Table 2 was defined for the evaluation. The responses to the questionnaire were measured on a five-point Likert scale ranging from 1 (strongly disagree) to 5 (strongly agree). The experts were also asked to rate the system from 0 (minimum) to 10 (maximum) and there was an additional open question to write comments or remarks.

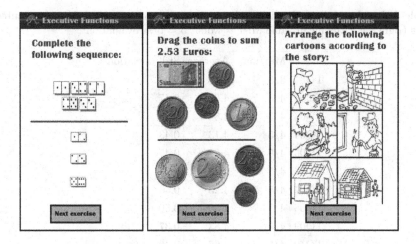

Fig. 6. Examples of exercises in the executive functions module

Table 2. Questionnaire designed for the evaluation of the application with caregivers

Technical quality
TQ01. The system offers enough interactivity
TQ02. The system is easy to use
TQ03. It is easy to know what to do at each moment
TQ04. The amount of information that is displayed on the screen is adequate
TQ05. The arrangement of information on the screen is logical
TQ06. The system is helpful
TQ07. The system is attractive
TQ08. The system reacts in a consistent way
TQ09. The system complements the activities without distracting or interfering with them
TQ010. The system provides adequate verbal feedback
TQ011. The system provides adequate non-verbal feedback
Rehabilitative potential
RP01. The system fulfills the objective of helping patients suffering from Alzheimer's
RP02. The contents worked in the activities are relevant for this objective
RP03. The design of the activities was adequate for these patients
RP04. The activities support significant cognitive abilities
RP05. The feedback provided by the system improves understanding
RP06. The system encourages continuing using it after errors

The results of this questionnaire are summarized in Table 3 (top). As can be observed from the responses to the questionnaire, the satisfaction with technical aspects was high, as well as the perceived potential to stimulate cognitive abilities. The application was considered attractive and adequate and the caregivers felt that the system is appropriate and the activities relevant. The global rate for the system was 8.6 (in the scale from 0 to 10).

Table 3. Results of the evaluation of the application by caregivers (left) and recruited users (right). For the mean value M: 1 = worst, 5 = best evaluation

	Min/max	Average	Std. deviation
TQ01	3/5	4.18	0.67
TQ02	4/5	4.67	0.47
TQ03	4/5	4.83	0.37
TQ04	4/5	4.13	0.43
TQ05	4/5	4.67	0.47
TQ06	4/5	4.83	0.37
TQ07	4/5	4.23	0.43
TQ08	4/5	4.50	0.50
TQ09	4/5	4.83	0.37
TQ10	4/5	4.67	0.46
TQ11	3/5	4.01	0.76
RP01	5/5	5.00	0.00
RP02	4/5	4.67	0.45
RP03	4/5	4.83	0.37
RP04	5/5	5.00	0.00
RP05	4/5	4.67	0.47
RP06	4/5	4.83	0.37
UQ1	4/5	4.56	0.47
UQ2	4/5	4.67	0.35
UQ3	4/5	4.12	0.58
UQ4	3/5	3.74	0.39
UQ5	3/5	3.49	0.51
UQ6	4/5	4.77	0.38
UQ7	3/5	4.02	0.27

Although the results were very positive, in the open question the caregivers also pointed out desirable improvements. One of them was to make the system listen constantly in spoken exercises instead of using the push-to-talk interface. However, we believe that this would cause many recognition problems, taking into account the range of exercises. Also, although they considered the contents useful and attractive and its feedback adequate.

We have already completed a preliminary evaluation of the application with 17 recruited users (avg. age 58.3, 10 male and 7 female) and a set of scenarios covering the different functionalities of the system. The total of users have previous knowledge about mobile devices, and more than half of them have previously worked with rehabilitative applications. We asked them to complete a questionnaire to assess their opinion about the interaction. The questionnaire had seven questions: (i) UQ1: *How well did the system understand you?*; (ii) UQ2: *How well did you understand the system messages?*; (iii) UQ3: *Was it easy for you to get the requested information?*; (iv) UQ4: *Was the interaction with the system quick enough?*; (v) UQ5: *If there were system errors, was it easy for you to correct them?*; (vi) UQ6: *Do the proposed activities support significant cognitive abilities?*; (vii) UQ7: *In general, are you satisfied with the performance of the system?* The possible answers for each questions were the same: *Never/Not at all, Seldom/In some measure, Sometimes/Acceptably, Usually/Well,* and *Always/Very Well.* All the answers were assigned a numeric value between one and five (in the same order as they appear in the questionnaire).

Table 3 (bottom) shows the average results of the subjective evaluation using the previous questions. It can be observed that the users perceived that the system understood them correctly. Moreover, they expressed a similar opinion regarding the easiness to understand the system responses. In addition, they assessed that it was easier to obtain the information specified for the different objectives, and that the interaction with the system was adequate and adapted to their preferences. An important point remarked by the users was related to the difficulty of correcting the errors and misunderstandings generated by the ASR and NLU processes in some scenarios. Finally, the satisfaction level also shows the correct operation of the system.

4   Conclusions

In this paper, we have described a mobile application created for helping patients suffering from Alzheimer. The application allows stimulating patients' cognitive abilities by means of different exercises organized into several categories. Such categories have been envisaged following a detailed study of the bibliography describing cognitive training and rehabilitation therapies for persons with different degrees of dementia.

Thanks to its multimodal interface, it provides the user combinations of input and output modalities to communicate with the system, which are particularly useful for the elderly and for people with visual or motor disabilities. This makes the application intuitive and handy, not only for people who suffer some form of dementia in the first or moderate phases, but also for informal caregivers (e.g. relatives), as well as the caregivers working in day centers for elderly.

Another important benefit of the application is its extensibility, as the proposed exercises are decoupled from the logic of the application, which facilitates the modification, deletion and incorporation of new exercises according to the patient's preferences and specific requirements.

We are currently undergoing the next phases in the deployment of the application. First, we want to conduct a comprehensive evaluation of the system's functionalities and different exercises with patients suffering from Alzheimer's. We also want to extend user awareness functionalities using a register to store the previous user's interactions with the application and adapting its operation according to their preferences, mistakes and advances in each of the categories.

With the results of these activities, we will optimize the system, and make it available the in Google Play, which will help to build a bigger user community that will allow to incorporate new exercises and experiences.

Acknowledgements. This work was supported in part by Projects MINECO TEC2012-37832-C02-01, CICYT TEC2011-28626-C02-02, CAM CONTEXTS (S2009/TIC-1485).

References

1. Pieraccini, R.: The Voice in the Machine: Building Computers that Understand Speech. MIT Press, Cambridge (2012)
2. McTear, M., Callejas, Z.: Voice Application Development for Android. Packt Publishing, Birmingham (2013)
3. Bickmore, T., Giorgino, T.: Health dialog systems for patients and consumers. J. Biomed. Inform. **39**(5), 556–571 (2006)
4. Pfeifer, L., Bickmore, T.: Designing embodied conversational agents to conduct longitudinal health interviews. In: Proceedings of IVA, pp. 4698–4703 (2010)
5. Hubal, R., Day, R.: Informed consent procedures: an experimental test using a virtual character in a dialog systems training application. J. Biomed. Inform. **39**, 532–540 (2006)
6. Glanz, K., Shigaki, D., Farzanfar, R., Pinto, B., Kaplan, B., Friedman, R.: Participant reactions to a computerized telephone system for nutrition and exercise counseling. Patient Educ. Couns. **49**, 157–163 (2003)
7. Migneault, J.P., Farzanfar, R., Wright, J., Friedman, R.: How to write health dialog for a talking computer. J. Biomed. Inform. **39**(5), 276–288 (2006)
8. Bickmore, T., Puskar, K., Schlenk, E., Pfeifer, L., Sereika, S.: Maintaining reality: relational agents for antipsychotic medication adherence. Interact. Comput. **22**, 276–288 (2010)
9. Delichatsios, H., Friedman, R., Glanz, K., Tennstedt, S., Smigelski, C., Pinto, B.: Randomized trial of a talking computer to improve adults eating habits. Am. J. Health Promot. **15**, 215–224 (2000)
10. Farzanfar, R., Frishkopf, S., Migneault, J., Friedman, R.: Telephone-linked care for physical activity: a qualitative evaluation of the use patterns of an information technology program for patients. Biomed. Inform. **38**, 220–228 (2005)
11. Ramelson, H., Friedman, R., Ockene, J.: An automated telephone-based smoking cessation education and counseling system. Patient Educ. Couns. **36**, 131–143 (1999)
12. Saz, O., Yin, S.C., Lleida, E., Rose, R., Vaquero, C., Rodrguez, W.R.: Tools and technologies for computer-aided speech and language therapy. Speech Commun. **51**(10), 948–967 (2009)
13. Williams, J., Plassman, B., Burke, J., Holsinger, T., Benjamin, S.: Preventing Alzheimer's Disease and Cognitive Decline. Evidence Report/Technology Assessment, Agency for Healthcare Research and Quality (2010)
14. Choi, J., Twamley, E.: Cognitive rehabilitation therapies for Alzheimer's disease: a review of methods to improve treatment engagement and self-efficacy. Neuropsychol. Rev. **23**(1), 48–62 (2013)
15. Bahar-Fuchs, A., Clare, L., Woods, B.: Cognitive training and cognitive rehabilitation for persons with mild to moderate dementia of the Alzheimer's or vascular type: a review. Alzheimer's Res. Ther. **5**(35), 1–14 (2013)

An Agent-Based Model for the Role of Social Support in Mood Regulation

A.H. Abro, M.C.A. Klein, and S.A. Tabatabaei[✉]

Artificial Intelligence Section, Vrije Universiteit Amsterdam, De Boelelaan 1081,
1081 HV Amsterdam, The Netherlands
{a.h.abro,michel.klein,s.tabatabaei}@vu.nl

Abstract. In this paper, a computational model of a human agent is presented which describes the effect of social support on mood. According to the literature, social support can either refer to the social resources that individuals perceive to be available or to the support that is actually provided in problematic situations. The proposed model distinguishes between both roles of social support. Simulation experiments are done to analyze the effect of the different types of support in different scenarios. It is shown that support can help to reduce the induced stress and thus can contribute to healthy mood regulation and prevention of depression. This presented model provides a basis for an intelligent support system for people with mood regulation problems that take the social network of people into account.

Keywords: Social support · Stress buffering · Human ambient agent

1 Introduction

Social support is one of the major factors that can help people in their life, especially during stressful events that may ultimately lead to depression. Social support plays a beneficial role in the mental wellbeing human beings through its impact on emotions, cognitions and behaviors [1], and through this even contributes to good physical health. Effective social support provided through adequate social networks can alleviate the effect of stress on an individual's psychological situation [2]. A person who is well integrated in social networks is less vulnerable to stress or depression.

Social support is often used in a broad sense, referring to any process through which social relationships might promote health and wellbeing. It is still a scientific questions by which mechanism the social support actually influences people's mental health. The psychological literature on social support and health includes multiple points of view, descriptions and effects. According to Gray et al. [3], subjective perception that support would be available if needed may reduce and prevent depression and unnecessary suffering. Literature [4, 5] differentiated structural and functional support measures. Structural supports refer to measures describing the existence and types of relationships (e.g. marital status, number of relationships). Functional support assesses whether interpersonal relationships serve particular functions (e.g. provide affection, feeling of belongings). According to Glanz et al. [6], social support is one of the important functions

© Springer International Publishing Switzerland 2015
J. Bajo et al. (Eds.): PAAMS 2015 Workshops, CCIS 524, pp. 15–27, 2015.
DOI: 10.1007/978-3-319-19033-4_2

of the web of social relationship around an individual (its social network). People may provide social support either in the form of emotional or tangible support. In [7], it is explained that social support is associated with how networking helps people to cope with stressful events moreover it can enhance psychological wellbeing. Social isolation and low level of social support have been shown to be associated with medical illness (e.g. depression).

In this paper, we extend an existing model for mood regulation to describe the different types of effect of social support on mood regulation. The model involves different cognitive states of a human being that are considered as important for mood and appraisal of the situations. The model is used to investigate the difference in effect of perceived (expected) and received (actual) support [5, 7] from a social network during a period of stress.

This paper is structured as follows. In Sect. 2 contains a more detailed discussion of social support and its effect on mental health and wellbeing. The conceptual model of mood dynamics with extension of social support concepts are discussed in Sect. 3. In Sect. 4, a number of hypotheses about the effect of different types of support are formulated, which are then investigated by simulation experiments with the model. The results of the experiments and the consequences for the hypotheses are discussed in Sect. 5. Finally, Sect. 6 concludes the paper with a discussion about the usage of this model in agent-based support systems and an outlook to future work.

2   Background

The increasing interest of researchers in the concept of social support and its role in psychological and physical health opened several dimensions of research in the field of social, psychological and health sciences. Literature over the last decades demonstrated notable research in the field of social support and its effects on health and wellbeing [8]. Many studies have shown that stress is generated when an individual appraises a situation as stressful or threatening and does not have proper coping response [9, 10]. Moreover, if an individual appraises a stressful situation with a feeling of helplessness or hopelessness (e.g., without the perception or reception of support), the situation become more stressful to deal with [11].

Social support is a coping resource to handle stressful events. The protective mechanism of social support in the face of psychosocial stress is called a buffering mechanism. Social support may play a role at different points in the process of relating the occurrence of stressful events to illness [5, 7, 12]. Support may intervene between stressful events (or expectation of it) and a stress response by attenuating or preventing a stressful appraisal. The perception of support by others through a network will provide necessary resources and may redefine the potential for harm posed by a stressful situation and strengthen one's capability to cope with imposed stressful demands. Support may alleviate stress appraisal by providing a solution to the problem, by reducing the perceived importance of the problem. Thus social support prevents a particular situation from being appraised as highly stressful. Moreover, sufficient support may intervene between experience of stress and the beginning of the pathological outcome of illness by reducing the stress reaction or by directly influencing accompanying psychological and physiological processes; so people are less reactive to perceived stress or by facilitating healthful behaviors [12].

According to literature [5, 7, 13] there are two hypothesis about the nature of the relationships between social support and health. First, the *main effect hypothesis* describes that social relationships have a beneficial effect regardless of whether individuals are under stress, as large social networks provide individuals regular positive experiences and socially rewarded roles in the community. This kind of support (i.e., a sense of identity, of purpose, and of meaning, belonging, and self-esteem) could be related to overall wellbeing because it provides positive effects during stressful events on self esteem, so integration in a social network may also help one to avoid negative experiences of life; otherwise that would increase the probability of psychological or physical disorder. Second, the *stress buffering hypothesis* describes that the social relationships are related to wellbeing only for individuals under stress. The buffering process takes into account both the variety of coping requirements that may be required by a stressful event and the range of resources that may (or may not) be provided by social relationships. Buffering effects occur when an individual perceives the availability of resources that will help him to respond to stressful events. Whereas it has been suggested that structural aspects of relationships might operate through the main effect model, functional aspects of relationships might operate through the stress buffering mechanism, and perceived availability of functional support is thought to buffer the effects of stress by enhancing individuals coping capabilities. The model proposed below simulates the stress buffering model as described in [8].

3   Model of a Human Agent

The human agent model (see Fig. 1) describes how the stress buffering affects different cognitive states and helps a person to deal with a bad event, and how this can increase

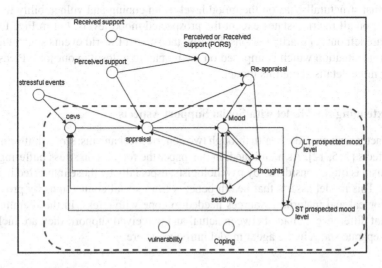

Fig. 1. Conceptual agent model of mood dynamics and social support

his/her coping skills. The model adopts an existing model for the dynamics of mood [14], and extends it by concepts of social support. In this section, the model of mood dynamics is described first, and then the extension parts are explained.

3.1 The Model of Mood Dynamics

The model of mood dynamics is depicted in the lower part of Fig. 1 (illustrated in the dashed box). The main concepts include the *mood level, appraisal* and *coping* skills of a person, and how the levels for these states affect the external behavior in the form of selection of situations over time (objective emotional value of situation). The model is based upon a number of psychological theories; see [14] for a mapping between the literature and the model itself. A short definition of each state and its role is explained in Table 1.

In the model a number of states are defined, whereby to each state at each point in time a number from the interval [0,1] is assigned. First, the state objective emotional value of situation (*oevs*) represents the value of the situation a human is in (without any influence of the current state of mind of the human). The state *appraisal* represents the current judgment of the situation given the current state of mind (e.g., when you are feeling down, a pleasant situation might no longer be considered pleasant). The *mood* level represents the current mood of the person, whereas *thoughts* indicates the current level of thoughts (i.e., the positivism of the thoughts). The *long term prospected mood* indicates what mood level the human is striving for in the long term, whereas the *short term prospected mood level* represents the goal for mood on the shorter term (in case you are feeling very bad, your short term goal will not be to feel excellent immediately, but to feel somewhat better). The *sensitivity* indicates the ability to select situations in order to bring the mood level closer to the short term prospected mood level. *Coping* expresses the ability of a human to deal with negative moods and situations, whereas *vulnerability* expresses how vulnerable the human is for negative events and how much impact that structurally has on the mood level. Both coping and vulnerability have an influence on all internal states except the prospected mood levels; but in Fig. 1 those arrows are left out for clarity reasons. Finally, the stressful world events state indicates an external situation which is imposed on the human (e.g. losing your job). Please see [14] for more details about this model.

3.2 Extending the Model with Social Support Aspects

Social factors can promote health through two generic mechanisms: stress-buffering and main effects [1, 5, 12]. As mentioned, in this paper the focus is on stress buffering; this mechanism is often considered by psychologists, especially by those interested in intervention. This model asserts that health benefits from social connections by providing psychological and material resources needed to cope with stress. In the literature, an important difference is made between actual and perceived support; they are included as two separate states in the agent model introduced here.

Table 1. Definition of states of conceptual model

Short name	Definition
Stressful event	Circumstances in the world that affect the situation in a stressful manner (e.g. losing his job)
OEVS	The objective emotional value of situation (OEVS) represents how an average person would perceive the situation
Appraisal	The current judgment of the situation given the current state of mind (e.g., when you are feeling down, a pleasant situation might no longer be considered pleasant)
Mood	The complex notion of mood is represented by the simplified concept *mood level*, ranging from low corresponding to a bad mood to high corresponding to a good mood
Thoughts	The mood level influences and is influenced by *thoughts*. Positive thinking has a positive effect on the mood and vice versa
Sensitivity	This node represents the ability to change or choose situations in order to bring mood level closer to prospected mood level. A high sensitivity means that someone's behavior is very much affected by thoughts and mood, while a low sensitivity means that someone is very unresponsive
St-prospected mood level	The mood level someone strives for, whether conscious or unconscious is represented by *prospected mood level*. This notion is split into a *long term (LT) prospected mood level*, an
Lt-prospected mood level	evolutionary drive to be in a good mood, and a *short term (ST) prospected mood level*, representing a temporary prospect when mood level is far from the prospected mood level
Vulnerability	Having a predisposition for developing a disorder
Coping	*Coping* is used in the model presented in this deliverable by means of continuously trying to adapt the situation in such a way that an improvement is achieved
Received support	The actual support which person received from his social network
Perceived support	The perception that others will provide appropriate aid if it is needed. The belief that others will provide necessary resources may bolster one's perceived ability to cope with demands, thus changing the appraisal of the situation and lowering its effective stress [9]
Perceived or received support	Whole amount of social support (both received and perceived received)
Re-appraisal	Reappraisal process occurs when a person, reappraises the stress experience in the presence of actual support as well as perceived support

Actual Support: This state presents the value of actual support which person received from his social network (e.g., your friend provides some money when you temporary loss your job).

Perceived Support: According to the psychological literature, the critical factor in social support operating as a stress buffer is the perception that others (even one reliable source) will provide appropriate aid [1, 5, 15]. A belief that (s)he can ask a friend for help changes the person's opinion about the situation. According to [16], the perceived availability of social support in the face of a stressful event may lead to a more benign appraisal of the situation, thereby preventing a cascade of ensuing negative emotional and behavioral responses. As a result, the value of this state has effect on *appraisal* in the proposed model.

In addition to these two kinds of support states, some additional states are added to the previous mood model.

Perceived or Received Support: The value of this state shows the whole amount of social support (both perceived and actually received). According to the psychological literature, the belief that others will provide necessary resources may bolster one's perceived ability to cope with demands [5, 17, 18]. For instance, the perceived availability of functional support is thought to buffer the effects of stress by enhancing an individual's coping abilities [16]. So, this state has effect on the coping skills of person. Please note that the value of this state has influence on the state *coping*; however this is not shown as an arrow in Fig. 1.

Re-appraisal: The *reappraisal* state uses the concept of the perception of the support in addition to the appraisal state. More specifically, the reappraisal state uses the concept perception as well as actual reception of the support; a reappraisal process occurs when a person reappraises the stress experience (generated by the appraisal) in the presence of actual support as well as perceived support. Reappraisal intervenes between the actual and perceived support and stress and the pathological illness.

3.3   Numerical Details of the Agent Model

As mentioned, for the model of mood dynamics (the lower part of Fig. 1, illustrated in the dashed box) an existing model was adopted. In the simulations, the settings of this model were also adopted. Due to the lack of space, we have to refer to original article [14] for the numerical details of this part of model. In the simulations weights of arrows which connect the new states to each other or to old states have been set at the following values: $w_{perceived,appraisal}$ 0.2, $w_{perceived,appraisal}$ 0.2, $w_{perceived,PORS}$ 1, $w_{received,PORS}$ 1. The weights of all arrows to the *reappraisal* are the same as arrows to/from *appraisal*, except $w_{PORS,Reappraisal}$ which is 0.2. Moreover, in this new model the *mood* states thoughts and *sensitivity* are affected by an average value of *appraisal* and *reappraisal* instead of only *appraisal*. Furthermore, the initial for the simulation, are as follows: *coping* 0.1, *vulnerability* 0.9, *LT_prospected* 0.6, *ST_prospected* 0.6, *oevs* 0.6, *appraisal* 0.8, and *sensitivity* 0.6.

In each iteration, the value of each state (except *coping*), V_{new}, is defined according the weighted sum of its inputs from other, connected states and its old value (V_{old}):

$$V_{new} = V_{old} + af * (w_1 V_1 + W_2 V_2 + ..)$$

The adaptation factor *af* for all states in the mood model is 0.1. The new value of coping is calculated by this formula ($af_{coping} = 0.0005$):

$$\text{Coping}_{new} = \text{coping}_{old} + af_{coping} * \text{coping}_{old} * (0.55 - \text{coping}_{old}) * \text{PORS}$$

4   Simulation Experiments

The human agent model presented above is used to make a comparison between what the model predicts for the human agent, and what actually holds in the real world (according to the literature).

4.1   Hypotheses

The objective of this paper is proposing a cognitive model that is consistent with related theories about social support. A number of expected behaviors of the model can be formulated:

H1. Social support (both perceived and actual) leads to less negative mood.
H2. A person who has a suitable social support will be more robust against bad events.
H3. Perception that others will provide appropriate aids during bad events (perceived support) is more helpful than the actual support itself.
H4. Social support can help people to learn how to cope with bad events. It means that at the very first times which a bad event happen, (s)he needs social support to cope with. But, after some successful experiences to handle the problem, (s)he will be more robust to cope with events with almost same demands.

4.2   Assumptions Behind the Example Simulations

To do the simulation experiments, some simplifying assumptions about the availability of *actual* and *perceived supports* and their affect on the *coping* have been made:

- Perception about the availability of support starts meanwhile the stressful event and fades out gradually after the event.
- In cases that actual support occurs, it starts meanwhile the event, and fades out gradually (10 times faster than perceived support) after the event.
- Both kinds of social support have a positive effect on coping.

4.3   Simulations

In the **first experiment**, a scenario is simulated which one bad event (stressful_event with value 0.2) occurs for the person and lasts for 3 days. Figure 2 shows the changes in mood and appraisal for four different conditions:

(a) No perceived support, no actual support
(b) No perceived support, just actual support
(c) Just perceived support, no actual support
(d) Both perceived and received support

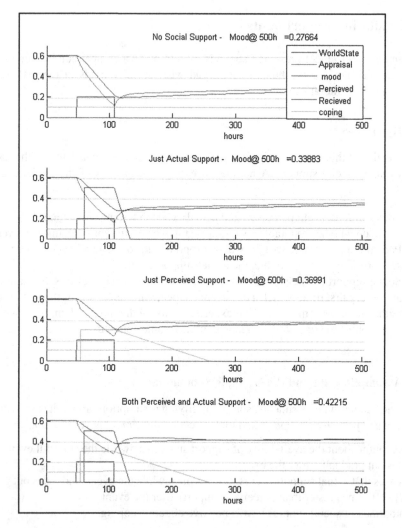

Fig. 2. Simulation results of the first experiment. Studying the influence of perceived and actual support on handling a bad event. Value of mood after 500 h is mentioned above each graph. The value of each state is a value between [0,1]

As it can be seen, the value of mood and appraisal decrease much when there is not any kind of support (a). In contrast, only a minimal decrease in the value of mood happens when both perceived and received are available (d). Moreover, comparison between situations in which just one kind of support is available shows that the perception of support has a more positive effect on mood than actual support.

In the **second experiment**, we consider three different scenarios. In the first scenario the person experiences a very stressful event (value 0.2). In the next scenarios, two and four events happen, but the events are less negative (value of 0.3 and 0.1 respectively). In all scenarios, the bad event lasts for 2.5 days.

The scenarios are simulated for three types of persons with different personalities. For each of the persons, we consider 5 different combinations of perceived and actual support: no support, a (little) perceived support, a (little) actual support. Together this results in $3 \times 3 \times 5$ is 45 simulations.

The following types of persons are used first, an emotionally stable person, defined by having good coping skills that balance out any vulnerability, and by having the desire to have a good mood: coping value is 0.5, vulnerability 0.5 and LT prospected mood level 0.8. An emotionally slightly unstable person is defined by having some vulnerability and bad coping skills and the desire to have a medium mood: settings 0.9, 0.1 and 0.6 respectively. The third type, an emotionally very unstable person, is characterized by settings 0.01, 0.99 and 0.6. For type 1 the OEVS is 0.8, for type 2 it is 0.94 and for type 3 the stable OEVS is 0.999.[1] The results of the 45 simulations are presented in Table 2 and Fig. 3, the figure depicts the maximum value of mood during simulation given different increasing values for support. The idea behind this is that the maximum value of the mood is an indicator for the recovery of a person from a depression.

According to some literature, depression is defined as a mood level below a threshold (usually 0.5) during at least 336 h (two weeks). Table 2 shows the length of period that the mood is bellow two particular thresholds (0.5 and 0.25), the cases that the length is higher than 336 h are highlighted, and the average of value of mood in the first two weeks of depression is mentioned in the second line of cell. Lower values of mood refer to a stronger depression, which is shown by darker colors. The table illustrates that social support in some cases prevents the depression; and in some other cases it decrease the depth.

As in can be seen in Fig. 3 the social support is beneficial mostly for a person number 2, but not for a very stable or very unstable person. A very stable person seems not to need to social support; on the contrary, social support cannot help a very unstable person. The exception is for a very unstable person: when some moderate events happen for this person, a high value of perceived social support can help to recovery after the event.

On the other hand, by focusing on the graphs related to person 2, we can see that the graph of perceived social support has a higher gradient. This suggests that the same amount of perceived social support is more effective than actual support.

In **the third experiment**, the long-term effect of social support is studied. Handling a bad event by help of social support may lead to bolster one's perceived ability to cope with demands, and the person will be more ready to deal with next events (with almost the same kinds of demands). In this simulation, several bad events occur with interval of one month. Each bad event lasts for 2.5 days; during each event, the value of

---

[1] The start value for OEVS needs to be calculated for each type so that when no events occur, the person stays balanced with al variables equal to LT prospected mood level.

Table 2. Length and depth of period which mood is less than threshold (in hours). First number: the length of period when mood is bellow threshold; second number: average mood value during this period. Situations in which length >336 h are highlighted.

Personality	Perceived or Actual Support	Threshold = 0.5			Threshold = 0.25		
		Scenario 1	Scenario 2	Scenario 3	Scenario 1	Scenario 2	Scenario 3
Stable Person	P=0,A=0	119 / 0.322	93 / 0.407	0 / -	37 / 0.196	0 / -	0 / -
	P=0.25,A=0	103 / 0.331	57 / 0.445	0 / -	29 / 0.205	0 / -	0 / -
	P=0.5,A=0	86 / 0.341	17 / 0.484	0 / -	19 / 0.220	0 / -	0 / -
	P=0,A=0.25	117 / 0.327	83 / 0.422	0 / -	34 / 0.2	0 / -	0 / -
	P=0,A=0.5	113 / 0.334	69 / 0.439	0 / -	30 / 0.206	0 / -	0 / -
Slightly Unstable Person	P=0,A=0	1286 / 0.075	1281 / 0.065	1261 / 0.233	1273 / 0.064	1257 / 0.043	1139 / 0.116
	P=0.25,A=0	1286 / 0.091	1280 / 0.090	1241 / 0.363	1273 / 0.081	1252 / 0.066	50 / 0.241
	P=0.5,A=0	1286 / 0.126	1279 / 0.14	1056 / 0.456	1013 / 0.117	849 / 0.118	0 / -
	P=0,A=0.25	1286 / 0.078	1281 / 0.072	1256 / 0.287	1273 / 0.067	1255 / 0.049	675 / 0.167
	P=0,A=0.5	1286 / 0.083	1281 / 0.085	1245 / 0.342	1273 / 0.072	1253 / 0.060	174 / 0.234
Unstable Person	P=0,A=0	1287 / 0.035	1282 / 0.039	1265 / 0.131	1275 / 0.022	1261 / 0.015	1172 / 0.032
	P=0.25,A=0	1287 / 0.041	1281 / 0.048	1249 / 0.246	1274 / 0.028	1257 / 0.021	1077 / 0.064
	P=0.5,A=0	1287 / 0.047	1280 / 0.063	1147 / 0.346	1274 / 0.033	1251 / 0.032	756 / 0.136
	P=0,A=0.25	1287 / 0.038	1282 / 0.042	1261 / 0.162	1275 / 0.025	1260 / 0.017	1158 / 0.046
	P=0,A=0.5	1287 / 0.039	1282 / 0.046	1254 / 0.212	1275 / 0.026	1258 / 0.02	1132 / 0.075

stressful_event is 0.2. It is assumed that both perceived and received social supports are available during all events.

Figure 3 shows the result of this simulation experiment. As it can be seen, the value of coping skills is increasing during each event. As a result, the last events have less effect on mood and appraisal, in comparison to the first ones. In fact, during the first event, the value of mood is decreased by 0.235; while it is decreased only by 0.164 during the last event.

5 Discussion

The results of the experiments described previous section are used to validate the hypotheses about our model about the relation between support and mood. Based on the literature, four different hypotheses have been defined.

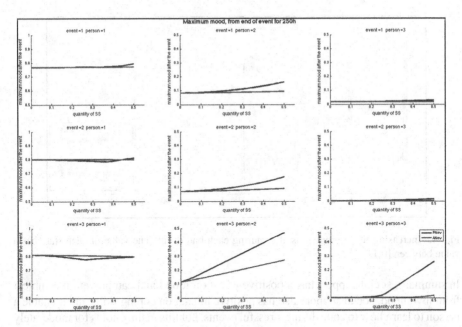

Fig. 3. The maximum value of mood for different amount of social support (perceived and actual)

H1. The first hypothesis states that social support (both perceived and actual) leads to less negative mood. The simulations in Fig. 2 show that mood goes down when a stressful event occurs. However, when a person has a perception of adequate social support he appraises the situation less negative and the lowest value of the mood is less negative. Actual support doesn't have much effect on the appraisal, but still reduces the effect of the stressful event. Thus, both types of supports leads to less depression in our model and H1 is validated

H2. The second hypothesis states that a person who has a suitable social support, will be more robust against bad events. Figure 3 shows that this only holds for a moderately stable person (there we see that the mood value increases with additional support), but not for very stable or very unstable persons (except for scenario 3). A similar patterns is visible in Table 2. The hypothesis partly holds

H3. The third hypothesis says that perceived support is more helpful than actual support. Figure 3 indeed shows that – when there is a positive effect – the perceived support is more helpful than the actual support (in the figure the blue line is above the green line). Thus, this hypothesis holds

H4. The fourth hypothesis states that social support can help people to learn how to cope with bad events. Indeed Fig. 4 clearly shows that the coping skills increase after negative events. As a result, the last events have less effect on mood and appraisal, in comparison to the first ones.

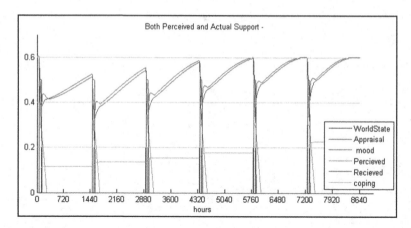

Fig. 4. Increasing the coping skills after during each bad event. The value of each state has a value between [0,1].

In summary, social support has a positive effect on mood and can prevent the subject from low mood, social support also has positive impact on coping skills and it enable a person to learn how to cope during stressful events, but this mainly holds for moderately stable persons.

6   Conclusion and Future Work

The computational model presented in this paper is the part of ongoing work on social support and its effects on health and psychological wellbeing, particularly on stress and depression. In this paper an extension of a human agent model of mood dynamics is presented that takes social support into account. It distinguishes between actual support and perceived support. The simulation experiments show that the effect of different types of support are in line with the literature.

This model can form the basis of a support system that provides advices for persons based on a prediction of the effect of situations on a person's mood. For such a system, it is important to be able to be able to estimate whether a person has social support and how large that is. For this, it might be possible to use data from social media. In the current decade, many electronic social environments have been developed in the form of social media or social network sites (e.g., Facebook, Twitter, Myspace). These social media provide a social environment where people can communicate with each other through forming their own social networks or groups, and thus integrating with these social networks. Such social media environments can be used for data collection (e.g., network size, frequency of the contacts, locations, etc.) to develop, analyze, and validate predictive models.

In future work, it is planned to investigate the relationships between measureable aspects of social environment (e.g. size and structure of a social network), and the factors used in the current model about the influence of social support on the cognitive states of a human. This could lead to a support system that is able to exploit social network data for predicting the mood of a person. Moreover, the effects of different kinds of intervention on persons and social networks can be analyzed and evaluated through empirical data.

References

1. Cohen, S.: Psychosocial models of the role of social support in the etiology of physical disease. Health Psychol. **7**, 269–297 (1988)
2. Aneshensel, C.S., Frerichs, R.R.: Stress, support, and depression: a longitudinal causal model. J. Commun. Psychol. **10**, 363–376 (1982)
3. Grav, S., Hellzèn, O., Romild, U., Stordal, E.: Association between social support and depression in the general population: the HUNT study, a cross-sectional survey. J. Clin. Nurs. **21**, 111–120 (2012)
4. House, J.S., Kahn, R.L.: Measures and concepts of social support. In: Cohen, S., Syme, S.L. (eds.) Social Support and Health, pp. 83–108. Academic Press, Orlando (1985)
5. Cohen, S., Wills, T.A.: Stress, social support, and the buffering hypothesis. Psychol. Bull. **98**, 310–357 (1985)
6. Glanz, B.K., Lewis, K., Rimer, F.M.: Health Behavior and Health Education: Theory, Research and Practice. Wiley, San Francisco (2002)
7. House, J.S.: Work Stress And Social Support. Addison-Wesley, Reading (1981)
8. S. Cohen and S. L. Syme, "Issues in the study and application of social support," in *Social support and health*, vol. 3, 1985, pp. 3–22
9. Cohen, S., Syme, S.L.: Social Support and hEalth, pp. 3–22. Academic Press, New York (1985)
10. Lazarus, R.S.: Psychological Stress and the Coping Process, p. 466. McGraw-Hill, New York (1966)
11. Lazarus, R.S., Launier, R.S.: Stress-related transactions between persons and environment. In: Pervin, L.A., Lewis, M. (eds.) Perspectives in Interactional Psychology, pp. 287–327. Plenum, New York (1978)
12. Garber, M.E.P., Seligman, J.: Human Helplessness: Theory and Applications. Academic Press, New York (1980)
13. Turner, R.J.: Direct and indirect moderating effects of social support upon psychological distress and associated conditions. In: Kaplan, H.B. (ed.) Psychosocial Stress: Trends in Theory and Research, pp. 105–156. Academic Press, New York (1983)
14. Both, F., Hoogendoorn, M., Klein, M.C., Treur, J.: Modeling the dynamics of mood and depression. In: Proceeding of ECAI'08, pp. 266–270 (2008)
15. Cohen, S., Underwood, L., Gottlieb, B.H.: Social Support Measurement and Intervention: A Guide for Health and Social Scientists, p. 334. Oxford University Press, Oxford (2000)
16. Wethington, E., Kessler, R.C.: Perceived support, received support, and adjustment to stressful life events. J. Health Soc. Behav. **27**, 78–89 (1986)
17. Uchino, B.N., Cacioppo, J.T., Kiecolt-Glaser, J.K.: The relationship between social support and physiological processes: a review with emphasis on underlying mechanisms and implications for health. Psychol. Bull. **119**, 488–531 (1996)
18. Thoits, P.A.: Social support as coping assistance. J. Consult. Clin. Psychol. **54**, 416–423 (1986)

Human-Agent Dialogues on Health Topics - An Evaluation Study

Jayalakshmi Baskar$^{(\boxtimes)}$ and Helena Lindgren

Department of Computing Science, Umeå University, SE-901 87 Umeå, Sweden
{jaya,helena}@cs.umu.se

Abstract. A common conversation between an older adult and a nurse about health-related issues includes topics such as troubles with sleep, reasons for walking around nighttime, pain conditions, etc. This dialogue emerges from the participating human's lines of thinking, their roles, needs and motives, while switching between topics as the dialogue unfolds. This paper presents a dialogue system that enables a human to engage in a dialogue with a software agent to reason about health-related issues in a home environment. The purpose of this work is to conduct a pilot evaluation study of a prototype system for human-agent dialogues, which is built upon a set of semantic models and integrated in a web application designed for older adults. Focus of the study was to receive qualitative results regarding purpose and content of the agent-based dialogue system, and to evaluate a method for the agent to evaluate its behavior based on the human agent's perception of appropriateness of moves. The participants include five therapists and 11 older adults. The results show users' feedback on the purpose of dialogues and the appropriateness of dialogues presented to them during the interaction with the software agent.

Keywords: Human-agent interaction · Human-agent dialogue · Health · Active assistive technology · Evaluation · User experience

1 Introduction

Assistive technology aims to support an individual in accomplishing activities, which they need to be able to do in the presence of decreased functionality or ability. In this work the definition of *active* assistive technology, used by Kennedy and co-workers [1], is applied to distinguish systems, which includes automated processing of health information during a human agent's interaction with the system and which may output tailored responses to the human agent in the process. The purposes of active assistive technology include the following: to increase knowledge, assist in deciding about actions to make, and promote changes of unhealthy behavior (i.e., in the form of *behavior change systems*).

Our work focuses on dialogues between a human actor and an active assistive technology in the form of an intelligent software agent. The concept of Embodied Cognitive Agents (ECA) is generally used for such systems. The ECA uses a

© Springer International Publishing Switzerland 2015
J. Bajo et al. (Eds.): PAAMS 2015 Workshops, CCIS 524, pp. 28–39, 2015.
DOI: 10.1007/978-3-319-19033-4_3

virtual representation of a human with the ability to send information through body language in addition to linguistic messages. However, we restrict the focus in this work to structured linguistic dialogues based on semantic models of relevant knowledge.

In this article, a dialogue system is presented, which enables a human actor to conduct a dialogue with a software agent for the purpose of handling health-related issues in a home environment. The aim is to enable the dialogues between a human agent and a software agent, which are tailored to the human's needs, preferences and goals. The goal is to build a software agent that interacts with the human as their personal coach, friend or a discussion partner, i.e., as a *Coach Agent* as described in [2]. A prototype dialogue system was implemented and integrated in a web-based support application designed for older adults, which enables the human actor to conduct a dialogue with the Coach Agent in their home environment. The prototype was evaluated in a pilot study involving a group of older adults and a group of therapists.

This paper is organized as follows. In the following section the methods are described and in Sect. 3, a brief description of the human-agent dialogue system is provided. The results of the pilot evaluation study is presented in Sect. 4. In Sect. 5, the results are discussed in the perspective of related active assistive technologies described in literature. The article ends with conclusions and comments on future work.

2   Methods

A pilot evaluation study was conducted involving a group of five female professionals in occupational therapy and physiotherapy, specialized in the needs of older adults, and a group of eleven older adults, six women and five men. The study was formative, with the results aimed to inform further development. The main research questions, which were targeted by the evaluation study, were related to the overall idea of a dialogue system for supporting everyday issues, how a sense-making dialogue would unfold and what topics would be interesting to elaborate upon. Other research questions were related to interaction design of the dialogue system.

The evaluation study was limited to the initiation of inquiry dialogues and the conduction of nested information-seeking dialogues [3], in the context of a use case scenario of an older adult called Ruth [2]. The information about Ruth forms the base for the Coach Agent's user model and the priorities of goals and tasks. An example is given in Fig. 1. This information and consequently, the user model changed during the testing, depending on how the participants interacted with the system.

Observation of use and interviews were the methods used for collecting the data.

During the study, the older adults and two of the therapists were individually given the tasks to play the role of either the persona in our scenario, some other person or themselves. The participants could also play both the roles one after

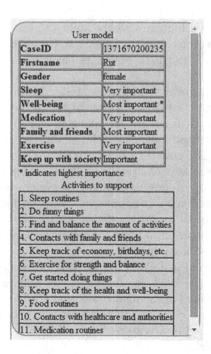

User model	
CaseID	1371670200235
Firstname	Rut
Gender	female
Sleep	Very important
Well-being	Most important *
Medication	Very important
Family and friends	Most important
Exercise	Very important
Keep up with society	Important

* indicates highest importance

Activities to support
1. Sleep routines
2. Do funny things
3. Find and balance the amount of activities
4. Contacts with family and friends
5. Keep track of economy, birthdays, etc.
6. Exercise for strength and balance
7. Get started doing things
8. Keep track of the health and well-being
9. Food routines
10. Contacts with healthcare and authorities
11. Medication routines

Fig. 1. Screenshot of a user model generated by the Coach Agent based on the preferences and needs of the individual.

the other. After deciding the role they play, they were asked to select topics of interest to initiate a dialogue and respond the way they wished. The user was also asked to evaluate the appropriateness of each statement of the Coach Agent within its context where it was stated by marking one of four alternatives on a Likert scale, presented in connection to each of the Coach Agent's statements. A purpose of the pilot study was also to evaluate this method. The system and the scenario were demonstrated to the remaining three therapists in a focus group session and discussed. The data was analyzed qualitatively using content analysis.

3   The Human-Agent Dialogue System

The human-agent dialogue system is developed as a part of the architecture of the agent-based ambient assistive living system presented in [2]. The architecture integrates knowledge repositories, developed using ACKTUS (Activity-Centered modeling of Knowledge and interaction Tailored to USers) [4,5]. ACKTUS is a platform for end-user development of knowledge-based systems in the medical and health domain. These repositories are built on semantic models represented using RDF/OWL[1], which were in [6] extended to integrate components vital for

---

[1] http://www.w3.org/.

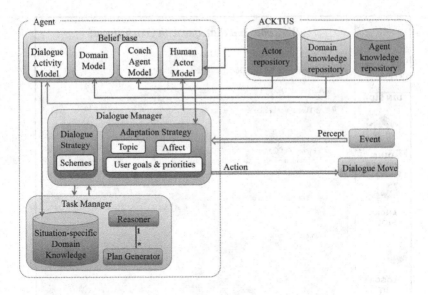

Fig. 2. Architecture of the human-agent dialogue system.

enabling the agent dialogues, based on the canonical model for agent architectures presented by Fox and coworkers [7].

The software agent comprises of a belief base, a dialogue manager and a task manager (Fig. 2). The agent builds its belief base upon information retrieved from the relevant ACKTUS repositories depending on the topic and who the user is. The human actor and the software agent interact with each other via events and dialogue moves, which are displayed in the graphical user interface (Figs. 2 and 3).

The ACKTUS knowledge repositories were created by domain experts in the rehabilitation domain [5] among other. The knowledge consists of both factual knowledge related to a user, which is used for creating a baseline user model, and procedural knowledge, in the form of rules obtained from domain knowledge repositories. Moreover, interactive templates, or protocols for assessment of different aspects can be retrieved from the domain knowledge repositories, which formed the basis of an earlier dialogue system presented in [8]. The knowledge was structured and implemented by the domain experts, to be used as assessment protocols by therapists in clinical interviews, or in human-agent dialogues. As a consequence, the topics and associated knowledge are structured, in that there is typically a set of answer-alternatives defined by the domain expert associated to each question in the knowledge base (e.g. Fig. 3). Each constructed piece of information is also associated to a concept, which is organized in an ontology, and which provides the theme of a topic to the software agent.

A generic model of purposeful human-agent dialogues about health-related topics builds the base for the human-agent dialogue system. The model was based on analyses of scenarios, personas and models of human behavior. The resulting

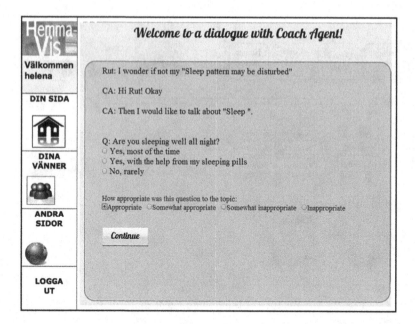

Fig. 3. Screenshot from the human-agent dialogue system. The agent collects the perceived appropriateness/inappropriateness of each of its question posed during the dialogue.

conceptual model includes four models, which are included in the software agent's belief base; (i) a user model, (ii) a model of the domain knowledge related to the topic of the dialogue, (iii) an agent model, and (iv) a dialogue activity model [9]. The architecture for a human-agent dialogue system presented in [10] was extended with the agent and dialogue activity models and is partially implemented. The system is integrated in a web-based support application designed for older adults, which is also used for therapist-lead assessments through structured interview-protocols (Fig. 3).

4   Results

The main research questions addressed in the evaluation study is related to the overall idea of a dialogue system for supporting everyday issues, how a sense-making dialogue would unfold and what topics would be interesting to elaborate upon. Other research questions are related to interaction design of the dialogue system. Since the evaluation study was limited to a subset of the models described in this article, and the study sample was small, the results are only indicative, aimed to inform further development.

A purpose was also to evaluate the method to allow the user to evaluate the appropriateness of each of the Coach Agent's statements within its context where it was stated. A question about the appropriateness of the agent's behavior was associated to a four-item Likert scale with the values *inappropriate (1), somewhat inappropriate (2), somewhat appropriate (3)* and *appropriate (4)*. The 13 participants' interaction with the dialogue application was logged, and resulted in a corpus with a total of 28 dialogues, 156 complete turns, and a total elapsed time of 2 h (approximately 10 min per participant). The examples from the dialogues presented in this section have been translated from the participants' native language into English. The results are divided into results related to the interaction design, the purposes of dialogues, and the appropriateness of the agent's behavior in the following sections.

4.1   Interaction Design

The older adults did not comment on the visualization of dialogues in the graphical interface. By contrast, the therapists put significantly more interest in how the dialogues would appear to the user. They commented on what parts of the dialogue line were visible at different phases in the dialogue, the unfolding of dialogues, on how the responses would be given by the user, etc. Their main concern was, how to reduce the amount of information presented to the user, while not losing the information about in which context the dialogue was situated. The interface design will be improved based on their comments and suggestions.

One therapist mentioned the concept of an "avatar", sometimes used for representing an Embodied Cognitive Agent (ECA). She viewed the Coach Agent as such, and discussed how body language could be added to the static figure used in the graphical user interface for representing the Coach Agent. Other comments related to the benefits of, and how to mediate, the dialogues through spoken language instead of text. Testing voice-based dialogues will be a natural step towards a more adaptive human-agent dialogue system, considering the large proportion of older adults who have sight impairments. One obvious benefit from using the ontology-based semantics of dialogues, was illustrated in the pilot evaluation study, since it allowed to apply the two languages needed by the participants. This will also facilitate the inclusion of additional modalities in the interaction design, which will be evaluated in future studies.

4.2   Purposes of Dialogues

The dialogues were based on the fictive persona Ruth's health and priorities. Most of the participants could personally relate to the dialogue topics, a few referred to a family member. In general, the available dialogue topics were considered interesting and relevant.

A generic attitude among the participants was that there is need for supportive dialogue systems, on various themes. Additional health-related topics, which were suggested were topics related to eating habits and eating disorders. Besides having healthcare issues to discuss, some pointed out the need in particular situations, when getting lost in the forest, or misplaced a car in the forest or bike in the city center. Others pointed out the potential benefits relating to getting access to social networks, having dialogues about societal issues such as politics, weather, golf and other sports.

A few expressed enthusiasm and curiosity about the idea and wanted to use the dialogue system merely for the fun of it: "...this is fun, let me try another one!"

Two of the older adults expressed skepticism, and did not see the point in using the dialogue system. One of these had also some difficulties using a smart phone, which may indicate a threshold for using new technology in general. By contrast, the other skeptical older adult was already using alternative ways to accomplish potential dialogue purposes, by using search engines for health issues, GPS for navigating, etc. Consequently, the group of participating older adults, including the two skeptical persons, illustrates the broad heterogeneity of the group of older adults.

The therapists highlighted the potential benefits of using a proactive human-agent dialogue system for providing active support for improving strength and balance, e.g., by supplementing the dialogues with sensor information from daily activities and physical exercises performed, analyzed over time.

4.3   Perceived Appropriateness of the Agent's Moves

One of the therapists who tested the system perceived the approach to evaluate the moves within the context it occurs, as highly beneficial. She compared it to structured clinical interviews, where it is typically not known how the patient perceives the appropriateness of the question asked.

The question, which was used for evaluating the appropriateness of the agent's moves, was found to be used in two different ways. Based on this observation, we distinguish between two types:

1. *Context-related appropriateness:* the appropriateness based on the immediate context of the agent's move, e.g., placement in the dialogue line, and
2. *Topic-related appropriateness:* appropriateness related to the topic of the dialogue.

The moves, which were categorized as the first kind and valued inappropriate to some level, were considered a failure of the agent, and are aimed to be minimized by improved strategies for the agent to use when choosing behavior. Consequently, these were removed, when analyzing the second kind, which was considered relating to the domain knowledge and not behavior issues.

Context-Related Appropriateness: Regarding the context-related appropriateness, some of the agent's moves were considered as inappropriate to some extent due to the agent's inadequate understanding of the human's responses. The agent needs to understand the context of human's response, update its belief base and act accordingly. Therefore the agent needs strategies for wisely selecting moves based on the human's response and the unfolding of the dialogue line.

Table 1. Total number of dialogue turns (Turns), number of Contextual Appropriateness Errors (CAE: turns, which are to some extent inappropriate), and mean of errors

User	1	2	3	4	5	6	7	8	9	10	11	12	13	Total	Mean
Turns	13	13	8	9	13	28	28	9	9	9	8	9	11	167	12.8
CAE	1	1	1	4	1	0	3	2	0	1	1	1	0	16	1.2

Table 2. Perceived topic-related appropriateness: inappropriate (✔), somewhat inappropriate (✓), somewhat appropriate(✓) and appropriate(✔). The abbreviation (n/a) (not available) represents missing information where a particular question was not asked to the user or the user chose not to give feedback.

Ques \ Users	1	2	3	4	5	6	7	8	9	10	11	12	13
Sleeping well all night	✔	✔	✓	n/a	✔	✓	✔	✓	✔	✗	✓	n/a	✔
Cause of getting up at night	✔	✔	✓	✔	✓	✓	✔	✔	✓	✔	n/a	✔	✔
Severity of pain	✔	✔	✓	n/a	✔	✔	✔	✔	✓	n/a	n/a	✔	✓
Having worries	✗	n/a	n/a	✔	n/a	✓	✓	✔	✓	n/a	n/a	✓	✓
Severity of worries	✓	✗	n/a	✔	✓	✓	✔	n/a	✓	✗	✗	n/a	✓
Taking some medication	✔	n/a	✔	n/a	✔	✓	n/a	n/a	✓	✔	n/a	n/a	✓
Handling medications	n/a	n/a	✗	✔	n/a	✓	✓	✓	✓	n/a	n/a	✓	✓

For evaluating the agent's improvement of behavior for future studies, a Contextual Appropriateness Value was defined and tested on this data sample. The total contextual appropriateness value for the complete corpus was 90.4 %, and consequently, the error rate was 9.6 % (16 of 167 moves) (Table 1).

Topic-Related Appropriateness: To what extent the agent's moves were perceived by the participants to be relevant to the overall dialogue topic was analyzed. The agent uses the domain knowledge, which it retrieves from a domain knowledge repository modeled by domain experts, to build a model of the knowledge domain, related to the selected topic of a dialogue. The domain experts have in their modeling created a knowledge model with interrelated topics following their view on to what extent different phenomenon are relevant to each other. However, human individuals who have a dialogue with the agent may perceive the level of appropriateness differently. We evaluated this topic-related appropriateness based on the participants' answers to the question about appropriateness, and mapped them to the concept associated to the content of the agent's move.

The most common topic, which the participants selected was the topic *sleep patterns may be disturbed*. The corresponding concept is *sleep*. Table 2 provides a summary of the participants' responses about appropriateness of different moves in relation to sleep. After removing the contextual errors and missing information (marked as not available (n/a) in Table 2), we can observe that most of the turns made by the agent were considered as appropriate to the topic sleep.

5   Discussion and Related Work

A software agent may have the capability to adapt to user's pace of communication and interacts in a nonjudgmental manner as described in [10–13]. Research literature shows an increasing number of applications of software agents that interact with the human actors for health-related purposes (e.g., [11,14–18]). A review of behavior change systems utilizing personalization technologies for accomplishing active assistance is provided in [1]. It was concluded that an agent provides an effective interface modality especially for the applications that require repeated interactions over longer period of time, which is crucial for applications supporting behavior change [1,12]. One example is the system, which has been developed for older adults with cognitive impairment described in [14]. However, it focuses mainly on generating reminders about the activities of their daily living and takes no part in a complex dialogue with the user. Agent-based systems which interact with human actors through dialogues are less common. They are typically developed for a specific task or for a limited domain, and the dialogues are tested in specialized environments [11,17].

Bickmore et al. [11] developed an animated conversational agent that provides information about a patient's hospital discharge plan in an empathic fashion. The patients rated the agent very high on measures of satisfaction and ease of use, and also as being the most preferred over their doctors or nurses in the hospital when receiving their discharge information. One of the reasons for the positive results in this study was the amount of time that the agent spent with users helped them to establish a stronger emotional bond. Our approach has the same potential, in that there is no time limit, and the dialogues can reoccur whenever the older adult may wish to have a dialogue. The prototypic graphical user interface used in our study was commented upon by the therapists, who suggested that an animated agent would be an interesting improvement, as well as using spoken language. A difference in evaluation methodology is that their analysis was carried out after the dialogue had been completed with a summative purpose, using questionnaires with no particular focus on the software agent's interactive behavior in dialogue situations. Our method aims at tuning the behavior to the human agent's experience, which was also received positively by the therapists in our study.

The counseling dialogue system discussed in [12] also uses an ontology to represent the user model and the domain knowledge. The domain knowledge is based on behavioral medicine. However, the domain experts are not directly involved in the modeling of the agent's knowledge in this system. As a consequence, it lacks features for modifications, such as future changes in domain knowledge and also it lacks the representation of goals, which drives the behavior of the dialogue system.

Different approaches to developing and implementing behavior change systems in healthcare for older adults have been documented in the literature [1,11,18–20], but to our knowledge, there has been no attempt to design a method for a software agent to analyze its own behavior for improving its behavior when interacting with the older adult. For instance, [16] tested their dialogue system by letting the users use the system for 2 months and at the end of 2 months, an experimenter conducts a follow-up meeting. During the meeting, they used questionnaires to evaluate various aspects of intervention. However, this study lacks in exploring the behavioral aspects especially focusing on the agent, which they point out to be very important. The same authors in another work [15], evaluate a conversational agent based on behavioral measures such as rate of speech and type of utterance but not the relevance of the utterance to that of the previous utterance or the overall dialogue topic. Hence, we evaluated our agent based on the appropriateness of the agent's move as a behavioral measure.

Identifying the topic-related appropriateness of a participant's moves is to a large extent dependent on the perspective of an individual. Some participants considered the questions related to pain and the presence of worries as appropriate while some others considered the same topics as inappropriate to different extent. Some comments by the participants indicated that they associated these questions to their own situation and health conditions, rather than the persona Ruth's situation, which was the reason for why these moves were perceived as inadequate. Consequently, if the participants had been able to create their own profile in the system for the agent to build a user model from in the dialogues, then some of these less appropriateness evaluations had been different. The question about reasons for why getting up at night had a broad range of answering alternatives, among which a few participants found less relevant alternatives.

The overall goal of our human-agent dialogue system is to minimize the contextual appropriateness errors and maximize the topic-related appropriateness. To attain this goal, future work includes developing strategies for the agent to wisely select moves based on changes in its belief base. Moreover, these improvements will be evaluated with a group of older adults who create their own profiles in the system, for evaluating to what extent the perceived inappropriateness is related to the domain knowledge, and the differences in the view on this. If the differences are significant, a machine learning method will be built for the agent to learn how an individual values the topic-related appropriateness and adapt its selection of moves to that individual.

To summarize the results regarding the described method of valuing the appropriateness of the agent's behavior within its context where it occurs, the approach was found to add significant value to the evaluation study, without disturbing the participant from participating in the dialogue. The advantage of this method is that a software agent can learn (1) what an individual user thinks is appropriate, also (2) learn based on a number of people with different characteristics, how some topics are perceived more or less appropriate, depending on the context (human's age, gender, type and/or severity of disease, current main topic, etc.). However, considering the limitations of the pilot study, in particular the quantified analyses in relation to the limited number of participants, and the two possible ways to interpret the question, the method will also be further developed and evaluated in future studies.

6 Conclusions

In this paper, a dialogue system that enables a human to engage in a dialogue with a software agent to reason about health-related issues in a home environment was presented. The main contributions of this paper are the insights about the perception of this human-agent dialogue system by older adults and therapists. A new method for an agent to evaluate the appropriateness of each of its move was also presented. Finally, an evaluation of the initial prototype system was presented, which was evaluated by therapists and a group of older adults. The study shows results related to users' feedback on the purpose of dialogues and the appropriateness of dialogues presented to them, during the interaction with the software agent. Future work involves evaluation of the proposed method with different topics such that it can be generic for selecting appropriate behavior, to test the agent's capability of selecting what is perceived appropriate to talk about in different contexts. Future work also includes the development of the dialogue and reasoning strategies for the agent to improve its ability to adapt to the individual and the situatedness of contextual and natural dialogues.

References

1. Kennedy, C.M., Powell, J., Payne, T.H., Ainsworth, J., Boyd, A., Buchan, I.: Active assistance technology for health-related behavior change: An interdisciplinary review. J. Med. Internet Res. **14**(3), e80 (2012)
2. Lindgren, H., Surie, D., Nilsson, I.: Agent-supported assessment for adaptive and personalized ambient assisted living. In: Corchado, J.M., Pérez, J.B., Hallenborg, K., Golinska, P., Corchuelo, R. (eds.) Trends in PAAMS. AISC, vol. 90, pp. 25–32. Springer, Heidelberg (2011)
3. Walton, D., Krabbe, E.: Commitment in Dialogue: Basic Concepts of Interpersonal Reasoning. SUNY Press, Albany (1995)
4. Lindgren, H., Winnberg, P.J., Winnberg, P.: Domain experts tailoring interaction to users – an evaluation study. In: Campos, P., Graham, N., Jorge, J., Nunes, N., Palanque, P., Winckler, M. (eds.) INTERACT 2011, Part III. LNCS, vol. 6948, pp. 644–661. Springer, Heidelberg (2011)
5. Lindgren, H., Nilsson, I.: Towards user-authored agent dialogues for assessment in personalised ambient assisted living. Int. J. Web Eng. Technol. **8**(2), 154–176 (2013)
6. Lindgren, H.: Towards context-based inquiry dialogues for personalized interaction. In: Demazeau, Y., Pechoucek, M., Corchado, J.M., Pérez, J.B. (eds.) Adv. on Prac. Appl. Agents and Mult. Syst. AISC, vol. 88, pp. 151–161. Springer, Heidelberg (2011)
7. Fox, J., et al.: Towards a canonical framework for designing agents to support healthcare organisations. In: Proceedings of the European Conference of AI (ECAI) Workshop Agents Applied in Healthcare (2006)
8. Baskar, J., Lindgren, H.: Towards personalised support for monitoring and improving health in risky environments. In: VIII Workshop on Agents Applied in Health Care (A2HC 2013), Murcia, Spain, pp. 93–104 (2013)
9. Baskar, J.: Adaptive human-agent dialogues for reasoning about health, Licentiate Thesis, Umea University (2014)

10. Baskar, J., Lindgren, H.: Cognitive architecture of an agent for human-agent dialogues. In: Corchado, J.M., et al. (eds.) PAAMS 2014. CCIS, vol. 430, pp. 89–100. Springer, Heidelberg (2014)
11. Bickmore, T., Mitchell, S., Jack, B., Paasche-Orlow, M.: Response to a relational agent by hospital patients with depressive symptoms. Interact. Comput. **22**, 289–298 (2010)
12. Bickmore, T.W., Schulman, D., Sidner, C.L.: A reusable framework for health counseling dialogue systems based on a behavioral medicine ontology. J. Biomed. Inform. **44**, 183–197 (2011)
13. Yan, C., Lindgren, H.: Hypothesis-driven agent dialogues for dementia assessment. In: VIII Workshop on Agents Applied in Health Care (A2HC 2013), Murcia, Spain, pp. 93–104 (2013)
14. Pollack, M., Brown, L., Colbry, D., McCarthy, C.E., Orosz, C., Peintner, B., Ramakrishnan, S., Tsamardinos, I.: An intelligent cognitive orthotic system for people with memory impairment. Robot. Auton. Syst. **44**, 273–282 (2003)
15. Bickmore, T., Cassell, J.: Social dialogue with embodied conversational agents. In: Advances in Natural, Multimodal Dialogue Systems, pp. 4–8 (2005)
16. Bickmore, T., Caruso, L., Clough-Gorr, K., Heeren, T.: 'It's just like you talk to a friend' relational agents for older adults. Interact. Comput. **17**, 711–735 (2005)
17. Susan, R., Traum, D.R., Ittycheriah, M., Henderer, J.: What would you ask a conversational agent? observations of human-agent dialogues in a museum setting. In: International Conference on Language Resources and Evaluation, pp. 69–102 (2008)
18. Alistair, K., Vlugter, P.: Multi-agent human-machine dialogue: issues in dialogue management and referring expression semantics. In: Trends in Artificial Intelligence, vol. 172(2–3), pp. 69–102. Elsevier Science Publishers Ltd., Essex (2008)
19. Isern, D., Sánchez, D., Moreno, A.: Agents applied in health care: A review. Int. J. Med. Inform. **79**, 145–166 (2010)
20. Vedel, I., Akhlaghpour, S., Vaghefi, I., Bergman, H., Lapointe, L.: Health information technologies in geriatrics and gerontology: a mixed systematic review. J. Am. Med. Inform. Assoc. (JAMIA) **20**, 1109–1119 (2013)

Workshop on Agent-Based Solutions for Manufacturing and Supply Chain

A Holonic Multiagent Model Based on a Combined Genetic Algorithm—Tabu Search for the Flexible Job Shop Scheduling Problem

Houssem Eddine Nouri[(✉)], Olfa Belkahla Driss, and Khaled Ghédira

Stratégies d'Optimisation et Informatique IntelligentE (SOIE),
Higher Institute of Management of Tunis, Tunis, Tunisia
houssemeddine.nouri@gmail.com,
{olfa.belkahla,khaled.ghedira}@isg.rnu.tn

Abstract. The Flexible Job Shop scheduling Problem (FJSP) is an extension of the classical Job Shop scheduling Problem (JSP) that allows to process operations on one machine out of a set of alternative machines. It is an NP-hard problem consisting of two sub-problems which are the assignment and the scheduling problems. This paper proposes a holonic multiagent model based on a combined genetic algorithm and tabu search for the FJSP. Firstly, a scheduler agent applies a Neighborhood-based Genetic Algorithm (NGA) for a global exploration of the search space. Secondly, a cluster agents set uses a local search technique to guide the research in promising regions. Numerical tests are made to evaluate our approach, based on two sets of benchmark instances from the literature of the FJSP: Kacem and Hurink. The experimental results show the efficiency of our approach in comparison to other approaches.

Keywords: Scheduling · Flexible job shop · Genetic algorithm · Local search · Multiagent

1 Introduction

The Job Shop scheduling Problem (JSP), which is among the hardest combinatorial optimization problems [14], is a branch of the industrial production scheduling problems. The Flexible Job Shop scheduling Problem (FJSP) is an extension of the classical JSP that allows to process operations on one machine out of a set of alternative machines. Hence, the FJSP is more computationally difficult than the JSP, presenting an additional difficulty caused by the operation assignment problem to a set of available machines. This problem is known to be strongly NP-Hard even if each job has at most three operations and there are two machines [6].

To solve this problem, some authors used the metaheuristics to find near-optimal solutions for the FJSP with acceptable computational time. Hurink et al. [7] developed a Tabu Search procedure for the job shop problem with multi-purpose machines. Mastrolilli and Gambardella [13] used Tabu Search techniques and presented two neighborhood functions allowing an approximate resolution for the FJSP. Bozejko et al. [2]

© Springer International Publishing Switzerland 2015
J. Bajo et al. (Eds.): PAAMS 2015 Workshops, CCIS 524, pp. 43–54, 2015.
DOI: 10.1007/978-3-319-19033-4_4

presented a Tabu Search approach based on a new golf neighborhood for the FJSP. A novel hybrid Tabu Search algorithm with a fast Public Critical Block neighborhood structure (TSPCB) was proposed by [12] to solve the FJSP. For the Genetic Algorithm, it was adopted by [3], where their chromosome representation of solutions for the problem was divided into two parts. The first part defined the routing policy and the second part took the sequence of operations on each machine. Kacem et al. [9] presented a hybridization of an evolutionary algorithm with the fuzzy logic to solve jointly the assignment and job shop scheduling problems with total flexibility. Gao et al. [5] adapted a hybrid Genetic Algorithm (GA) and a Variable Neighborhood Descent (VND) for FJSP. The GA used two vectors to represent a solution and the disjunctive graph to calculate it. Then, a VND was applied to improve the GA final individuals. Zhang et al. [16] presented a model of low-carbon scheduling in the FJSP considering three factors, the makespan, the machine workload for production and the carbon emission for the environmental influence. A metaheuristic hybridization algorithm was proposed combining the original Non-dominated Sorting Genetic Algorithm II (NSGA-II) with a Local Search algorithm based on a neighborhood search technique. Moreover, a Knowledge-Based Ant Colony Optimization (KBACO) algorithm was presented by [15] for the FJSP. Furthermore, a new heuristic was developed by [17] for the FJSP. This heuristic is based on a constructive procedure considering simultaneously many factors having a great effect on the solution quality. Furthermore, distributed artificial intelligence techniques were used for this problem, such as the multiagent model proposed by [4] composed by three classes of agents, job agents, resource agents and an interface agent. This model is based on a local search method which is the tabu search to solve the FJSP.

In this paper, we propose a holonic multiagent model based on two combined metaheuristics for the flexible job shop scheduling problem. This new approach follows two principal steps. In the first step, a genetic algorithm is applied by a scheduler agent for a global exploration of the search space. In the second step, a local search technique is used by a set of cluster agents to improve the quality of the final population. Numerical tests were made to evaluate the performance of our approach based on two data sets of [7, 9] for the FJSP, where the experimental results show its efficiency in comparison to other approaches.

The rest of the paper is organized as follows. In Sect. 2, we define the formulation of the FJSP with its objective function and a simple problem instance. Then, in Sect. 3, we detail the holonic multiagent levels with its two combined metaheuristics. The experimental and comparison results are provided in Sect. 4. Finally, Sect. 5 ends the paper with a conclusion.

2 Problem Formulation

The flexible job shop scheduling problem (FJSP) could be formulated as follows. There is a set of n jobs $J = \{J_1, ..., J_n\}$ to be processed on a set of m machines $M = \{M_1, ..., M_m\}$. Each job J_i is formed by a sequence of n_i operations $\{O_{i,1}, O_{i,2}, ..., O_{i,ni}\}$ to be performed successively according to the given sequence. For each operation $O_{i,j}$, there is a set of alternative machines $M(O_{i,j})$ capable of performing it. The main objective of this problem is to find a schedule minimizing the end date of the last operation of the jobs set which is the makespan. The makespan is defined by *Cmax* in Eq. (1), where C_i is the completion time of job J_i.

$$Cmax = max_{1 \leq i \leq n}(C_i) \tag{1}$$

To explain the FJSP, a sample problem of three jobs and five machines is shown in Table 1, where the numbers present the processing times and the tags "-" mean that the operation cannot be executed on the corresponding machine.

Table 1. A simple instance of the FJSP

Job	Operation	M1	M2	M3	M4	M5
J1	O_{11}	2	9	4	5	1
	O_{12}	–	6	–	4	–
J2	O_{21}	1	–	5	–	6
	O_{22}	3	8	6	–	–
	O_{23}	–	5	9	3	9
J3	O_{31}	–	6	6	–	–
	O_{32}	3	–	–	5	4

3 A Holonic Multiagent Model Based on a Combined Genetic Algorithm—Tabu Search

In this work, we propose a combined metaheuristic approach processing two general steps: a first step of exploration using a genetic algorithm to find promising areas in the search space and a clustering operator allowing to regroup them in a set of clusters. In the second step, a tabu search algorithm is applied to find the best individual solution for each cluster. The global process of the proposed approach is implemented within a holonic multiagent model, named a combination of a Genetic Algorithm with a Tabu Search in a Holonic Multiagent model (GATS + HM), see Fig. 1. This new approach follows the paradigm of Master/Workers, where it is divided into two holonic levels of agents: a first level composed by the Master which is a Scheduler Agent and a second level containing a set of Workers which are N Cluster Agents, where N is the number of clusters generated by the clustering operator. Each holonic level of this model is responsible to process a step of the proposed approach and to cooperate between them to attain the global solution of the problem.

In fact, the choice of this new metaheuristic combination is justified by that the standard metaheuristic methods use generally the diversification techniques to generate many different solutions distributed in the search space. But they did not guarantee to attain promising areas with good fitness despite the repetition of many iterations, that is why they need to be more optimized. So, the novelty of our approach is to launch a genetic algorithm based on a diversification technique to only explore the search space and to select the best promising part by the clustering operator. Then, applying the

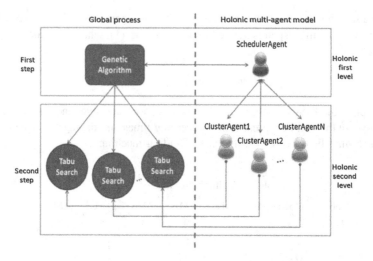

Fig. 1. A holonic multiagent model based on two combined metaheuristics

intensification technique of the tabu search allowing to relaunch the search from an elite solution of each cluster autonomously to attain more dominant solutions of the search space.

In addition, the use of a multiagent model gives the opportunity for a distributed and parallel treatment which is very complimentary for the second step of the proposed approach. Indeed, our combined metaheuristic approach follows the paradigm of "Master" and "Workers" which are two hierarchical levels adaptable for a holonic multiagent model, where the Master is the Scheduler Agent and the Workers are the Cluster Agents. Also, our algorithm needs a distributed, parallel and especially recursive treatment between the two global steps, that is why the holonic multiagent model is considered in our case and not the simple multiagent model.

3.1   Scheduler Agent

The Scheduler Agent (SA) is responsible to process the first step of the combined approach by using a genetic algorithm called NGA (Neighborhood-based Genetic Algorithm) to identify areas with high average fitness in the search space. In fact, the goal of using the NGA is only to explore the search space, but not to find the global solution of the problem. Then, a clustering operator is integrated to divide the best identified areas by the NGA in the search space to different parts where each part is a cluster $CL_i \in CL$ the set of clusters, where $CL = \{CL_1, CL_2, ..., CL_N\}$. In addition, this agent plays the role of an interface between the user and the system (initial parameter inputs and final result outputs). According to the number of clusters N obtained after the integration of the clustering operator, the SA creates N Cluster Agents (CAs) preparing the passage to the next step of the global process. After that, the SA remains in a waiting state until the reception of the best solutions found by the CAs for each cluster. Finally, it finishes the process by displaying the final solution of the problem.

Individual's solution presentation. The flexible job shop problem is composed by two sub-problems: the machine assignment problem and the operation scheduling problem, that is why the chromosome representation is encoded in two parts: Machine Assignment part (MA) and Operation Sequence part (OS). The first part MA is a vector V_1 with a length L equal to the total number of operations and where each index represents the selected machine to process an operation indicated at position pos, see Fig. 2(a). For example $pos = 2$, $V_1(2)$ is the selected machine M_4 for the operation $O_{1,2}$. The second part OS is a vector V_2 having the same length of V_1 and where each index represents an operation $O_{i,j}$ according to the predefined operations of the job set, see Fig. 2(b). For example the operation sequence $1 - 2 - 1 - 3 - 2 - 3 - 2$ can be translated to: $(O_{1,1}, M_5) \rightarrow O_{2,1}, M_1) \rightarrow (O_{1,2}, M_4) \rightarrow (O_{3,1}, M_3) \rightarrow (O_{2,2}, M_3) \rightarrow (O_{3,2}, M_1) \rightarrow (O_{2,3}, M_2)$.

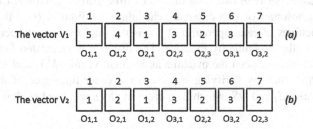

Fig. 2. The chromosome representation

To convert the chromosome values to an active schedule, we used the priority-based decoding of [5]. This method considers the idle time which may exist between operations on a machine m, and which is caused by the precedence constraints of operations belonging to the same job i. Let $S_{i,j}$ is the starting time of an operation $O_{i,j}$ (which can only be started after processing its precedent operation $O_{i,(j-1)}$) with its completion time $C_{i,j}$. In addition, we have an execution time interval $[t_m^S, t_m^E]$ starts form t_m^S and ends at t_m^E on a machine m to allocate an operation $O_{i,j}$. So, if $j = 1$, $S_{i,j}$ takes t_m^S, else if $j \geq 2$, it takes $max\{t_m^S, C_{i,(j-1)}\}$. In fact, the availability of the time interval $[t_m^S, t_m^E]$ for an operation $O_{i,j}$ is validated by verifying if there is a sufficient time period to complete the execution time p_{ijm} of this operation, see Eq. (2):

$$\begin{aligned} t_m^S + p_{ijm} \leq t_m^E && \text{if } j = 1 \\ max\{t_m^S, C_{i,(j-1)}\} + p_{ijm} \leq t_m^E && \text{if } j \geq 2 \end{aligned} \quad (2)$$

The used priority-based decoding method allows in each case to assign each operation to its reserved machine following the presented execution order of the operation sequence vector V_2. Also, to schedule an operation $O_{i,j}$ on a machine m, the fixed idle time intervals of the selected machine are verified to find an allowed available period to its execution. So, if a period is found, the operation $O_{i,j}$ is executed there, else it is moved to be executed at the end of the machine m.

Noting that the chromosome fitness is calculated by *Fitness(i)* which is the fitness function of each chromosome i and *Cmax(i)* is its makespan value, where $i \in \{1, \ldots, P\}$ and P is the total population size, see Eq. (3).

$$Fitness(i) = \frac{1}{Cmax(i)} \tag{3}$$

Population initialization. The initial population is generated randomly following a uniform law and based on a neighborhood parameter to make the individual solutions more diversified and distributed in the search space. In fact, each new solution should have a predefined distance with all the other solutions to be considered as a new member of the initial solution. The used method to determinate the neighborhood parameter is inspired from [2], which is based on the permutation level of operations to obtain the distance between two solutions. Let *Chrom1(MA₁, OS₁)* and *Chrom2(MA₂, OS₂)* two chromosomes of two different scheduling solutions, $M(O_{i,j})$ the alternative number of machines of each operation $O_{i,j}$, L is the total number of operations of all jobs and *Dist* is the dissimilarity distance. The distance is calculated firstly by measuring the difference between the machine assignment vectors MA_1 and MA_2 which is in order of $O(n)$, then by verifying the execution order difference of the operation sequence vectors OS_1 and OS_2 which is in order of $O(1)$, we give here how to proceed:

```
Begin
  Dist=0, k=1
  For k from 1 to L
    If Chrom1(MA₁(k)) ≠ Chrom2(MA₂(k))
      Dist = Dist + M(Oᵢ,ⱼ)
    End if
    If Chrom1(OS₁(k)) ≠ Chrom2(OS₂(k))
      Dist = Dist + 1
    End if
  End for
  Return Dist
End
```

Noting that *Dist_max* is the maximal dissimilarity distance and it is calculated by Eq. (4), representing 100 % of difference between two chromosomes.

$$Dist\_max = \sum_{i,1}^{i,ni} [M(Oi,j)] + L \tag{4}$$

Selection operator. The selection operator is used to select the best parent individuals to prepare them to the crossover step. This operator is based on a fitness parameter allowing to analyze the quality of each selected solution. But progressively the fitness values will be similar for the most individuals. That is why, we integrate the neighborhood parameter, where we propose a new combined parent selection operator named Fitness-Neighborhood Selection Operator (FNSO) allowing to add the dissimilarity distance criteria to the fitness parameter to select the best parents for the crossover step. The FNSO chooses in each iteration two parent individuals until engaging all the population to create the next generation. The first parent takes successively in each case a solution i, where $i \in \{1,\ldots,P\}$ and P is the total population size. The second parent obtains its solution j randomly by the roulette wheel selection method based on the two Fitness and Neighborhood parameters relative to the selected first parent, where $j \in \{1,\ldots,P\} \setminus \{i\}$ in the P population and where $j \neq i$. In fact, to use this random method, we should calculate the Fitness-Neighborhood total FN for the population, see Eq. (5), the selection probability sp_k for each individual I_k, see Eq. (6), and the cumulative probability cp_k, see Eq. (7). After that, a random number r will be generated from the uniform range [0,1]. If $r \leq cp_1$ then the second parent takes the first individual I_1, else it gets the kth individual $I_k \in \{I_2,\ldots,I_P\} \setminus \{I_i\}$ and where $cp_{k-1} < r \leq cp_k$.

- The Fitness-Neighborhood total for the population:

$$FN = \sum_{k=1}^{P} [1/(Cmax[k] \times Neighborhood[i][k])] \tag{5}$$

- The selection probability sp_k for each individual I_k:

$$sp_k = \frac{1/(Cmax[k] \times Neighborhood[i][k])}{FN.} \tag{6}$$

- The cumulative probability cp_k for each individual I_k:

$$cp_k = \sum_{h=1}^{k} p_h \tag{7}$$

$\Longrightarrow$ For Eqs. (5–7), $k = \{1,2, \ldots,P\} \setminus \{i\}$.

Crossover operator. The crossover operator has an important role in the global process, allowing to combine in each case the chromosomes of two parents in order to obtain new individuals and to attain new better parts in the search space. In this work, this operator is applied with two different techniques successively for the parent's chromosome vectors MA and OS. For the machine vector crossover, a uniform crossover is used to generate in each case a mixed vector between two machine vector parents, Parent1-MA1 and Parent2-MA2, allowing to obtain two new children, Child1-MA1' and Child2-MA2'. This uniform crossover is based on two assignment cases, if the generated number is less than 0.5, the first child gets the current machine value of parent1 and the second child takes the current machine value of parent2. Else, the two children change their assignment direction, first child to parent2 and the second child to parent1. For the operation vector crossover, an improved precedence preserving order-based on crossover (iPOX), inspired from [11], is adapted for the parent operation vector OS. This iPOX operator is applied following four steps, a first step is selecting two parent operation vectors (OS_1 and OS_2) and generating randomly two job sub-sets Js_1/Js_2 from all jobs. A second step is allowing to copy any element in OS_1/OS_2 that belong to Js_1/Js_2 into child individual OS'_1/OS'_2 and retain them in the same position. Then the third step deletes the elements that are already in the sub-set Js_1/Js_2 from OS_1/OS_2. Finally, fill orderly the empty position in OS'_1/OS'_2 with the reminder elements of OS_2/OS_1 in the fourth step.

Mutation operator. The mutation operator is integrated to promote the children generation diversity. In fact, this operator is applied on the chromosome of the new children generated by the crossover operation. Also, each part of a child chromosome MA and OS has separately its own mutation technique. The machine mutation operator uses a random selection of an index from the machine vector MA. Then, it replaces the machine number in the selected index by another belonging to the same alternative machine set. The operation mutation operator selects randomly two indexes index1 and index2 from the operation vector OS. Next, it changes the position of the job number in the index1 to the second index2 and inversely.

Replacement operator. The replacement operator has an important role to prepare the remaining surviving population to be considered for the next iterations. This operator replaces in each case a parent by one of its children which has the best fitness in its current family.

Clustering operator. By finishing the last iteration of the genetic algorithm, the Scheduler Agent applies a clustering operator using the hierarchical clustering algorithm of [8] to divide the final population into N Clusters, to be treated by the Cluster Agents in the second step of the global process. The clustering operator is based on the neighbourhood parameter which is the dissimilarity distance between individuals. The clustering operator starts by assigning each individual $Indiv(i)$ to a cluster CL_i, so if we have P individuals, we have now P clusters containing just one individual in each of them. So, for each case, we fixe an individual $Indiv(i)$ and we verify successively for each next individual $Indiv(j)$ from the remaining population (where i and j $\in \{1, \dots, P\}$, i $\neq$ j) if the dissimilarity distance $Dist$ between $Indiv(i)$ and $Indiv(j)$ is less than or equal to a fixed threshold $Dist\_fix$ (representing a percentage of difference X% relatively to $Dist\_max$, see Eq. (8)) and where $Cluster(Indiv(i)) \neq Cluster(Indiv(j))$. If it is the case, $Merge(Cluster(Indiv(i)), Cluster(Indiv(j)))$, else continue the search for new combination with the remaining individuals. The stopping condition is by browsing all the population individuals, where we obtained at the end N Clusters.

$$Dist\_fix = Dist\_max \times X\% \tag{8}$$

3.2 Cluster Agents

Each Cluster Agent CA_i is responsible to apply successively to each cluster CL_i a local search technique which is the Tabu Search algorithm to guide the research in promising regions of the search space and to improve the quality of the final population of the genetic algorithm. In fact, this local search is executed simultaneously by the set of the CAs agents, where each CA starts the research autonomously from an elite solution of its cluster searching to attain new more dominant individual solutions separately in its assigned cluster CL_i. The used Tabu Search algorithm is based on an intensification technique allowing to start the research from an elite solution in a cluster CL_i (a promising part in the search space) in order to collect new scheduling sequence minimizing the makespan. Let E the elite solution of a cluster CL_i, $E' \in N(E)$ is a neighbor of the elite solution E, CL_i plays the role of the tabu list with a dynamic length and $Cmax$ is the makespan of the obtained solution. So, this algorithm applies in each case two steps, a *move and insert* first step inspired from [13] to generate new scheduling combination and a second step to save the best found solution in the tabu list (which is CL_i) after each generation case, we give here how to proceed:

```
Begin
  E ← Elite(CL_i)
  While N(E) ≠ ∅
    E' ← {Move and insert(E) | E' ∈ N(E)}
    If Cmax(E') < Cmax(E) and E' ∉ CL_i
      E ← E'
      CL_i ← E'
    End if
  End while
  Return E
End
```

By finishing this local search step, the CAs agents terminate the process by sending their last elite solutions to the SA agent, which considers the best one of them the global solution for the FJSP.

4 Experimental Results

4.1 Experimental Setup

The proposed GATS + HM is implemented in Java language on a 2.10 GHz Intel Core 2 Duo processor and 3 Gb of RAM memory, using the *eclipse* IDE to code the approach and the multiagent platform *Jade* [1] to create the holonic multiagent model. To evaluate its efficiency, numerical tests are made based on two sets of benchmark instances from the literature of the FJSP: the *Kacem data* [9] consisting of 5 problems considering a number of jobs ranging from 4 to 15 with a number of operations for all jobs ranges from 12 to 56, which will be processed on a number of machines ranging from 5 to 10. The *Hurink edata* [7] consisting of 40 problems (la01–la40) inspired from the classical job shop instances of [10], where three test problems are generated: rdata, vdata and edata which is used in this paper. Due to the non-deterministic nature of the proposed approach, we run it five independent times for each one of the two instances in order to obtain significant results. The computational results are presented by four metrics such as the best makespan (*Best*), the average of makespan (*Avg Cmax*), the average of CPU time in seconds (*Avg CPU*), and the standard deviation of makespan (*Dev %*) which is calculated by Eq. (9). The Mko is the makespan obtained by Our approach and Mkc is the makespan of an approach that we chose to Compare to. The used parameter settings for our approach are adjusted experimentally and presented as follow: Crossover probability = 1.0, Mutation probability = 1.0, Maximum number of iterations = 1000. The population size ranged from 15 to 400 depending on the complexity of the problem.

$$\text{Dev} = [(\text{Mkc} - \text{Mko})/\text{Mkc}] \times 100\% \tag{9}$$

4.2   Experimental Comparisons

To show the efficiency of our GATS + HM approach, we compare its obtained results from the two previously cited data sets with other well known algorithms in the literature of the FJSP. The chosen algorithms are the N1-1000 of [7], the AL + CGA of [9], the MATSLO + of [4], the Hybrid NSGA-II of [16] and the Heuristic of [17]. The different comparative results are displayed in the Tables 2 and 3, where the first column takes the name of each instance, the second column gives the size of each instance, with *n* the jobs number and *m* the machines number (*n* × *m*), and the remaining columns detail the experimental results of the different chosen approaches in terms of the best Cmax (*Best*) and the standard deviation (*Dev %*). The bold values in the tables signify the best obtained results and the N/A means that the result is not available.

Discussion about the Kacem and Hurink instance results. By analyzing the Table 2, it can be seen that our approach GATS + HM is the best one which solves the fives instances of Kacem. In fact, the GATS + HM outperforms the AL + CGA in four out of five instances, the Hybrid NSGA-II in two out of five instances, and the Heuristic in three out of five instances. Also, our approach attains the same results obtained by the chosen approaches, such as in the case 1 (4 × 5) for the Hybrid NSGA-II and the Heuristic; in the case 4 (10 × 10) for all the three algorithms; in the case 5 (15 × 10) for the Hybrid NSGA-II. From Table 3, the comparison results show that the GATS + HM obtains seven out of ten best results for the Hurink edata instances (la01-la05) and (la16-la20). Indeed, our approach outperforms the N1-1000 in eight out of ten instances. Moreover, our GATS + HM outperforms the MATSLO + in seven out of ten instances. For the comparison with the literature lower bound LB, the GATS + HM attains the same results for the la01, la02, la04, la05, la16, la17 and la20 instances, but it gets slightly worse result for the la03, la18 and la19 instances. Furthermore, by solving this second data set, our GATS + HM attains the same results obtained by the chosen approaches such as in the la01 for the MATSLO +; in the la02 for the N1-1000 and the MATSLO +; in the la05 for the N1-1000 and the MATSLO +. By analyzing the computational time in seconds and the comparison results of our approach in term of makespan, we can distinguish the efficiency of the new proposed GATS + HM relatively to the literature of the FJSP. This efficiency is explained by the flexible selection of the promising parts of the search space by the clustering operator after the genetic algorithm process and by applying the intensification technique of the tabu search allowing to start from an elite solution to attain new more dominant solutions.

Table 2. Results of the Kacem instances

Instance	Problem n×m	AL+CGA		Hybrid NSGA-II		Heuristic		GATS+HM		
		Best	Dev (%)	Best	Dev (%)	Best	Dev (%)	Best	Avg Cmax	Avg C.P.U (in seconds)
case 1	4×5	16	31,250	11	0	11	0	11	11,00	0,05
case 2	8×8	15	6,666	15	6,666	15	6,666	14	14,20	0,36
case 3	10×7	15	26,666	N/A	--	13	15,384	11	11,40	0,72
case 4	10×10	7	0	7	0	7	0	7	7,60	1,51
case 5	15×10	23	52,173	11	0	12	8,333	11	11,60	29,71

Table 3. Results of the Hurink edata instances

Instance	Problem n×m	LB		N1-1000		MATSLO+		GATS+HM		
		Best	Dev (%)	Best	Dev (%)	Best	Dev (%)	Best	Avg Cmax	Avg C.P.U (in seconds)
la01	10×5	609	0	611	0,327	609	0	609	609,00	24,64
la02	10×5	655	0	655	0	655	0	655	655,00	4,65
la03	10×5	550	-3,091	573	1,047	575	1,391	567	567,40	10,67
la04	10×5	568	0	578	1,730	579	1,900	568	569,60	22,13
la05	10×5	503	0	503	0	503	0	503	503,00	10,22
la16	10×10	892	0	924	3,463	896	0,446	892	909,60	73,14
la17	10×10	707	0	757	6,605	708	0,141	707	709,60	116,58
la18	10×10	842	-0,119	864	2,431	845	0,237	843	848,60	34,98
la19	10×10	796	-1,005	850	5,412	813	1,107	804	813,40	36,88
la20	10×10	857	0	919	6,746	863	0,695	857	859,80	70,36

5   Conclusion

In this paper, a new holonic multiagent model based on two combined metaheuristics, called GATS + HM, is proposed for the flexible job shop scheduling problem (FJSP). In this approach, a Neighborhood-based Genetic Algorithm is adapted by a Scheduler Agent (SA) for a global exploration of the search space. Then, a local search technique is applied by a set of Cluster Agents (CAs) to guide the research in promising regions. To measure its performance, numerical tests are made using two well known data sets from the literature of the FJSP. The experimental results show that the proposed approach is efficient in comparison to others approaches. In the future work, we will integrate new constraints of other extensions of the FJSP, such as the transportation resources. So, we will make improvements to our approach to adapt it to this new transformation and study its effects on the makespan.

References

1. Bellifemine, F., Poggi, A., Rimassa, G.: JADE - a FIPA-compliant agent framework. In: The fourth International Conference and Exhibition on The Practical Application of Intelligent Agents and Multi-Agent Technology, pp. 97–108 (1999)
2. Bozejko, W., Uchronski, M., Wodecki, M.: The new golf neighborhood for the flexible job shop problem. In: The International Conference on Computational Science, pp. 289–296 (2010)
3. Chen, H., Ihlow, J., Lehmann, C.: A genetic algorithm for flexible job-shop scheduling. In: The IEEE International Conference on Robotics and Automation, pp. 1120–1125 (1999)
4. Ennigrou, M., Ghédira, K.: New local diversification techniques for the flexible job shop problem with a multi-agent approach. Auton. Agent. Multi-agent Syst. 17(2), 270–287 (2008)
5. Gao, J., Sun, L., Gen, M.: A hybrid genetic and variable neighborhood descent algorithm for flexible job shop scheduling problems. Comput. Oper. Res. 35(9), 2892–2907 (2008)
6. Garey, M.R., Johnson, D.S., Sethi, R.: The complexity of flow shop and job shop scheduling. Math. Oper. Res. 1(2), 117–129 (1976)
7. Hurink, J., Jurisch, B., Thole, M.: Tabu search for the job-shop scheduling problem with multi-purpose machines. Oper. Res. Spektrum 15(4), 205–215 (1994)
8. Johnson, S.C.: Hierarchical clustering schemes. Psychometrika 32(3), 241–254 (1967)
9. Kacem, I., Hammadi, S., Borne, P.: Pareto-optimality approach for flexible job-shop scheduling problems: hybridization of evolutionary algorithms and fuzzy logic. Math. Comput. Simul. 60(3–5), 245–276 (2002)
10. Lawrence, S.: Supplement to resource constrained project scheduling: an experimental investigation of heuristic scheduling techniques. Technical report, GSIA, Carnegie-Mellon University, Pittsburgh (1984)
11. Lee, K., Yamakawa, T., Lee, K.M.: A genetic algorithm for general machine scheduling problems. In: The second IEEE international Conference on Knowledge-Based Intelligent Electronic Systems, pp. 60–66 (1998)
12. Li, J., Pan, Q., Suganthan, P., Chua, T.: A hybrid tabu search algorithm with an efficient neighbourhood structure for the flexible job shop scheduling problem. Int. J. Adv. Manuf. Technol. 52(5), 683–697 (2011)
13. Mastrolilli, M., Gambardella, L.: Effective neighbourhood functions for the flexible job shop problem. J. Sched. 3(1), 3–20 (2000)
14. Sonmez, A.I., Baykasoglu, A.: A new dynamic programming formulation of (nm) flow shop sequencing problems with due dates. Int. J. Prod. Res. 36(8), 2269–2283 (1998)
15. Xing, L., Chen, Y., Wang, P., Zhao, Q., Xiong, J.: A knowledge-based ant colony optimization for flexible job shop scheduling problems. Appl. Soft Comput. 10(3), 888–896 (2010)
16. Zhang, C., Gu, P., Jiang, P.: Low-carbon scheduling and estimating for a flexible job shop based on carbon footprint and carbon efficiency of multi-job processing. J. Eng. Manuf. 39 (32), 1–15 (2014)
17. Ziaee, M.: A heuristic algorithm for solving flexible job shop scheduling problem. Int. J. Adv. Manuf. Technol. 71(1–4), 519–528 (2014)

Heuristics for Non-dominated Sets
of Two-Agent Scheduling on a Single
Parallel-Batching Machine

Jun-qiang Wang[1,2(✉)], Cheng-wu Zhang[1,2], Guo-qiang Fan[1,2],
and Shu-dong Sun[1,2]

[1] Performance Analysis Center of Production and Operations Systems (PacPos),
Northwestern Polytechnical University, Xi'an 710072, Shaanxi
People's Republic of China
wangjq@nwpu.edu.cn
[2] Key Laboratory of Contemporary Design and Integrated Manufacturing
Technology, Ministry of Education, Northwestern Polytechnical University,
Xi'an 710072, Shaanxi, People's Republic of China

Abstract. We study a bi-objective problem of scheduling the jobs from two
agents on a single parallel-batching machine with the objective of minimizing
the makespans of the both agents. All jobs have an equal processing time and
non-identical job sizes. We define a boundary of Pareto-optimal set and then
present two metrics to evaluate the quality of a non-dominated set. Based on two
different strategies, two heuristics are proposed to generate non-dominated sets.
Furthermore, we compare the performance of the heuristics with the widely used
non-dominated sorting genetic algorithm (NSGA-II), and evaluate the quality
of the obtained non-dominated set based on the proposed metrics. The results
show that the proposed heuristics outperform NSGA-II, and the obtained non-
dominated set is very close to the Pareto-optimal set.

Keywords: Two-agent scheduling · Heuristics · Pareto-optimal set · Parallel-
batching machine · Makespan

1 Introduction

Parallel-batching machines are encountered in many industries, such as the burn-in
oven in the semiconductor industry [1], the heat-treatment furnace in the meta working
industry [2], and the harden oven in the aircraft industry [3]. This type of parallel-
batching machines is often a bottleneck due to some inevitable factors such as
equipment cost, energy consumption, installation space limitation, environmental
requirement and high competition, etc. Hence, they are numbered. Furthermore, the
operations on parallel-batching machines typically have longer processing times than
other operations, yet they play a critical role to improve the physical or chemical
properties of materials. Therefore, the orders from different customers, or agents, often
compete for the use of the parallel-batching machines for their own interests.

Two-agent scheduling problem was firstly introduced by Baker and Smith [4] in
2003 and Agnetis et al. [5] in 2004, and has attracted a large amount of attentions in

© Springer International Publishing Switzerland 2015
J. Bajo et al. (Eds.): PAAMS 2015 Workshops, CCIS 524, pp. 55–68, 2015.
DOI: 10.1007/978-3-319-19033-4_5

recent years [6], but few work on parallel-batching machines. Related work on two-agent scheduling on a single parallel-batching machine can be classified into three categories. With regards to the linear combination problem of objectives, Yazdani Sabouni and Jolai [7] considered a linear combination of the makespan of the first agent and the maximum lateness of the other agent. Feng et al. [8] further studied a special case of [7] where the machine capacity is unbounded and two agents are incompatible, and presented a polynomial-time algorithm.

With regards to the constraint problem that optimize one objective on the condition that the other objectives meet certain constraints, Mor and Mosheiov [9] designed an optimal algorithm to minimize the total flowtime of the first agent subject to an upper bound on the total flowtime of the other agent. Li and Yuan [10] minimized the makespan of the first agent subject to an upper bound on the makespan of the other agent. Later, Fan et al. [11] studied the problem with the same objective as that in [10] but with identical job sizes, and showed that the problem with incompatible agents can be solved in polynomial-time. However, when the two agents are compatible, the problem becomes NP-hard, for which they a dynamic programming algorithm and a fully polynomial-time approximation scheme (FPTAS).

With regards to the bi-objective problem of obtaining a non-dominated set, Tan et al. [12] developed an improved ant colony algorithm to search the non-dominated set. To the best of our knowledge, there is no study on the deterministic algorithm for the bi-objective optimization problem to obtain the non-dominated set of two-agent scheduling on a single parallel-batching machine. Such a deterministic heuristic algorithm is the focus of this paper.

We consider a problem that schedules the jobs from two agents on a single parallel-batching machine. Two agents, denoted as agent A and agent B, have their own jobs to be processed. Agent A has n_A jobs, denoted as $\mathcal{J}^A = \{J_1^A, J_2^A, \ldots, J_{n_A}^A\}$. Agent B has n_B jobs, denoted as $\mathcal{J}^B = \{J_1^B, J_2^B, \ldots, J_{n_B}^B\}$. The total number of jobs is n, $n = n_A + n_B$. All jobs are available for processing at time zero. Preemption and splitting are not allowed. Let p_j^X and s_j^X denote the processing time and the size of job J_j^X respectively, where $j = 1, 2, \ldots, n_X$, $X \in \{A, B\}$. All jobs have an equal processing time, i.e., $p_j^X = 1$, and $s_j^X \leq C$ for all J_j^X, where C denotes the machine capacity. The two agents are compatible, i.e., jobs from different agents can be processed in one batch. The machine can process a number of jobs simultaneously as a batch provided that the total size of all the jobs in the batch cannot exceed C. The processing time of each batch on the parallel-batching machine is equal to 1. The objective is to minimize the makespans of the both agents. Our problem is denoted as $1|p - batching, p_j^X = 1, s_j^X \leq C|ND$ $(C_{\max}^A, C_{\max}^B)$, where $C_{\max}^X$ is the makespan of agent X. $ND(C_{\max}^A, C_{\max}^B)$ indicates that the objective is to minimize $C_{\max}^A$ and $C_{\max}^B$, obtaining non-dominated set. Even we consider the problem that the objective is to minimize the makespan of one agent, this single objective problem is equivalent to bin packing problem, which is NP-hard in the strong sense [13]. Therefore, our problem is more complicated.

The rest of the paper is organized as follows: A boundary of Pareto-optimal set is presented in Sect. 2. Two metrics to evaluate the quality of a non-dominated set are presented in Sect. 3. Based on two different strategies, two heuristics are presented to generate non-dominated sets in Sect. 4. Computational experiments are conducted to evaluate the performance of the proposed heuristics and the quality of the obtained non-dominated set in Sect. 5. Finally, we conclude in Sect. 6.

2 Boundary of Pareto-Optimal Set

According to Deb [14], feasible solution s_1 dominates feasible solution s_2 ($s_1 \succ s_2$) if and only if $C_{\max}^A(s_1) \leq C_{\max}^A(s_2)$ and $C_{\max}^B(s_1) \leq C_{\max}^B(s_2)$ with at least one strict inequality. Among a set of solutions P, the non-dominated set of solutions E is a set in which each solution is not dominated by any solution in the set P. When the set P is the entire space, the resulting non-dominated set E is called the Pareto-optimal set. It is clear that a Pareto-optimal set is always a non-dominated set, not vice versa.

Definition 1. Boundary of Pareto-optimal set. The boundary of Pareto-optimal set is a set of points that enclose a closed region in which all Pareto-optimal solutions are included.

For our problem, the boundary of Pareto-optimal set is illustrated in Fig. 1. The u-axis and v-axis are the makespan of jobs from agent A and agent B, respectively. Point $P_i(u_i, v_i)$ represents a feasible solution. Therefore both u_i and v_i are integer.

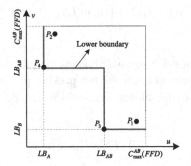

Fig. 1. Boundary of Pareto-optimal set

We give two points: $P_1(u_1, v_1)$ and $P_2(u_2, v_2)$. The point P_1 denotes a solution that the makespan of jobs from agent A is minimum provided that the makespan of jobs from agent B is optimal. Similarly, the point P_2 denotes a solution that the makespan of jobs from agent B is minimum provided that the makespan of jobs from agent A is optimal. There is no Pareto-optimal set in the region $\{(u, v) | u \geq u_1\} \cup \{(u, v) | v \geq v_2\}$, otherwise it is dominated by solution P_1 or solution P_2. Furthermore, there is no feasible solution in the region $\{(u, v) | u < u_2\} \cup \{(u, v) | v < v_1\}$, otherwise v_1 and u_2 are not the optimal makespan of agent B and agent A respectively. Let $C_{\max}^A(FFD)$ and $C_{\max}^B(FFD)$ be the makespan of jobs from agent A and agent B, respectively, which is obtained by the First Fit Decreasing (FFD) rule [15], where FFD arranges the jobs in a decreasing order according to their sizes firstly, then assign a job at a time from the head and place the job to the first batch with enough space to accommodate it. We denote $C_{\max}^A(FFD) + C_{\max}^B(FFD)$ as $C_{\max}^{AB}(FFD)$. Let LB_A and LB_B be a lower bound of the makespan of jobs from agent A and agent B, respectively. Obviously, for point P_1, $u_1 \le C_{\max}^{AB}(FFD)$, $v_1 \ge LB_B$; for point P_2, $u_2 \ge LB_A$, $v_2 \le C_{\max}^{AB}(FFD)$. Therefore, the Pareto-optimal set is in the region of R_1,

$$R_1 = \{(u,v)|LB_A \le u \le C_{\max}^{AB}(FFD),\ LB_B \le v \le C_{\max}^{AB}(FFD)\} \tag{1}$$

Then, we cut the region of R_1 to make it smaller. We mix jobs from agent A and agent B together and treat them as undifferentiated jobs. Let LB_{AB} be a lower bound of the makespan of these undifferentiated jobs. Thus, there is no feasible solution in the region $\{(u,v)|u<LB_{AB}\} \cap \{(u,v)|v<LB_{AB}\}$. Therefore, the Pareto-optimal set is in the region of R_2,

$$R_2 = \{(u,v)|u \ge LB_{AB}\} \cup \{(u,v)|v \ge LB_{AB}\} \tag{2}$$

Thus, the closed region, $R_1 \cap R_2$, is the efficient region in which all Pareto-optimal solutions are included. Furthermore, we define the red broken line shown in Fig. 1 as a lower boundary of Pareto-optimal set for our problem, which is denoted as follows..

$$\{(u,v)|u = LB_A, LB_{AB} \le v \le C_{\max}^{AB}(FFD)\} \cup \{(u,v)|LB_A \le u \le LB_{AB}, v = LB_{AB}\} \cup$$
$$\{(u,v)|u = LB_{AB}, LB_B \le v \le LB_{AB}\} \cup \{(u,v)|LB_{AB} \le u \le C_{\max}^{AB}(FFD), v = LB_B\} \tag{3}$$

For determining each of the three lower bounds LB_A, LB_B and LB_{AB}, we obtain two lower bounds based on the results for the bin packing problem from Dósa [16] and Martello [17] and choose the bigger one, which are denoted as LB^1 and LB^2 respectively,

$$LB^1 = \lceil (9 \cdot FFD(I) - 6)/11 \rceil \tag{4}$$

$$LB^2 = \max_{0 \le K \le C/2} \left\{ |N_1| + |N_2| + \max\left\{0, \left\lceil \left(\sum_{i \in N_3} s_i - (|N_2|C - \sum_{i \in N_2} s_i)\right)\Big/ C \right\rceil \right\} \right\} \tag{5}$$

where K is an integer, $0 \le K \le C/2$, C is the bin capacity, s_i is the size of item i, I is the set of items, $N_1 = \{i \in I : s_i > C - K\}$, $N_2 = \{i \in I : C/2 < s_i \le C - K\}$ and $N_3 = \{i \in I : K \le s_i \le C/2\}$.

Therefore, $LB_A = \max\{LB_A^1, LB_A^2\}$, $LB_B = \max\{LB_B^1, LB_B^2\}$ and $LB_{AB} = \max\{LB_{AB}^1, LB_{AB}^2\}$.

Here, we analyze two important points P_3 and P_4 in Fig. 1, and have Theorem 1.

Theorem 1. Let E be a non-dominated set, $E = \{P_3, P_4\} \Rightarrow E$ is the Pareto-optimal set.

Proof. Because all the Pareto-optimal solutions are in the region of $R_1 \cap R_2$, and $E = \{P_3, P_4\}$ dominate all the solutions in the region of $R_1 \cap R_2$, there is no solution that can dominate the solutions in E. Therefore, E is the Pareto-optimal set.   □

3 Metrics of Non-dominated Sets

To evaluate the quality of a non-dominated set, we present two metrics, D_{avg} and D_{max}, on the basis of the proposed lower boundary of Pareto-optimal set in Sect. 3 and the well-known distance metrics in [18]. D_{avg} and D_{max} represent the average distance and maximum distance from the non-dominated set to the lower boundary of Pareto-optimal set, respectively.

$$D_{avg} = \sum_{P_T \in T} \min_{P \in E} d(P, P_T) \Big/ |T| \tag{6}$$

$$D_{max} = \max_{P_T \in T} \left\{ \min_{P \in E} d(P, P_T) \right\} \tag{7}$$

where T is the set of integer points on the lower boundary of Pareto-optimal set. $d(P, P_T) = \max\{(u - u_T)/\Delta_u, (v - v_T)/\Delta_v\}$, $P \in E$, $P_T \in T$, Δ_u and Δ_v are the range of u-axis and v-axis respectively among all the solutions in set E and set T.

As for the points P_3 and P_4 as shown in Fig. 1, we get Theorem 2.

Theorem 2. $E = \{P_3, P_4\} \Leftrightarrow D_{avg}=0 \Leftrightarrow D_{max}=0$

Proof. If $E = \{P_3, P_4\}$, for $\forall P_T \in T\backslash\{P_3, P_4\}$, P_T is dominated by P_3 or P_4. If P_T is dominated by P_3, $u_3 - u_T \leq 0, v_3 - v_T = 0$ or $u_3 - u_T=0, v_3 - v_T \leq 0$, thus $d(P_3, P_T) = \max\{(u_3 - u_T)/\Delta_u, (v_3 - v_T)/\Delta_v\}=0$. Similarly, if P_T is dominated by P_4, $d(P_4, P_T) = \max\{(u_4 - u_T)/\Delta_u, (v_4 - v_T)/\Delta_v\}=0$. Therefore, $\forall P_T \in T$, $\min_{P \in E} d(P, P_T)=0$, that is $D_{avg}=0$, $D_{max}=0$.

If $D_{avg}=0$ or $D_{max}=0$, for $\forall P_T \in T$, $P \in E$, $\min_{P \in E} d(P, P_T)=0$. We proof $\{P_3, P_4\} \subset E$ by contradiction. Without loss of generality, we assume $P_3 \notin E$, then for $\forall P_k \in E$, $v_k - v_3 > 0$, $d(P_k, P_3) = \max\{(u_k - u_3)/\Delta_u, (v_k - v_3)/\Delta_v\} > 0$ and $\min_{P \in E} d(P, P_T) \neq 0$, it is a contradiction. Therefore, $\{P_3, P_4\} \subset E$. Because P_T is dominated by P_3 or P_4 for all $P_T \in T\backslash\{P_3, P_4\}$, there is no other point belong to E except P_3 and P_4, i.e. $E = \{P_3, P_4\}$.   □

4 Heuristics

Based on ε-constraint method [19], we select C_{max}^A as primary objective, and transform the objective C_{max}^B into the constraint $C_{max}^B \leq \varepsilon$ where ε is an integer. This ε-constraint problem is denoted as $1|p - batching, p_j^X = 1, s_j^X \leq C|C_{max}^A, C_{max}^B \leq \varepsilon$ and is tackled by our heuristic strategies: Reserved-Space-Heuristic (RSH) and Dynamic-Mix-Heuristic (DMH). Then, two corresponding heuristics, named $H1$ and $H2$, are proposed to generate non-dominated sets.

4.1 Heuristic Strategies

RSH and DMH are both developed based on the FFD rule, but employ different strategies for satisfying the hard constraint of $C_{max}^B \leq \varepsilon$. RSH emphasizes the minimization of the makespan of agent A without occupying the reserved space for agent B. While DMH focuses on maximizing the utilization of the batches by mixing together as many jobs from agent A and agent B as possible, provided that the jobs from agent B must be assigned before ε. Furthermore, DMH reserves a part of space in each batch for the jobs from agent B rather than reserves a number of whole batches as what RSH does.

(1) Heuristic Strategy RSH

In order to satisfy the constraint of $C_{max}^B \leq \varepsilon$, RSH reserves enough batches in advance for the jobs from agent B, and then assigns as many of the jobs from agent A as possible to the remaining batches. If there are remaining space in the batches only filled with the jobs from agent A, RSH assigns the jobs from agent B to these batches in order to improve their utilization. After that, the remaining jobs from agent B are assigned to the reserved batches. Finally, the remaining jobs from agent A are assigned. The following is a detailed description of RSH.

Step 1. Suppose the number of batches that assigning the jobs from agent B using the FFD rule is p, $0 \leq p \leq \varepsilon$, then reserve the batches from $B_{\varepsilon-p+1}$ to B_{ε} for the jobs from agent B.

Step 2. Assign the jobs from agent A to the batches starting from B_1 to $B_{\varepsilon-p}$ using the FFD rule. Then, the remaining jobs from agent A that cannot be assigned to the batches from B_1 to $B_{\varepsilon-p}$ are stored into set L_A. If L_A is empty, go to Step 3; otherwise, go to Step 4.

Step 3. Rearrange the batches occupied by the jobs from agent A in a non-increasing order according to their remaining space. Then, assign the jobs from agent B to the batches starting from B_1 using the FFD rule. RSH stops.

Step 4. Rearrange the batches from B_1 to $B_{\varepsilon-p}$ in a non-increasing order according to their remaining space. Then, assign the jobs from agent B to the batches starting from B_1 to $B_{\varepsilon-p}$ using the FFD rule, and the remaining jobs from agent B that cannot be assigned to the batches from B_1 to $B_{\varepsilon-p}$ are stored into set L_B.

Step 5. Assign the jobs in L_B to the batches backwards from B_{ε} using the FFD rule.

Step 6. Rearrange the batches from $B_{\varepsilon-p+1}$ to B_{ε} in a non-increasing order according to the remaining space. Then assign the jobs in L_A to the batches from $B_{\varepsilon-p+1}$ using the FFD rule.

(2) Heuristic Strategy DMH

The idea of DMH comes from an observation that scheduling all jobs together, without any distinction between agent A and agent B, may generate a schedule with a better use of machine capacity, which may result in a shorter makespan of agent A. In order to implement mix strategy while satisfying the constraint of $C_{max}^B \leq \varepsilon$, DMH reserves a part of space in each batch for the jobs from agent B. Then, DMH mixes all the remaining jobs from agent B and agent A, and assigns them to the remaining space in each batch. DMH employs a dynamic adjustment strategy to determine the number of jobs from agent B that are assigned to the reserved space in each batch.

Before describing DMH in detail, we first define two parameters: N and M. N is the number of remaining, unassigned jobs from agent B, and the initial value is n_B. M is the number of empty batches before B_ε, and the initial value is ε. $\lceil N/M \rceil$ is the maximal number of jobs from agent B to be assigned to the reserved space in each batch, and the value is changing dynamically with the ongoing assignment procedure. DMH focuses on one batch at a time, i.e., it assigns jobs to B_1, then to B_2, and then to B_3, etc. In this way, a schedule that some batches only filled with jobs from agent A are in the back parts and some batches only filled with jobs from agent B are in the front part, from B_1 to B_ε, may be generated. Therefore, DMH exchanges these batches to ensure that the jobs from agent A can be processed as early as possible. The following is a detailed description of DMH.

Step 1. $N = n_B$, $M = \varepsilon$, $i = 1$.

Step 2.   Assign the jobs from agent B to B_i using the FFD rule, until the number of jobs in B_i reaches $\lceil N/M \rceil$ or no more jobs from agent B can be assigned to B_i.

Step 3.   Assign the remaining jobs from agent B and agent A together to B_i using the FFD rule, until B_i cannot accommodate any job.

Step 4.   Update the value of N and M, N is the number of unassigned jobs from agent B, $M = M - 1$. $i = i + 1$. If all jobs from agent A and agent B have been assigned, go to Step 5; otherwise, go to Step 2.

Step 5.   Adjust the sequence of the batches from B_1 to B_ε, so that the batches only filled with jobs from agent B are the last batches before B_ε.

4.2   Heuristics $H1$ and $H2$

Based on RSH and DMH, two corresponding heuristics, $H1$ and $H2$, are proposed to generate non-dominated sets for $1|p - batching, p_j^X = 1, s_j^X \le C|ND(C_{max}^A, C_{max}^B)$ by solving $1|p - batching, p_j^X = 1, s_j^X \le C|C_{max}^A, C_{max}^B \le \varepsilon$ iteratively with different value of ε. The value of ε varies from the upper bound ε_{max} to the pseudo lower bound ε_{min} of C_{max}^B. When $\varepsilon > \varepsilon_{max}$, the function of $C_{max}^B \le \varepsilon$ become invalid for generating a non-dominated solution. When $\varepsilon < \varepsilon_{min}$, no feasible solution can be obtained for the ε-constraint problem by RSH and DMH.

Since $H1$ and $H2$ are similar except for the heuristic strategy. For simplicity, we describe them as $H1$ ($H2$) corresponding to RSH (DMH). Let l be the index of non-dominated solutions, and S_{H1} (S_{H2}) be the non-dominated set obtained by $H1$ ($H2$). The following is a detailed description of heuristic $H1$ ($H2$).

Step 1.   Calculate ε_{max} and ε_{min}.

     (1)   Assign the jobs from agent A to the batches starting from the first batch using the FFD rule, and rearrange these batches in a non-increasing order according to their remaining space. Then assign the jobs from

         agent B to the batches starting from the first batch using the FFD rule. The makespan of agent B is $\varepsilon_{\max}$.

    (2) Assign the jobs from agent B to the batches starting from the first batch using the FFD rule. The makespan of agent B is $\varepsilon_{\min}$.

Step 2.   Initialization. $\varepsilon = \varepsilon_{\max}$, $l = 1$, $S_{H1} = \emptyset$ $(S_{H2} = \emptyset)$.

Step 3.   Use RSH (DMH) to solve $1|p - batching, p_j^X = 1, s_j^X \leq C|C_{\max}^A, C_{\max}^B \leq \varepsilon$, and output solution $s_{H1}(l)$ $(s_{H2}(l))$.

Step 4. $S_{H1} = S_{H1} \cup \{s_{H1}(l)\}$ $(S_{H2} = S_{H2} \cup \{s_{H2}(l)\})$, $\varepsilon = C_{\max}^B(s_{H1}(l)) - 1$ $(\varepsilon = C_{\max}^B(s_{H2}(l)) - 1)$, $l = l + 1$. If $\varepsilon \geq \varepsilon_{\min}$, go to Step 3; otherwise, go to Step 5.

Step 5.   Delete the dominated solutions in S_{H1} (S_{H2}) and output S_{H1} (S_{H2}).

5 Performance Comparison and Analysis

5.1 Experimental Design

We randomly generate the testing instances and vary the four factors: the machine capacity C, the sizes of the jobs s_j^X, the total number of jobs n and the number of jobs from agent A n_A. We set the machine capacity to 100, i.e., $c = 100$, for all instances. The sizes of all jobs are generated using a Poisson distribution, i.e., $s_j^X \sim P(50)$. If a randomly generated value s_j^X is greater than 100, we set $s_j^X = 100$. The total number of jobs has five different cases: $n = 10, 20, 30, 40, 50$. The number of jobs from agent A has four cases: $n_A/n = 0.2, 0.4, 0.6, 0.8$.

We use the widely used non-dominated sorting genetic algorithm (*NSGA-II*) [20] for performance comparison. In *NSGA-II*, we encode the chromosomes based on the job sizes. In order to identify different jobs from agent A and agent B in decoding operator, we add a fractional number $1/(C \times 100)$ to the size of each job only for agent B, and increase the machine capacity to $c + 1$. In one batch, the total added size of jobs from agent B is no more than 0.01, which is much less than the added space of each batch (0.1). Furthermore, any job from either agent A or agent B cannot be assigned to the added space of each batch (0.1) since all their sizes are integers. Thus, it is convenient to decode chromosomes according to these decimal marks. We adopt a linear order crossover with a crossover probability $p_c = 0.9$ and a swap mutation with a mutation probability $p_m = 0.15$. For the selection operator, we employ an elitism strategy based on the non-dominated sorting and crowded-comparison operator [20].

The proposed heuristics and *NSGA-II* are coded in MATLAB 8.3.0 and run on Intel(R) Pentium(R) CPU G640 @ 2.80 GHz with 2 GB RAM under Windows 7 environment.

5.2 Performance Comparison Among *H1*, *H2* and *NSGA-II*

To evaluate the performance of heuristics, we use the coverage metric $C(X, Y)$ of two sets X and Y, which is defined as follows [21].

$$C(X,Y) = \frac{|\{y \in Y | \exists x \in X : x \succeq y\}|}{|Y|} \qquad (8)$$

where $x \succeq y$ means solution x dominates or equal to solution y.

Obviously, $C(X,Y) \in [0,1]$. When $C(X,Y) = 1$, all solutions in Y are dominated by or equal to the solutions in X. When $C(X,Y) = 0$, all solutions in Y cannot be dominated by the solutions in X. The smaller the value of $C(X,Y)$ is, the better the set Y is. Note that $C(X,Y)$ and $C(Y,X)$ are not symmetrical. Therefore, we also calculate $C(Y,X)$ in the experiments.

Based on the coverage metric, we have four ratios: $C(S_{H1}, S_{H2})$, $C(S_{H2}, S_{H1})$, $C(S_{H1\&H2}, S_{NSGA-II})$ and $C(S_{NSGA-II}, S_{H1\&H2})$, where $S_{H1\&H2}$ is the non-dominated set of $S_{H1} \cup S_{H2}$ and $S_{NSGA-II}$ is the non-dominated set obtained by NSGA-II.

The performance comparison results are shown in Table 1. We generate 1000 random instances in total. For each problem, 50 instances are randomly generated and the average of 50 instances is calculated as shown in Table 1.

Table 1. Performance comparison results

n	n_A/n	$C(S_{H1}, S_{H2})$	$C(S_{H2}, S_{H1})$	$C(S_{H1\&H2}, S_{NSGA-II})$	$C(S_{NSGA-II}, S_{H1\&H2})$
10	0.2	0.9700	0.6500	1.0000	0.6900
	0.4	0.9600	0.6167	1.0000	0.5883
	0.6	0.9667	0.5683	1.0000	0.5250
	0.8	1.0000	0.6400	1.0000	0.7100
20	0.2	0.9600	0.5900	1.0000	0.5033
	0.4	0.9033	0.5183	0.9700	0.4467
	0.6	0.9317	0.5117	1.0000	0.3817
	0.8	0.9400	0.5567	1.0000	0.4700
30	0.2	0.9867	0.4850	1.0000	0.4017
	0.4	0.9250	0.4970	1.0000	0.2250
	0.6	0.9267	0.4900	1.0000	0.1783
	0.8	0.9400	0.4983	1.0000	0.3033
40	0.2	0.8665	0.5012	1.0000	0.1220
	0.4	0.8113	0.5173	1.0000	0.1107
	0.6	0.8570	0.4963	0.9800	0.0897
	0.8	0.8800	0.4917	1.0000	0.1717
50	0.2	0.8733	0.5333	1.0000	0.0750
	0.4	0.9180	0.4777	1.0000	0.0000
	0.6	0.8173	0.5317	0.9900	0.0067
	0.8	0.8907	0.5067	1.0000	0.0683

As for the performance comparison between $H1$ and $H2$, from columns 3 and 4 in Table 1, we notice that $C(S_{H2}, S_{H1}) < C(S_{H1}, S_{H2})$ holds for all testing instances, which means that $H1$ finds more non-dominated solutions than $H2$. Therefore, $H1$ is better than $H2$ from the perspective of the number of non-dominated solutions. Furthermore, we can conclude that $H2$ is still useful for obtaining non-dominated solutions, because $C(S_{H1}, S_{H2})$ is not equal to 1 except for the case that $n = 10$ and $n_A/n = 0.8$. It means that $H2$ can generate some non-dominated solutions that are different from the solutions obtained by $H1$ in the most cases. Therefore $H2$ is a beneficial complement to $H1$. This fact inspires us to adopt $S_{H1} \cup S_{H2}$ to generate a more complete non-dominated set $S_{H1\&H2}$.

We further compare $S_{H1\&H2}$, with $S_{NSGA-II}$. From the column 5 in Table 1, we find that $C(S_{H1\&H2}, S_{NSGA-II})$ is equal to 1 in the most instances, which means that $NSGA-II$ rarely generate a solution that dominates the solutions in $S_{H1\&H2}$. From the column 6, we find that $C(S_{NSGA-II}, S_{H1\&H2})$ is not equal to 0 in the most instances, which means that $NSGA-II$ can generate some solutions belonging to $S_{H1\&H2}$. But, as the number of jobs increases, the ability of $NSGA-II$ for generating non-dominated solutions decreases sharply since $C(S_{NSGA-II}, S_{H1\&H2})$ drop markedly. Specially, for the case where $n = 50$ and $n_A/n = 0.4$, we find that $C(S_{H1\&H2}, S_{NSGA-II}) = 1$ and $C(S_{NSGA-II}, S_{H1\&H2}) = 0$ for all the 50 instances. It implies that the solutions obtained by $NSGA-II$ are completely dominated by the solutions in $S_{H1\&H2}$. Therefore, we conclude that the proposed heuristics outperform NSGA-II.

5.3   Performance Analysis of $S_{H1\&H2}$

We generate 2000 random instances and conduct a statistical analysis of $S_{H1\&H2}$ based on D_{avg} and D_{max}. The parameters $(C, s_j^X, n_A/n)$ are the same as those in Sect. 6.1 except the total number of jobs, $n = 10 : 10 : 100$. For each case, 50 instances are randomly generated.

The computational results of D_{avg} and D_{max} are shown in Figs. 2 and 3. In each figure, there are four subgraphs representing the cases of $n_A/n = 0.2$, $n_A/n = 0.4$,

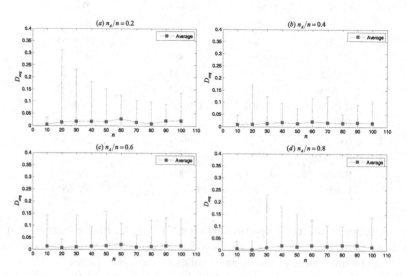

Fig. 2. Computational results of D_{avg}.

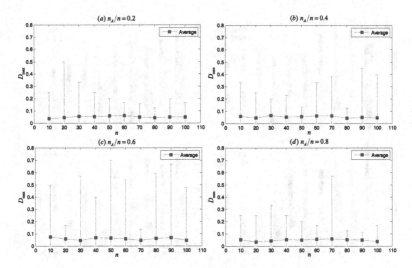

Fig. 3. Computational results of $D_{\max}$.

$n_A/n = 0.6$ and $n_A/n = 0.8$, respectively. In each subgraph, the x-axis is the total number of jobs varying from 10 to 100, and the y-axis is the value of D_{avg} ($D_{\max}$) in Figs. 2 and 3. Each data point in the graph is the average value of the 50 instances. The maximum and minimum values are also illustrated by the error bar. The smaller values of D_{avg} ($D_{\max}$) indicate the better $S_{H1\&H2}$.

From Figs. 2 and 3, we can see that the average values of both D_{avg} and $D_{\max}$ are very small (less than 0.1). The solutions in $S_{H1\&H2}$ are very close to the lower boundary of Pareto-optimal set in the most instances. In addition, the average values of D_{avg} and $D_{\max}$ do not change greatly with the increasing number of jobs. Therefore, the ability of generating non-dominated set ($S_{H1\&H2}$) by $H1$ and $H2$ is steady.

In order to further explore whether the obtained $S_{H1\&H2}$ is the Pareto-optimal set, we count the number of instances satisfying the condition of $D_{avg} = 0$ and $D_{\max} = 0$, which is denoted as N_{PO}. According to Theorem 1 and Theorem 2, if $D_{avg} = 0$ and $D_{\max} = 0$, $S_{H1\&H2}$ is the Pareto-optimal set, i.e., $S_{H1\&H2} = \{P_3, P_4\}$. Also, we count the number of instances that all solutions in $S_{H1\&H2}$ are on the lower boundary of Pareto-optimal set, which is denoted as N_{LB}. $N_{LB} \geq N_{PO}$ since both P_3 and P_4 are on the lower boundary of Pareto-optimal set.

The statistical results are illustrated in Fig. 4. The four subgraphs represent the cases of $n_A/n = 0.2$, $n_A/n = 0.4$, $n_A/n = 0.6$ and $n_A/n = 0.8$ respectively. In each subgraph, the x-axis is the total number of jobs, varying from 10 to 100, and the y-axis is value of number of instances. The blue and red bar represent N_{PO} and N_{LB}, respectively. The bigger the values of N_{PO} and N_{LB} are, the better $S_{H1\&H2}$ is.

As shown in Fig. 4, there exist a certain number of instances on which the proposed heuristics can obtain the Pareto-optimal set. Take the case of $n_A/n = 0.2$ among 10 problems for example. The maximum, minimum and average values of N_{PO} are 42, 12 and 24, respectively. Furthermore, there exist a large number of instances on which the proposed heuristics obtain non-dominated solutions on the lower boundary of

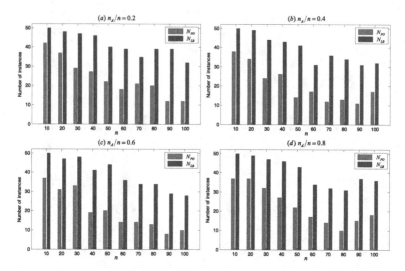

Fig. 4. Statistical results of N_{PO} and N_{LB}.

Pareto-optimal set. As an example, for the case of $n_A/n = 0.6$, the maximum, minimum and average values of N_{LB} are 50, 28 and 40, respectively. We further count N_{PO} and N_{LB} among the 2000 instances. For more than 900 instances (45%), the proposed heuristics can get their Pareto-optimal sets, and for more than 1650 instances (82.5%), the proposed heuristics can get non-dominated solutions on the lower boundary of Pareto-optimal set. In addition, both N_{PO} and N_{LB} slightly decrease and gradually level off as the number of jobs increases regardless of the ratio of n_A/n. Based on the above analysis, we can conclude that the obtained non-dominated set $S_{H1\&H2}$ is very close to the Pareto-optimal set, or is the exact Pareto-optimal set for some instances.

6   Conclusion

We studied the bi-objective problem of scheduling two agents on a single parallel-batching machine with equal processing time and non-identical job sizes. The objective is to minimize the makespans of the both agents, i.e., to obtain a Pareto-optimal set. We defined the boundary of Pareto-optimal set and gave two metrics to evaluate the quality of a non-dominated set. We designed two strategies, RSH and DMH, to solve the ε-constraint problem and presented two corresponding heuristics to generate non-dominated sets. The proposed heuristics were compared with NSGA-II on 1000 randomly generated instances. The results illustrate that the proposed heuristics outperform NSGA-II. Furthermore we analyzed the performance of the proposed heuristics based on the proposed metrics using 2000 random instances. The results show that the proposed heuristics can produce a good non-dominated set that is very close to the Pareto-optimal set. Furthermore, they obtained the exact Pareto-optimal set for more than 45% of the 2000 instances.

In the further work, we study the general problem when the processing times of the jobs are arbitrary. Designing a good approximation algorithm for the general problem does not seem to be easy. Another interesting topic is related to other unexplored objectives, such as the total completion time.

References

1. Lee, C.Y., Uzsoy, R., Martin-Vega, L.A.: Efficient algorithms for scheduling semiconductor burn-in operations. Oper. Res. **40**(4), 764–775 (1992)
2. Mathirajan, M., Chandru, V., Sivakumar, A.I.: Heuristic algorithms for scheduling heat-treatment furnaces of steel casting industries. Sadhana **32**(5), 479–500 (2007)
3. Van De Rzee, D.J., Van Harten, A., Schuur, P.C.: Dynamic job assignment heuristics for multi-server batch operations-a cost based approach. Int. J. Prod. Res. **35**(11), 3063–3094 (1997)
4. Baker, K.R., Smith, J.C.: A multiple-criterion model for machine scheduling. J. Sched. **6**(1), 7–16 (2003)
5. Agnetis, A., Mirchandani, P.B., Pacciarelli, D., et al.: Scheduling problems with two competing agents. Oper. Res. **52**(2), 229–242 (2004)
6. Agnetis, A., Billaut, J.-C., Gawiejnowicz, S., Pacciarelli, D., Soukhal, A.: Multiagent Scheduling-Models and Algorithms. Springer, Heidelberg (2014)
7. Yazdani Sabouni, M.T., Jolai, F.: Optimal methods for batch processing problem with makespan and maximum lateness objectives. Appl. Math. Model. **34**(2), 314–324 (2010)
8. Feng, Q., Yuan, J., Liu, H., et al.: A note on two-agent scheduling on an unbounded parallel-batching machine with makespan and maximum lateness objectives. Appl. Math. Model. **37** (10), 7071–7076 (2013)
9. Mor, B., Mosheiov, G.: Single machine batch scheduling with two competing agents to minimize total flowtime. Eur. J. Oper. Res. **215**(3), 524–531 (2011)
10. Li, S., Yuan, J.: Unbounded parallel-batching scheduling with two competitive agents. J. Sched. **15**(5), 629–640 (2012)
11. Fan, B.Q., Cheng, T.C.E., Li, S.S., et al.: Bounded parallel-batching scheduling with two competing agents. J. Sched. **16**(3), 261–271 (2013)
12. Tan, Q., Chen, H.P., Du, B., et al.: Two-agent scheduling on a single batch processing machine with non-identical job sizes. In: 2011 2nd International Conference on Artificial Intelligence, Management Science and Electronic Commerce (AIMSEC), pp. 7431–7435. IEEE (2011)
13. Garey, M.R., Johnson, D.S.: Computers and Intractability: A Guide to the Theory of NP-completeness. W. H. Freeman & Co, San Francisco (1979)
14. Deb, K.: Multi-objective Optimization Using Evolutionary Algorithms. Wiley, Chichester (2001)
15. Johnson, D.S.: Near-optimal bin packing algorithms. Massachusetts Institute of Technology (1973)
16. Dósa, G., Li, R.H., Han, X., et al.: Tight absolute bound for First Fit Decreasing bin-packing: FFD(L) ≤ 11/9 OPT(L) + 6/9. Theoret. Comput. Sci. **510**, 13–16 (2013)
17. Martello, S., Toth, P.: Lower bounds and reduction procedures for the bin packing problem. Discrete Appl. Math. **28**, 59–70 (1990)
18. Czyak, P., Jaskiewicz, A.: Pareto simulated annealing-A metaheuristic technique for multiple objective combinatorial optimization. J. Multi-criteria Decis. Anal. **7**, 34–47 (1998)

19. Haimes, Y.Y., Lasdon, L.S., Wismer, D.A.: On a bicriterion formulation of the problems of integrated system identification and system optimization. IEEE Trans. Syst. Man Cybern. **1**, 296–297 (1971)
20. Deb, K., Pratap, A., Agarwal, S., et al.: A fast and elitist multiobjective genetic algorithm: NSGA-II. IEEE Trans. Evol. Comput. **6**(2), 182–197 (2002)
21. Zitzler, E., Thiele, L.: Multiobjective evolutionary algorithms: a comparative case study and the strength Pareto approach. IEEE Trans. Evol. Comput. **3**(4), 257–271 (1999)

Selected Activity Coordination Mechanisms in Complex Systems

Katarzyna Grzybowska[✉]

Faculty of Engineering Management, Chair of Production Engineering
and Logistics, Poznan University of Technology, Strzelecka 11,
60-965 Poznan, Poland
katarzyna.grzybowska@put.poznan.pl

Abstract. The article is a presentation of the research results regarding selected activity coordination mechanisms. The research was carried out independently and within the framework of a research project. Reference coordination models, which serve further simulation works, are their result. The article consists of several parts. The first part discusses the most important issues regarding coordination theory. The second part discusses activity coordination in complex systems, multi-agent systems. Selected activity coordination mechanisms and their comparisons were presented in the third part. The article is concluded with a summary.

Keywords: Coordination · Coordination mechanisms · Supply chain · Complex systems

1 Introduction

A supply chain, as a sequence of organisations collaborating to provide the largest possible amount of a product or service for the customer, can create very complex interrelation networks at every stage [1]. Supply chain management is defined as "the systemic, strategic coordination of the traditional business functions and the tactics across these business functions within a particular company and across businesses within the supply chain, for the purposes of improving the long term performance of the individual companies and the supply chain as a whole" [2]. But the supply chain management is a decision process that not only integrates all of its participants, but also helps to coordinate the basic flows: products/services, information and funds [3]. Coordination defined as the process of managing dependencies among activities. Starting with the individual activity it is easily recognized that the industrial reality contains a multitude of various activities. When focusing solely on individual activities, these might seem to have a generic value, for example considering a production or exchange activity [13].

The author was interested in the topic of activity coordination in the supply chain and undertook research on the topic in 2011. Up to now works, which have been documented in relation to several issues have been led:

© Springer International Publishing Switzerland 2015
J. Bajo et al. (Eds.): PAAMS 2015 Workshops, CCIS 524, pp. 69–79, 2015.
DOI: 10.1007/978-3-319-19033-4_6

- Coordination in the Supply Chain - An Indication of Logistic Management – A Theoretical Approach, 2011 - It was noted that the effective coordination of activities of independent companies is the key to achieve flexibility and speed in completing the activities. These may become the source of the improvement of logistics processes as well as the competitive advantage necessary for processing on a global market. Weak coordination between the participants in the supply chain can cause a dysfunction of the operational activities.
- The Role of Coordination in the Supply Chain – Experimental Research, 2011 – It was observed that along with the acquisition of experience in the simulated supply chain, the number of verbal messages in total and the number of verbal task messages was subject to a decrease and the supervision (control) in the form of transferring verbal task messages (type: orders, guidelines) was weakened. Along with the gaining of experience, the internalization of standards takes place, i.e. the process of the systematic assimilation and acceptance of patterns of procedure, which are allocated to indicated conditions and are connected with the completion of the allocated rile in the supply chain. From this it follows that the more experienced participants of the supply chain, who achieved a certain level of identification and coordination with other elements in the system, require the relatively week level of control through verbal messages, with the maintenance of the expected quality and timely efficiency.
- Coordination Methods in the Supply Chain, 2012 – Four types of coordination have been distinguished and ten coordination techniques have been developed.
- Coordination in the Supply Chain – an Indication of Logistic Management, 2013 - The aim of the article is the indication of activity coordination techniques that are applied by the enterprises. Fifty enterprises, unrelated to each other in their business activities took part in the conducted research. The respondents had the possibility of indicating more than one answer. The application of three coordination techniques was most often noted: coordination (28 % indication), the application of six or seven techniques (4 % each) was least common. 16 % of the research respondents apply eight of the ten coordination techniques.
- Logistics Process Modelling in Supply Chain – algorithm of coordination in the supply chain – contracting, 2014 – The aim of the article is to discuss the selected process modelling methods in the supply chain on the example of one of the coordination mechanisms, i.e. contracting. In supply chain type structures, the coordination technique commonly referred to as contracting, is popular. This is a classic form of coordination in the case of a decentralized market. It can be applied in the case in which the order (undertaking or task to be accomplished) has a well defined structure of sub-orders or sub-tasks. It is also important to be able to subject the order to a decomposition into a series of sub-tasks [4].
- The meaning of activity coordination in the supply chain, 2014 – The presented results are a continuation of the research from 2013 and show the meaning and essence of coordination in the business environment. The respondents participating in the research indicating the significant impact of activity coordination on logistics at the operational level (1. activity coordination improves the processes occurring at this level, ca. 79 % - the total number of responses for I fully agree and I agree, 2. activity coordination decreases the order completion time, ca. 83 % - the total

number of responses for I fully agree and I agree) and point to the significant impact of activity coordination of the logistics carried out at the strategic level (activity coordination allows for the harmonisation of the applied logistics strategies, ca. 73 % - the total number of responses for I fully agree and I agree) [5].

- Reference models of selected activity coordination mechanisms in the supply chain, 2015 – The result of the work is a prepared model as well as its description in the use of Business Process Modeling Notation (BPMN). The presented model is a demonstrative model. It presents the general course of the business process, without probing into technical issues. This model allows for an understanding of the changes taking place, and also their automation in the future. This will serve future research works [6].

However, the material presented below is the result of the author's further works on activity coordination in the supply chain. The author is participating in the LOGOS entitled "Coordination model of virtual supply chains fulfilling the requirements of corporate social responsibility", intra-university program, within the framework of the first competition entitled Applied Research Program, announced by the National Centre for Research and Development. The project is being implemented by four scientific institutes: (1) The Institute of Logistics and Warehousing, (2) The Poznan University of Technology, (3) The University of Economics in Katowice, (4) The Gdansk University of Technology.

The project with the acronym LOGOS is aimed at preparing the virtual supply chain coordination model, which is to fulfil the requirements of corporate social responsibility.

The task carried out by the author entailed the elaboration of a activity coordination model, on the basis of which conducting simulation works will be possible.

The works within the framework of the task entailed:

- indication of the simulation criteria - including a definition of the objectives, key performance indicators, key decision variables as well as the scope of the simulation (borders, the border assumptions, operational assumptions),
- elaboration of selected activity coordination mechanisms in the supply chain with graphic notation help, serving to describe the business processes,
- conducting simulation experiments.

Works within the framework of the executed LOGOS project have been divided into three sub-tasks (Fig. 1):

- layer 1 - elaboration of the activity coordination models, The idea of process modeling is to construct a model, i.e., create a formal representation of a process that can subjected to a thorough analysis To perform this task, modeling languages are used. In the present work, an assumption has been made that a map of a process is its model [7]
- layer 2 - elaboration of a transport model, The majority of multiechelon systems presented in the literature usually explicitly consider the routing problem at the last level of the transportation system, while a simplified routing problem is considered at higher levels [8]. Modeling of the road in three ways shown in the article [9]. By analyzing the flow of transport should pay attention to the existence of a series of

distortions that affect the implementation of transport order. Quoting Hoffa And Pawlewskiego: "Analyzing the supply chain and, to be more exact, the transport turnaround time, it is Necessary to take into account a number of variables. The time of finishing the race depends on many factors, dry as the type of road on Which the Means of transportation is traveling, the weather conditions, driving skills, capabilities of Means of transportation and other factors." [9]. In addition, the authors present a list of interference with a description and method of modeling.

- layer 3 - elaboration of a route model and an optimisation of the GEO routes.

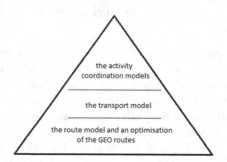

the activity coordination models

the transport model

the route model and an optimisation of the GEO routes

Fig. 1. The project layer sub-tasks

2   Activity Coordination - Basic Issues

The coordination and integration of activities are recommendations regarding efficient operations [10]. The coordination of activities recommends the linking of the individual system elements from the quantitative and time point of view [10]. The integration constitutes a postulate for the introduction of all and only those elements of the system that are required for it to achieve success to the » course of activities « . They should be included in such a manner so that the elements (in accordance with the meaning of the organisation) will contribute to the maximum success of the entire system [11]. Zieleniewski indicates the meaning of the coordination of events, which he understands (in a general manner) as a significant factor protecting the system against loses, which threaten the destruction of the potential organisational effect [11]. Coordination understood in such a manner is a necessary condition, although insufficient for the occurrence of this effect. Mutual information about how the implementation of the mutually intertwined system elements or that which is subject to coordination is also a necessary condition. The mutual information binds the individual parts with the help of feedback.

The research results regarding the assessment and the modelling of factors impacting the diverse cooperation and integration of the companies cooperating within the multi-agent systems (Fig. 2), conducted in Poland and Canada, indicate that sharing information and coordination are the most important [12].

Two key statements on coordination theory can be differentiated. The first of them states that coordination dependencies and mechanisms are of a general nature. This means that they can be found in various systems and organisations.

	Enablers	Mean score
1	Information sharing	4.45
2	Coordination	4.35
3	Trust	4.20
4	Willingness to collaborate	4.20
5	Communication	4.15
6	Common business goals	4.05
7	Responsibility sharing	3.90
8	Planning of supply chain activities	3.85
9	Flexibility	3.75
10	Benefit sharing	3.65
11	Joint Decision Making	3.65
12	Organizational culture	3.65
13	Organisational compatibility	3.60
14	Resource sharing (integration)	3.55
15	Top management support	3.25
16	Technological readiness	3.20
17	Training	3.10

Fig. 2. Enablers applied in the research [12]

The second statement of the coordination theory indicates that various coordination methods can be applied to the same problem. Alternative processes can occur for different coordination mechanisms. The second coordination theory statement indicates that by applying alternative coordination mechanisms, it is possible to create alternative processes.

3   Coordination of Activities in Complex Multi-agent Systems

In expanding the concept of activity coordination into the cooperation of two or more companies, the need arises for coordination at a higher level - business relations among others. Coordination presented as activity links [13] occurs between enterprises. The activity links (Fig. 3c) lead do co-dependent activities, which are synchronised and matched. The activities carried out by two (or more) enterprises in business relations become more or less interlinked due to the development of these relations. Such activities are much more efficient, as they are subject to coordination and rationalisation (they decrease the costs of performing the activities and/or increase the final result of the activity).

The coordination of activities in multi-agent systems can be related to the coordination of business activities of millions of people. Friedman claimed that there are in fact only two manners of coordinating activities.

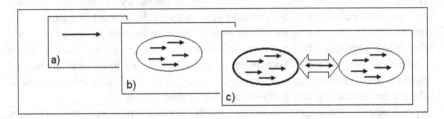

Fig. 3. Coordination (a) Individual activity, presented as an arrow, (b) Business operation, which uses five individual activities, (c) Activity links between the two enterprises; [13]

One of them is central coordination, with the "use" of a special coordination body (Fig. 4). Coordination centres are usually the leading centres. Friedman states that the central coordination must be connected with the use of coercion - just as in the military [14]. A special coordination body (lider, customer) has data sets about project. These data sets are also often complex and unstructured. Analysis of this data and acquisition of knowledge with the use of manual methods is slow, expensive, subjective, and prone to errors [15, 16].

The second manner of activity coordination is self-coordination, understood as the voluntary cooperation of units- as during an open market fair. "The possibility of coordination through voluntary cooperation is based on the fundamental truth, although often negated - that both parties to the transaction gain a benefit from it, under the condition that this is a transaction that is voluntary and conscious from both sides" [14]. One of the methods of the voluntary cooperation of entities is the Open Method of Coordination – OMC. The open method of coordination is based on:

- the mutual identification of aims to be achieved in a complex, multi-agent system,
- the joint establishment of means aimed at the achievement of goals (in the form of statistics, indicators and guidelines),
- analyses, which entail the comparison of system element activities and the exchange of good practices.

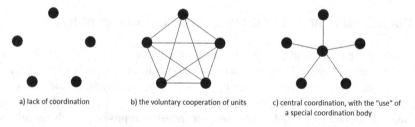

a) lack of coordination   b) the voluntary cooperation of units   c) central coordination, with the "use" of
                                                                    a special coordination body

Fig. 4. Coordination forms in multi-agent systems [17]

The condition of such a "self-coordination" is either the fully unchanged repetition of the cycle of activities with the unconditional compliance with the plan known to all of the system elements, or either very succinct and fast mutual information.

There are several reasons why multiple agents need to be co-ordinated [18, 19].

- Preventing anarchy or chaos — co-ordination is necessary or desirable because, with the decentralisation in agent-based systems, anarchy can set in easily.
- Agents need to co-ordinate their behaviour if they are to meet global constraints.
- Distributed expertise, resources or information — agents may have different capabilities and specialised knowledge in a similar manner to paediatricians, neurologists and cardiologists. Alternatively, they may have different sources of information, resources, reliability levels, responsibilities, etc.
- Dependencies between agents' actions — agents' goals are frequently interdependent.

4   Selected Activity Coordination Elements - Comparison

In mechanical engineering, the mechanism can be referred to as the group of machine or device integral parts cooperating with each other, which fulfil a specific task, for example the transfer the movement. The mechanism can also be referred to as the manner of acting or the order of the events. The coordination mechanism serves to describe the manner of activities of the enterprises that cooperate with each other. A presentation of the selected mechanisms is found below.

4.1   Coordination with the Use of an Electronic Bulletin Board

The coordination mechanism with the use of the electronic bulletin board is a modified form of the classic form of coordination - contracting. Coordination with the use of an electronic bulletin board is applied when the order has a very well defined sub-order or sub-task structure. As a result, the order can be structured into its simpler sub-tasks.

The structuring of the order entails its decomposition into a series of sub-orders in order to separate the structure of the order. This is a strictly indicated system resulting from the combining of sub-orders of the entire order. Structuring enables:

- the creation of a complete overview of the entire order and its aim,
- the division of the order into smaller sub-orders, which can be given for completion to sub-contractors,
- the indication of borderline conditions for the planning, steering and supervision over the completion of the order,
- the indication of all of the resources necessary to complete the order,
- the enabling of the current review of the costs of the order,
- the establishment of the control points of the order,
- placing the efficiency gauges in order.

First variant – orderly nature.

The occurrence of two roles is visible during coordination with the use of the electronic bulletin board. The first role comes down to the ordering party, which decomposes the order into sub-orders (tasks). They also organize the allocation of these sub-orders among the cooperating counter parties, already verified as being reliable. They use their own (most often closed) database of sub-contractors as well as the so called bulletin board. The role of the subcontractor (counter party and subcontractor) is complementary to the role of the ordering party. The subcontractor carries out sub-orders directly. It can also change the role to the ordering party of a lower rank, by placing sub-sub-orders (decomposed sub-orders) in the same or different electronic bulletin board. They also use their own subcontractor database (also closed).

In analysing this variant, one can indicate the so-called distance – the distance between one cell and the remaining ones. In the presented example, Fig. 5 presents 5 enterprises (cells) and 4 channels (connections). Cells A and E are in the worst situation. They communicate directly with the sole closest cell.

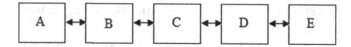

Fig. 5. Orderly nature (own work)

Second variant focused nature.

The second coordination variant with the use of the electronic bulletin board is maintaining the coordination and supervision of all of the works, even those at the lowest level of complexity, by the main ordering party. In such a case, when a sub-contractor is found for some sub-order, the scope of the works of this sub-order is decomposed into sub-sub-orders by the main sub-contractor. One can observe a repeating action (most often repeated multiple times) of the same instruction (schedule of activities) in the loop.

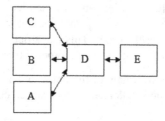

Fig. 6. Concentrated nature (own work)

In such a layout, cell D, who is the main ordering party, has the most advantageous position, having the full coordination of the activities and control over the completion of the order (Fig. 6).

4.2   Building of Structures with the Help of an Agent

It should be assumed that this is one of the simplest coordination mechanisms. It assumes that the enterprises in the built structure possess a hierarchy, previously provided. In order for it to function effectively, the execution of the following tasks is necessary:

- Initiating the creation of a database of enterprises that will operate within the structure
- Defining the scope of activities of the individual entities
- Specifying the rights and obligations of the individual entities (regulations)
- Expanding the database of enterprises through own actions (sending information through the available communication channels, i.e. e-mail, press, internet…)
- Registration of structure participants
- Approving the participants
- Agreement
- Establishing priorities and dependencies between the enterprises

The benefit of relations between enterprises defined in such a manner is the legible and explicit indication of the role that each enterprise is to play in the created structure. The building of structures with the help of an assistant most often assume the hierarchical master/slave structure. In such a case the agent master plans and sends out information on the orders to the individual subordinate agents (slave). And each of these agents transfers return information on the status of the completion of their order. The defect of such an approach is the small amount of autonomy for the slave agents. Coordination through the organisation works ideally in the coordination of the tasks of agents connected by strong hierarchical relations.

4.3 Comparison of Selected Mechanisms

Coordination with the use of an electronic bulletin board of a concentrated nature as well as the building of structures with the help of an agent are directed towards systems, in which a visible hierarchy among the partners is visible and they possess a coordinating body in the form of a main ordering party or agent (Fig. 7).

Criteria	Coordination with the use of a bulletin board		Building of structures with the help of an agent
	Orderly nature	Concentrated nature	
Manner of the coordination activities	Voluntary co-operation of the entities	With the "use" of the special coordinating body	With the "use" of the special coordinating body; agent
Hierarchy of the business partners	No	Yes	Yes
Structuring of the order	Yes	Yes	Yes
Interference in the activities of the business partner	None/small	Moderate	Strong
Cohesion of the established relationship	Loose	Moderate	Strong

Fig. 7. Criteria coordination (own work)

This body has a dominating impact on the remaining enterprises and their scope of works. They are also directed to the systems of a cohesive and well concentrated structure.

5 Conclusion

The presented activity coordination mechanism regard the problem of coordination in complex systems, which are the supply chain, at the stage of concluding trade contracts between business partners. The partners establish the terms and conditions of their mutual cooperation within the framework of these contracts. The contracts concluded between them are at the same time the result of the market tactics, in which each party takes independent decisions. Their aim is the maximising of one's own benefits and at the same time ensuring the greatest possible efficiency of the created system.

References

1. Kramarz, M.: The nature and types of network relations in distribution of metallurgical products. LogForum **4**, 57–66 (2010)
2. Awasthi, A., Grzybowska, K., Chauhan, S., Goyal, S.K.: Investigating organizational characteristics for sustainable supply chain planning under fuzziness. In: Kahraman, C. (ed.) Supply Chain Management Under Fuzziness. STUDFUZZ, vol. 313, pp. 81–100. Springer, Heidelberg (2014)
3. Sitek, P., Wikarek, J.: A hybrid framework for the modelling and optimisation of decision problems in sustainable supply chain management. Int. J. Prod. Res., 1–18 (2015). doi:10.1080/00207543.2015.1005762
4. Grzybowska, K., Kovács, G.: Logistics process modelling in supply chain – algorithm of coordination in the supply chain – contracting. In: de la Puerta, J.G., Ferreira, I.G., Bringas, P.G., Klett, F., Abraham, A., de Carvalho, A.C., Herrero, Á., Baruque, B., Quintián, H., Corchado, E. (eds.) International Joint Conference SOCO'14-CISIS'14-ICEUTE'14. AISC, vol. 299, pp. 311–320. Springer, Heidelberg (2014). doi:10.1007/978-3-319-07995-0_31
5. Grzybowska, K.: Znaczenie koordynacji działań w łańcuchach dostaw. Gospodarka Materiałowa i Logistyka **11**, 29–37 (2014)
6. Grzybowska, K.: Reference models of selected action coordination mechanisms in the supply chain. LogForum **11**(2), 151–159 (2015). doi:10.17270/J.LOG.2015.2.3
7. Pawlewski, P.: Multimodal approach to modeling of manufacturing processes. In: Procedia CIRP Variety Management in Manufacturing — Proceedings of the 47th CIRP Conference on Manufacturing Systems, vol. 17, pp. 716–720 (2014)
8. Sitek, P., Wikarek, J.: A hybrid approach to the optimization of multiechelon systems. Mathematical Problems in Engineering 2015, Article ID 925675 (2015). doi:10.1155/2015/925675
9. Hoffa, P., Pawlewski, P.: Agent based approach for modeling disturbances in supply chain. In: Corchado, J.M., Bajo, J., Kozlak, J., Pawlewski, P., Molina, J.M., Gaudou, B., Julian, V., Unland, R., Lopes, F., Hallenborg, K., García Teodoro, P. (eds.) PAAMS 2014. CCIS, vol. 430, pp. 144–155. Springer, Heidelberg (2014)
10. Zieleniewski, J.: Organizacja Zespołów Ludzkich: wstęp do Teorii Organizacji i Kierowania. PWN, Warszawa (1967)
11. Saniuk, A., Saniuk, S., Jasiulewicz-Kaczmarek, M., Kuźdowicz, P.: Efficiency control in industrial enterprises. Appl. Mech. Mater. **708**, 294–299 (2015)
12. Grzybowska, K., Awasthi, A., Hussain, M.: Modeling enablers for sustainable logistics collaboration integrating Canadian and Polish perspectives. In: Ganzha, M., Maciaszek, L., Paprzycki, M. (eds) Proceedings of the 2014 Federated Conference on Computer Science and Information Systems. ACSIS, vol. 2, pp. 1311–1319 (2014). http://dx.doi.org/10.15439/2014F90
13. Bankvall, L.: Activity coordination from a firm perspective -towards a framework. In: Proceedings IMP-Conference in Uppsala, Sweden (2008)
14. Friedman, M.: Kapitalizm i wolność, Fundacja im. A. Smitha, Warszawa (1993)

15. Relich, M.: Knowledge acquisition for new product development with the use of an ERP database. In: The Federated Conference on Computer Science and Information Systems, Krakow, Poland, pp. 1285–1290 (2013)
16. Relich, M., Muszynski, W.: The use of intelligent systems for planning and scheduling of product development projects. Procedia Computer Science **35**, 1586–1595 (2014)
17. Buxmann, P., Diaz, L.M., von Ahsen, A.: Ökonomische Bewertungsansätze und Anwendung eines Simulationsmodells. Wirtschaftsinformatik **45**(5), 509–514 (2003)
18. Nwana, H.S.: 'Negotiation Strategies: An Overview', BT Laboratories internal report (1994)
19. Jennings, N.R.: Coordination techniques for distributed artificial intelligence. In: O'Hare, G. M.P., Jennings, N.R. (eds.) Foundations of Distributed Artificial Intelligence, pp. 187–210. Wiley, London (1990)

A Multi-agent Hybrid Approach to Decision Support in Job Groups Handling

Jarosław Wikarek[1] and Izabela Ewa Nielsen[2(✉)]

[1] Department of Control and Management Systems,
Kielce University of Technology, Kielce, Poland
j.wikarek@tu.kielce.pl
[2] Department of Mechanical and Manufacturing Engineering,
Aalborg University, Aalborg, Denmark
izabela@m-tech.aau.dk

Abstract. This study deals with scheduling groups of jobs, their arrival and delivery, and individual processing of each of them. All jobs in a group should be delivered at the same time after processing. One of the objectives is to minimize the average delivery time of the group containing that job (waiting period). The new way of modeling and solving the decision problem - a multi-agent hybrid approach is presented. This approach includes the design and implementation of two agent types: MP-agents (Mathematical Programming) and CLP-agents (Constraint Logic Programming). The iterative algorithm for solving the model under dynamic emergence of new orders is also included. This structure enables managers to ask all kinds of questions.

In addition, the paper proposes new functionalities based on the CLP environment and numerical experiments for illustrative examples.

Keywords: Decision support systems · Mathematical programming · Constraint logic programming · Optimization · Group work

1 Introduction

In the current daily management, there are also problems that require management to ask questions like: *What .. if? Is it possible ..? What is the minimum ..? What is the number ..?* etc. and efficiently obtain the answers. Specialized modules for optimization or analyses based on data mining are available for purchase. However, they are costly and refer to selected areas such as scheduling or planning.

One of the common problems that appear in front of managers is the job groups handling. A very good illustration of the handling of jobs in groups is the process of preparing and serving food in a restaurant [1]. Guests enter the restaurant in different groups at different moments. Each group chooses a table and all orders of the group members are taken simultaneously. After the accomplishment of these processes, all meal items ordered by a group are served simultaneously. The quality of service and the rate of customer satisfaction are raised if a meal item is served as soon as it is ready. In a restaurant, a group of meal items ordered by guests sitting at a table should be delivered together. Thus, the cooked meal items for a specific group have to wait until

© Springer International Publishing Switzerland 2015
J. Bajo et al. (Eds.): PAAMS 2015 Workshops, CCIS 524, pp. 80–89, 2015.
DOI: 10.1007/978-3-319-19033-4_7

the last item of that group is cooked and is ready to be served. The proposed research problem finds many applications in industrial companies, including but not limited to food, ceramic tile, textile production industries, distributions, supply chain management, installation of bulky equipment, manufacturing of complex devices, etc. as well as operating systems and databases.

It can be noticed in many production and logistic industries that have different types of customers. Assume that each customer has different type of orders [15]. Each order has a different process function and resources, but all items ordered by a customer or group of customers should be delivered at the same time in one package to reduce the transportation costs, subsequent processing steps time and costs or/and assure proper quality of the product/service and customer satisfaction.

One of the solving methods for this problem at the operational level includes scheduling methods. Scheduling methods for optimal and simultaneous provision of service to groups of customers are usually proposed in the flexible flow-shop system (FFS). In the FFS system, processing is divided into several stages with parallel resources at least in one stage. All of the tasks should pass through all stages in the same order (preparing meals) [2, 3]. The exemplified objectives of the problem [3] are minimizing the total amount of time required to complete a group of jobs and minimizing the sum of differences between the completion time of a particular job in the group and the delivery time of this group containing that job (waiting period).

The motivation was to implement a method that allows modeling and support decisions for problems handling incoming orders in groups with the same date of completion for various forms of organization (not only flow-shop). Development of decision-making models, whose implementation using the proposed method will allow obtaining quick answers to key questions asked by a service manager. The method takes into account the dynamics resulting from the coming of new groups of orders while previous orders are handled.

The remainder of the article is organized as follows. Problem statement, research methodology, mathematical model and contribution are provided in Sect. 2. Computational examples, tests of the implementation platform and discussion are presented in Sect. 3. Possible extensions of the proposed approach as well as the conclusions are included in Sect. 4.

2 Problem Statement, Methodology and Contribution

The majority of models presented in the literature refer to a single problem and optimization according to the set criterion. Fewer studies are devoted to multiple-criteria optimization by operations research (OR) methods [3]. Declarative environments such as CP/CLP facilitate problem modeling and introduction of logical and symbolic constraints [4–8]. Unfortunately, high complexity of decision-making models and their integer nature contribute to poor efficiency of modeling in OR methods and inefficient optimization in CLP. This is particularly important when such questions as *What is the minimum ..? What is the maximum ..?* are asked. Therefore, a new approach to modeling and solving these problems was developed. A multi-agent environment was chosen as the best structure for this approach [4, 7, 9]. Mathematical programming environment was used for optimization questions [10] and constraint logic programming environment was applied for general questions and to frame the whole. This multi-agent hybrid approach is the basis for the creation of the implementation environment to support managers. Such environment allows asking various questions while processing the groups of orders.

The main contribution on our part is the new method for the modeling and decision support problems for handling orders in groups. It is based on the integration of CLP and MP agents in the CLP environments (Sect. 2.4). One of the possible objective functions of the constructed decision model is minimizing the average service/waiting time for each group. Based on the proposed method and model, we designed the framework that allows managers to ask questions and get fast answers in the process of handling groups of orders. The iterative algorithm proposed enables dynamic use of this method. The algorithm is designed in such a way that allows you to run framework in subsequent periods in which there are orders. The algorithm also updates every period the availability of resources.

2.1   Problem Description

This problem can be stated as follows (Fig. 1). Orders ($j = 1..M$) enter the system in groups at different periods ($h = 1..V$). Each order should be processed by specific resources, including parallel resources ($k = 1..E$). The orders ($j = 1..M$) in each group should be delivered. It is assumed that all processors in the last stage are eligible to process all jobs. This assumption is valid due to the fact that processors in the last stage (waiters at restaurants who deliver meals or packers in a factory, or quality control) are the same in most of the application areas of the proposed problem. Special points at which orders are submitted and then delivered are introduced/e.g. tables, assembly points, etc. ($i = 1..N$). (These points can be aggregated in groups $a = 1..A$). The problem does not cover configuration of the points but relates to handling orders, as many orders may come from one customer (orders several items from the menu). Each order may be processed by a different resource set in any order.

The objective function is stated as the minimization of the average delivery time for each group. Possible questions for this model (but not limited to) are:

- Q1 – What is the minimum average waiting time in each group?
- Q2 – What is the minimum waiting time?
- Q3 – What is the minimum number of resources Rzt for timely execution of orders?
- Q4 – What is the minimum number of groups of points for timely execution of orders?
- Q5 – How much will the order execution time extend if the number of resourced is extended by 20 %, by 50 %?
- Q6 – What number of resources $d1$, $d2$, $d3$, … is needed to execute the orders when the waiting time is no longer than g?
- Q7 – Can m orders at n points be executed within time g so that the waiting time does not exceed T?

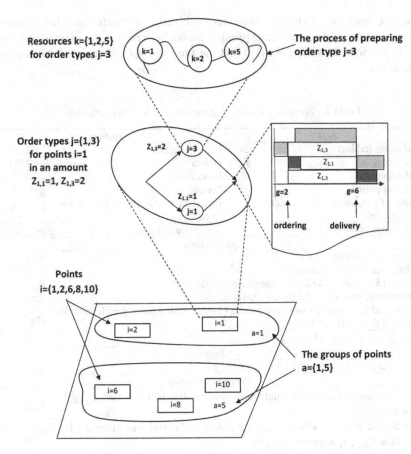

Fig. 1. Scheme for the problem of handling orders in a restaurant

2.2 Mathematical Model

A mathematical model is developed for the research problem. The sets, indices, parameters, decision variables are presented in Table 1.

Objective function. Minimization of average waiting time at each point i (1a) or the minimization of the total waiting time for all points i (1b).

Constraints. Constraint (2) specifies the starting time of handling order j from point i. Delivery/processing/handling of order j cannot start before moment St, at which demand appears (3). Only available number of resources k can be used in any period of time (4). When order j for point i is delivered using resource k in period g, the resources have to be reserved for a period of time (5). Determining the end times for resource jobs – constraints (6), (7) ensure the value of variable $Y_{i,j,k,g}$ and continuous handling/processing of the order. All orders j for point i should end at the same moment (8). Constraint (9) binds variable $X_{i,j,k,g}$ (setting its value to be 1 where index g takes values ranging from $S_{i,j}$ to Tkp_i) (9). Constraint (10) specifies the number of different type of resources. Constraint (11) is responsible for the binarity of selected decision variables. Two random points i from the same group a cannot be served at the same period Tkp_i, which is provided by constraint (12) and the properties of resources of different typ (e.g. waiters).

Table 1. Summary indices, parameters and decision variables

Sets		Indices		
Set of points (tables)	N	Points (tables)		$i = 1..N$
Set of orders	M	Orders		$j = 1..M$
Set of resources	E	Resources		$k = 1..E$
Number of periods	U	Period		$g = 1..U$
Number of periods in which orders can be entered	V	Period in which orders can be entered		$h = 1..V$
Set of groups of points	A	The group of points		$a = 1..A$
parameters				
Time for execution of order j				t_j
Available number of resources k				d_k
Number of k resources needed for execution of order j				$R_{j,k}$
The number of resources of different type (waiters)				Rzt
Number used to convert periods to moments (for connecting index g with variable $S_{i,j}$, if $S_{i,j}=7$ then index $g=7$)				pp_g
The group number a to which point i belongs				alo_i
Inputs				
The number of orders j at point i during period g				$Z_{g,i,j}$
Decision variables				
If the execution of order j for point i uses resource k in period g then $X_{i,j,k,g}=1$, otherwise $X_{i,j,k,g}=0$				$X_{i,j,k,g}$
If g is the last period in which resource k is used in the execution of order j for point i then $Y_{i,j,k,g}=1$, otherwise $Y_{i,j,k,g} = 0$				$Y_{i,j,k,g}$
If g is the last period in which orders are executed for point i then $W_{i,g}=1$, otherwise $W_{i,g}=0$				$W_{i,g}$
Calculated number of periods g (using pp_g) delivery of all orders for point i.				Tkp_i
Calculated number of periods g (using pp_g) starting time of order j delivery for point i.				$S_{i,j}$
Auxiliary variables needed for the linearization of constraint that the group points do not complete the task at the same time				$\_P1_{i1,i2}$, $\_P2_{i1,i2}$

$$Fc = \min \frac{1}{N} \sum_{i=1}^{N} Tkp_i \tag{1a}$$

$$Tk \geq Tkp_i \text{ for } i = 1..N$$
$$Fc = \min Tkp_i \tag{1b}$$

$$S_{i,j} + t_j = Tkp_i \text{ for } i = 1..N, j = 1..M, z_{i,j} > 0 \quad S_{i,j} = 0 \text{ for } i = 1..N, j = 1..M, z_{i,j} = 0 \tag{2}$$

$$S_{i,j} \geq St \text{ for } i = 1..N, j = 1..M \tag{3}$$

$$\sum_{i=1}^{N} \sum_{j=1}^{M} \left(X_{i,j,k,g} \cdot R_{j,k} \cdot z_{i,j} \right) \leq d_k \text{ for } k = 1..E, g = 1..U \tag{4}$$

$$\sum_{g}^{U} X_{i,j,k,g} = t_j \text{ for } i = 1..N, j = 1..M, k = 1..E, z_{i,j} > 0, R_{j,k} > 0$$

$$X_{i,j,k,g} = 0 \text{ for } i = 1..N, j = 1..M, k = 1..E, z_{i,j} = 0$$

$$X_{i,j,k,g} = 0 \text{ for } i = 1..N, j = 1..M, k = 1..E, R_{j,k} = 0 \tag{5}$$

$$\sum_{g}^{U} Y_{i,j,k,g} = 1 \text{ for } i = 1..N, j = 1..M, k = 1..E, z_{i,j} > 0, R_{j,k} > 0 \tag{6}$$

$$X_{i,j,k,g-1} - X_{i,j,k,g} \leq Y_{i,j,k,g-1} \text{ for } i = 1..N, j = 1..M, k = 1..E, g = 2..U, z_{i,j} > 0, R_{j,k} > 0$$

$$Y_{i,j,k,g} = 0 \text{ for } i = 1..N, j = 1..M, k = 1..E, g = U$$

$$Y_{i,j,k,g} = 0 \text{ for } i = 1..N, j = 1..M, k = 1..E, g = 1 \tag{7}$$

$$Y_{i,j,k1,g} = Y_{i,j,k2,g} \text{ for } i = 1..N, j = 1..M, k1, k2 = 1..E, g = 1..U, z_{i,j} > 0, R_{j,k} > 0 \tag{8}$$

$$X_{i,j,k,g} = \begin{cases} 1 & \text{for } i = 1..N, j = 1..M, k = 1..E, g = 1..U, g \geq S_{i,j}, g \leq Tkp_i \\ 0 & \text{otherwise} \end{cases} \tag{9}$$

$$\sum_{i=1}^{N} \sum_{j=1}^{M} \sum_{k=1}^{E} Y_{i,j,k,g} \leq Rzt \text{ for } g = 1..U \tag{10}$$

$$X_{i,j,k,g} = \{0, 1\} \text{ for } i = 1..N, j = 1..M, k = 1..E, g = 1..U$$

$$Y_{i,j,k,g} = \{0, 1\} \text{ for } i = 1..N, j = 1..M, k = 1..E, g = 1..U \tag{11}$$

$$Tkp_{i_1} \neq Tkp_{i_2} \text{ for } i_1 = 1..N, i_2 = 1..N, alo_{i_1} = alo_{i_2} \tag{12}$$

2.3 Linearization of the Model

The mathematical model presented in 2.2 is non-linear. To linearize this model, an ancillary variable was used, $W_{i,g} = \{0,1\}$, determined according to formula 13 (where coefficients/factors pp_g are determined by the CLP). Additional constraints (14), (15), (16) and (17) were introduced to replace constraints (9) and (12). After the linearization, the model was formulated in the form of the mixed integer linear programming (MILP) problem.

$$\text{Tkp}_i = \sum_{g=1}^{U} \text{pp}_g \cdot W_{i,g} \text{ for } i = 1..N \tag{13}$$

$$Y_{i,j,k,g} = W_{i,g} \text{ for } i = 1..N, j = 1..M, k = 1..E, g = 1..U, z_{i,j} \geq 0, R_{j,k} \geq 0 \tag{14}$$

$$\sum_{g=1}^{U} W_{i,g} \leq 1 \text{ for } i = 1..N \tag{15}$$

$$W_{i,g} = \{0, 1\} \text{ for } i = 1..N, g = 1..U \tag{16}$$

$$\begin{aligned}
&\text{Tkp}_{i_1} - \text{Tkp}_{i_2} \leq \_P1_{i_1,i_2} - 0.1 \text{ for } \text{alo}_{i_1} = \text{alo}_{i_2}, i_1 = 1..N, i_2 = 1..N \\
&\text{Tkp}_{i_2} - \text{Tkp}_{i_1} \leq \_P2_{i_1,i_2} - 0.1 \text{ for } \text{alo}_{i_1} = \text{alo}_{i_2}, i_1 = 1..N, i_2 = 1..N \qquad (17) \\
&\_P1_{i_1,i_2} + \_P2_{i_1,i_2} = 1 \text{ for } \text{alo}_{i_1} = \text{alo}_{i_2}, i_1 = 1..N, i_2 = 1..N
\end{aligned}$$

2.4 A Multi-agent Hybrid Approach to Modeling, Solving and Optimization

The multi-agent approach was chosen for the implementation of the CLP and MP integration [13, 14]. This approach seems the most suitable for integrating and hybridizing of various environments. In this way, the framework with two types of agents and multiple interconnections between them was created (Fig. 2).

It can be used to implement specific decision models (Sect. 2.3) as well as ask questions related to these models. The questions and the additional constraints are implemented in the form of CLP and MP agents in Eclipse and Eplex environments [12]. Examples of question that can be asked are presented in Sect. 2.1. The CLP agents are used to model the problem, linearize and transform it. They are also effective in terms of receiving answers to general questions, such as *Is it possible ..? Is it enough ..?*. For optimization and specific questions, such as *What is the minimum ..? What is the shortest time ..?*, after the initial "domain" solving, the problem is finally solved by the MP agents.

3 Numerical Experiments

In order to verify and evaluate the proposed approach, many numerical experiments were performed for the illustrative example. All the experiments relate to the restaurants with fifteen points (tables) ($i = 1..15$), twenty five order types ($j = 1..25$), twenty resource types ($k = 1..20$), thirty time periods ($g = 1..30$), five groups ($a = 1..5$) and fifteen orders $Z_{g,i,j}$ Computational experiments consisted in asking questions Q1..Q7 for the model (Sect. 2.2) implemented in the framework (Sect. 2.4) iteratively run with interactive algorithm. Orders are ordered in groups during periods marked $h_1 = 2$, $h_2 = 6$. Figure 3 shows the implementation schedule of all orders for this example while

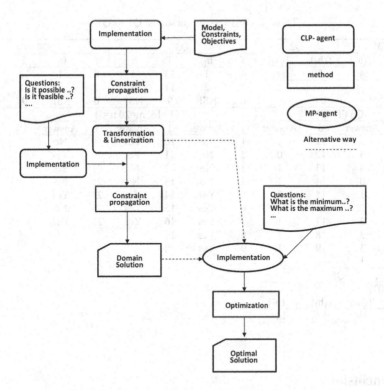

Fig. 2. The scheme of the implementation framework

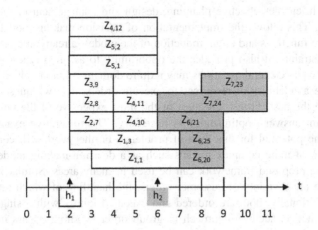

Fig. 3. Gantt chart for illustrative example ($Z_{i,j}$) for $g = h_1$, $g = h_2$

minimizing the average waiting time. The answer to question Q1, i.e. the minimum waiting time for each order of period h_1 is from $Tpk = 4$ to $Tpk = 7$, for the period h_2 is from $Tpk = 9$ to $Tpk = 11$. Average waiting time for h_1 and h_2 is shown in Table 2.

The values of answers to the remaining questions, Q2 to Q7, are shown in Table 2.

Table 2. Answers to questions, Q1 to Q7

Q1		Q2		Q3				Q4			
$T(h_1)$	$T(h_2)$	$T(h_1)$	$T(h_2)$	T	h_1	T	h_2	T	h_1	T	h_2
3.4	4	7	11	8	1	13	1	8	1	13	1
				7	2	11	1	7	2	11	1
				6	NSF	9	NSF	6	NSF	9	NSF

Q6 (T=15)				Q7 (T=18, m=20 n=5)					
d	Answer	d	Answer	j	Answer	j	Answer	j	Answer
1	5	11	1	1	No	10	Yes	19	No
2	5	12	0	2	No	11	Yes	20	Yes
3	4	13	1	3	No	12	No	21	Yes
4	0	14	1	4	No	13	No	22	No
5	1	15	1	5	Yes	14	Yes	23	Yes
6	2	16	0	6	Yes	15	Yes	24	No
7	3	17	1	7	Yes	16	Yes	25	Yes
8	3	18	1	8	Yes	17			
9	3	19	1	9	Yes	18			
10	1	20	1						

Q5			
20%		50%	
$T(h_1)$	$T(h_2)$	$T(h_1)$	$T(h_2)$
4	10	5.6	14

4 Conclusion

The presented multi-agent hybrid framework, which is an implementation of the proposed approach, enables effective planning, design and management of the processes by a manager. This allows the implementation of decision-making models with different objective functions and the introduction of the models already implemented with additional constraints. It also provides the opportunity to ask two types of questions and obtain answers. General questions may require domain solution, which in practice determines the availability of resources to execute orders. The wh-questions will in practice define the best, fastest, cheapest or the most expensive of the possible solutions. To obtain answers, optimization is necessary. The illustrative example shows only part of the potential for this kind of problems. Further work will consist in the implementation of more complex models such as a decision-making model covering operations. The proposed framework can be used in many areas. Similar issues exist wherever there are a variety of customer orders, the handling of which requires processes and additionally, both are ordered and executed jointly with a single delivery deadline. In practice, such an approach to group order handling occurs in manufacturing, services, logistics, supply chain and project management [11, 16]. Introduction of precedence constraints to operations and orders, uncertainty, fuzzy logic and others intelligent methods is considered. New questions will be implemented to broaden the scope of decision support.

References

1. Guerriero, F., Miglionico, G., Olivito, F.: Strategic and operational decisions in restaurant revenue management. Eur. J. Oper. Res. **237**, 1119–1132 (2014)
2. Ribas, I., Leisten, R., Framinan, J.M.: Review and classification of hybrid flow shop scheduling problems from a production system and a solutions procedure perspective. Comput. Oper. Res. **37**, 1439–1454 (2010)
3. Tadayon, B., Salmasi, N.: A two-criteria objective function flexible flow-shop scheduling problem with machine eligibility constraint. Int. J. Adv. Manuf. Technol. **64**(5–8), 1001–1015 (2013)
4. Apt, K., Wallace, M.: Constraint Logic Programming Using Eclipse. Cambridge University Press, Cambridge (2006)
5. Sitek, P., Wikarek, J.: A hybrid approach to the optimization of Multiechelon systems. Math. Probl. Eng. **2015**, 1–12 (2015). doi:10.1155/2015/925675. Article ID 925675
6. Sitek, P., Wikarek, J.: A hybrid approach to modeling and optimization for supply chain management with multimodal transport. In: Proceedings of the 18th International Conference on Methods and Models in Automation and Robotics (MMAR 2013), pp. 777–782 (2013)
7. Sitek, P., Wikarek, J.: Hybrid solution framework for supply chain problems. In: Omatu, S., Bersini, H., Corchado Rodríguez, J.M., González, S.R., Pawlewski, P., Bucciarelli, E. (eds.) Distributed Computing and Artificial Intelligence 11th International Conference. AISC, vol. 290, pp. 11–18. Springer, Heidelberg (2014)
8. Sitek, P.: A hybrid CP/MP approach to supply chain modelling, optimization and analysis. In: Proceedings of the 2014 Federated Conference on Computer Science and Information Systems, pp. 1345–1352 (2014). DOI:10.15439/2014F89
9. Sitek, P.: A hybrid approach to the Two-Echelon Capacitated Vehicle Routing Problem (2E-CVRP). Recent Adv. Autom. Rob. Measuring Tech. Adv. Intell. Syst. Comput. **267**, 251–263 (2014)
10. Schrijver, A.: Theory of Linear and Integer Programming. Wiley, New York (1998)
11. Relich, M.: Knowledge acquisition for new product development with the use of an ERP database. In: The Federated Conference on Computer Science and Information Systems, pp. 1285–1290 (2013)
12. Eclipse, Eclipse - The Eclipse Foundation open source community website (2014). www.eclipse.org. Accessed 12 Nov 2014
13. Pawlewski, P., Dossou, P.-E., Golinska, P.: Using simulation based on agents (ABS) and DES in enterprise integration modelling concepts. In: Rodr\'ıguez, J.M., Pérez, J.B., Golinska, P., Giroux, S., Corchuelo, R. (eds.) Trends in PAAMS. AISC, vol. 157, pp. 75–84. Springer, Heidelberg (2012)
14. Barbati, M., Bruno, G., Genovese, A.: Applications of agent-based models for optimization problems, a literature review. Expert Syst. Appl. **39**, 6020–6028 (2012)
15. Relich, M., Jakabova, M.: A decision support tool for project portfolio management with imprecise data. In: 10th International Conference on Strategic Management and its Support by Information Systems, pp. 164–172 (2013)
16. Grzybowska, K., Kovács, G., Lenart, B.: The supply chain in cloud computing – the natural future. Res. Log. Prod. **4**(1), 33–44 (2014)

Simulation of Supply Chain with Disturbances Using Flexsim - Case Study

Patycja Hoffa[✉] and Pawel Pawlewski

Poznan University of Technology, ul.Strzelecka 11, 60-965 Poznań, Poland
patrycja.hoffa@doctorate.put.poznan.pl,
pawel.pawlewski@put.poznan.pl

Abstract. The aim of the paper is to present a simulation model of transportation which includes different disturbances. The paper describes in detail modeled route and way of modeling some disturbances. In article authors presented influence of distinguished distortion to time of realization transport task. Authors create own object with using Discrete Event Simulation and Agent Based Simulation approach. The research highlights of the performed works are as follows: showing influence of disturbances to transportation time and present a description to build objects, which represent disturbances.

Keywords: Supply chain · Disturbances · Creation of special objects · Simulation

1 Introduction

Paper presents author's work on supply chain modeling method with including the some disturbances. Given the wide range of aspects included in the supply chain, authors decided to concentrate on the selected area - transport processes and disturbances occurring in them and how they can be modeled. In the literature, many articles about modeling a supply chain can be find. Popular methods of modeling route/supply chain are: creation paths by using graph, by using algorithms and neural networks and others. However, describing the disruptions in transportation and how they can be modeled is not enough.

Authors in this article are presenting a simulation model of realization a transport order (route of this transport). This model takes into account some disturbances. It was created by using a modern software Flexsim, that allows build models of various degrees of complexity [26]. In order to present a discussed issues, authors integrate Discrete Event Simulation (DES) with an Agent Based Simulation approach (ABS). Authors created their own objects, which map some interference. This objects have a certain intelligence, which have been given by creator.

The main aim of this article is to present a simulation for chosen transport route, taking into account some disturbances and detailed description of a method of modeling those distortions. Authors also demonstrate in practice how they create these objects, not just a theoretical description. Important is also to show the relationship between disturbances and time of realization the transport task.

© Springer International Publishing Switzerland 2015
J. Bajo et al. (Eds.): PAAMS 2015 Workshops, CCIS 524, pp. 90–101, 2015.
DOI: 10.1007/978-3-319-19033-4_8

An article consists of six parts. Section 2 contains a literature background about a supply chain, way of route modelling and about disturbances in transport. A Section 3 presents detail descriptions of planned route as a case study. It includes description of method of modeling disturbances, and how they can be modeled in practice. Parts 4 and 5 refer to simulation experiments and results of them. An article ends with conclusions and plans for further work.

2 Supply Chain and Disturbances – Literature Background

Modern supply chains are dispersed systems [6, 19, 23]. In order to confirm the complexity of aspects in supply chain, few definition about them are presented. Recalling Umeda: "A supply chain system is a chain of processes from the initial raw materials to the ultimate consumption of the finished product spanning across multiple supplier-customer links. It provides functions within and outside a company that enable the value chain to make products and provide services to the customers." [22]. Other definition is: „a supply chain is a worldwide network consisting of suppliers, manufacturers, ware-houses, distribution centers and retailers through which raw materials are purchased, transformed and delivered to customers" [10]. So, the supply chain is represented by a number of actors and many factors (inside and outside the company [13]) which have an impact of its functioning. It can consist of two participants (sender and receiver), but it is more complicated often, as: wholesalers, storage or transport service providers.

Because of wide range of supply chain issue, in the literature can be found many articles about methods of describing and modeling a network. The most known are:

– modeled transport routes by using different type of network, for example Petri net [20];
– by using algorithm like Dijkstra and/Floyd-Warshall algorithms [9];
– and of course in mathematical description [24].

To model processes in supply chain, two methods are using: Discrete-Event Simu-lations (DES) and Agent-Based Simulation (ABS). DES models are characterized by the process approach – they focus on the modeling of the system in detail, not on the independent units. More information about this method can be found in [3, 7, 18]. Whereas, ABS focuses on individual elements (resource, participants in the process), which are characterized by their own distinct behaviors [14]. In ABS approach we should pay attention to: attributes and behaviors of individual agents, relations and interactions between agents and the environment that we model. Agent-Based Simulation is discussed in more detail in [2, 8, 13, 14].

Describing about disturbances in transportation issues, it should be noted that usually they involve of the transport of hazardous materials and the associated with this transport risks [5, 11, 16, 21]. Of course, it can be find articles about disturbances not related to transportation of hazardous material, for example about car accident [1, 17]. Very inter-esting approach to robustness of Multimodal Transportation Networks is presented in [4]. Author distinguished two types disruptions in supply and demand: structural and behavioral.

But there is a little number of articles devoted to modeling a disturbances, describing how to model them, not only to calculate the risk of their occurrence. Therefore, the authors decided to engage in the topic of disruptions modeling. A list of featured disturbances by authors with method of modeling them can be found in [12].

3   Simulation Model of Supply Chain - Description

The simulation model of the selected transport route was built using the Flexsim software. In this software we can simulate, analyze, optimize every systems and processes. The model is created in 3D visualization. Using Flexsim is very simple by build-in tool and objects [26]. In order to make the best representation of reality, some assumptions were made, for example about vehicle speed and the presence of interfering elements transport mileage. Detailed assumptions are described in the next part of article.

3.1   Model of Transport Route - Definition of the Problem and the Assumptions

General information about the modeled transport routes are included in Table 1. This route includes travel from Jarogniewice city to Zgierz city, both of them are located in Poland.

Table 1. Modeled transport route – general information.

Transport route				
Loading place	Zip code	Unloading place	Zip code	Distance [km]
Jarogniewice	64-020	Zgierz	95–100	222

Figure 1 presents the route.

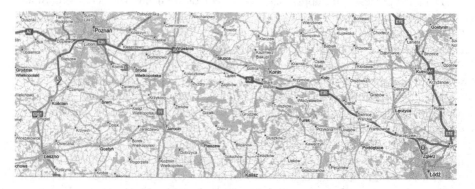

Fig. 1. Jarogniewice – Zgierz route. Source: [30].

The planned route includes journey using motorway A2. Part of the road (from Komorniki to Konin) is managed by Autostrada Wielkopolska [25]. At this section of route some toll collection points are, so fee should be pay. Further section (Konin - Emilia node) is managed by GDDKiA, and therefore fees are collected through an electronic system viaTOLL [27]. Table 2 shows the places where there are manually toll point. In those points, in relation to pay a fee, there is slow traffic. Therefore, authors treat these situations (these points) as a disturbance.

Table 2. Manual Toll Collection Point at the route. Source: based on [25, 27].

Toll collection point	
Administrator	Place
AW	Nagradowice
AW	Lądek
GDDKiA	Konin Wschód
GDDKiA	Emilia

In present simulation model, assumes that speed of a mean of transport is 80 km/h (+ - Acceleration/Deceleration). This speed is intentionally not a random value, because authors want to clearly show the influence of various disturbances on the modeled route - at the time of realization the transport order.

The purpose of the simulation model is show the transport time from the start to the final point, in the event of the occurrence of different, random disruptions. In this model includes three types of disturbances:

(1) Driver working time - in conjunction with the applicable provisions [29] time of driver working should be considered; authors treat this as a certain disruption (time of working between next break are well known and duration of break are know too; these breaks increase the time interval of the order realization);

(2) Time of fee payment in Toll Collection Point (TCP) - in connection with moving by motorway, we are faced with a manual toll collection points; time spent at these points is variable - it depends on the volume of traffic;

(3) Road accident - List of "Black points", which is widely available, can be used for defining the dangerous places in Poland [28]. At the planned route the black point doesn't exist, but authors decided to take into account this disturbance in some point as a random incident.

3.2 Selected Disturbances - Description and Method of Modeling

For the above-mentioned interference, detailed method of modeling will be presented. Authors, in order to model a particular interference, created own objects with special labels and some assigned intelligence. Each disruption is described in detail in next part of this work.

Driver working time. In accordance with current regulations, the driver at the specified interval has to stop and make a break (during which he can not to do any other
operations - e.g. loading processes) [29]. In the present model, the time of driver
working starts at time, when vehicle received the message about new transport order
to its completion. Therefore, loading and unloading operations are included. The
authors treat the break as the disturbance - an element extending the time of realization
order. But they have to be made. Analyzing the driver work time, in the basic terms,
the driver after 4.5 hours of driving/work is required to make a 45 minutes break, then
after a further 4.5 hours driving/working a break is equal 11 hours. This approach has
been simulated in the model (the authors did not take into account other cases of breaks
in work, because this disturbance is like a reminder to modeler that the driver must
have breaks!! Besides at the market, specialized programs for time management driver
can be founded.

Driver working time in the simulation model is mapped by using individually created
object called Driving_Work_time_Measure (Fig. 2). This object has 7 labels: the first
specifies the time interval between subsequent measurements, the second and the third
contains information on what time after the start of the work is have to be a break; lables
4 and 5 contain information about time duration of each break; 6 and 7 are supplemented
with the start time (time of receipt message about starting transport order by the
vehicle = start time), and with the end time (end of transportation order = stop time).

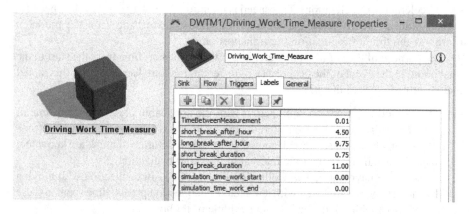

Fig. 2. Driving_Work_Time_Measure-Object.

In presented labels, important information are written. Thanks to them object
manages of mean of transport, when the break have to be made. This object contact with
vehicle by sending messages. Driving_Work_time_Measure Object, after receiving
information from a vehicle that it started a work - sends information to itself about next
break (break type and duration). In situation when a break should be made, created object
sends a message to vehicle (about stop it) and to itself. And after appropriate time (equal
time of break) it sends next message to mean of transport about unlocking and to itself
about next step in measurement. This cycle is shown schematically at Fig. 3.

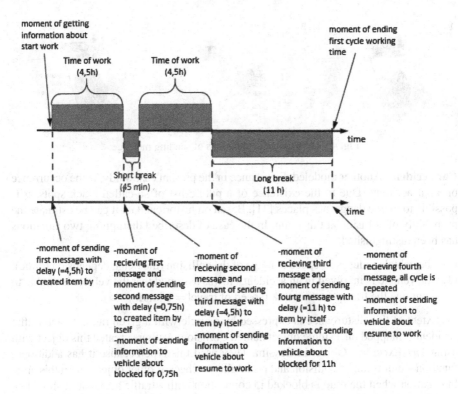

Fig. 3. Driving_Work_time_Measure Object - mechanism of sending message.

Toll collection point. In connection with moving motorways in the presented case study, toll collection points should be take into account. In these points, speed of travel are slowed down because of stop for the fee payment. Authors had created new object (TCP) to map this situation. TCP has four labels, in which the values for the stop operations at the fee payment point are defined (mean, deviation, min, max). On the basis of these labels, value of the blocking time is defined with using normal distribution. When the vehicle comes to toll collection point, it is stopped for established time. The slow down of the speed around the toll point is not included - it is included to stop time at point.

Disruption is modeled as follows: created object named TCP is combined with network, in which is a toll point. At the moment of the reset a model, a stop time at TCP is defined, by using normal distribution (in relation to values in labels). At the time of arrival the vehicle to the point, information about this situation is sending to TCP object (1). In response, the TCP object sends the information about stopped to the vehicle, and it sends to itself delayed information, delay is equal defined time of stopping (2). After this time, the TCP object receives a message from itself and sends information to vehicle to unlocked it (3). The described situations are shown in Fig. 4.

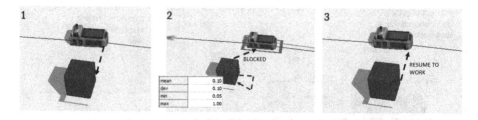

Fig. 4. TCP_Object – situations of sending message.

Car accident. Another modeled disturbance in the present case study, is the occurrence of a car accident. Due to the existence of a public list of so-called black spots, it is possible to define dangerous places [31]. Based on historical data it can be estimate the probability of collision at this point. In the case of described disruption, two situations has been distinguished:

(1) the vehicle reduces its speed at range of the collision (the range depends on traffic);
(2) the vehicle is involved in an accident - it was assumed that the vehicle is unable to continue the transportation task (speed of travel = 0 km/h).

Extent of this disturbance is expressed by a circle with a given radius. Each traffic accident is mapped on a single object named Collision. Authors created this object with using TaskExecuters Object in flexsim. They used this type because it has additional function – definition of collision and possibility to check if other object are in this area. In situation when the road is blocked in connection with a traffic accident, it should be take into account the additional time required to complete the order (in the event of failure to comply with the delivery date could mean a financial penalty).

Authors, using the ABS approach, created object with defined properties, which are stored in the labels. This created object has 17 labels (Fig. 5).

Label 1 contains information about type of accident (involving a car which realizes the order or no) - this value is defined according to the information contained in the other labels.

Label 2 - is a part of the information that describes the type of accident.

Labels 3 and 4 - they are places, where the probability of occurrence of a given type of accident at a given point, have to be defined.

Labels 5–8 - they are contained information about the speed of the vehicle in the event of a car accident without the participation of our vehicle; a speed is defined on the basis of these data.

Labels 9–12 - they included information about car accident range (radius), a radius is defined by this information, with using a normal distribution.

Label 13 - is equal 0 - in the case of an accident involving our car, it is assumed that it can not to continue further drive (does not move).

Labels 14–15 contain randomly selected values for each elements. In case of accident type 2 radius is 1.

Label 16 - allows you to change the stream of random numbers.

Label 17 - it gets information about that if in a disruption range is another object or not.

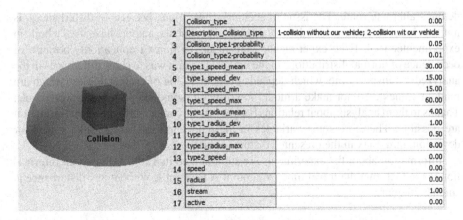

1	Collision_type	0.00
2	Description_Collision_type	1-collision without our vehicle; 2-collision wit our vehicle
3	Collision_type1-probability	0.05
4	Collision_type2-probability	0.01
5	type1_speed_mean	30.00
6	type1_speed_dev	15.00
7	type1_speed_min	15.00
8	type1_speed_max	60.00
9	type1_radius_mean	4.00
10	type1_radius_dev	1.00
11	type1_radius_min	0.50
12	type1_radius_max	8.00
13	type2_speed	0.00
14	speed	0.00
15	radius	0.00
16	stream	1.00
17	active	0.00

Fig. 5. Created collision object.

In case of a traffic accident, the range of them is defined by values in labels and with using normal distribution. In the same way the speed in range of disturbances is defined. This object, of every certain time interval, checks if in defined range appeared another object, if so then performing a specific action - changes the speed of travel in a foreign object. In the moment, when it is determined that the foreign object (mean of transport) is no longer in a disturbance range, created object again changes the speed of the vehicle, to value as which a vehicle had before it came to this disruption. Checking the area of interference occurs very often (currently 0.01 time unit). Thanks to this, the moment when the vehicle has left the disturbance is quickly noticed. Figure 6 shows described situations.

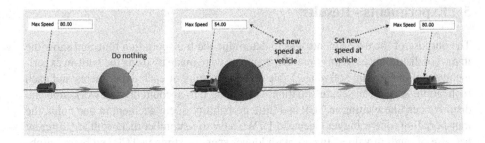

Fig. 6. Collision object – mode of action.

4   Simulation Experiment – Description

Simulation model with a selected route (described in Sect. 3) was created, in order to show the effect of various disturbances on the duration of the transport order. For a choosen route, few experiments were made, in which the values of the different variables have been changed. In preset case authors do not take into account the possibility of a detour - alternate route. The issue of seeking a new route, because of disturbances, is not the aim of this study. In order to carry out experiments, authors have used a built-in experimenter tool. Each experiments were made 10 times (replications) because of occurrence of normal distributions in the model. The aim was to show differences in the analyzed a transport time, which depends of the duration of each activities (which are random values). To not make a model too difficult, some simplifications were made. Thanks to them analysis about relations between disturbances and time of transportation are possible. Therefore some variables in the model left unchanged (like values for deviation, min, max in the presented disturbances).

Information about the experiments are summarized in Table 3. Important information is the fact, that the travel time from point A to point B without any disturbance is equal 2.78 hour.

Table 3. Definition of simulation experiments.

Experiment				
No	Take into account the driver's working time	Mean Time in every TCP	Probability of type 1 collision	Probability of type 2 collision
1	yes	0,1	0,1	0,01
2	yes	1	0,8	0,01
3	yes	1	0.1	1

5 Experiments - Results

The purpose of the experiments was to determine the transportation time and show the impact of disturbances to this time. Experiments were made by using the built-in experimenter tool in Flexsim software. Table 4 shows results of each experiments and each replication. As we can see, in situation with taking into account driving work time and disturbances like waiting in TCP and little probability of car accident in one point, the transportation time is bigger (scenario 1). We have to remember that result are different because of random values. In case with longer spending time in TCP and bigger probability of type 1 car accident, the time of transport is much longer. Of course in normal situation we will not stay in every TCP about 1 hours – it was defined so big to show a relation and to show the defined state at graph (Fig. 7). For scenario 3 the transport time is equal 0 – it is true, because mean of transport is involved in a car accident and can not continue the realization of work – it never comes to unload point. By using built-in experimenter tool we have information about interval of values of the analyzed time for the confidence interval as 90 % (Fig. 8).

Table 4. Results of simulation experiments. Source: results obtained from Flexsim model.

	Transportation Time [h]				
	Rep 1	Rep 2	Rep 3	Rep 4	Rep 5
Scenario 1	3,34	4,96	3,09	3,22	3,22
Scenario 2	8,55	8,98	7,34	7,39	8,72
Scenario 3	0	0	0	0	0
	Rep 6	Rep 7	Rep 8	Rep 9	Rep 10
Scenario 1	3,28	3,27	3,25	9,15	3,20
Scenario 2	29,37	23,84	24,04	23,31	7,39
Scenario 3	0	0	0	0	0

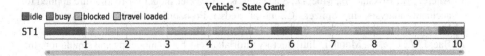

Fig. 7. State of vehicle. Source: results obtained from Flexsim model.

	Mean (90% Confidence)			Sample Std Dev	Min	Max
Scenario 1	2.9 <	4.0	< 5.1	1.9	3.1	9.1
Scenario 2	9.7 <	14.9	< 20.1	9.0	7.3	29.4
Scenario 3	N/A <	0.0	< N/A	0.0	0.0	0.0

Fig. 8. Confidence interval for analyzed time. Source: results obtained from Flexsim model.

Figure 7 present states of vehicle. State BLOCKED is when mean of transport is waiting in TCP. State BUSY is when the driver has a break (in accordance to law regulation).

6   Conclusion and Further Investigations

This article presents in detail a method of transport routes modeling, including distur-bances. In the case study authors show the effect of disturbances on the duration of the transport task. Using the simulation model, we can observe and experiment with the process - which gives a chance to improve it. Besides using the built-in Experimenter tool, it is possible to determine the range of values describe transport time for a given confidence interval. An important aspect of this article is a detailed description of way of modeling the individual disturbance and present how they work in practice (in the model) and not just in theory (description).

Obviously, there is an opportunity for further development of the proposed work: modelling next disturbances in described way (with combining ABS and DES approach). Besides experiment with them at created routes, and check influence of them to the transport time. By building a library of possible disruptions, we can fast build a model of routes and play (experiment) with them. And then, search a range of the time needed to travel by vehicle from point A to B at a given confidence interval will be possible. Information about needed time to travel from point A to B taking into account different disturbances, are very useful for transport companies and other.

Acknowledgements. Presented research are carried out under the LOGOS project (Model of coordination of virtual supply chains meeting the requirements of corporate social responsibility) under grant agreement number PBS1/B9/17/2013.

References

1. Alteren, B., Hokstad, P., Moe, D., Sakshaug, K.: A barrier model for road traffic applied to accident analysis. In: Spitzer, C., et al. (eds.) Probabilistic Safety Assessment and Management, pp. 3603–3608. Springer, London (2004)
2. Bae, J.W., Lee, G., Moon, I.: Introductory tutorial: agent-based modeling and simulation. In: Winter Simulation Conference, pp. 3809–3820 (2012)
3. Banks, J., Carson II, J.S., Nelson, B.L., Nicol, D.M.: Discrete-Event System Simulation, 4th edn, pp. 68–86. Prentice Hall, Upper Saddle River (2004). ISBN 0-13-144679-7
4. Bocewicz, G.: Robustness of multimodal transportation networks. Eksploatacja i Niezawodność-Maintenance and Reliability **16**(2), 259–269 (2014)
5. Brussaard, L.A., Kruiskamp, M.M., Oude Essink, M.P.: The Dutch Model for the quantitative risk analysis of road tunnels. In: Spitzer, C., et al. (eds.) Probabilistic Safety Assessment and Management, pp. 2660–2665. Springer, London (2004)
6. Caddy, I.N., Helou, M.M.: Supply chains and their management: application of general systems theory. J. Retail. Consum. Serv. **14**, 319–327 (2007)
7. Cassandras, C.G., Lafortune, S.: Introduction to Discrete Event Systems, 2nd edn, pp. 557–615. Springer, Heidelberg (2008). ISBN 978-0-387-33332-8
8. Chan, W.K.V., Son, Y., Macal, C.M.: Agent-based simulation tutorial – simulation of emergent behavior and differences between Agent-Based Simulation and Discrete-Event Simulation. In: Winter Simulation Conference, pp. 135–150 (2010)
9. Chen, S., Peng, H., Liu, S.: Yang, Y.: A Multimodal Hierarchical-based Assignment Model for Integrated Transportation Networks. J. Transp. Syst. Eng. Inf. Technol. **9**(6), 130–135 (2009)
10. Fung, R.Y.K., Chen, T.: A multiagent supply chain planning and coordination architecture. Int. J. Adv. Manuf. Technol. **25**(7–8), 811–819 (2004)
11. Gheorghe, A., Birchmeier, J., Kröger, W.: Advanced spatial modelling for risk analysis of transportation dangerous goods. In: Spitzer, C., et al. (eds.) Probabilistic Safety Assessment and Management, pp. 2499–2504. Springer, London (2004)
12. Hoffa, P., Pawlewski, P.: Agent based approach for modeling disturbances in supply chain. In: Corchado, J.M., et al. (eds.) Highlights of Practical Applications of Heterogeneous Multi-Agent Systems. The PAAMS Collection, pp. 144–155. Springer, Heidelberg (2014)
13. Jasiulewicz-Kaczmarek, M.: Role and contribution of maintenance in sustainable manufacturing. In: Bakhtadze N., Chernyshov K., Dolgui A., Lototsky V., (eds.) 7th IFAC Conference on Manufacturing Modelling, Management, and Control, part 1, vol. 7, pp. 1146–1151 (2013)
14. Kim, S.-H., Robertazzi, T.G.: Modeling Mobile Agent Behavior. Comput. Math. Appl. **51**, 951–966 (2006)
15. Macal, C.M., North, M.J.: Introductory tutorial: agent-based modeling and simulation. In: Winter Simulation Conference, pp. 362–376 (2013)

16. Marseguerra, M., Zio, E., Bianchi, M.: A fuzzy model for the estimate of the accident rate in road transport of hazardous materials. In: Bedford, T., van Gelder, P.H.A.J.M. (eds.) Safety and Reliability, pp. 1085–1092. Swets & Zeitlinger, Lisse (2003)
17. Orlandelli, C.M., Vestrucci, P.: Development of a road transportation risks data base for Italy: methodology, models and results. In: Spitzer, C., et al. (eds.) Probabilistic Safety Assessment and Management, pp. 2269–2274. Springer, London (2004)
18. Siebers, P.O., Macal, C.M., Garnett, J., Buxton, D., Pidd, M.: Discrete-event simulation is dead, long live agent-based simulation! J. Simul. **4**(3), 204–210 (2010)
19. Sitek P., Wikarek J.: A hybrid approach to supply chain modeling and optimization. In: Federated Conference on Computer Science and Information Systems, pp. 1223–1230 (2013)
20. Skorupski, J.: Sieci Petriego jako narzędzie do modelowania procesów ruchowych w transporcie, Prace Naukowe Politechniki Warszawskiej, Transport, z.78, pp.69–84 (2011)
21. Tixier, J., et al.: Development of a risk knowledge platform dedicated to accident of dangerous goods transportation. In: Guedes Soares, G., Zio, E. (eds.) Safety and Reliability for Managing Risk, pp. 117–122. Taylor & Francis Group, London (2006)
22. Umeda, S.: Simulation analysis of supply chain systems with reverse logistics. In: Winter Simulation Conference, pp. 3375–3384 (2013)
23. Wieland, A., Wallenburg, C.M.: Supply-Chain-Management in stürmischen Zeiten, Berlin. (2011)
24. Wilhelm, T., Hollunder, J.: Information theoretic description of networks. Phys. A **385**(1), 385–396 (2007)
25. http://autostrada-a2.pl. Accessed Jan 2015
26. https://www.flexsim.com/. Accessed Jan 2015
27. http://www.gddkia.gov.pl. Accessed Jan 2015
28. http://gddkia.gov.pl/pl/aprint/6636/mapa-i-spis-czarnych-punktow. Accessed Jan 2015
29. http://isap.sejm.gov.pl/. Accessed Jan 2015
30. https://mapa.targeo.pl. Accessed Jan 2015
31. http://www.rmf24.pl/fakty/polska/news-szokujacy-raport-o-polskich-drogach-zobacz-mape-czarnych-odc,nId,769924. Accessed Jan 2015

A Multi-agent System for Selecting Portfolio of New Product Development Projects

Marcin Relich[1(✉)] and Pawel Pawlewski[2]

[1] Faculty of Economics and Management, University of Zielona Gora, Zielona Gora, Poland
m.relich@wez.uz.zgora.pl
[2] Faculty of Engineering Management, Poznan University of Technology, Poznan, Poland
pawel.pawlewski@put.poznan.pl

Abstract. This paper is concerned with designing a multi-agent approach for evaluating new products and selecting product portfolio. In today's companies it is widespread to execute many new product projects simultaneously. As these projects require resources that are available in the limited quantities, there is the need to select the most promising set of new product for development. The evaluation of new product projects involves many agents that analyse the customer requirements and information acquired from an enterprise system, including the fields of sales and marketing, research and development, and production. The company's resources, performance metrics, and the identified relationships are stored in knowledge base that is specified according to the framework of constraint satisfaction problem. The relationships are sought with the use of fuzzy neural system and described in the form of if-then rules.

Keywords: Knowledge acquisition · Data mining · Fuzzy neural system · Project management · Decision support system

1 Introduction

Nowadays, project companies generate an increasing number of products and services, as the response to market trends that impose to shorten product life cycle, increase variety of products, and fulfil customer requirements. Consequently, new product development (NPD) is one of the most important processes to maintain company's competitive position and continue business success. Contribution of NPD to the growth of the companies, its influence on profit performance, and its role as a key factor in business planning has been widely considered [1–3]. Nevertheless, it is still reported that the success rate of product development projects is unsatisfactory, with more cost and time than expected to achieve the project goals.

The main reasons of NPD failures can consider in the context of extrinsic and intrinsic problems. Extrinsic problems include flops in the market, changes in regulations or simply competition develops product first [4]. Intrinsic problems concern the limited resources (e.g. funds, specialists) and result in the difficulties to meet the project goals, including time of product launch and product innovativeness. Although unsatisfactory success rate of NPD projects depends on the environmental uncertainties as

© Springer International Publishing Switzerland 2015
J. Bajo et al. (Eds.): PAAMS 2015 Workshops, CCIS 524, pp. 102–114, 2015.
DOI: 10.1007/978-3-319-19033-4_9

market competition and product technology advancement are often intense [5], companies should try to improve the NPD process through taking into account both external and internal agents.

New product development requires numerous decisions by many individuals and groups, including customers, analysts, project managers, R&D employees, chief marketing and production officers, etc. These decisions can be supported through an integrated business information system that combines the different agents and enables their communication. An enterprise information system consists of enterprise resource planning (ERP) system, project management software, customer relationship management (CRM) system, computer aided design (CAD) system, and knowledge acquired from the experts and company's databases. The advancement of information technology helps today's organisations in business management processes and collecting data. As a result, enterprise systems generate and store a huge amount of data that is potential source of information [6, 7]. A key challenge faced by NPD projects is how to acquire knowledge, sustain success rate among the products, and manage the project in order to reduce the risk of failure of the product [4].

Knowledge creation and management through the new product development and management processes is of significant interest in the context of recent technology and infrastructure changes. Data mining applications have vastly increased the amount of information available and the ease of manipulating and using it [8]. However, the use of data mining techniques require expert knowledge, for example, to select a set of variables to an analysis among enormous number of possible variables in an enterprise system, or to choose a suitable data mining technique for the stated problem. The use of data mining techniques aims to discover patterns, improve expert knowledge, and finally, increase a chance to make a proper decision. As in the knowledge discovery process is not possible to eliminate a human dimension, a multi-agents approach seems to be suitable framework to model the problem of selecting new product portfolio on the basis of an enterprise system.

Multi-agent systems are intelligent distributed approach suited for applications that are modular, complex, and changeable, for example, for management of the NPD projects. These systems have capabilities such as autonomy, integration, reactivity and flexibility, and they are an emerging sub-field of artificial intelligence that is concerned with a society of agents interacting in order to solve a common problem [9]. Agent approach replaces the conventional centralized systems (for manufacturing, product design etc.) with a network of agents that are endowed with a local view of its environment and the ability to respond locally to that environment. The overall system performance is not globally planned, but emerges through the dynamic interactions between agents in real time [10].

Despite the popularity and applications of the agent technology in the business domain have grown over the recent years, there is a lack of unifying framework that would used the paradigm of multi-agent system for selecting new product portfolio. This study aims to develop an approach that bases on the multi-agent paradigm and uses an enterprise system (ERP, CRM, etc.) providing a foundation for conceptual analysis. The model of new product portfolio selection is specified in term of a constraint satisfaction problem as a set of variables, domains, and constraints. The constraint satisfaction problem can be considered as a knowledge base enabling the design of a knowledge-based system that includes the identified patterns, expert knowledge, and routine queries such as what is the most promising set of products for development? Knowledge base and inference engine of the proposed approach has been developed with the use of constraint programming environment.

Many attempts have been made in recent years to introduce data mining techniques for improvement of the NPD process. Agard and Kusiak [11] used a data mining based method to analyze the requirements for the design of product families. Jiao and Zhang [12] proposed product portfolio identification with the use of an association rule mining system. In turn, Yu and Wang [13] described product portfolio identification with data mining based on multi-objective genetic algorithm. Although many data mining based methods have been developed to support product portfolio identification, there is a scarcity in the context of using a multi-agent approach with data mining agent to new product portfolio selection.

This study is concerned with the use of a multi-agent system to identify the customers' requirements and select a set of the best concepts of new products taking into account information of the previous projects that are retrieved from an enterprise system database. The relationships between net profit of past products and metrics of the NPD process are sought with the use of a fuzzy neural system that enables the description of the identified relationships in form of if-then rules. The rules acquired from an enterprise system and agents, as well as facts (e.g. company's resources, performance metrics) are stored in knowledge base that is specified according to the framework of constraint satisfaction problem. The proposed approach uses the knowledge base to estimating net profit for new products, and proposing a set of the most promising products for further development. A portfolio of new product projects is sought with the use of constraint programming according to project manager's preferences.

The remaining sections of this paper are organised as follows: Sect. 2 presents the use of multi-agent systems in project management. A model of selecting new product portfolio in terms of constraint satisfaction problem is presented in Sect. 3. The proposed multi-agent architecture to evaluating the product success and selecting new product portfolio is shown in Sect. 4. An example of the proposed approach is illustrated in Sect. 5. Finally, some concluding remarks are contained in Sect. 6.

2 Multi-agent Systems in Project Management

An agent is defined as a computer system that is situated in an environment, and that is capable of autonomous actions in order to meet its design objectives [14]. Agents are commonly modeled in terms of knowledge, belief, intention, obligation, while objects are modeled through their internal structure as methods and attributes. The degree to which agents and objects are autonomous is quite different. Objects do not have control over their behaviours, because they are invoked by others. On the contrary, agents are able to decide whether or not to execute an action after receiving request. Ontology is frequently used for internal knowledge representation in agents that furthermore enables knowledge sharing, inference etc. Multi-agent systems are systems with multiple agents and are suitable for complex problems that have alternative problem solving techniques, involve reasoning with multiple models at different levels of abstraction and representations, and usually involve distributed knowledge sources [15].

The paradigm of multi-agent systems (MAS) provides a very suitable architecture for a design and implementation of integrative business information systems. The complex information systems development can be supported with the use of agent-based technology in the context of natural decomposition, abstraction and flexibility of management for organisational structure changes [16]. MAS consists of a set of autonomous agents that can define their own goals and actions and can interact and collaborate each other through communication. As in a MAS environment agents work collectively to solve specific problems, the MAS paradigm provides an effective platform or coordination and cooperation among multiple functional units in a company [17]. The communication is an important part of any MAS to achieve its desired functionality [18].

The use of the MAS paradigm in the context of knowledge management includes such tasks as [19]: knowledge search, acquisition, analysis and classification from various data sources; information given to human and computing networks once usable knowledge is ready to be consulted; negotiation on knowledge integration or exclusion into the system; explanation of the quality and reliability which are related to the system integrated knowledge; learning progressively all along the knowledge management process. Such services are mostly implemented to create two MAS categories devoted to knowledge management. The first MAS type is based upon an agent cooperation to solve complicated problems related to the knowledge types. The second MAS category gathers management assistant agents depending on the actors' needs.

Project team members and other actors incorporated in the NPD process are usually located at different places. In contrast, planning and control of projects is often centralized. All information relevant to the project should be passed to the project manager. Information of interest for other team members is often transferred through the project manager as well, even if it is not crucial from the project's point of view. Centralized project management creates long communication paths and makes the exchange of information cumbersome, redundant and unreliable. Agent approach can replace the central database and the central control computer with a network of agents that are responsible for a local domain and have the ability and authority to respond locally to range of their domains. The overall system performance is not globally planned, but emerges through the dynamic interaction of agents. Knowledge is integrated into agent to deal with uncertainty and computational complexity [10].

A multi-agent system considered from the perspective of a tool can be used by project managers as an aid to decision making and problem solving. The NPD process includes tasks such as evaluating project parameters, selecting the most promising projects, scheduling and monitoring, which involve considerable skills and experience to plan the activities, time, people, equipment, material and the money required. A task-oriented decision support system may assist project managers in indicating what is likely to happen in future, presenting facts in a manner that makes judgment easier, and showing what has happened and why.

3 Reference Model of New Product Portfolio Selection

The product design process depends on many factors that derive from the external environment and the field of enterprise. The external environment includes customer's demand, force of competition, sources of supply, changes in regulations, technology or financial limitations. In turn, the internal factors concern the resources and processes that appear in the different fields of an organization. Specifications of the previous products, design parameters, product portfolios, and customer requirements are registered and stored in an enterprise system that mainly includes ERP, CRM or CAD system and that is used nowadays by more and more enterprises. The selected attributes of an enterprise system, resources, and the identified relationships are stored in knowledge base that aims to facilitate the project manager to evaluate the success of a new product, and finally, select a set of the most promising products for further development. Figure 1 illustrates the reference model of new product selection in the context of the external and internal environment of an enterprise as well as an enterprise system.

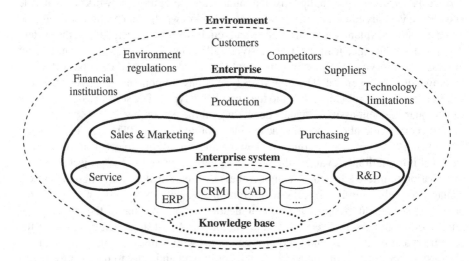

Fig. 1. Reference model of new product portfolio selection

The presented model contains a set of decision variables, their domains, and the constraints that can be referred to the company's resources and performance indicators. The decision problem concerning the selection of the most promising set of products for development has been described in terms of a constraint satisfaction problem (CSP). The model description encompasses the limitations of a company, parameters of new products that are considered for development, and a set of routine queries (the instances of decision problems) that are formulated in the framework of CSP. The structure of the constraint satisfaction problem may be described as follows [20]:

$$CSP = ((V, D), C)$$

where:

$V = \{v_1, v_2, ..., v_n\}$ – a finite set of n variables,

$D = \{d_1, d_2, ..., d_n\}$ – a finite set of n discrete domains of variables,

$C = \{c_1, c_2, ..., c_k\}$ – a finite set of k constraints limiting and linking variables.

Consider a set of new products for development $P = \{P_1, ..., P_i, ..., P_I\}$, where P_i consists of J activities. The input variables are as follows: duration of new product development (PD_i) and its cost (PC_i), production unit cost of the product (PUC_i), duration of marketing campaign of the product (MCD_i) and its cost (MCC_i), percentage of customer requirements translated into technical specification (PTS_i). The decision variable is net profit of the product (PNP_i). The company's resources include the total number of employees directly involved in the NPD projects $C_{1,t}$ and financial means $C_{2,t}$ in the t-th time unit $(t = 0, 1, ..., T)$. The decision criterion for product portfolio selection is maximization of the total net profit from product portfolio by the given constraints.

The constraint satisfaction problem can be considered in the context of a knowledge base. The knowledge base is a platform for query formulation as well as for obtaining answers, and it comprises of facts and rules that are relevant to the system's properties and the relations between its different parts. As a knowledge base can be considered in terms of a system, at the input of the system are the variables concerning basic characteristics of an object that are known and given by user [21]. The model description in terms of constraint satisfaction problem enables the design of a decision support system taking into account the available specifications, routine queries, and expert knowledge. Consequently, the model integrates technical parameters, available resources, expert experience, identified relationships (rules) and user requirements in the form of knowledge base [22]. The problem solution is connected with seeking the answer to the following question: what products should be chosen to the product portfolio to obtain the maximal net profit from the products by a fixed amount of resources? The methodology of finding solutions for the above-described problem in the context of multi-agent architecture is presented in the next section.

4 The Proposed Multi-agent Architecture for Selecting Product Portfolio

The enterprise system generates routinely an enormous amount of data according to the business processes in a company. The amount of available data and easiness of data retrieval results in increasing awareness of an opportunity to derive valuable information from their databases, which can further be used to improve business processes in a company [23]. As analysis of huge amount of data and knowledge acquisition with the use of manual methods is slow, expensive, subjective, and prone to errors, there is a need to automate the process through using data mining techniques [24, 25]. Data mining is a stage of the knowledge discovery process and its aim is to identify nontrivial, novel, and potentially useful patterns in data. Data mining techniques can be considered as an extension of OLAP (OnLine Analytical Processing) tools that enable users to carry out multidimensional analysis interactively taking into account different perspectives.

The process of selecting product portfolio can be divided into a few sub-processes, for example, selection of key customers, identification of key customer requirements, estimation of the NPD parameters, and evaluation of the NPD projects. These sub-processes require cooperation and communication between the agents involved. Figure 2 illustrates the framework of a multi-agent approach for product portfolio selection.

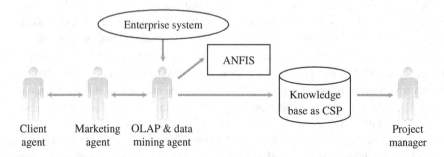

Fig. 2. Framework of multi-agent system for product portfolio selection

The sub-process of selecting key customers is initiated by an OLAP agent on the bases of information from an enterprise system, e.g. sales analysis and sales forecast in the customer perspective. In the next sub-process, i.e. identification of key customer requirements, an OLAP agent communicates with a marketing agent that investigates the requirements of key customers in the context of new product demand. OLAP and data mining agent selects a set of variables from the enterprise databases, variables that are suspected of significant impact on the success of previous products. These variables are led to inputs and outputs of fuzzy neural system that estimates the NPD parameters such as duration and cost of the NPD projects, and net profit from a new product.

The fuzzy neural system has the advantages of both neural networks (e.g. learning abilities, optimization abilities and connectionist structures) and fuzzy systems (e.g. if-then reasoning, simplicity of incorporating expert knowledge). The outcome of a fuzzy neural system is a set of if-then rules that can be used to perform nonlinear predictive modelling, simulation, and forecasting. One well-known structure of fuzzy neural networks is the adaptive neuro-fuzzy inference system (ANFIS) that has been used in this study.

A data mining agent evaluates the importance of relationships identified by ANFIS, and makes decision to store a relationship in a knowledge base. The knowledge base stores the identified relationships as well as the resource constraints (financial, temporal, personal, etc.) that are used to estimate the success of a potential product and further used to select the most promising products for development. The output of the presented multi-agent system is the proposal of project portfolio for the project manager. More-over, the decision-maker can carry out what-if analysis and check whether the product portfolio will be changed in the case of others values of the input variables.

The agents possess the different objectives and constraints, and they do not have a global view of the entire NPD process. As a result, there is needed cooperation to allow the agents to adjust their local tasks in order to achieve global objectives. The contract net protocol is a high level protocol for achieving efficient cooperation based on a market-like protocol [9]. The contract net protocol is proposed for inter-agent cooperation in the context of selecting new product portfolio. Table 1 presents an example of information that is specified in the messages between the agents.

Table 1. An example of message description

Item	Description
Sender:	OLAP agent
Receiver:	Marketing agent
Message type:	Selecting key customers
Message task:	Investigating key customers' requirements
Deadline:	Time by which the marketing agent has to respond
Content:	The description of the sales volume in the customer and product dimension

The negotiation algorithm between marketing agent and client agent is executed until the requirements of new product are sent. These requirements are sent to data mining agent that verifies them in the context of technology limitations and the potential success of new products on the basis of information acquired from an enterprise system. In the next step, data mining agent sends the message to marketing agent with description of the rejected requirements. The negotiation algorithm between marketing agent and client agent is repeated until the requirements are rejected. In the case of approving all requirements by data mining agent, information is stored in the knowledge base and used in selecting new product portfolio.

In this study, the knowledge base is specified in terms of constraint satisfaction problem that can be implemented effectively in a constraint programming environment. Constraint programming (CP) is an emergent software technology for a declarative constraints satisfaction problem description and can be considered as a pertinent framework for the development of decision support system software. Moreover, the impact of real-life constraints on decision-making is of great importance, especially for designing an interactive decision support system. In the case of extensive search space, the processing time of calculations can be significantly reduced with the use of constraints programming techniques [26]. CP is qualitatively different from the other programming paradigms, in terms of declarative, object-oriented and concurrent programming. Compared to these paradigms, constraint programming is much closer to the ideal of declarative programming: to state what we want without stating how to achieve it [27].

A constraints satisfaction problem can always be solved with exhaustive search, where all possible values of all variables are enumerated and each is checked to in the context of a solution. Except for trivial problems, the number of candidates is usually too large to enumerate them all. Constraint programming has embedded ways to solve constraints satisfaction problems with greatly reduction of the amount of search needed [27]. This is sufficient to solve many practical problems such as supply chain problem [28–30] or scheduling problem [26, 31, 32].

A multi-agent approach can be successfully used to solving of constraint satisfaction problems, such as n-queen problems and coloring problems. In solving a CSP with this approach, each agent can represent a variable and its position corresponds to a value assignment for the variable. The environment for the whole multi-agent system contains all the possible domain values for the problem. The conducted research shows that the performance of a multi-agent approach in solving CSPs for approximate solution is time-efficient [33]. A multi-agent system can be implemented in the constraint programming environment, e.g. with the use of Oz programming language.

In the context of the presented approach, the domain of a CSP can be represented into a multi-agent environment. Thus, finding a solution of the CSP is reduced to local behaviour-governed moves within such an environment. There is a need to examine how exact solution of CSP can be self-organized by a multi-agent system that consists of environment, reactive rules, and agents. All agents inhabit in an environment, where there positions indicate values of certain variables [33]. The next section presents an illustrative example of the use of ANFIS to seeking relationships in order to develop knowledge base, and the use of CP techniques to selecting product portfolio.

5   Illustrative Example

An illustrative example consists of two parts: the use of ANFIS to seeking relationships that describe the success of a product and the use of CP to selecting the most promising set of new products for development. On the basis of information about the previous NPD projects, ANFIS seeks the relationships between variables selected by data mining agent and output variable, i.e. net profit from a product (PNP). These relationships are further used to estimate net profit from product concepts. In the example, the following input variables have been selected: NPD project duration (PD), NPD project cost (PC), production unit cost of the product (PUC), marketing campaign duration of the product (MCD), marketing campaign cost of the product (MCC), and percentage of customer requirements translated into technical specification (PTS).

In order to eliminate the overtraining of ANFIS and increase the estimation quality, the data set of the previous NPD projects has been divided into learning and testing sets. In studies, the ANFIS has been trained according to subtractive clustering method that was implemented in the Matlab® software. The identified relationships are specified in form of fuzzy if-then rules and used to estimating net profit from a new product. Figure 3 presents the membership functions for 7 rules that are used to estimating net profit from a product.

The estimated net profits are used further to seeking the NPD portfolios according to the available resources (the number of employees involved in the NPD projects and financial means) and selecting a NPD portfolio that ensures the maximal total net profit from all products. Let us assume that the R&D department generated 35 concepts for

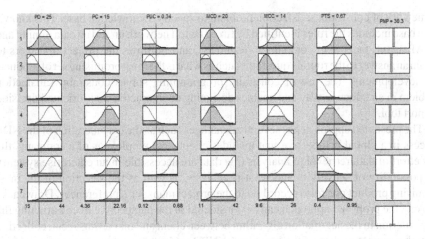

Fig. 3. The use of ANFIS to estimating net profit from a product

new products that are evaluated according to net profit per month. In the NDP projects can participate 14 employees (C_1), and the total budget for NDP projects (C_2), including the R&D and marketing campaign budget, equals 155,000 €. The number of possible solutions, i.e. combinations of new product portfolio, is very large. This imposes the use of techniques that enable the reduction of the amount of search needed, such as constraint programming. The considered problem has been implemented in the Oz Mozart programming environment that includes CP paradigms. The number of the admissible solutions equals 4,058 instances. The set of the NPD projects that ensures the maximal total net profit (64,000 € per month) consists of product P_8, P_{15}, and P_{17}.

6 Concluding Remarks

The continuous development and launching of new products is an important determinant of sustained company performance. The development of new product projects involves many agents in the field of customers, marketing, production, research and development, etc. As in the NPD process is required knowledge acquisition from the different local areas and communication between these areas, the use of a multi-agent system seems to be a pertinent framework to select a portfolio of new product development projects. The proposed system takes a global perspective concerning the NPD process and presents a mechanism of interaction between agents. As an enterprise system stores the data connected with the various areas of business, including customers' demand and specification of the past NPD projects, its database can be used to seeking the relationships between these areas and the success of a product. In this study, fuzzy neural system has been used to seek these relationships that can be used further to evaluating concepts for new products and selecting product portfolio for development.

The characteristics of the presented approach includes the use of expert domain knowledge to select variables used in the knowledge discovery process, fuzzy neural networks to seek the relationships and their description in the form of if-then rules, and framework of constraint satisfaction problem to specify a knowledge base. This knowledge base includes the rules identified by fuzzy neural network or/and an data mining and OLAP agent, facts (e.g. company's resources), and it allows the project managers to obtain an answer to the routine questions such as what is the most promising set of products for development? The use of constraint programming solves constraint satisfaction problem in an effective way and enables designing an interactive task-oriented decision support tool.

The presented approach has several advantages such as the consideration of the NDP process in a global perspective that includes clients and employees of a company, the low effort of data retrieval to analysis (the data are accessible in an enterprise system), the possibility of sensitivity and what-if analysis, as well as the selection of the most promising product portfolio according to the project manager's preferences. Drawbacks of using the proposed approach can be considered in the perspective of constructing the stop criterion in the negotiation algorithm between client and marketing agent, collecting enough amounts of data of the past similar NPD projects, and ambiguous principles to build structure of a fuzzy neural system. The subject of future research includes the extension of the assumptions presented in this study. For instance, the proposed approach assumes one agent for each process, but in real world more agents can work at a process. The improvement of the negotiation algorithm between client and marketing agent is also considered as further research.

References

1. Cooper, R., Edgett, S.: Maximizing productivity in product innovation. Res. Technol. Manage. **51**(2), 47–58 (2008)
2. Ulrich, K.T., Eppinger, S.D.: Product Design and Development. McGraw-Hill, Boston (2011)
3. Spalek, S.: Improving industrial engineering performance through a successful project management office. Inzinerine Ekonomika-Engineering Economics **24**(2), 88–98 (2013)
4. Cooper, L.P.: A research agenda to reduce risk in new product development through knowledge management: a practitioner perspective. J. Eng. Tech. Manage. **20**(1), 117–140 (2003)
5. McCarthy, I.P., Tsinopoulos, C., Allen, P., Rose-Anderssen, C.: New product development as a complex adaptive system of decisions. J. Prod. Innov. Manage **23**(5), 437–456 (2006)
6. Doskocil, R.: Microsoft project as a knowledge base for project management. In: 22nd International Business Information Management Association Conference on Creating Global Competitive Economies, pp. 1412–1418, Rome (2013)
7. Relich, M.: Using ERP database for knowledge acquisition: a project management perspective. In: International Scientific Conference on Knowledge for Market Use, pp. 263–269, Olomouc (2013)
8. Zahay, D., Griffin, A., Fredericks, E.: Sources, uses, and forms of data in the new product development process. Ind. Mark. Manage. **33**(7), 657–666 (2004)
9. Fazel Zarandi, M.H., Ahmadpour, P.: Fuzzy agent-based expert system for steel making process. Expert Syst. Appl. **36**, 9539–9547 (2009)
10. Yan, Y., Kuphal, T., Bode, J.: Application of multiagent systems in project management. Int. J. Prod. Econ. **68**, 185–197 (2000)
11. Agard, B., Kusiak, A.: Data-mining-based methodology for the design of product families. Int. J. Prod. Res. **42**, 2955–2969 (2004)

12. Jiao, J., Zhang, Y.: Product portfolio identification based on association rule mining. Comput. Aided Des. **37**, 149–172 (2005)
13. Yu, L., Wang, L.: Product portfolio identification with data mining based on multi-objective GA. J. Intell. Manuf. **21**, 797–810 (2010)
14. Wooldridge, M.: An Introduction to Multiagent Systems. Wiley, Chichester (2002)
15. Madhusudan, T.: An agent-based approach for coordinating product design workflows. Comput. Ind. **56**, 235–259 (2005)
16. Kishore, R., Zhang, H., Ramesh, R.: Enterprise integration using the agent paradigm: foundations of multi-agent-based integrative business information systems. Decis. Support Syst. **42**(1), 48–78 (2006)
17. Lavbic, D., Rupnik, R.: Multi-agent system for decision support in enterprises. J. Inf. Organ. Sci. **33**(2), 269–284 (2009)
18. Adhau, S., Mittal, M.L., Mittal, A.: A multi-agent system for distributed multi-project scheduling: an auction-based negotiation approach. Eng. Appl. Artif. Intell. **25**, 1738–1751 (2012)
19. Monticolo, D., Miaita, S., Darwich, H., Hilaire, V.: An agent-based system to build project memories during engineering projects. Knowl.-Based Syst. **68**, 88–102 (2014)
20. Rossi, F., van Beek, P., Walsh, T.: Handbook of Constraint Programming. Elsevier Science, Amsterdam (2006)
21. Bocewicz, G., Nielsen, I., Banaszak, Z.: Iterative multimodal processes scheduling. Ann. Rev. Control **38**(1), 113–132 (2014)
22. Woolliscroft, P., Relich, M., Caganova, D., Cambal, M., Sujanova, J., Makraiova, J.: The implication of tacit knowledge utilisation within project management risk assessment. In: 10th International Conference of Intellectual Capital, Knowledge Management and Organisational Learning (ICICKM 2013), pp. 645–652. Washington, DC (2013)
23. Li, T., Ruan, D.: An extended process model of knowledge discovery in database. J. Enterp. Inf. Manage. **20**(2), 169–177 (2007)
24. Han, J., Kamber, M.: Data Mining Concepts and Techniques. Morgan Kaufmann Publishers, San Francisco (2006)
25. Cios, K.J., Pedrycz, W., Swiniarski, R.W., Kurgan, L.A.: Data Mining: A Knowledge Discovery Approach. Springer, New York (2007)
26. Banaszak, Z., Zaremba, M., Muszynski, W.: Constraint programming for project-driven manufacturing. Int. J. Prod. Econ. **120**, 463–475 (2009)
27. Van Roy, P., Haridi, S.: Concepts, Techniques and Models of Computer Programming. Massachusetts Institute of Technology, Massachusetts (2004)
28. Grzybowska, K., Kovács, G.: Logistics process modelling in supply chain – algorithm of coordination in the supply chain – contracting. In: International Joint Conference SOCO 2014-CISIS 2014-ICEUTE 2014, Advances in Intelligent Systems and Computing, vol. 299, pp. 311–320 (2014)
29. Grzybowska, K., Awasthi, A., Hussain, M.: Modeling enablers for sustainable logistics collaboration integrating Canadian and Polish perspectives. In: the Federated Conference on Computer Science and Information Systems, pp. 1311–1319, Warsaw (2014)
30. Sitek, P., Wikarek J.: A hybrid framework for the modelling and optimisation of decision problems in sustainable supply chain management. Int. J. Prod. Res. **53**, 1–18 (2015). doi: 10.1080/00207543.2015.1005762
31. Baptiste, P., Le Pape, C., Nuijten, W.: Constraint-Based Scheduling: Applying Constraint Programming to Scheduling Problems. Kluwer Academic Publishers, Norwell (2001)

32. Relich, M.: Identifying relationships between eco-innovation and product success. In: Golinska, P., Kawa, A. (eds.) Technology Management for Sustainable Production and Logistics, pp. 173–192. Springer, Berlin Heidelberg (2015)
33. Liu, J., Jing, H., Tang, Y.Y.: Multi-agent oriented constraint satisfaction. Artif. Intell. **136**, 101–144 (2002)

DES/ABS Approach to Simulate Warehouse Operations

Pawel Pawlewski[✉]

Poznan University of Technology, ul.Strzelecka 11,
60-965 Poznań, Poland
pawel.pawlewski@put.poznan.pl

Abstract. The paper presents the results of research performed in the area of modeling and simulation of warehouse operations in a supply chain. Author defines in details main problems concerning warehousing. "Old" and "new" approaches to modeling and simulating are compared based on available simulation programs on the market. Main goal of the paper is to answer the question how to prepare in a very short time the motion of forklifts in a defined simulation model based on picking lists. Author proposes a method based on mixing DES (Discrete Event) and ABS (Agent Based Simulation). As result the library of agents objects (LogABS) is described and explained.

Keywords: Agent based modeling · Simulation · Supply chain · Warehouse

1 Introduction

The paper presents results of research performed over the last few years in the area of modeling and simulating of warehouse operations in a supply chain. Each supply chain is composed of three main stages: procurement, manufacturing and distribution. Warehousing has an important role at the procurement and distribution stages. Some authors state that warehousing is one of the three separated strategies for the distribution out of a factory in a supply chain [1]:

– direct transmission: shipment from vendors to retails is executed without the services of distribution center,
– warehousing: goods are delivered based on customer orders, goods are stored in devices such as pallet rackets or shelving,
– using cross-docking system: based on customer demands, goods are delivered to a warehouse by receiving trucks, goods are loaded into shipping trucks. Usually goods are not stored in a warehouse; if an item is held in storage, the time of storage is less than 10–15 h.

At the procurement stage the role of warehousing is similar to the distribution stage: raw materials, parts, components etc. are delivered, stored and shipped to producers.

© Springer International Publishing Switzerland 2015
J. Bajo et al. (Eds): PAAMS 2015 Workshops, CCIS 524, pp. 115–125, 2015.
DOI: 10.1007/978-3-319-19033-4_10

The major objectives of the present paper are:

– to define main problems concerning warehousing – in details
– to present the comparison between "old" and "new" approaches to modeling and simulating warehousing operations based on simulation programs available on the market
– to solve the problem of how to model and simulate main warehousing operations - picking and replenishment.

Our main research goal is how to prepare in a very short time the motion of forklifts in a defined simulation model based on picking lists.

The main contribution of the paper is to present and combine two approaches to model and simulate picking operations in a distribution center. To do it, author proposes a method based on mixing DES (discrete event system) and ABS (agent based system) approaches. DES approaches are based on FlexSim Simulation Package available on the market. ABS approach called LogABS is the solution proposed by the author as an additional part of FlexSim. The paper answers question why mixing these two approaches (DES and ABS) is necessary to simulate this kind of operations. The highlights are:

– presenting the the main features of picking operations in warehouse,
– demonstrating that the DES (discrete-event simulation) method is insufficient to modeling picking process in warehouse/distribution center and identify areas where ABS is more appropriate,
– describing the structure of LogABS approach.

The paper structure is as follows. Section 2 describes the literature background of warehouse operations problems in supply chains. Section 3 defines the problem to solve. Section 4 discusses DES and ABS approaches to solve these kinds of problems. The implementation of the designed solution is described in Sect. 5. The final conclusions are stated in Sect. 6.

2 Warehouse Operations – Literature Background

As mentioned in previous section, warehousing is one of main strategies for procurement and distribution in a supply chain. Warehouses are complex structures that are used for storing goods. Warehousing involves large capital expenditures. Equipment from various suppliers used in a single warehouse, needs to be tested as an integrated system. Basic operations in any warehouse can be summarized as:

– receiving,
– inspection/acceptance,
– proper storage,
– order/preparation/picking,
– dispatching/delivery,
– inventory management.

There are two types of material handling system:

- vehicle types – use a transporter to carry the load along a path that may or may not be predefined e.g.: fork trucks, pallet jacks, AS/RS, AGVs, Bridge Cranes etc.,
- non vehicle types: they usually have a fixed path and do not require a vehicle to transport the load, they may not consist of multiple sections e.g. conveyors.

The author focuses on the vehicle type material handling system, in this case based on forklifts. Around 75 % of the warehouses are manually served by forklifts [2]. This kind of operation receives significantly less attention in research than full- or partly automated systems [3]. In [4] it was pointed out, that modeling large-scale non-automated distribution warehouse with forklifts is much more difficult in comparison to AS/RS-systems due to their complexity.

According to the objective and operating cycle, the related works are categorized into three improvement fields [5]: aspects with regards to the loaded run, to the unloaded run and blocking operations.

Generally three types of data necessary for modeling must be collected about the real system [6]:

- technical data – including the topology and structure of the system e.g. layout, equipment, capacities, process time,
- organizational data – including scheduling rules for working time, allocation of resources to tasks, restrictions of handling operations,
- system load data – including the amount of handled pallets concerning time and volume aspects.

There are many simulation packages which support warehouse operations. Generally, we can classify them into two groups – packages dedicated to warehouse operations (CLASS) and general purpose packages which have dedicated objects to model a warehouse infrastructure like racks, forklifts, AGV, conveyors etc. (FlexSim, Simio, Arena, Anylogic and other). Table 1 presents the comparison between CLASS and FlexSim. The author selected FlexSim due to the following features [7]:

- ease of use in a real size with drag and drop technology,
- loading an.dwg file from the layout directly to a model,
- objects ASRS vehicle, Crane, Robot, Elevator,
- extended possibilities to model conveyors
- fitting the shape of trucks and their parameters – in real values,
- integrating built-in experimenter tool with OptQuest,
- including task sequence technology.

The order-picking time components in a typical picker-to-parts warehouse are as follow: travel (50 %), search (20 %), pick (15 %), setup (10 %) and other (5 %) [3]. The travel time (equivalently travel distance) is often considered as a primary objective in warehouse design and optimization. Another important objective would be minimizing the total cost. Other objectives which are often taken into consideration in warehouse design and optimization are [3]:

- minimize the throughput time of an order,
- minimize the overall cycle time (e.g. to complete a batch of orders),

- maximize the use of space,
- maximize the use of equipment,
- maximize the use of labor,
- maximize the accessibility to all items.

Table 1. Comparison between simulation programs: CLASS and FlexSim

Capability	CLASS Warehouse Simulation	FlexSim
Graphics technology	old technology – 2D (3D as postprocesor) 3D only for visualisation	New (state of the art) technology – real 3D – animation and kinematics
Layout	Layout – to draw using simple 2D tools	Imported from dwg (autocad)
3D shapes	For 3D – standard shapes – textures from bitmaps, cl3D -format	Shapes from all 3D CAD programs (practically all 3D formats) – extended textures, reflections etc.
Ability to customize	Non, only objects providedt	Complete, all parameters available, can create objects
Script language	No scripts	Script language – FlexScript/C ++
Statistics	Standard statistics, flow analysis	Standard and designed-by-users statistics
Animation	No operators animation,	Operator animation – possible to analyze the motion of a part of body – very detailed analysis
Extended Objects	No extended objects like ASRS vehicle, Crane, robots, elevator	ASRS vehicle, Crane, Robot, Elevator etc.
Optimizer	Without Experimentator and Optimizer	Experimentator – build-in Optimizer – OptQuest
		Tool to define many scenarios for automate experimentation process
Agent technology	No Agents	New technology – based on agents (Logistics GEO) to model processes in warehouse as exact as in the real world
		Possibility to mix many technologies – using conveyors, operators, forklifts, ASRS etc.
		AGV module
Interface	Interface (no data)	To/from Excel, SQL, ODBC
Reports	Reports – no data – on the screen	Csv (Excel), html
	Only to solve standard problems defined by authors of CLASS	No limits

Companies make decisions on the design and control of order picking systems at a tactical or operational level, with a different time horizon [8]. Common decisions at these levels are:

- layout design and dimensioning of the storage system (tactical level),
- assigning products to storage locations (storage assignment) (tactical and operational level),
- assigning orders to pick batches and grouping aisles into work zones (batching and zoning) (tactical and operational level),
- order picker routing (routing) (operational level),
- sorting picked units per order and grouping all picks of the orders (order accumulation/sorting) (operational level).

3   Problem Definition

The problem to solve is defined as follows: based on data which are obtained from logistics operator - the owner of the analyzed warehouse, we want to propose solution to shorten the time of modeling and preparing motion of forklifts in a warehouse simulation model. The logistics operator prepared the following data for us:

- layout of a warehouse in.dwg format (from AutoCad),
- data of racks – size, number of levels,
- data of operators, forklifts,
- picking lists in an excel file,
- picking process – start position of forklifts and end position of output buffer.

The whole process can be divided into two steps:

- modeling the infrastructure of a warehouse – racks positions and forklifts routes,
- preparing motion of forklifts based on the obtained picking list.

In this paper we focus on step 2 – preparing the motion of forklifts, operators, transporters in a warehouse simulation model. Step 1 was prepared with use of FlexSim simulation program and using standard activities and objects offered by this program.

Figure 1 shows the screen from a simulation model of a warehouse prepared in FlexSim in step 1. This model was built based on the layout from AutoCad, which we obtained from the logistics operator. This model contains the set of racks in real size and transportation network which define the routes for forklifts, operators or transporters.

Our main research goal is determine how to prepare in very short time the motion of forklifts in a defined simulation model based on picking lists. It means that we want to build special object which automate many activities which are necessary to transform the paths of forklifts defined in external pick list into the path saved in mobile objects.

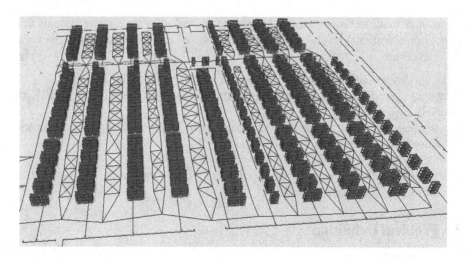

Fig. 1. Model of a warehouse with racks and transportation network prepared in FlexSim based on layout from autocad

4   DES/ABS Concept to Model Warehouse Operations

As mentioned in previous section, we have chosen FlexSim program as the main simulation environment. FlexSim is DES (Discrete-Event-Simulation) program. DES has been the main way for the process simulation of manufacturing and logistics for about four decades. This is adequate for problems that consist of queuing simulations and a variability is represented through stochastic distributions [9]. This approach is applicable in simulating the manufacturing and supply chain processes. DES models are characterized by [10] a process oriented approach (the focus is on modeling the system in detail, not the entities). They are based on a top-down modeling approach and have one thread of control (centralized). They contain passive entities (i.e. something is done to the entities while they move through the system) and intelligence (e.g. decision making) is modeled as part of the system. In DES, queues are the crucial element; a flow of entities through a system is defined; macro behavior is modeled and input distributions are often based on collected/measured (objective) data. In case of picking operation we think that the process approach is insufficient.

Operator, forklift are task executers. It means that they have the list of tasks to do. The operator decides what he will do next based on this list. So we think about operator as an agent. To do it we use approach based on ABS (Agent Based Systems). ABS modeling seems to be useful for modeling operators, and forklifts which have their own "intelligence", where the intelligence means the ability to complete changeable task lists (in our case – the picking list). In this case, an operator must have the ability to receive and send messages to the adoption of a task list, and to send a message about the execution or termination of the implementation of the task list. In the literature this approach is also referred to as Task Driven [7].

ABS is a simulation technique that models the overall behavior of a system through the use of autonomous system components (also referred to as agents) that communicate with each other [11]. The behavior incorporated into an agent determines its role in the environment, its interaction with other agents, its response to messages from other agents, and indeed whether its own behavior is adaptable [12].

5   Implementation

To solve the defined problem we designed three special agents:

- schedule control,
- schedule generator,
- contractor.

The information flow between them is showed in Fig. 2.

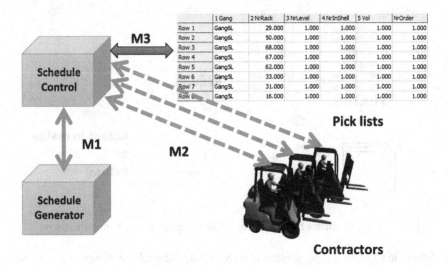

Fig. 2. Flow of orders between agents

Pick lists are built based on an excel file obtained from logistics operator. The structure of this file is as follow:

- a row in a table – one pick from the location indicated by columns,
- columns contain the name of a sector of racks (the sector represents a line of racks), the number of a rack in a sector, the number of a level (the shield of a rack), the number of item position on the level (Fig. 3).

An additional column contains the number of order.

The main agent is ScheduleControl: it prepares the list of tasks (according to order number) based on the set of rows from PickLists table (M3 arrow from Fig. 2) and sends this list to Contractor (M2 arrows from Fig. 2). ScheduleControl agent works as an answer to a request from ScheduleGenerator (M1 arrow from Fig. 2) and manages the

A –B – C – D

Where: A – name of the sector
          B – number of the rack in a sector
          C – number of the level of a rack
          D – number of the position of an item on the level

Fig. 3. Adressing of item in warehouse

set of Contactors which are connected to ScheduleControl. ScheduleGenerator based on time list tries to send the request to ScheduleControl – if it is not possible, Schedule-Generator forms the queue of requests Fig. 4.

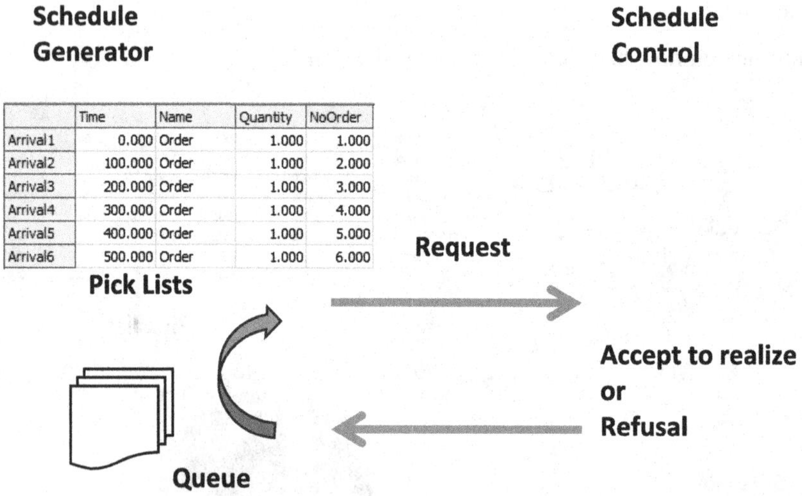

Schedule Generator   **Schedule Control**

	Time	Name	Quantity	NoOrder
Arrival1	0.000	Order	1.000	1.000
Arrival2	100.000	Order	1.000	2.000
Arrival3	200.000	Order	1.000	3.000
Arrival4	300.000	Order	1.000	4.000
Arrival5	400.000	Order	1.000	5.000
Arrival6	500.000	Order	1.000	6.000

Pick Lists

Request

Accept to realize or Refusal

Queue

Fig. 4. Request scheme between agents: schedule generator and schedule control

Schedule Control accepts request from Schedule Generator in the case one or more Contractors connected to Schedule Control are free – it means that it is ready to receive and perform the order. If all Contractors are busy, the Schedule Control waits for first free Contractor and refuses the request from Schedule Generator. Schedule Generator agent uses a queue to save all the waiting requests.

If Schedule Control can accept the request (one or more Contactors are ready to work), it prepares the list of tasks based on Pick lists. This list is sent (loaded) to Contractor, then Contractor starts to work, i.e. to implement this list task by task independently of other agents. It means that Contractor has its own "intelligence" to realize the tasks and to react on independencies. Figure 5 shows the Contractor Properties Window with a loaded list of tasks. If Contractor finishes its work, it sends the message to Schedule Control that is ready to receive next order.

At this stage of the research, the Contractor has the following skills:

– to travel – it moves to a defined address – for example the address of a rack,
– to load – it picks and loads the item from the address,

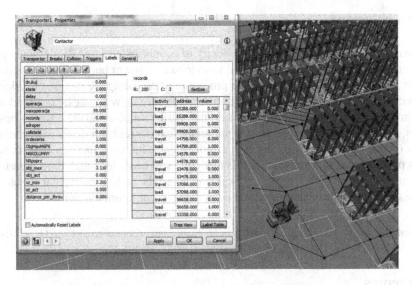

Fig. 5. The Contractor properties window with list of tasks

- to unload – it unloads the item to the defined address
- to park – it moves to the parking address
- to check load – it loads the item from the address if the conditions are fulfilled – for
  example the weight of the picked item is less than the defined limit.

All the described agents form the LogABS library. Figure 6 shows this library in FlexSim
layout.

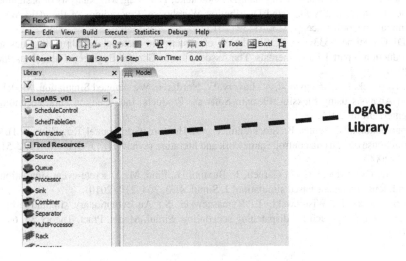

Fig. 6. The new layout of FlexSim with LogABS library

6   Conclusions

The paper presents the program of the library of agents called LogABS designed and implemented in FlexSim DES. Our goal to shorten the time of building the simulation model was obtained because the whole procedure of preparing the motion of forklifts (Contractors) in a defined model of warehouse needs only a few minutes. The user drags and drops the agents from a library, connects them using a mouse and the system is ready to run. It is a very useful and easy to use solution. Next our research works will focus on step 1 (defined in Sect. 3 of this paper), i.e. modeling the infrastructure of a warehouse – racks positions and forklifts routes. This modeling still needs too much time, therefore we want to automate this step. In a typical warehouse the racks form regular structures so we suppose that this feature can be used as the basis for future solutions.

Aknowledgement.   Presented research works are carried out under the project - 503213/11/140/ DSPB/4129 in Poznan University of Technology

References

1. Simchi-Levi, D., Kaminsky, P., Simchi-Levi, E.: Designing and Managing the Supply Chain: Concepts Strategies and Case Studies. McGraw-Hill/Irwin, Boston (2002)
2. Chan, F.T.S.: Design of material handling equipment selections system: an integration of expert system with analytic hierarchy process approach. Integr. manuf. Syst. **13**(1), 58–68 (2002)
3. De Koster, R., Le-Duc, T., Roodbergen, K.J.: Design and control of warehouse order picking: a literature review. Eur. J. Oper. Res. **182**(2), 481–501 (2007)
4. Takakuwa, S., Takizawa, H., Kumiko, I., Hiraoka, S.: Simulation of distribution systems: simulation and analysis of non-automated distribution warehouse. In: Proceedings of the 32nd Conference on Winter Simulation, pp. 1177–1184 (2000)
5. Clausen, U., Dabidian, P., Diekman, D., Goedicke, I., Poting, M., Analysis of assignment rules in an Manually Operated Distribution Warehouse, Proceedings of the 2013 Winter Simulation Conference, p. 3430–3439 (2013)
6. VDI Guideline 3633 part 1. Simulation of systems in material handling, logistics and production – part 1 Fundamentals. The Association of Gemran Engineers (ed.), Dusseldorf (2010)
7. Beaverstock, M., Greenwood, A., Lavery, E., Nordgren, W.: Applied Simulation. Modeling and Analysis using Flexsim. Flexsim Software Products, Inc., Canyon Park Technology Center, Orem (2011)
8. Rouwenhorst, B., Reuter, B., Stockrahm, V., van Houtum, G.J., Mantel, R.J., Zijm, W.H.M.: Warehouse design and control: framework and literature review. Eur. J. Oper. Res. **122**, 515–533 (2000)
9. Siebers, P.O., Macal, C.M., Garnett, J., Buxton, D., Pidd, M.: Discrete-event simulation is dead, long live agent-based simulation! J. Simul. **4**(3), 204–210 (2010)
10. Korytkowski, P., Wisniewski, T., Rymaszewski, S.: An evolutionary simulation-based optimization approach for dispatching scheduling. Simul. Model. Pract. Theory **35**, 69–85 (2013)

11. North, M.J., Macal, C.M.: Managing business complexity: discovering strategic solutions with agent-based modeling and simulation. Oxford University Press, New York (2007)
12. Mustafee, N., Bischoff, E.E.: A multi-methodology agent-based approach for container loading. In: Jain, S., Creasey, R.R., Himmelspach, J., White, K.P., Fu, M. (eds.) Proceedings of the 2011 Winter Simulation Conference (2011)

The Use of Multi-agent Systems for Improving a Logistic Platform in a GRAI Environment

Paul-Eric Dossou[1(✉)], Pawel Pawlewski[2], and Philip Mitchell[1]

[1] ICAM, Site de Paris-Sénart, 2 Allée des Savoirs,
77127 Lieusaint, France
paul-eric.dossou@icam.fr, philip.mitchell704@orange.fr
[2] Poznań University of Technology, ul. Strzelecka 11,
60-965 Poznań, Poland
pawel.pawlewski@put.poznan.pl

Abstract. The lack of growth in Europe is one of the reasons behind the dire economic situation facing many European countries today. This economic situation can also be seen as the cause of political turmoil in many countries and the consequences could be radical as in Greece with the success of a far left party. The social situation in Europe is equally worrying and enterprises have been severely impacted. They have to resist the crisis and prepare for the future, hoping to find effective solutions very quickly to enable them to reorganize and be more competitive during and after the crisis. The research of ICAM (School of Engineering) in industrial organization aims to satisfy the needs of enterprises, public and private organisms, establishments and departments. It is based on GRAI Methodology, one of the three main methodologies for enterprise modeling. GRAIMOD is a software tool being developed by ICAM for supporting GRAI Methodology. A general typology is proposed for enterprises and general public entities, then for facilitating the improvement during the design phase a reference model is proposed for each enterprise, public establishment or department domain. This paper presents the latest concepts of GRAIMOD. The combination of CBR reasoning with multi-agent systems is also presented. An example is given to illustrate how to use concepts for developing the tool and improving enterprise performance.

Keywords: Multi-agent systems · Expert system · Simulation · Reference models · Rules · Knowledge

1 Introduction

The dire economic situation is the consequence of the lack of growth in Europe. Indeed the high level of the Euro together with the high rate of unemployment imply extremely harsh conditions for many enterprises and individuals especially in the worst-hit countries such as Greece. The atmosphere is not conducive to facilitate growth. People are reluctant to spend money because of the social situation and enterprises are equally hesitant to invest for the same reasons. The question is how to help enterprises resist the

© Springer International Publishing Switzerland 2015
J. Bajo et al. (Eds.): PAAMS 2015 Workshops, CCIS 524, pp. 126–135, 2015.
DOI: 10.1007/978-3-319-19033-4_11

present crisis and improve their economic situation, creating wealth and jobs at the same time. How best to prepare them for being more competitive and better equipped to thrive in the context of globalisation?

One of the difficulties for these enterprises is that they find it difficult to penetrate the European market and export their products. This is due to many reasons, the main one being global manufacturing costs. In fact with globalisation it is less expensive to produce in China or India rather than in France or Germany. There are also other reasons which are subjective reasons corresponding to quality of the products, brand awareness, the desire to export and product promotion. In this context research has been carried out for integrating the environmental dimension into the supply chain of the enterprises of the west of France.

GRAI (Interrelated Activity Network Graph) Methodology allows to reorganise enterprises in order to adapt them to globalisation. Enterprise Modelling methodologies permit a detailed analysis of an enterprise and, thereby, to pinpoint the strengths and weaknesses. Nowadays, enterprise performance criteria are not only cost, quality and lead time but also carbon management, together with all environmental and societal issues. GRAIMOD (GRAI for modelling) is a tool being developed for supporting GRAI Methodology [4, 5]. In an enterprise supply chain, carbon management could be considered as a new criterion in addition to quality, cost and delivery date. How to redefine the optimum of the enterprise by integrating the environmental dimension with efficiency? For instance, GRAIQUAL (GRAI for quality improvements), a module of GRAIMOD, is designed to implement, manage and improve quality in enterprises. It contains norms and certifications. Quality could be improved in each part of the supply chain by distinguishing processes, products and supplier quality and quality management. The reduction of cost and lead time simultaneously with improvement in quality is also achieved. Moreover the global reduction of carbon in the supply chain allows to obtain a green and sustainable supply chain adapted to the future.

In fact, it is important for enterprises to prepare themselves for the end of the current crisis in order to be efficient in future circumstances. So they have to take into account the changes in our world and anticipate them by introducing into the management of their supply chain the social, societal or environmental dimensions. In this paper the concept of GRAIMOD is presented together with a detailed example.

2   GRAIMOD: Existing Concepts and Architecture

GRAI Methodology is one of the three main methodologies used for analyzing and designing enterprises. The GRAI approach is composed of four phases: An initialization phase to start the study, a modeling phase where the existing system is described, an analysis phase to detect the inconsistencies of the studied system and a design phase during which the inconsistencies detected are corrected and a new system proposed. These concepts could be used to ensure the transformation of enterprises to meet real market needs (globalization, relocation, capacity to be proactive, cost optimization, lead time, quality, flexibility, etc.) and need to be constantly improved and updated.

An enterprise is completely described according to GRAI Methodology by finding five models: functional (functions of the enterprise and their links), physical (the production system), informational (the net, tools and informational flows), process (series of sequences or tasks), and decisional (structure of orders, hierarchic organisation). Then these models could be improved for increasing enterprise performance.

GRAIMOD is a new tool being developed by ICAM School of Engineering for proposing concrete solutions to improve enterprises according to new market evolutions. Nowadays, it contains five modules working around three sub modules (Fig. 1).

GRAIKERN is a graphic editor, an interface used for representing the different models associated to GRAI methodology. GRAIWORKER is the work base elaborated for managing, modifying and capitalising knowledge about the case studied. GRAI-TRANS is a Transfer Interface used for putting the new case in GRAIXPERT in order to improve its Cases Base [1–3]. The reference model elaborated for each enterprise domain will be improved by the acquisition of this new model in GRAIXPERT between the different modules.

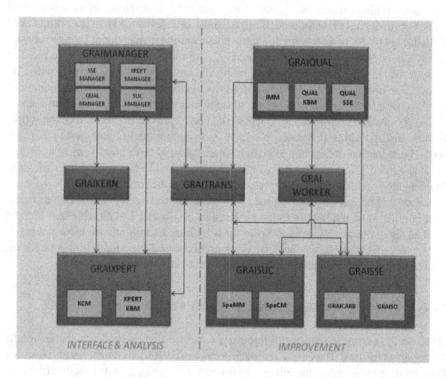

Fig. 1. Architecture of GRAIMOD

GRAIXPERT is a hybrid expert system for managing the analysis of the existing system and proposing a new system [12, 16]. It is composed of two sub-modules in interaction with GRAIKERN: the Knowledge Capitalization (KCM) and the Knowledge Based System (XPERTKBM).

GRAIMANAGER is a management module used for organising the different interactions between the modules of GRAIMOD. It controls and manages the system's interactions with the users [5, 6].

GRAISUC is a module used for managing the choice of an ERP or SCM tool for an enterprise. It is composed of two sub-modules SpeMM and SpeCM. The Specification Management Module (SpeMM) is used for choosing the appropriate ERP or SCM Tool of an enterprise. The specifications obtained are capitalised in the Specification Capitalisation Module (SpeCM).

GRAIQUAL is a module used for managing quality approach implementation or quality improvement in an enterprise [7]. It contains two sub-modules IMM and QUALKBM. The Improvements Management Module (IMM) is used for managing the different quality action plans of the enterprise. The Quality Knowledge Base Module (QUALKBM) is being elaborated for containing the rules related to quality certifications in order to use them for improving or elaborating quality in an enterprise. The module GRAIQUAL of GRAIMOD is both able and efficient for defining how to improve enterprises based on criteria such as quality, lead time and cost. Indeed, a fourth criterion allowing carbon management has been put forward. Then this criterion has to be combined to the others to really improve enterprises according to the actual context of enterprises today.

GRAI_SSE is the new module being developed specifically for integrating social, societal and environmental dimensions in the improvement of enterprises. It is composed of a sub-module GRAICARB destined to manage the carbon footprint and GRAI_SO being elaborated for improving the other aspects of environmental, social and societal dimensions.

It is useful to focus needs on the use of this criterion. A new module GRAI_SSE is being added to GRAIMOD in order to pinpoint the environmental, societal and social dimensions in enterprises. This module would integrate, for example, changes associated to carbon management, ISO 26000, ISO 14000 implementations, social and societal evolutions impacts on enterprises but also impact on local authorities (states, associations, districts, etc.) [9]. The objective is not to dissociate this criterion but to obtain the best combination by really studying this aspect of the enterprise in order to propose appropriate solutions. The difficult enterprise context due to the crisis and the search for alternative solutions to the basic QCD optimization are the cause of this new focus on how important social, societal and environmental dimensions have indeed become and how beneficial it is for enterprises to find a new optimized solution by focusing on these aspects.

The architecture of this system contains three different bases for managing the study of a new case. A model base is used for managing elaborated reference models. A rule base is used for analyzing the models of the system in question. And a case base is defined for capitalizing different studies for future use. This tool proposes the combination of CBR (Case Based Reasoning) and Multi-agent systems [14] for solving enterprise modeling problem and improving enterprise performance.

It is clear that the agents defined for the phases related to enterprise performance improvement have to learn quickly in accordance with the possible changes (previous cases, reference models associated to typology, etc.). Indeed, the choice was difficult because of the advantages of BDI architecture, but we chose the training agents because of their particularity to learn [13]. This system is used for defining how to improve the enterprise performance and for capitalizing the process followed. The language associated to Jade platform is FIPA ACL (Agent Communication Language) [10, 11, 14]. The training agent structure is adapted to the requirements of GRAIMOD. This choice is in coherence with the problem solving method used for defining concepts of GRAIMOD.

For instance, the agents are used for production system diagnosis and improvement. The objective is to use these agents for elaborating models of an enterprise, making diagnosis of these models and designing new models and appropriate improvements.

GRAIMOD is being developing by using Java. The platform used for multi-agent systems is JADE. This method combines different reasoning such as Case Based Reasoning, decomposition reasoning, generalization and particularization reasoning and transformation reasoning.

3 Developing GRAIMOD

The global structure of the tool is described in a handbook. All the functions needed in GRAIMOD are defined. The planning of developing, the release hypotheses are presented. Then each step of GRAI approach is explained with the particularity and the way to use GRAIMOD. The context acquisition is used for capitalising interviews carried out in an enterprise on the existing system. In addition, the list of enterprise characteristics is also capitalised.

So the objectives targeted by the enterprise would be recorded in order to be used for analysing the existing system.

The function intended to elaborate the models of the enterprise is used. Each model is considered as an object which could be decomposed into sub-objects. An agent is associated to each sub-object. This function uses essentially the graphic editor for modelling the models. The modelling rules defined into GRAIMOD are used at this step. An agent is defined for applying these rules. The data associated to enterprise performance criteria are also recorded at this stage.

The analysis function is used for extracting rules from GRAIXPERT and launching them in order to analyse the existing models. These rules are for verifying models elaborated. The output of this function is the list of inconsistencies. A multi-agent is used for making this step. Then subsequently the points to improve and strengths are presented. The dashboard containing performance criteria measures is compared to objectives and shows the improvement expected at the end of the study. A manual addition of inconsistencies, points to improve or strengths is possible.

The function design is used for elaborating the new system. This function defines how the enterprise could be reorganised for better performance. GRAIQUAL is used for a QCD improvement. Norms according to process improvements or quality approach are used for building the future enterprise models. GRAISUC presents the approach for choosing a software tool. The use of this tool depends on the necessity to integrate software tools of the enterprise. A handbook is defined for regrouping specifications needed by the enterprise. GRAI_SSE presents criteria associated to social, societal and environmental dimensions. This function extracts norms corresponding to the case studied, and applies parameters associated to these norms in order to define the structure of the new system. The concepts and approaches needed to manage carbon, to implement ISO 26000 norm, to manage energy and propose alternative solutions are used. The points to improve are studied in detail and improvements defined according to objectives. An action plan is elaborated with deadlines in short, medium and long terms. The dashboard containing performance measures is used for evaluating the performance expected after the design phase.

The function implementation records each improvement action and serves for managing this action. The approach used is PDCA (Plan, Do, Check, Act) allowing to continuously improve the enterprise performance. This function also serves for managing the global improvement implementation project. The dashboard containing performance measures is used for recording the real performance obtained after implementation. A decision aiding tool is needed for analysing implementation scenarios and suggesting ideas for best use.

4 Example

Each step of this tool needs to be defined in detail. An example is elaborated for defining the way to refine GRAIMOD. The objective of this example is to present to developers the global coherence of the tool. The first step is the same as any tool: the login step management. Then the welcome page allows the user to choose what he wants to do: introducing a new case, visiting an existing case, accessing reference models or existing cases for modifying them, and managing rights. All this part is coordinated by the GRAIMANAGER module.

The access for a new case allows to obtain the possibility for acquiring enterprise context. An acquisition aided tool and interview saver is available. The format of information required is defined in order to obtain for each case the same parameters and to be able to compare them. One of the questions which has to be solved is how to take into account innovation aspects during all the design and modeling. The objective is to allow the enterprise to improve itself but by keeping its DNA and also introducing other innovations. Presently different hypotheses are being explored.

Then the objectives of the enterprise are entered. This page is also used for obtaining the indicators used for measuring the existing system: the dashboard. What is hoped for is the existing measures, the objectives, and the gap between them in order to know exactly what is expected during the modelling. The following pages are for the graphic editor GRAIKERN for elaborating models of the existing system (Fig. 2).

The analysis page is one of the most important because of the necessity to find inconsistencies and define points to improve (Fig. 3). The possibility for exporting the list of inconsistencies is given. The possibility of a manual addition is also given but this aspect could introduce in the analysed model other constraints. This part is added to respect the DNA of the enterprise studied.

The next page shows how to design a new version of each model by taking into account the result of analysis but also the objectives. Three possibilities are given in order to respect the problem solving method elaborated: design rules, reference models or previous cases (Fig. 4).

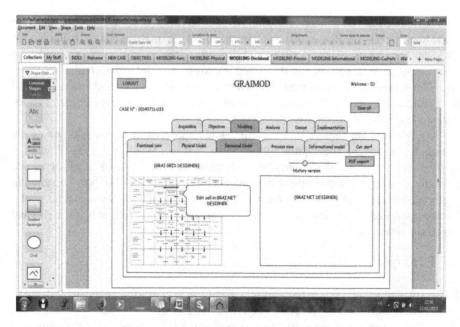

Fig. 2. Modelling editor of GRAIMOD

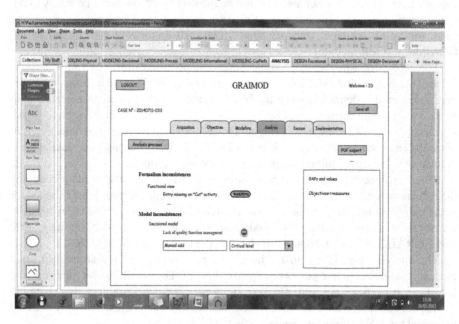

Fig. 3. Analysis module of GRAIMOD

If the user needs to fully maintain the control of the design and elaborate an original model he can. Should he prefer to be guided, the design-aided tool composed of GRAIQUAL, GRAI_SSE and GRAISUC would be used. Reference models or previous

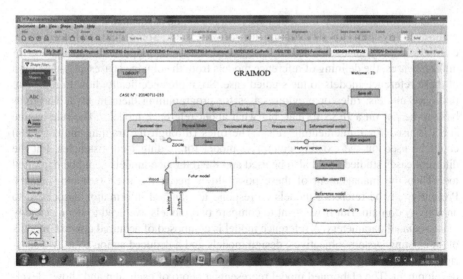

Fig. 4. Design module of GRAIMOD

cases are also available as support during this phase. The results of this part will be translated into action plans and expected measures on the dashboard.

The last page is about implementation (Fig. 5). Here the action plan is managed by using the previous modules. The dashboard is used once again for measuring the real level of indicators and checking if the decisions related to the action plan improve the enterprise performance.

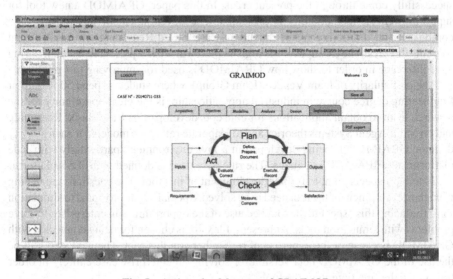

Fig. 5. Action plan Manager of GRAIMOD

The problem solving process and different reasoning associated are combined with multi-agent systems for developing the software tool. Some questions need to be clarified. For instance, the use of case based reasoning implies the acquisition of different cases, the defining of reference models from the obtained cases and adaptation of these reference models to the studied case. So, more specifically, how to represent reference models, rules or previous cases for programming them in Java. The rules have to be put on a JESS format, but what about reference models? The rule engine JESS is used for implementing rules. The rules (through the training multi-agents) could be used on the existing enterprise model for finding inconsistencies, but the different cases studied could also be used and the reference models could be exploited too. Then the management of these possibilities needs the use of training agents. Presently, all the reference models correspond to standard information associated to an activity domain. But if we want to compare two models, we need to define exactly the associated parameters. A reference model is composed of acquired context, models of an existing system, objectives, design models and a deduced action plan. A discussion is now taking place for translating this structure into standard parameters for development. The elaborated model represents a photo of each step and shows developers what is expected in terms of structure, efficiency, usability, etc. For instance, each page of the tool must insist on the representation used but also the links with the other pages and the data acquisition process.

5 Conclusion

Enterprise modelling is one of the main tools available for enterprises to help them successfully come through the present crisis. In this paper, GRAIMOD a new tool for supporting GRAI methodology is presented. The development of this tool needs a combination of different concepts including Case Based Reasoning and Multi Agent Systems theories. The example of the logistic platform will be presented in detail during the conference in order to show how GRAIMOD is used for improving this platform.

The particularity of Icam Vendee (Icam Group), where students spend 50 % of their Engineering degree course in industrial apprenticeship, is the great opportunity for the research team to obtain applications for concepts developed on Case Based Reasoning and on Multi Agent Systems theories and to elaborate reference models for each activity domain. GRAIMOD is being developed in a Java environment, particularly with Jade platform and FIPA-ACL Language. The rule base used is defined with JESS platform.

Future prospects point to further development of this tool. The questions emanating from the development of the tool need to be solved. Special attention is paid to simulation for introducing this aspect in the tool because of the opportunities in enterprises to solve problems with simulation tools. At present, Flexsim is chosen for being connected with GRAIMOD because of the expertise of researchers on this tool. The next step will be the use of the GRAIMOD beta version for solving an enterprise case entirely in order to validate the functioning of the tool.

References

1. Aamodt, A.: Case-based reasoning: foundational issues, methodological variations, and system approaches. Artif. Intell. Commun. **7**(1), 39–59 (1994)
2. Burke, E.K., et al.: Structured cases in case-based reasoning – reusing and adapting cases for time-tabling problems. J. KBS **13**(2–3), 159–165 (2000)
3. Brown, D.C., Chandrasekaran, B.: Expert system for a class of mechanical design activities. In: Gero, J.S. (ed.) Knowledge Engineering in CAD. Elsevier, Amsterdam (1985)
4. Chen, D., Doumeingts, G., Vernadat, F.B.: Architectures for enterprise integration and interoperability: past, present and future. Comput. Ind. **59**, 647–659 (2008)
5. Dossou, P.-E., Pawlewski, P., Mitchell, P.: Combining simulation and multi-agent systems for solving enterprise process flows constraints in an enterprise modeling aided tool. In: Corchado, J.M., Bajo, J., Kozlak, J., Pawlewski, P., Molina, J.M., Gaudou, B., Julian, V., Unland, R., Lopes, F., Hallenborg, K., García Teodoro, P. (eds.) PAAMS 2014. CCIS, vol. 430, pp. 156–166. Springer, Heidelberg (2014)
6. Dossou, P.-E., Mitchell, P.: Implication of reasoning in GRAIXPERT for modeling enterprises. In: Omatu, S., Rocha, M.P., Bravo, J., Fernández, F., Corchado, E., Bustillo, A., Corchado, J.M. (eds.) IWANN 2009, Part II. LNCS, vol. 5518, pp. 374–381. Springer, Heidelberg (2009)
7. Dossou, P.E., Mitchell, P.: How Quality management could improve the supply chain performance of SMES. In: FAIM 2009, Middlesbrough, UK (2009)
8. Dossou, P.-E., Pawlewski, P.: Using multi-agent system for improving and implementing a new enterprise modeling tool. In: Demazeau, Y., Dignum, F., Corchado, J.M., Bajo, J., Corchuelo, R., Corchado, E., Fernández-Riverola, F., Julián, V.J., Pawlewski, P., Campbell, A. (eds.) Trends in PAAMS. AISC, vol. 71, pp. 225–232. Springer, Heidelberg (2010)
9. European Commission: Responsabilité sociale des entreprises: une nouvelle stratégie de l'UE pour la période 2011–2014, Brussels, Belgium (2011)
10. Ferber, J.: Multi-agent System: An Introduction to Distributed Artificial Intelligence. Addison Wesley Longman, Harlow (1999). ISBN 0-201-36048-9
11. Friedman-Hill, E.: JESS, the rule engine for the JAVA platform, version 7.1p2. Sandia National Laboratories (2008)
12. Russell, S.J., Norvig, P.: Artificial Intelligence: A Modern Approach. Prentice-Hall, Englewood Cliffs (1995)
13. Sen, S., Weiss, G.: Learning in multiagent systems (Chapitre 6). In: Weiss, G. (ed.) MultiagentSystems : A Modern Approach to Distributed Artificial Intelligence, pp. 259–298. The MIT Press, Cambridge (1999)
14. Sycara, K.P.: Multi-agent systems. AI Magazine, American Association for Artificial Intelligence, 0738-4602-1998 (1998)
15. Wooldridge, M.: Intelligent agents (Chapitre 1). In: Weiss, G. (ed.) Multiagent Systems: A Modern Approach to Distributed Artificial Intelligence, pp. 27–77. The MIT Press, Cambridge (1999)
16. Xia, Q., et al.: Knowledge architecture and system design for intelligent operation support systems. J. Expert Syst. Appl. **17**(2), 115–127 (1999)

Workshop on MAS for Complex Networks and Social Computation

Weaver: A Multiagent, Spatial-Explicit and High-Performance Framework to Study Complex Ecological Networks

José Román Bilbao-Castro[1]($\boxtimes$), Gabriel Barrionuevo[1], Dolores Ruiz-Lupión[2],
Leocadio G. Casado[1], and Jordi Moya-Laraño[2]

[1] Department of Informatics, University of Almería
(Campus de Excelencia Internacional Agroalimentario, CEiA3),
Carretera de Sacramento S/N, Almería, Spain
{jbc747,gbarrionuevo,leo}@ual.es
[2] Department of Functional and Evolutionary Ecology, Estación Experimental de
Zonas Áridas, EEZA-CSIC, Carretera de Sacramento S/N, Almería, Spain
{loli.ruiz,jordi}@eeza.csic.es

Abstract. This work presents a new agent based simulation tool specifically designed to study ecological networks. It includes many unique features like genetics, evolution, space-explicit simulation domain, flexible environmental modeling, etc. Written in C++, it yields a high performance experience and allows extremely large and complex simulations to be run, with up to hundreds of thousands of individuals moving and interacting in different ways to feed, reproduce or attack each other. It can be used to study ecosystems at different scales, from microscopic to superior animals whether alive or extinct.

Keywords: Ecology · Agent based model · Individual based model

1 Introduction

Ecological networks [2] study is of vital importance to quantify relationships and dependencies among animals and their surrounding environment [1]. This is a central objective of ecology and it has profound implications in our knowledge about how life networks are established, how do they evolve and how do they eventually collapse. All these three stages do occur in nature following evolutionary and ecological rules. Nowadays, anthropogenic interventions, although also natural to a degree, are now a major factor contributing to destabilize this natural order of things. For example, global warming is a major threat at different levels as climate variables are changing too fast, negatively impacting the capacity of individuals and populations (and as a consequence consequence, ecological networks) to adapt properly or rapidly enough. As life can be depicted as an entangled set of more or less interdependent ecological networks -whose interactions are modulated by the environment conditions- the impact of abrupt changes can unexpectedly affect the whole system. Thus, disentangling ecological

© Springer International Publishing Switzerland 2015
J. Bajo et al. (Eds.): PAAMS 2015 Workshops, CCIS 524, pp. 139–150, 2015.
DOI: 10.1007/978-3-319-19033-4_12

interactions is of central interest not only to study the origins and mechanisms of biodiversity but also to assess future trends risks and act consequently when negative consequences are expected [3].

Ecological networks have been traditionally studied in situ through direct observation under natural conditions as well as under controlled environments in laboratories for simple experiments [7]. Although these methods allow us to measure and quantify some variables, the complexity of the natural environments and the large number of individuals and species involved make it a daunting and virtually impossible task to build a full cause and effect matrix.

With the development of computer science, different approaches were attempted in order to simulate organisms interactions in silico. Usually, individual and group behaviors are observed in situ and a more or less precise mathematical model is developed that is mainly based on differential equations [4]. Despite the undeniable usefulness of such models, not all variables can be easily modeled into an equations-based model and other alternatives must be taken into consideration. Multiagent Based Models (MABM) is one of them. Here, agents ("actors") are modeled as individuals interacting with each other and their environment following a set of rules. Regarding our field of interest, such rules include; (a) environmental factors such as temperature and moisture, (b) individual internal factors (state variables) such as hunger, age or energy tank and, (c) presence of predators and or preys, etc.

MABMs allow a precise control at the level of an individual. Nonetheless, for extremely large simulations, where even millions of individuals co-exist, the computational demands grow very fast, making it virtually impossible to model complex enough systems. Thus, using High Performance Computing (HPC) techniques becomes a must when certain level of complexity is desired. Another important aspect is that individuals interact following a spatial distribution where soil, water and/or air characteristics vary from point to point. Explicitly including space in the MABM models provides interesting tools to analyze the effect of changes in the environment and how individuals adapt following different strategies like, for example, migrating towards more friendly places.

Weaver is a new MABM framework specifically written from scratch to provide a spatial-explicit simulation space. It can simulate one, two or three-dimensional (1D, 2D, 3D) worlds where animals, fungi and plants do interact, move, grow, reproduce, hunt, etc. Surface, underwater, underground or hybrid scenarios can be defined and individuals of different species can populate them. HPC has been taken into account since the beginning and all methods are designed in order to benefit from it at any point in the future. This makes Weaver a one of a kind piece of software where individuals are modeled through a broad range of variables. Next sections describe Weaver in detail. Weaver binaries are available for free at the project's web page (http://www.eeza.csic.es/foodweb/Simulators_FWEE.html).

1.1   State-of-the-art in MABMs Applied in Life Studies

The design and implementation of a MABM comprises a deep understanding of the state-of-the-art in the techniques and tools that already exist. Numerous frameworks have been -and are still being- developed so as to provide the optimal kit for implementing and building these sort of models. By utilizing these toolkits, the user is able to produce his/her own model and run his/her own experiments. Different communities tend to make use of the most popular frameworks. Among them we can find NetLogo [10], which seems to be the most advanced platform in matter of graphical interaction and documentation in this field of knowledge. However, this tool is primarily focused on providing easy mechanism for educational environments, thus becoming relatively inefficient when it comes to computational performance if we compare it with other options [11]. Some of these efficient alternatives are RePast/RePast-HPC [12,13] and MASON [14]. RePast is a robust, extensible and easy-to-use library written in Java, an intent on surpassing the performance and features of its Objective-C predecessor, Swarm [15]. Repast-HPC is written in C++ and includes MPI as a mechanism parallelize work among processes and improve performance and scalability. To our knowledge, it does not currently include shared-memory capabilities, which reduces its parallel computing potential and increases memory needs by using processes and not threads on local processors. MASON is a smaller library also written in Java, which focuses on performance and reproducibility. Another framework which also looks towards high-performance applicability is FLAME [28]. In fact, some implementations on GPGPUs have already been built over FLAME [29]. Several other frameworks exist in the scene. Here we have merely mentioned some of the most popular.

The development of such tools is actually a consequence of the solid interest and dedication the scientific community has shown on implementing ABMs for a wide variety of topics. These topics range from sociology [17,18] to economics [16,19,20] and environmental sciences [21,22]. The developing of ABMs is a study field on its own [23–25] and some articles about its educational potential have already been published [26,27].

Regarding our concerns, there are several instances of ABMs applied to the life sciences. In ecological modeling, the systems which use agents -i.e. individuals- as the atomic entities for implementation are described as *individual-based models* (IBM) [30]. IBMs have been used for relatively long time to simulate, reproduce or detect patterns emerging from the interactions between the elements of populations [34]. Thus, these kind of simulations become an important tool when studying evolutionary and ecological dynamics [31]. Some examples of research carried on using IBMs are the study of interactions between soil fauna species [6] and its further development using the framework presented in this article [7]; the evaluation of the effects of the temperature and surface water on spatiotemporal dynamics of stream salamanders [33]; or even some research including human interactions can be found [32].

2   Weaver History and Characteristics

Weaver was born as a continuation and improvement of the work initiated with Mini-Akira [6]. Mini-Akira was developed using the R language by scientists in the field of Ecology. It worked well but, as a proof of concept, rapidly hit different computational walls. Relatively simple simulations took days to run and just a few specimens could be processed in one-dimensional worlds. The Mini-Akira team decided then to contact a group of computer scientists with a strong applied computing background and having HPC as one of their main strengths. Soon, requirements were defined and development started. Nowadays, Weaver is a very complex piece of software accounting for several thousands of lines of code that is able to run 10000 times faster than the original Mini-Akira even with much more complex simulations.

Weaver is based on C/C++ and reduces as much as possible its dependence on external libraries which in turn maximizes its portability to other platforms. After checking the most important existing MABM frameworks, we decided to go ahead on implementing a new one from scratch. There where three main reasons to do that; (a) Maximizing performance at different levels (single processor, multiple processors, accelerators and multiple nodes) was a priority so any generic framework should be discarded because too much flexibility made it difficult a priori to achieve our performance goals; (b) A tight control on the core source code was needed and while some of the most popular packages are open sourced, making changes to them was not straightforward and could make it difficult any further upgrade; and (c) Our spatial-explicit model added quite a lot of functionality (soil moisture, basal resources, etc.) to the spatial cells whose implementation using agents would not be as efficient. Our platform has been tested for UNIX/Linux systems but porting it to Windows systems should be straightforward.

2.1   Defining Everything

Weaver allows a fully customized run of simulations. The user decides, based on proper bibiographical documentation, which parameters to use for each element of the simulation, from space to animals and climate. While this can be a complete nightmare for extremely complex simulations, Weaver adopted a human-friendly description language based on the standard JSON [5] which also allows to seamlessly interchange data with other software packages when needed.

Next we show a short example of how a simulation could be defined using JSON for Weaver.

```
1  {
2      "world": {
3          "soil": {
4              "dimensions": {
5                  "depth": "10",
6                  "length": "20",
7                  "width": "20",
8                  "cellSize": "1"
9              },
10             "moisture": {
11                 "patches": [
12                     {
13                         "type": "sphere",
14                         "radius": "5",
15                         "xPos": "15",
16                         "yPos": "15",
17                         "zPos": "5",
18                         "value": "87.5"
19                     },
20                     {
21                         "type": "sphere",
22                         "radius": "5",
23                         "xPos": "15",
24                         "yPos": "35",
25                         "zPos": "5",
26                         "value": "87.5"
27                     }
28                 ]
29             },
30             "nutrients": {
31                 "minC": "0",
32                 "maxC": "23",
33                 "minN": "0",
34                 "maxN": "23",
35                 "minP": "0",
36                 "maxP": "23"
37             },
38             "temperature": "18",
39             "maxK": "9.6",
40             "minK": "0.1",
41             "timelapseForChemostatEffect": "1",
42             "thresholdForChemostatEffect": "0.05",
43             "increaseForChemostatEffect": "1.0"
44         },
45         "life": {
46             "animals": [],
47             "fungi": [
48                 {
49                     "name": "Fungus_X",
50                     "sporeMass": "4",
51                     "minimumFungus": "0",
52                     "ACTIVATION_ENERGY": "0.68",
53                     "NORMALIZATION_B": "25.98",
54                     "minHR": "85",
55                     "maxHR": "90",
56                     "maxRScale": "0.5",
57                     "zeroFungi": "8",
58                     "patches": [
59                         {
60                             "type": "sphere",
61                             "radius": "5",
62                             "xPos": "15",
63                             "yPos": "15",
64                             "zPos": "5",
65                             "value": "1.0"
66                         },
67                         {
68                             "type": "sphere",
69                             "radius": "5",
70                             "xPos": "15",
71                             "yPos": "35",
72                             "zPos": "5",
73                             "value": "1.0"
74                         }
75                     ]
76                 }
77             ]
78         }
79     },
80     "simulation": {
81         "runDays": "20",
82         "outputDirectory": "omnivores_50x50_rep1",
83         "saveIntermidiateVolumes": "false",
84         "saveIntermidiateVolumesPeriodicity": "100000",
85         "encountersMatrixFilename": "encountersMatrix",
86         "predationsMatrixFilename": "predationsMatrix",
87         "nodesMatrixFilename": "nodesMatrix",
88         "predationEventsOnOtherSpeciesFilename": "predatOnSpecies"
89     }
90 }
```

Code Listing 1. Example of a simple Weaver simulation definition file written using JSON.

2.2   Space-Explicit Model

Weaver is strictly space-explicit which means that agents always interact within a finite space that plays a central role in simulations. The simulation space (in our case, soil, water, air or an hybrid scenario) is defined as a homogeneous grid of equally-spaced, same sized voxels (volume elements). The voxel is the minimum unit of space that can hold animals and basal resources. We can arrange as many voxels as we want (with the only restriction being that imposed by memory limits), from one to three dimensions scenarios (width x height x depth). Each voxel represents a portion of our simulation space and its size is user-defined.

Basal Resources. Basal resources are distributed across voxels. Those can be water, fungi, chemical elements (mainly C, N and P) and compounds, etc. and represent the basic elements that sustain some of our living organisms that form the base of the trophic pyramid.

Basal resources evolve over time based on different parameters. For example, moisture can change with new rains or droughts, fungi population will grow depending on temperature, moisture and competition from other fungi species, etc. The case of fungi species is particularly complex as different species will co-exist and compete for resources and space. At the same time, if conditions are good, the fungi will outgrow the voxel limits and settle in neighbor voxels.

The way each basal resource is initialized is quite flexible. It can go from fully randomized to totally defined by hand. The user can say "let us create 5 fungus spherical patches at random positions, with fungus quantities at each patch decreasing with the sphere radius following a Gaussian distribution with a given σ and μ. Now let us add this patch of other species with this exact amount and shape at this position. Finally, let us add a minimum moisture of 20 % to all voxels while this part of terrain will have another amount".

2.3   Animals and Interactions

Each animal species taking part in the simulation will be defined by a broad set of parameters using JSON. Those include size, growth rate, phenological states, movement speed, distance sensing capabilities, genre, eating behavior (omnivore, fungivore, herbivore, etc.), reproduction characteristics, metabolism, etc. Values for this parameters should be studied in situ or extracted from literature to obtain realistic results for simulations.

An interesting feature in Weaver is that it allows to define, for each animal species, which other (or same in the case of cannibalism) species can be predated. This is defined by means of a simple vector of edible preys that defines the initial food web structure to be simulated.

```
1  {
2      "animals": [
3          {
4              "name": "aca1",
5              "huntingMode": "active_hunting",
6              "genetics": {
7                  "NumberOfLoci": "20",
8                  "NumberOfAlleles": "10",
9                  "NumberOfTraits": "13",
10                 "TRAITS_PER_MODULE": "3"
11             },
12             "edibleAnimalSpecies": [
13                 "aca1",
14                 "enc2"
15             ],
16             "edibleFungusSpecies": [
17                 "Fungus_X"
18             ],
19             "initialPopulation": "414"
20         }
21     ]
22 }
```

Code Listing 2. Example of a partial animal definition in Weaver using JSON. It is named aca1 (mite) and we can see that it can predate on its own and another mite species. This code snippet could be inserted into line 46 at Code Listing 1.

All those parameters will drive animals behavior within a given range of uncertainty.

There is a certain degree of randomization at almost every step of the underlying algorithms. This ensures non-deterministic simulations and an improved resemblance with natural ecosystems. For example, a certain animal has to decide where to move to in the next step (if needed) in order to feed, reproduce or run away from dangers. Before moving, it "takes into consideration" different variables like the number of expected predators/preys at each potential location, the existence of basal resources when needed or the presence/absence of breeding mates if in a breeding phenological stage. Those variables join to define a series of equations that, based on observed models and parameters, suggests the most potentially advantageous decision. Nevertheless, this movement will be made only with a certain probability. The same happens with the probability of eating a prey, breeding with a potential partner, etc.

Genetics. Weaver stresses the importance of evolution when studying food webs and different ecosystems. Thus, the genetic information that defines the different traits is explicitly included for each animal. The genes of an individual are provided following a quantitative basis, which allows the conversion from the values stored as genes into an ecologically meaningful value for the trait. Importantly, the framework incorporates trait multidiminesionality, allowing for genetic positive and negative correrlations among tratis, thus mimicking real genetic trade-offs. The genes (and associated values) are passed on to the new generations of individuals by mimicking real recombinations. Genes are scattered across 13 chromosomes and each chromosome has a single chiasma (point for cross-over during recombination). Genetically speaking, the algorithm includes recombination, seggregation and fertilisation, therefore perfectly mimicking sexual reproduction. Natural selection occurs through the interactions the animals experience and these genetic background allows the effect of natural selection to endure through generations in the form of an evolutionary response.

 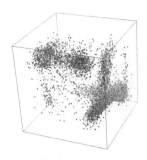

Fig. 1. Three-dimensional visualizations of a small soil portion simulated using Weaver. (**Left**) Spheres represent fungi with different species codified using different colors. Small red dots represent fungivores. They concentrate around fungi while leaving sterile zones free. Also, some fungi zones have already been eaten away and appear as small holes in the spheres. (**Right**) Preys and predators are represented by green and red points respectively. Here, preys occupy the whole space despite the existence of fungi patches (not depicted for clarity) as they also have to avoid predators (Colour figure online).

Genetic information in Weaver is stored as a set of chromosomes following an array structure. It is transmitted to new generations following simple recombination mechanisms where chromosomes (arrays) are randomly split and combined on the parents to generate new gametes that will define the new offspring genetic background (genome).

Hence, this important feature provides exceptional insight in how environmental pressure favors some individulas in detriment of others. It also shows interesting effects of evolution when populations live in isolation.

Code Listing 2 shows (lines 6 to 10) some genetics structure definition for an animal species. Each individual genetic makeup is unique and depends on user-defined ranges and variability for each trait. When sexual reproduction occurs, realistic inheritance rules are included as described above. More details on the algorithm for reproduction and genetics can be found in (Moya-Laraño et al. [6,7]).

2.4   Generated Data

Each time a simulation is run, a bunch of output files can be generated. The user decides where to store files and which ones to keep or discard through JSON directives.

Data output is the final product of the simulation process itself and the beginning stage of further research to reach different conclusions. This data summarizes all the interesting events that have happened during the simulation execution. All this raw data can be processed to extract valuable statistical information that supports or refutes a previous hypothesis.

Next there is a description of the most important files that can be obtained from a Weaver simulation:

- *animal_constitutive_traits.txt:* information relative to each animal traits that is born is kept in this file. This is used to study genetic variability of populations and its evolution. Currently, 13 traits are stored for each animal: **energy, growth, pheno, body, assim, vor, speed search, met, vorQ10, spdQ10, srchQ10, e_met**. Other information is also present in this file, including its unique identifier, (**id**), speciesl (**species**), generation based on parents ones (**g_numb_prt1** and **g_numb_prt2**), and parents unique identifiers (**ID_prt1** e **ID_prt2**).
- *extendedDailySummary.txt:* a daily summary is kept detailing, for each species, the number of individuals that fall within a given phenological state. Basal resources are also detailed (i.e. fungus biomass). Fields for this data file are: simulation day (**day**), fungus biomass, as **scientificName_biomass**, and the number of individuals at any phenological state as **scientificName_X**. Where **X** represents the state (0-to be born, 1-active, 2-starved to death, 3-predated, 4-reproducing, 5-background death, 6-natural death).
- *animals_each_day_end:* This is the most complete set of information regarding each individual. A file is kept for each day containing detailed information for them. Its structure is as **animals_day_X.txt** where **X** represents a given day. Each file is written after a simulation day is finished and contains a summary of each animal currently participating in the simulation: unique individual id (**id**), its species (**species**), spatial location (**x, y, z**), phenological state (**state**), instar for reproduction purposes (**instar**), the initial phenology value (**pheno_ini**), date of creation (**date_egg**), first reproduction date (**age_first_rep**), number of reproduction episodes (**rep_count**), number of descendants to date (**fecundity**), death date (**date_death**), its generation number based on parents ones (**g_numb_prt1** y **g_numb_prt2**), parents unique ids (**ID_prt1** and **ID_prt2**), the number of encounters with predators this day (**encounters_pred**), the accumulated number of encounters with predators along its life (**global_pred_encs**), time to finish digestion (**days_digest**) and all variables regarding genetic traits that can be modified (**energy, growth, pheno, body, assim, vor, speed search, met, vorQ10, spdQ10, srchQ10, e_met**).

Matrices: this file is generated upon completion of the simulation and its called *predationOnSpecies*. It stores a NxN matrix where N represent the number of different animal species. This matrix stores an all-to-all predation index with predators forming columns and preys forming rows.

2.5 Computational Requirements

Weaver was designed with performance in mind from the beginning. This involved moving from an interpreted language like R used with Mini-Akira to a compiled one like C/C++. Many code optimizations were included to make use of modern processors vectorial instructions (SSE, SSE2, etc.). This thorough development yielded performance gains of 5 orders of magnitude, making it possible to move to much more complex simulations including several hundreds of thousands of individuals living in three-dimensional worlds.

The impressive performance improvements obtained with Weaver over Mini-Akira presented its own drawbacks. More complex simulations implied a vast increase in runtime memory demands as well as disk space to store simulation results. Memory demands cannot be predicted a priori as animals reproduce at different rates and populations grow and deplete continuously. Data output is continuously generated by Weaver at a fast pace. This has two main implications. First, data bandwidth is limited by the I/O system and disk infrastructure which is a potential bottleneck that is being studied. Using optimized databases instead of plain files, parallel file-systems and distributed computing are the three main strategies under development. As data outputs must be analyzed afterwards, a distributed file-system (like Hadoop) is quite interesting and is being investigated. Another important source of memory consumption is the size of the simulation scenery. In 1D and 2D scenarios, memory consumption is mainly driven be the number of individuals while for three dimensions, the scenario storage itself represents a major contributor to storage requirements. The only realistic solution to improve the maximum size of simulation scenarios is to include distributed computing through MPI or similar alternatives and divide the whole scenario into smaller chunks where some information must be shared at different moments to build a coherent simulation. Locally, the huge number of individuals and interactions to be computed require of shared-memory parallel computing strategies like OpenMP, OpenTBB and plain POSIX Threads.

3   Results and Conclusions

Weaver has already been successfully used in simulation studies of Food Webs involving many different species and scenarios. A detailed example can be found in [8].

4   Future Work

Future work is centered on three main areas. First, extending HPC capabilities to include the most advanced technologies including GPGPUs, multi-threading, MPI and Cloud/Grid computing. Second, developing a graphical user interface to create and edit JSON files and make it easier to design new simulations. Finally, another graphical user interface application to visualize and analyze simulation data. The last two areas are devised to improve user experience and increase usability whilst the first one is aimed at increasing processing speed and/or simulations complexity.

Another important field of current work is centered on large data volumes management and analysis. Weaver is able to generate extremely big amounts of data that need to be stored, processed and converted to useful information. All three steps pose serious challenges that are being working on.

Acknowledgements. This work was funded by the Spanish Ministry Grants CGL 2010-18602 to J.M.-L and by Grant TIN2012-37483 and Junta de AndalucÁa Grant P11-TIC-7176 to L.G.C and RNM-1521 to J.M.-L. and Campus de Excelencia Internacional Agroalimentario (ceiA3). All grants have been funded in part by the European Regional Development Fund (ERDF). J.R.B.-C. is a recipient of a Ramón y Cajal fellowship awarded by the Spanish Ministry of Economy and Competitiveness (MINECO). D.R.L. is a recipient of a predoctoral fellowship awarded by the Spanish Ministry of Education, Culture and Sports (FPU13/04933).

References

1. Margalef, R.: On certain unifying principles in ecology. Am. Nat. **97**(897), 357–374 (1963)
2. Cohen, Joel E.: Food Webs and Niche Space. Princeton University Press, Princeton (1978)
3. Zhou, Y., Brose, U., Kastenberg, W., Martinez, N.D.: A New Approach to Ecological Risk Assessment: Simulating Effects of Global Warming on Complex Ecological Networks Unifying Themes in Complex Systems, pp. 342–350 (2011)
4. Ramsey, S., Orrell, D., Bolouri, H.: Dizzy: stochastic simulation of large-scale genetic regulatory networks. J. Bioinform. Comput. Biol. **3**(2), 415–436 (2005)
5. ECMA international: The JSON data interchange format. ECMA-404 (RFC 4627) (2013)
6. Moya-Laraño, J., Verdeny-Vilalta, O., Rowntree, J., Melguizo-Ruiz, N., Montserrat, M., Laiolo, P.: Climate change and eco-evolutionary dynamics in food webs. Adv. Ecol. Res. **47**, 1 (2012)
7. Verdeny-Vilalta, O., Moya-Laraño, J.: Seeking water while avoiding predators: moisture gradients can affect predator-prey interactions. Anim. Behav. **90**, 101–108 (2014)
8. Moya-Laraño, J., Bilbao-Castro, J.R., Barrionuevo, G., Ruiz-Lupión, D., Casado, L.G., Montserrat, M., Melián, C.J., Magalhães, S.: Eco-evolutionary spatial dynamics: rapid evolution and isolation explain food web persistence. Adv. Ecol. Res. **50**, 75–143 (2014)
9. Gandrud, C.: Reproducible Research with R and RStudio. Chapman & Hall/CRC Press (2013)
10. Tisue, S., Wilensky, U.: NetLogo: design and implementation of a multi-agent modeling environment. In: Proceedings of Agent 2004, Chicago, IL, pp. 7–9 (2004)
11. Railsback, Steven F., Lytinen, Steven L., Jackson, Stephen K.: Agent-based simulation platforms: review and development recommendations. SIMULATION **82**(9), 609–623 (2006)
12. Collier, N.: Repast: an extensible framework for agent simulation. Nat. Resour. Environ. Issues **8**(4), 17–21 (2001)
13. Collier, N., North, M.: Repast HPC: a platform for large-scale agent-based modeling, in large-scale computing. In: Dubitzky, W., Kurowski, K., Schott, B. (eds.). John Wiley & Sons Inc, Hoboken (2011). doi:10.1002/9781118130506.ch5
14. Luke, S., Cioffi-Revilla, C., Panait, L., Sullivan, K., Balan, G.: MASON: a multi-agent simulation environment. SIMULATION **81**(7), 517–527 (2005)
15. Minar, N., Burkhart, R., Langton, C., Askenazi, M.: The Swarm Simulation System: A Toolkit for Building Multi-Agent Simulations. Santa Fe Institute, Santa Fe (1996)

16. Cao, K., Feng, X., Wan, H.: Applying agent-based modeling to the evolution of eco-industrial systems. Ecol. Econ. **68**(11), 2868–2876 (2009)
17. Terna, P.: Simulation tools for social scientists: building agent based models with swarm. J. Artif. Soc. Soc. Simul. **1**(2), 1–12 (1998)
18. Macy, M.W., Willer, R.: From factors to actors: computational sociology and agent-based modeling. Ann. Rev. Sociol. **28**, 143–166 (2002)
19. Rashid, S., Yoon, Y., Kashem, S.B.: Assessing the potential impact of microfinance with agent-based modeling. Econ. Model. **28**(4), 1907–1913 (2011)
20. Roozmand, O., Ghasem-Aghaee, N., Hofstede, G.J., Nematbakhsh, M.A., Baraani, A., Verwaart, T.: Agent-based modeling of consumer decision making process based on power distance and personality. Knowledge-Based Syst. **24**(7), 1075–1095 (2011)
21. Zellner, M.L.: Embracing complexity and uncertainty: the potential of agent-based modeling for environmental planning and policy. Plan. Theory Prac. **9**(4), 437–457 (2008)
22. Bichraoui, N., Guillaume, B., Halog, A.: Agent-based modelling simulation for the development of an industrial symbiosis-preliminary results. Procedia Environ. Sci. **17**, 195–204 (2013)
23. North, M.J., Collier, N.T., Vos, J.R.: Experiences creating three implementations of the repast agent modeling toolkit. ACM Trans. Model. Comput. Simul. **16**(1), 1–25 (2006)
24. Macal, C.M., North, M.J.: Tutorial on agent-based modelling and simulation. J. Simul. **4**(3), 151–162 (2010)
25. Tobias, R., Hofmann, C.: Evaluation of free java-libraries for social-scientific agent based simulation. J. Artif. Soc.Soc. Simul. **7**, 6 (2004)
26. Ginovart, M.: Discovering the power of individual-based modelling in teaching and learning: the study of a predator-prey system. J. Sci. Edu. Technol. **23**(4), 496–513 (2014)
27. Shiet, A.B., Shiet, G.W.: An introduction to agent-based modeling for undergraduates. Procedia Comput. Sci. **29**, 1392–1402 (2014)
28. Holcombe, M., Coakley, S., Smallwood, R.: A general framework for agent-based modelling of complex systems. In: Proceedings of the 2006 European Conference on Complex Systems (2006)
29. Richmond, P., Coakley, S., Romano, M.: A high performance agent based modelling framework on graphics card hardware with CUDA. In: Proceedings of the 8th International Conference on Autonomous Agents and Multiagent Systems, AAMAS 2009, Budapest, Hungary, vol. 2, pp. 1125–1126 (2009)
30. Grimm, V.: Ten years of individual-based modelling in ecology: what have we learned and what could we learn in the future? Ecol. Model. **115**(2), 129–148 (1999)
31. Grimm, V., Steven, F.: Individual-based Modeling and Ecology. Princeton University Press, Princeton (2005)
32. Chion, C., Lamontagne, P., Turgeon, S., Parrott, L., Landry, J.-A., Marceau, D.J., Martins, C.C.A., Michaud, R., Ménard, N., Cantin, G., Dionne, S.: Eliciting cognitive processes underlying patterns of human-wildlife interactions for agent-based modelling. Ecol. Model. **222**(14), 2213–2226 (2011)
33. Girard, P., Parrott, L., Caron, C.-A., Green, D.M.: Effects of temperature and surface water availability on spatiotemporal dynamics of stream salamanders using pattern-oriented modelling. Ecol. Model. **296**, 12–23 (2015)
34. De Angelis, D.L., Grimm, V.: Individual-based models in ecology after four decades. F1000Prime Reports (2014)

On the Joint Modeling of the Behavior of Social Insects and Their Interaction with Environment by Taking into Account Physical Phenomena Like Anisotropic Diffusion

Nicolas Cazin[1], Aymeric Histace[1]([⊠]), David Picard[1], and Benoît Gaudou[2]

[1] ETIS, ENSEA, University of Cergy-Pontoise, CNRS, Cergy-pontoise, France
nicolas.cazin@inserm.fr, aymeric.histace@u-cergy.fr,
[2] IRIT, University of Toulouse, Toulouse, France
david.picard@ensea.fr, benoit.gaudou@ut-capitole.fr

Abstract. This work takes place in the framework of GEODIFF project (funded by CNRS) and deals with the general issue of the social behavior modeling of pest insects with a particular focus on Bark Beetles. Bark Beetles are responsible for pine trees devastation in North America since 2005. In order to stem the problem and to apply an adapted strategy, one should be able to predict the evolution of the population of Bark Beetles. More precisely, a model taking into account a given population of insects (a colony) interacting with its environment, the forest ecosystem, would be very helpful. In a previous work, we aimed to model diffusive phenomenons across the environment using a simple reactive Multi-agent System. Bark beetle use pheromones as a support for recruitment of other bark beetles in the neighborhood in order to achieve a mass attack over a tree. They are first attracted by the ethanol or other phytopheromones emitted by a sick, stressed or dead tree and reinforce the presence of other individuals amongst the targeted tree. Both ethanol and semiochemicals are transported through the forest thanks to the wind, thermic effects and this advection phenomenon is modulated by the topology of the environment, tree and other obstacles distribution. In other words, the environment is involved in the process of a bark beetle attack. The first modeling we used to tackle our objective was not spatially explicit as long as free space propagation only was taken into account (isotropic phenomenon) with no constraint imposed by the environment such as wind. This article is intended to take into account such physical phenomenons and push the modeling one step further by providing predictions driven by measures provided by a Geographical Information System.

1 Introduction

Modeling of the population dynamics is an essential part of both research and management of forest pest insects. These kind of complex objectives require prediction of population changes over long time intervals and over large areas. Of course, it is impossible to predict pest abundance at specific location ten years

© Springer International Publishing Switzerland 2015
J. Bajo et al. (Eds.): PAAMS 2015 Workshops, CCIS 524, pp. 151–164, 2015.
DOI: 10.1007/978-3-319-19033-4_13

ahead, but it may be possible to predict the change in average pest population density as a result of some change in environment.

Formerly, to tackle this objective, mathematical modeling was the major tool for predicting population dynamics and the reader could refer to Berryman and Millstein [1] for a complete overview of some of the most known models that are mainly based on modifications of discrete-time analog of the logistic model. The main advantage of such methods is that parameters of these models can be adjusted to fit available data.

Nowadays, mathematical modeling based approaches tend to be replaced by Multi-agent Modeling (MAM) based ones that has constituted an important research and development area for the past two decades [2].

Aim of this article is to propose a MAM based on a simple reactive Multi-agent System (MAS) [3,4] with possibility to take into account evolution physical laws related to the corresponding environment. More precisely, we want to show that by integrating the way the resources and the trail markers could naturally vanish, steered by a diffusive phenomenon parametrically described using a spatio-temporal like heat equation, we can obtain a more realistic modeling of the global behavior of the MAS dynamics.

Practically speaking, we focus our attention on the behavior modeling of a particular social pest insect: the "Bark beetle". Bark beetles or "Scolytes" are ecologically and economically significant [5] since outbreak species help to renew the forest by killing older trees and other species aid in the decomposition of dead wood. However, several outbreak-prone species are known as notorious pests that can cause tremendous damage to pine tree forests for instance [6]. As a consequence, a better understanding of the social behavior of this beetle would definitely be of some precious help to limit its damage capability.

This article is organized as follows: In Sect. 2, the model used for experiments is presented and detailed. In Sect. 3, different scenarios are considered for experiments in order to show that the proposed modeling is realistic and can adapt to non-classic situations including anisotropic phenomenons like wind. In the last section, conclusion and discussion are proposed.

2   Materials and Modeling

2.1   GAMA Platform

In the context of this work, the GAMA platform was used [7–9]. GAMA is a freely available modeling and simulation development environment for building spatially explicit agent-based simulations. GAMA platform allows to:

- Design, prototype and write models in the GAML agent-oriented language and its optional graphical modeling tool.
- Instantiate agents from any kind of dataset, including GIS data, and execute large-scale simulations (up to millions of agents).
- Couple discrete or continuous topological layers, multiple levels of agency and multiple paradigms (mathematical equations, control architectures, finite state machines).

- Define rich experiments on models and explore their parameters space for calibration and validation.
- Design rich user interfaces that support deep inspections on agents, user-controlled actions and panels, multi-layer 2D/3D displays and multiple agent aspects.

Because of the related flexibility and the possibility to enrich the existing functions in GAML language, the GAMA platform appears as the best solution, providing us the tools to create our complete environment, including complex phenomena as anisotropic ones (winds for instance).

2.2   Static Model

The static model considered in this work was introduced in [10]. Synthetically, the concentration of chemical agents in the environment is modeled according to a Gaussian law decreasing as and when the distance to the tree is increasing. The scolytes and trees behavior is controlled by a finite state automaton owned by each agent. This way, specific operation are realized by each agent, in accordance with a specific internal state at a given instant. The model is constituted of three species (Scolyte, Tree, Environment cell) and their description are mutually dependent. There is no optimal order for describing each one. In the following, each aspect of the model (environments, agents, interactions and related physical laws) are detailed.

Environment. The environment is discretized in a finite number of square cells noted (x, y). Each cell is characterized by two variables modeling (i) the amounts of ethanol and (ii) the quantity of pheromones in the cell.

Ethanol. The amount of ethanol available in cell (x, y) at time t is given by:

$$E(x, y, t) = \sum_{s \in S} E_s(t) e^{-\gamma[(x-x_s)^2 + (y-y_s)^2]} \tag{1}$$

with S being the set of trees in ALIVE state, $E_s(t)$ being the amount of ethanol emitted by the s tree (of spatial coordinate (x_s, y_s)), at time t, given by Eq. (5).

Pheromones. The amount of aggregation pheromones available in a (x, y) cell at time t is given by:

$$Ph(x, y, t) = \sum_{s \in S} Ph_s(t) e^{-\gamma[(x-x_s)^2 + (y-y_s)^2]} \tag{2}$$

with S being the set of trees in ALIVE state, $Ph_s(t)$ being the amount of aggregation pheromones emitted by the scolyte located in cell (x, y) given by the Eq. (7).

Attractiveness. The attractiveness of a cell (x, y) is defined as a convex combination of the amounts of contained chemical agents given by:

$$A(x, y, t) = \eta Ph(x, y, t) + (1 - \eta) E(x, y, t) \tag{3}$$

with η being the coupling coefficient chosen empirically between 0 and 1.

Tree. A tree lying in a (x_s, y_s) cell is noted $s(x, y)$. This tree represents an amount of resource for scolytes noted $R_s(t)$ and this variable is evolving according to the number of scolytes present in the $s(x, y)$ cell. For all experiments, we use the usual logistic law of Eq. (4) to model the evolution of the resources on a site.

$$R_s(t + 1) = R_s(t) - \alpha n_s(t) \tag{4}$$

– α being a constant representing the average consumption rate of the resource by a scolyte between two infinitesimal time steps.

Equation (4) is a positive or null amount. The behavior of a tree is described by two states:

ALIVE. The tree is alive. This is the initial state of each tree. All along its lifespan, it will rot and emit in the environment an amount of ethanol noted E_s, proportional to a fraction μ of the remaining ressources R_s. The ethanol amount emitted by a tree $s(x, y)$ at time t is given by:

$$E_s(t) = \mu R_s(t) \tag{5}$$

A tree will switch to the DEAD. state when $R_s(t) = 0$.

DEAD. The tree is dead. This is its final state. No more operation can arise.

Scolyte. A scolyte contained in a given cell (x, y) is noted $a(x, y)$. The behavior of a Scolyte [11–13] is described by three main states:

INIT. This is the initial state of a scolyte after its instantiation. This is a technical state added in order to work around a constraint of the GAML language stating that an initial state must be declared. More than anything, the initial state of a scolyte agent may be different according to its initial location or experiment constraints. It is impossible to force the initial state during the instantiation. A transition towards the FLYING state is trigged if the scolyte is in a cell containing an ALIVE tree. Otherwise, a transition towards the EATING state is trigged.

FLYING. In this state, the scolyte will choose the next cell he will visit by using its local perceptions. The immediate neighborhood of the cell occupied by the a agent is noted $N(a)$. The scolyte will fly towards the cell $(x\star, y\star)$ from the $N(a)$ cell with a probability related to the cell attractiveness. The probability for a scolyte to move in the cell $(x\star, y\star)$ is given by:

$$p_a(t)(x\star, y\star) = \frac{A(x\star, y\star, t)}{\sum_{(x,y) \in N(a)} A(x, y, t)} \tag{6}$$

with $A(x\star, y\star, t)$ the attractiveness of the $(x\star, y\star)$ cell, at instant t. Then, the target cell is determined thanks to a barrel roll algorithm, i.e. by scanning the attractivity of each possible in a 8-connectivity neighborhood. Several copies of each cell are inserted in a list. The number of copies of each cell is proportional to the associated transition probability towards this cell. If no cell is really attractive, all transitions are with same probability and the cell is thus randomly selected in $N(a)$. This probabilistic roaming gives the opportunity to each agent to move sometimes in a cell different than the most attractive cell. Since the new surrounding cells may be close to another potential well, the scolytes are allowed to separate from the colony and explore new areas of the environment.

EATING. When the scolyte lands in the cell $s(x, y)$ containing a tree, it consumes the R_s resource by eating a μ fraction and emitting a v amount of aggregation pheromones in the $s(x, y)$ cell. This cell becomes more attractive for the other scolytes. The amount of pheromones emitted by the scolytes in the $s(x, y)$ cell at time t is given by:

$$Ph_s(t) = \nu * n_s(t) \tag{7}$$

with ν the amount of aggregation pheromones emitted by a single scolyte.

At each iteration, the departure probability of the scolyte a to move from the s source is given by:

$$q_a(t) = 1 - \frac{R_s(t)}{R_s(0)} \tag{8}$$

The transition towards the FLYING state is related to the probability $q_a(t)$. A variable between 0 and 1 is randomly selected in a uniform distribution. If the result is less than (8), the transition to the FLYING state occurs. Otherwise, the scolyte stays in the EATING state.

2.3   Diffusion/Reaction

Formerly introduced in [14] for MAS Modeling, matter diffusion is an irreversible transport phenomenon and one may define it by the trend of a system to converge towards a homogenous concentration of chemical agents. The diffusion equation is given by:

$$\frac{\partial \phi(r, t)}{\partial t} = \nabla \cdot [D(\phi, r) \cdot \nabla(\phi(r, t))] \tag{9}$$

with r the cell where the ϕ density, sampled at time t, is set, $D(\phi, r)$ is the diffusion coefficient for the ϕ density sampled at place r, and $D(\phi, r)$ may be an input from a GIS.

By considering the diffusion coefficient as a constant value over the whole R map[1], the Eq. (9) may be rewritten as:

$$\frac{\partial \phi(r, t)}{\partial t} = D_\Phi \cdot \nabla^2 \cdot \phi(r, t) \tag{10}$$

This is the well known heat equation. By considering $r = (x, y)$, first order spatial derivatives along X and Y axis, the square cell hypothesis and the 8-connexity of the cells, Eq. 10 may be solved on the discrete time case by:

$$\Phi_R(t + 1) = \Phi_R(t) * G_D \tag{11}$$

---

[1] $D(\phi, r) = D_\Phi, \forall r \in R.$

with $\Phi_R(t) = (\phi(x, y, t))_{x \in R_x, y \in R_y}$ being the concentration of a given chemical reagent in the R space (square in this case), $G_D = \frac{D_\Phi}{16} \cdot \begin{pmatrix} 1 & 2 & 1 \\ 2 & \frac{16}{D_\Phi} - 12 & 2 \\ 1 & 2 & 1 \end{pmatrix}$ being a stencil describing the neighborhood influence in the diffusive phenomenon related to the constant diffusion coefficient D_Φ.

If the diffusion coefficient is a constant, then the diffusion equation is a simple convolution with a 3×3 mask. This mask is Gaussian for $D_\Phi = 1$. Knowing that trees emit ethanol while decaying and that scolytes emit pheromones during an attack to attract other agent of the same species, on may consider emission as a chemical diffusive phenomenon. Let $q_\phi(x, y, t)$ be the amount of chemical reagent ϕ at cell (x, y) and time t.

$$q_\phi(x, y, t) \begin{cases} > 0 & \text{when the chemical reaction is active.} \\ = 0 & \text{when there is no chemical reaction.} \\ < 0 & \text{when the chemical reaction is destroying reagents.} \end{cases}$$

The Eq. (11) is now extended by:

$$\Phi_R(t+1) = \Phi_R(t) * G_D + Q_{\Phi_R}(t) \tag{12}$$

with $Q_{\Phi_R}(t)$ being the amount of created (or vanished) chemical reagent ϕ by the chemical reactions happenings over the whole R map (It is also called the the reaction term), and $\Phi_R(t) * G_D$ is the diffusion term. It is a solution to the diffusion reaction equation.

2.4 Diffusion/Reaction/Evaporation

The current update Eq. (12) is still not so realistic. Suspended chemical agents may have a limited persistence. This persistence depends mainly on moisture and ambient temperature. Without a deep understanding of complex chemical reaction, we propose to simply model the evaporation as a progressive reduction of the current amount of chemical agent. The amount map $Q_{\Phi_R}(t)$ is simply extended as:

$$Q_{\Phi_R}^{Ev}(t) = Q_{\Phi_R}(t) - Ev_\Phi \cdot \Phi_R(t) * G_D \tag{13}$$

with Ev_Φ being the evaporation constant between 0 and 1. It represents the amount of diffused $\Phi_R(t)$ being evaporated, and $Q_{\Phi_R}(t)$ is the simple reaction term.

A fraction Ev_Φ of the diffused amount $\Phi_R(t) * G_D$ is subtracted from the current amount for chemical reagents $Q_{\Phi_R}(t)$. By plugging this extended reaction term (13) in Eq. (12), it comes:

$$\Phi_R(t+1) = (1 - Ev_\Phi) \cdot \Phi_R(t) * G_D + Q_{\Phi_R}(t) \tag{14}$$

Only a fraction $1 - Ev_\Phi$ of the diffusion term is kept. Like D_Φ, Ev_Φ is chosen constant over the whole R map for simplicity purpose but it may be kept variable, for instance by taking into account measures from a GIS.

2.5   Diffusion/Reaction/Evaporation/Advection

The wind phenomenon may be modeled by the advection equation. The advection of a scalar quantity may be written as the gradient of the average velocity vector moving a Φ amount of chemical agent. By using the finite elements method and first order spatial derivatives, the Eq. (14) becomes:

$$
\Phi_R(t+1) = (1 - Ev_\Phi) \cdot (\Phi_R(t) * G_D - v \cdot \begin{pmatrix} \Phi(x,y,t) * \begin{pmatrix} 0 & 0 & 0 \\ -1 & 0 & 1 \\ 0 & 0 & 0 \end{pmatrix} \\ \Phi(x,y,t) * \begin{pmatrix} 0 & -1 & 0 \\ 0 & 0 & 0 \\ 0 & 1 & 0 \end{pmatrix} \end{pmatrix}) + Q_{\Phi_R}(t)
$$

$$
= (1 - Ev_\Phi) \cdot (\Phi_R(t) * G_D - \Phi_R(t) * \begin{pmatrix} 0 & \frac{-v_x}{2} & 0 \\ \frac{-v_x}{2} & 0 & \frac{v_x}{2} \\ 0 & \frac{v_y}{2} & 0 \end{pmatrix}) + Q_{\Phi_R}(t)
$$

$$
= (1 - Ev_\Phi) \cdot (\Phi_R(t) * G_D - \Phi_R(t) * V) + Q_{\Phi_R}(t)
$$

$$
= \Phi_R(t) * (G_D - V) \cdot (1 - Ev_\Phi) + Q_{\Phi_R}(t) \tag{15}
$$

The advection is represented by a stencil V opposed to the diffusion stencil G_D. This scheme is unstable for $\|v\| > 1$. The initial model (11) is based on a forward Euler method with a unitary time-step[2]. One can rewrite the model using the Euler forward method or a higher order method (like the Runge-Kutta 4) in order to avoid numerical instability problems. In [15], the author proposes a method based on the reverse scheme. By considering the displacement vector as the variation of the $r(t)$ position of a particle during a short time-lapse, one may write:

$$
\frac{r(t+1) - r(t)}{\Delta t} = u(t) \tag{16}
$$

The $r(t+1)$ may be deduced from $r(t)$ and $u(t)$

$$
r(t+1) = r(t) + \Delta t \cdot u(t) \tag{17}
$$

Instead of moving an amount of chemical reagent from one point to another, the place r where the advected amount is originated will be determined by inverting the advection vector direction.

$$
q(r, t+1) = q(r - u(r,t) \cdot \Delta t, t) \tag{18}
$$

The point $r_{source} = r - u(r,t) \cdot \Delta t$ is not a exactly a discrete cell coordinate but a point located between the 4 adjacent cells of the source. The amount q advected from r_{source} is determined thanks to a bilinear interpolation between the amounts contained in the 4 adjacent cells of the source. This interpolated amount is added to $r_{destination}$ and subtracted from the 4 adjacent cells of the

---

[2] $\phi(r, t+h) = \phi(r,t) + h\frac{\partial \phi(r,t)}{\partial t}$ with $h = 1$.

source, proportionally to their contribution weighting in the bilinear interpolation. The advected amounts are conserved ([16]). The velocity map may be precomputed in order to take into account several obstacles such as trees in the environment.

3   Experiments and Results

The following experiments aim to exhibit the effect of wind on the colony's next move. Wind is advecting semiochemicals and ethanol. The attractiveness of an area from the point of view of the Scolyte is driven by the concentration of semiochemicals and ethanol. From a upper point of view, It may be interpreted by a concentration map of reagents on the forest ecosystem. Any modulation of the "density map" could lead to a different behavior of a colony and may have several consequences on the other actors of the ecosystem due to their tight coupling.

3.1   Double-Well Potential Function

This is the reference experiment. The colony converges towards the nearest tree, consumes all its resources and then forages for the next host tree. This is the straight implementation of the model introduced in Sect. (2). The only source of non determinism in this simulation is the stochastic probabilistic selection of the next cell, a random "walk" algorithm.

Description. The grid world is set up with a 50×50 empty array of semiochemicals and ethanol. Scolytes are initially consuming the first tree at coordinates $(20, 5)$ and each of the three provide the same amount of ressource (arbitrarly set to 1000). The Fig. 1 displays this configuration. The attraction map is colored according a logarithmic scale described by the following equation:

$$((h, s, v), x, y) = (((grid[x][y] - MIN)/(MAX - MIN), 1.0, 1.0), x, y) \quad (19)$$

With:

- $grid[x][y] = 10 \cdot log_{10}(attractiveness[x][y])$
- $MIN = -300\,dB$
- $MAX = 10 \cdot log_{10}(1000)\,dB$

The red color denotes a non attractive cell[3] and a pink cell denotes a very attractive cell[4]

---

[3] $attractiveness[x][y] = MIN$.
[4] $attractiveness[x][y] = MAX$.

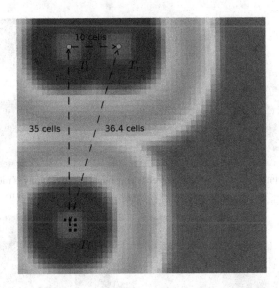

Fig. 1. Attractiveness map state at initial configuration. The initial tree is named T_r and have $(20, 5)$ grid coordinates, the leftmost tree is named T_l and have $(10, 5)$ grid coordinates, the rightmost tree is named T_i and have $(10, 40)$ grid coordinates.

Observations. Figure 2 depicts the colony's path through the forest.

1. The colony is initially set on the T_i tree (Fig. 2a). The surrounding cells are less attractive than the immediate neighborhood of T_i. The all colony is aggregated on this particular location of the map.
2. Scolytes are consuming T_i resources and will move towards the closest tree T_l once totally consumed (Fig. 2b). The tree stop emits ethanol and scolytes stops emit pheromones. After evaporation of the remaining amounts of reagents, the attractiveness gradient is now positive and scolyte will be trapped by the closest potential well.
3. According to the scolytes perception, the most interesting bearing is given by the closest tree. Almost the entire colony is consuming the T_l tree (Fig. 2c). Due to the randomized/probabilistic move of each agent, a small part of the population is sometimes set at a random location according to a given probability.
4. Colony is mostly located on the T_l tree (Fig. 2d) and the remaining agents are consuming the T_r tree.
5. Once T_l is left dead, the colony converges quickly towards the remaining T_r tree (Fig. 2e). The attractiveness around T_l decreases since all over no more ethanol nor pheromones are emitted. The remaining chemical products are evaporated. The gradient becomes positive and the colony is no longer trapped around T_l.
6. The whole colony is consuming the T_r tree resources (Fig. 2f). They are trapped but the potential well induced by ethanol and pheromones emission.

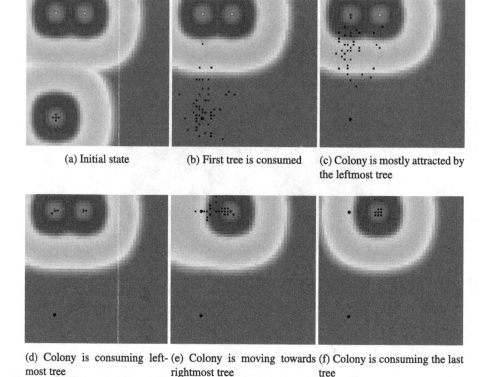

(a) Initial state   (b) First tree is consumed   (c) Colony is mostly attracted by the leftmost tree

(d) Colony is consuming left-most tree   (e) Colony is moving towards rightmost tree   (f) Colony is consuming the last tree

Fig. 2. False color attractiveness map, No wind experiment

Each agent is following the shortest path to the local maximum of attractiveness when not wandering. The random exploratory strategy is useful for handling the case where attractiveness gradient is not relevant. The path of the colony in this experiment is summarized by $(T_i \rightarrow T_l \rightarrow T_r)$.

3.2 Wind Influence

This experience aims to demonstrate the effect of the wind on the colony's trend in choosing the most attractive cells when flying.

Description. The same configuration as in the previous experiment is kept and is extended by adding a wind corridor. The Fig. 3 displays the effect of wind on the attractiveness map. Clearly, amounts of ethanol and pheromones are transported from one cell to another.

Observations. Figure 4 depicts the colony's path through the forest modified by the advection of semiochemicals.

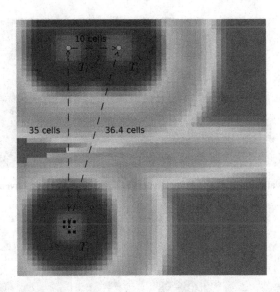

Fig. 3. Attractiveness map state at initial configuration with a wind corridor. The initial tree is named T_r and have $(20, 5)$ grid coordinates, the leftmost tree is named T_l and have $(10, 5)$ grid coordinates, the rightmost tree is named T_i and have $(10, 40)$ grid coordinates, the wind corridor is 10 cells wide and directed along the x axis.

1. The colony is initially set on the T_i tree (Fig. 4a). The surrounding cells are less attractive than the immediate neighborhood of T_i. The colony is focused those cells.
2. Scolytes are consuming T_i resources and will move towards the most interesting cells once totally consumed (Fig. 4b). The attractiveness gradient is now positive and scolyte will be trapped by the closest potential well.
3. According to the scolytes perception, the most interesting bearing is now towards the T_r tree which is not the closest tree. Almost the entire colony is consuming the T_r tree (Fig. 4c). Due to the randomized/probabilistic move of each agent, a small part of the population is sometimes set at a random location according to a given probability.
4. Colony is mostly located on the T_r tree (Fig. 4d) and the remaining agents are consuming the T_l tree.
5. Once T_r left dead, colony converges quickly towards the remaining T_l tree (Fig. 4e). The attractiveness around T_l is lowered since over the no more ethanol nor pheromones are emitted. The remaining chemical products are evaporated. The gradient becomes positive and the colony is no longer trapped around T_r.
6. The whole colony is consuming the T_l tree resources (Fig. 4f). They are trapped but the potential well induced by ethanol and pheromones emission.

The path of the colony in this experiment is summarized by $(T_i \rightarrow T_r \rightarrow T_l)$.

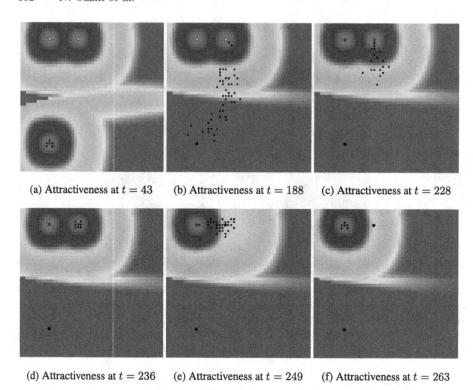

(a) Attractiveness at $t = 43$ (b) Attractiveness at $t = 188$ (c) Attractiveness at $t = 228$

(d) Attractiveness at $t = 236$ (e) Attractiveness at $t = 249$ (f) Attractiveness at $t = 263$

Fig. 4. False color attractiveness map with a wind corridor

4 Discussion, Conclusion, Perspectives

In this article, a MAS approach is proposed for modeling of the behavior of pest insects, not only considering their classic social interactions using hormones, but also by the taking into of the external physical phenomena that characterized the environment in which the agents are living (linear and non-linear diffusion). This work extends former work of Langlois et al. [14] in which only simple linear phenomenon were taken into account in chemical agents diffusion process modeling and is new considering applications to the modeling of ant-like insects' behavior. The Sect. 3.2 shows that modeling physical phenomenon by taking into account measurements extracted from a GIS allows the hybrid MAS-PDE simulator GAMA to provide more realistic forecasts. In other words, the agent's behavior is modified thanks to their interaction with the environment and their peer trough the environment. This environment is no longer static and have its own dynamic, like the other agents. Each cell from the grid world and each particle of chemical reagent may be considered as a particular agent. We use simplified fluid dynamics usual equations in order to demonstrate the feasibility of a joint MAS-PDE modeling tool. This work is easily extendable to GP-GPU fluid dynamics and MPI clustering in order to support larger scale problems. From a modeling point of view now, the current model have several limitations:

- The advection model is incomplete and have no support for viscosity. The amounts of chemical reagents are like teleported from one point or another without any resistance to advection. The velocity map needs to be updated at each step according by the perturbations resulting from the viscosity forces modeling.
- Pressure, topology, heat, moisture have a major influence on the velocity map and need.
- Real world is in three dimensions and our grid world have only two dimensions. Temperature differences play an important role in the determination of the velocity map.
- The size of the environment, agents and their parameters, different timescales have to be studied and fixed.
- The behavior of scolytes is incomplete: Eggs, larvaes, females, males scolytes have different behaviors and different needs. Other pheromones play an important role in local competition handling and colonies formation.
- Dynamic environments also have an influence on scolytes, such as wind carrying the agents.
- Other actors/phenomenons of the ecosystem need to be modeled. Especially, human and forest management, fires, water and temperature.

To overcome these limitations, tools inspired coming from large scale fluid dynamics simulations could be of real interest and integrating these real-time computing methods in the MAS-PDE simulator could permit to have a modeling of the insects' behavior always more realistic, which is of primary importance for an efficient and anticipated management of the pest insect populations.

References

1. Berryman, A.A., Millstein, J.A.: Population Analysis System, Pullman edn. Washington (1994). Version 4.0
2. Ferber, J.: Multi-Agent Systems: An Introduction to Distributed Artificial Intelligence. Addison-Wesley (1999)
3. Drogoul, A.: Résolution Collective de Problèmes: Une étude de l'émergence de structures d'organisations dans les systèmes multi-agents. Ph.D. thesis, Université Paris VI (1993)
4. Rouchier, J. In: Systèmes multi-agents et modélisation de systèmes sociaux, Hermes Science, pp. 285–299 (2002)
5. Bentz, B.: Climate change and bark beetles of the western united states and canada: direct and indirect effects. BioScience 8(60), 602–613 (2010). doi:10.1525/bio.2010.60.8.6
6. Robins, J.: Bark Beetles Kill Millions of Acres of Trees in West, New York Times, 17 November 2008
7. Amouroux, E., Chu, T.-Q., Boucher, A., Drogoul, A.: GAMA: an environment for implementing and running spatially explicit multi-agent simulations. In: Ghose, A., Governatori, G., Sadananda, R. (eds.) PRIMA 2007. LNCS, vol. 5044, pp. 359–371. Springer, Heidelberg (2009)

8. Taillandier, P., Vo, D.-A., Amouroux, E., Drogoul, A.: GAMA: a simulation platform that integrates geographical information data, agent-based modeling and multi-scale control. In: Desai, N., Liu, A., Winikoff, M. (eds.) PRIMA 2010. LNCS, vol. 7057, pp. 242–258. Springer, Heidelberg (2012)
9. Drogoul, A., Amouroux, E., Caillou, P., Gaudou, B., Arnaud, G., Marilleau, N., Taillander, P., Vavasseur, M., Duc-An, V., Jean-Daniel, Z.: Gama: multi-level and complex environment for agent-based models and simulations. In: Proceedings of the 2013 International Conference on Autonomous Agents and Multi-agent Systems, pp. 1361–1362 (2013)
10. Picard, D., Histace, A., Desseroit, M.C.: Joint MAS-PDE modeling of forest pest insect dynamics: analysis of the bark beetle's behavior (2013)
11. Byers, J.A.: Behavioral mechanisms involved in reducing competition in bark beetles. HOLARCT. ECOL. **12**, 466–476 (1989)
12. Bakke, A.: Using pheromones in the management of bark beetle outbreaks. In: Patterns of Interaction with Host Trees, pp. 371–377 (1991)
13. Harrington, T.C.: Ecology and evolution of mycophagous bark beetles and their fungal partners. In: Press, O.U., Vega, F.E., Blackwell, M. (eds.) Ecological and Evolutionary Advances in Insect-Fungal Associations, pp. 257–291 (2005)
14. Langlois, P., Daudé, E.: Concepts et modélisation de la diffusion géographique: cybergeo. Eur. J. Geogr. (2007). http://www.cybergeo.eu/index2898.html
15. Stam, J.: Real-time fluid dynamics for games. In: Proceedings of the Game Developer Conference (2003)
16. West, M.: Practical fluid dynamics: part 1. In: Game Developer Magazine (2008)

Reconstruction of Prehistoric Settlement Network Using Agent-Based Model in NetLogo

Kamila Olševičová[1](✉), Jan Procházka[1], and Alžběta Danielisová[2]

[1] University of Hradec Králové, Rokitanského 62, 50003 Hradec Králové, Czech Republic
{kamila.olsevicova,jan.prochazka}@uhk.cz
[2] Institute of Archaeology of Academy of Sciences of the Czech Republic, Letenská 4, 11801 Prague 1, Czech Republic
danielisova@arup.cas.cz

Abstract. We provide an overview of agent-based and network-based computational models in archaeology. Then we suggest a sample model of gradual spatial dispersion of late Iron Age settlement network regarding the probable existence of central sites and settlement hierarchies. The model is based on archaeological research hypotheses and fragmented archaeological evidence of sites in Central Europe. The aim of the model is to enable experimenting with relevant combinations of parameters and triggers and to provide the dynamic picture of the emergence of the prehistoric settlement network.

Keywords: Agent-based model · Archaeology · Emergence · Netlogo · Network

1 Introduction

Agent-based social simulations help us to capture the complexity of socio-economic behaviour of past cultures. Our project *Social modelling as a tool for understanding Celtic society and cultural changes at the end of the Iron Age* was focused on development of agent-based models of daily economic activities of inhabitants of late Iron Age settlements. We aimed to verify hypotheses about the self-substistence of prehistoric settlements by means of the set of models of the economics of the particular centre (Staré Hradisko in Bohemia) and its hinterland. Results were presented in (Danielisová et al. 2013; Machálek et al. 2013; Olševičová et al. 2012).

Our current interest is modelling social and economic interactions among settlements. The interpretation of fragmented and/or uncertain data from sites has to be based on statistical and visualization methods, and thus the agent-based approach has to be accompanied with network modelling. In this paper we provide an overview of classic archaeological agent-based models and we discuss the role of emulative and explorative simulation in archaeology. Then we present our model of gradual spatial dispersion of prehistoric settlement network. The model is based on archaeological evidence of sites in Central Europe in late Iron Age and it itegrates domain knowledge and hypotheses on formation of probable settlement networks.

© Springer International Publishing Switzerland 2015
J. Bajo et al. (Eds.): PAAMS 2015 Workshops, CCIS 524, pp. 165–175, 2015.
DOI: 10.1007/978-3-319-19033-4_14

2 State of the Art

Nowadays, computational models and social simulations are broadly accepted by archaeological community. Two main directions of modelling are under intensive development: agent-based models with roots in artificial intelligence and knowledge engineering, and network modelling, based on graph theory, statistics and probability theory. It is especially the dynamic aspect of computational models that makes them attractive for archaeologists: using models, it is possible to study spatial and temporal characteristics of development and adaptation of past societies.

2.1 Agent-Based Models

Application of the agent-based modelling contributed significantly to the exploration and interpretation of key archaeological questions and topics such as subsistence strategies of hunters and gatherers (Lake 2000; del Castillo and Barceló 2013), spreading of neolitic agriculture to Europe (Conolly et al. 2008; Shennan 2007; van der Vaart et al. 2006), human impact on landscape and natural environment (Axtell et al. 2002; Wainwright 2008; Barton et al. 2010) and socio-economic factors influencing the development and/or collapse of complex societies.

Iconic and frequently replicated project is *Artificial Anasazi*: model of disaperanace of Anasazi culture in south-western America (Axtell et al. 2002; Janssen 2009). Other projects were focused on exploration of political and social structures in ancient Mesopotamia (Altaweel 2007, 2008), where different stress scenarios were applied (e.g. long-term dry weather, economic crisis, demographic decline etc.) with the aim to test the resistance and sustainability of society with the given level of social complexity.

These models illustrate how results that were achieved by social simulation and agent-based modelling can make us uncertain about traditional theories of economic production, labour input and sustainability of preindustrial society and offer new research directions and archaeological questions. Among these projects, we have to mention also *Mesa Verde* project which studies the development of population at American middle-west (Kohler and Varien 2012).

2.2 Network Models

Networks consist of nodes and edges. Nodes represent various archaeological entities (e.g. sites) or their attributes, the edges represent relationships between entities (e.g. commercial or social contacts). The network analysis is based on the statistical evaluation of the network and visualisation with an emphasis to highlight important features (e.g. topology, communities), causal connections and possibly also the dynamics (growth) of the whole network. Apart from inductive network analysis of existing archaeological data, the network modelling can be used for capturing historical processes in order to simulate the missing data. Generally the strength of the synthetic use of network modelling is recreation of the no-longer-existent settlement patterns and analysis of their mutual socio-economic and political interactions on various spatial scales.

The network analysis represents the best method possible to explore the socio-economic interactions among the settlements of various ranks, complementing methods so far used, but often criticized (cf. Grant ed. 1986; Nakoinz 2010, 2012). Central place theory in geography was abandoned in the 1980s (Nakoinz 2010). Today a paradigmatic shift towards a network model is propagated in both geography (Meijers 2007) and archaeology (Nakoinz 2012; Östborn and Gerding 2014; Knappet 2013). Central place theory and computational network models can complement each other: central place theory asks for the given hierarchy of central sites, network models can explore this structure.

Network models are used to explain empirical data and analyse settlement patterns. Abundant literature can testify that network theory has found a significant position within the archaeological methodology (for list of references see Knappett 2013). It has given insights into archaeological data which could not have been obtained by other means. In addition, this analysis requires an expert pre-processing of the data and refor-mulating of the research questions.

2.3 Emulation Versus Exploration

In archaeological practice, there are two reasons to develop computational models: either we want to emulate (and verify hypotheses), or we want to explore (and build new theories).

Emulative models are complex, realistic models with large spaces of parameters. The main objective is to operate with hypotheses such as *"population A in region B in period C disappeared/change its structure due to climate changes/technological inno-vations"*. Throught the emulative model, it is possible to study emergence, to recognize trends or to find relationship between observations and their optional explanations. Simulation results are compared with empirical data, and if the similarity was significant, the hypothesis is confirmed. When building emulative models, the important question is how to define reliable representations of participants (agents or nodes) and their behaviour (sets of rules). Having the model, the main challenge is how to master systematic experiments with all relevant combinations of micro-behaviours of all types of agents and how to produce meaningful macrolevel patterns.

Explorative models are mainly methodological tools. Typically, models are much simpler and more abstract than emulative models, and are used to generate data on particular aspects of the society, without an ambition to explain complex phenomena and/or provide ultimate answers (see e.g. Bentley et al. 2005; Powel et al. 2009; Barton 2014; del Castillo and Barceló 2013; Lake and Crema 2012; Crema 2014; Angourakis et al. 2014; Salgado et al. 2014). Models help to extrapolate trends, and to better bound the optional emulative model.

As well as in the area of social simulations in general, archaeological computa-tional models are abstract: they work with the idea of past instead of the past itself, and generate data that optionally become sources of new hypotheses. Therefore models can serve as behavioral laboratories for experimental ethnoarchaeology (Premo 2010). By abstraction we mean the model often operate with artificial variables that have no real equivalents (e.g. *attractivity of the site, potential of the landscape, intensity of interactions*) and that cannot be sufficiently and indisputably grounded in empirical data.

Highly relevant argument against realistic emulative models is so called *equifinality*: the same effect can be achieved by different means or caused by various processes, i.e. same outputs can be obtained from different models (Premo 2010; Lake 2010; Madella et al. 2014). Other frequently discussed controversial topics are scales and levels of detail in models (often overrated) and nontrasparency of some models, i.e. blackboxes that give outputs but their internal structure is not presented.

3   Model

We propose the model of spatial dispersion of the network of prehistoric settlements during the late Iron Age (from the 4th century BC to the 1st century AD) in Central Europe, within the agricultural landscape around Staré Hradisko agglomeration. The settlements are seen as either self-sufficient economic units (*baseline*) or as partners cooperating within the network of neighbouring settlements (*alternative scenarios*). The reconstruction of the settlement structure and exploration of its complexity represents two sides of the same coin.

3.1   Background

Current archaeological evidence can lead to different ideas: (a) clusters of smaller settlements around agglomerations, (b) networks of settlements without any site with seemingly central function (Fig. 1). Therefore we may interpret the settlement network either as bipolar (village settlements and agglomerations) or with several more or less complex centres. However, the new findings in the field such as structural processes behind the circulation of goods (Thér-Mangel 2014), distribution of the coin finds (Militký 2011) and luxury materials such as glass suggest rather more complex structure of the settlements than what appears from the mere evaluation of the settlement pattern. This structure is becoming more complex during the middle/late Iron Age.

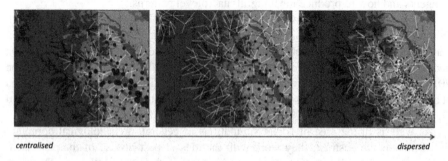

centralised   dispersed

Fig. 1. Different level of centralization/dispersal of settlements: nodes represent settlements, links connect parent-child pairs of settlements

Archaeological evidence (map of known settlements) is a source of fragmented, uncertain data on the original network of settlements. With respect to the existence of Staré Hradisko agglomeration, there are four categories of sites:

- abandoned before the agglomeration was founded,
- established simultaneously with the agglomeration,
- continuous from the earlier period,
- undated.

These four types of nodes of incomplete network are basis for our model, together with GIS data (primary and secondary map layers, see Fig. 2) that describe overall characteristics of the landscape in qualitative and quantitative sense (topography, accessibility – friction/cost surface, soil quality, land cover). The environment is defined by the grid of 100 × 100 m cells.

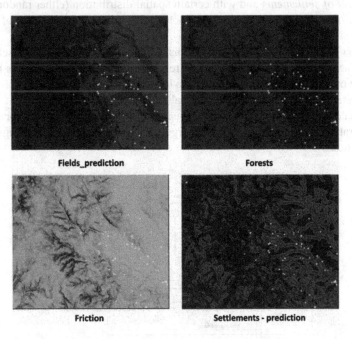

Fig. 2. Region of Staré Hradisko – map layers

The system of settlements is represented by two types of agents: *household agents* are atomic self-subsistent units of approx. 6 inhabitants; *settlement agents* are aggregations of household agents with certain position in the landscape. Directed links from parent settlements to their successors connect nodes and thus capture formation of the network.

Theoretically, the model builds on *scalar stress* (Bandy 2004) and requirements of new organizational structures. These are regarded as general explanatory mechanisms of gradual development of settlement spatial networks and formation of hierarchies with centres, i.e. emerging patterns that are object of our interest. Moreover, ecological, economic and population *potential of the landscape* can be calculated to express the relationship between renewable resources and energetic requirements of settlement of certain size in given location, according to general knowledge of agricultural and economic practices in the late Iron Age. The potential of the landscape is related to the action radius, which is derived from the friction distance in terrain. On one side, the maximum sustainable yield increases with the growing working capacity of the settlement (i.e. number and structure of *household agents*), on the other hand reserves of renewable resources can be exhausted and distant areas cannot be exploited at that stage of technological progress (the law of diminishing returns).

3.2   Inputs and Schedule

UML sequence diagram of model initialization is presented in Fig. 3. Model inputs are:

- Initial size of *population* in the region,
- Initial *set of settlements* and with certain spatial distribution (either random choice of locations with high socio-ecological potential or randomized selection of archaeological sites),
- *Triggers* which conduct the process of dispersion and/or aggregation of settlements (either achieving critical population size regarding the scalar stress value or requiring for one or more key resources in relation to local economic strategy),
- *Parameters* of the dispersion (operational and movement distances),
- Socio-economic *role of the main agglomeration* (attractivity factors for potential immigration, consummer/producer category in terms of the regional agricultural production).

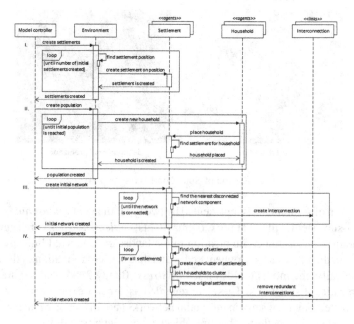

Fig. 3. Model initialization

The process of disperision emerges from the movement of *household agents*. It is natu-
raly assumed that populations move rationally, preferring areas with higher potential
(fertile lowlands, access to water, fuel wood reserves, sustainable, good connection to
the rest of the network):

- If the leaving group is small (couple of *household agents*), either a new settlement is
  expected to be founded closely to the older one, or migrants join existing sites, typically those with some kind of personal or social tights or highly attractive.
- Larger groups tend to move to larger distances.

These general expectations are covered by sets of movement rules which conduct
household agents' behavior. Simulation takes 120 yearly steps. In each step, following
procedures are applied on all *settlement agents* (see also Fig. 4):

- Update of the settlement size using the value of the annual population growth,
- Update of relevant energetic requirements: crop size and fuel wood reserves are
  compared with the population requirements and the estimation of the future production; further versions of model will operate with more constraints,
- Comparison of the settlement requirements with movement triggers and optional
  application of movement procedures: this leads to the dispersion of *settlement agents*
  and changes of their locations, i.e. *household agents* move, join settlements (or found
  new settlements), and *settlement agents* are optionally clustered.

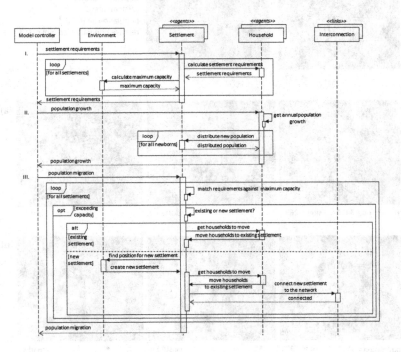

Fig. 4. Simulation schedule

3.3 Sample Experiment

Following experiment illustrates the usability of the model. The initial population of 1000 inhabitants is distributed over 97 sites, arbitrarily chosen from archaeological evidence and with acceptable friction distances among settlements. The movement trigger for settlement is 30 inhabitants, the size of moving group is 30 % of the population (two households, i.e. groups of migrants are small and tend to settle in the neighborhood of the parent site). Two scenarios are taken into account:

– *Scenario a*: migrants prefer foundation of a new settlement,
– *Scenario b*: migrants prefer joining settlement in the neighborhood.

For both scenarios, the same clustering procedure is applicable: if hinterlands of sites overlap, sites are merged and are understood as the establishing of the centre.

The main output of the simulation is the map of settlement network, with data on the gradual formation of this network. Data can be interpreted by domain experts, e.g. it is possible to explore positions of large clusters with topography or to compare degree of nodes with combinations of migration triggers. See Fig. 5 for sample output of the simulation.

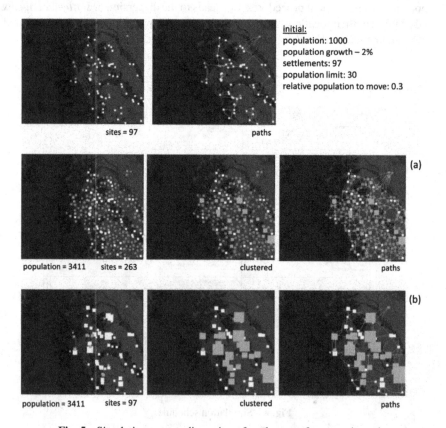

Fig. 5. Simulation output: dispersion of settlements for scenarios a, b

4 Conclusion

We want to enhance agent-based models of subsistence strategies of individual prehistoric agricultural settlements with principles of network modelling and network analysis. This method can provide the dynamic picture of the prehistoric socio-economic landscape. Our further intention is to involve more complex scenarios, i.e. to take into account optional economic specialization of households, different levels of interactions among settlements and different movement triggers. Also, we want to match the logic of the model (especially movement rules and triggers) with data from other locations to get deeper insight into the emergence of prehistoric settlement network patterns.

Acknowledgement. This work was supported by the Czech Science Foundation under Grant P405/12/0926 *"Social modelling as a tool for understanding Celtic society and cultural changes at the end of the Iron Age"* and UHK FIM specific research project 7/2015.

References

Altaweel, M.: Addressing the structures and dynamics of modeled human ecologies. In: Jeffrey, T.C., Emily, M.H. (eds.) Digital Discovery Exploring New Frontiers in Human Heritage, pp. 30–41. Computer Applications and Quantitative Methods in Archaeology, Budapest (2007)

Altaweel, M.: Investigating agricultural sustainability and strategies in northern Mesopotamia: results produced using a socio-ecological modeling approach. J. Archaeol. Sci. **35**, 821–835 (2008)

Angourakis, A., Rondelli, B., Stride, S., et al.: Land use patterns in central Asia. Step 1: the musical chairs model. J. Archaeol. Method Theory **21**, 405–425 (2014)

Axtell, R.L., et al.: Population growth and collapse in a multi-agent model of the kayenta anasazi in long house valley. Proc. Nat. Acad. Sci. **99**(3), 7275–7279 (2002)

Bandy, M.S.: Fissioning, scalar stress, and social evolution in early village societies. Am. Anthropol. **106**(2), 322–333 (2004)

Barton, C.M., Ullah, I.I., Mitasova, H.: Computational modeling and Neolithic socioecological dynamics: a case study from Southwest Asia. Am. Antiq. **75**, 364–386 (2010)

Barton, C.M.: Complexity, social complexity, and modeling. J. Archaeol. Method Theory **21**(2), 306–324 (2014)

Bentley, R.A., Lake, M.W., Shennan, S.J.: Specialization and wealth inequality in a model of a clustered economic network. J. Archaeol. Sci. **32**, 1346–1356 (2005)

Conolly, J., Colledge, S., Shennan, S.: Founder effect, drift, and adaptive change in domestic crop use in early Neolithic Europe. J. Archaeol. Sci. **35**, 2797–2804 (2008)

Crema, E.R.: A simulation model of fission-fusion dynamics and long-term settlement change. J. Archaeol. Method Theory **21**, 385–404 (2014)

Danielisová, A., Olševičová, K., Cimler, R., Machálek, T.: Understanding the iron age economy: sustainability of agricultural practices under stable population growth. In: Wurzer, G., Kowarik, K., Reschreiter, H. (eds.) Agent-based Modeling and Simulation in Archaeology. Advances in Geographic Information Science, pp. 205–241. Springer, Wien (2013)

Del Castillo, F., Barceló, J.A.: Why hunter and gatherers did not die more often? Simulating prehistoric decision making. In: Earl, G., Sly, T., Chrysanthi, A., Murrieta-Flores, P., Papadopoulos, C., Romanowska, I., Wheatley, D. (eds.) Archaeology in the Digital Era, pp. 154–163. Computer Applications and Quantitative Methods in Archaeology, Southampton (2013)

Grant, E. (ed.): Central Places Archaeology and History. University of Sheffield, Sheffield (1986)

Janssen, M.A.: Understanding Artificial Anasazi. J. Artif. Soc. Soc. Simul. 12(4), 13 (2009)

Knappett, C. (ed.): Network Analysis in Archaeology: New Approaches to Regional Interaction. Oxford University Press, Oxford (2013)

Kohler, T.A., Varien, M.D. (eds.): Emergence and Collapse of Early Villages Models of Central Mesa Verde Archaeology. University of California Press, Los Angeles (2012)

Lake, M.W.: Trends in archaeological simulation. J. Archaeol. Method Theory 21, 258–287 (2014)

Lake, M.: Computer Simulation of mesolithic foraging? In: Gumerman, G.J., Kohler, T.A. (eds.) Dynamics in Human and Primate Societies: Agent-Based Modeling of Social and Spatial Processes, pp. 107–143. Oxford University Press, New York (2000)

Lake, M.W.: The uncertain future of simulating the past. In: Costopoulos, A., Lake, M.W. (eds.) Simulating the Change Archaeology into the Twenty-First Century, pp. 12–20. University of Utah Press, Salt Lake City (2010)

Lake, M.W., Crema, E.R.: The cultural evolution of adaptive-trait diversity when resources are uncertain and finite. Adv. Complex Syst. 19, 1150013 (2012)

Madella, M., Rondelli, B., Lancelotti, C., et al.: Introduction to simulating the past. Archaeol. Method Theory 21, 251–257 (2014)

Machálek, T., Cimler, R., Olševičová, K., Danielisová, A.: Fuzzy methods in land use modeling for archaeology. Math. Methods Econ. 2, 536–542 (2013)

Meijers, E.: From central place to network model: Theory and evidence of a paradigm change. Tijdschrift voor Economische en Soc. Geogr. 98, 245–259 (2007)

Militký, J.: Nejstarší středoevropské mince – vzestup a pád keltské civilizace ve střední Evropě z pohledu numismatiky. *Kolaps a regenerace: cesty civilizací a kultur. Minulost, současnost a budoucnost komplexních společností*, Praha, pp. 139–172 (2011)

Nakoinz, O.: Concepts of central place research in archaeology. landscapes and human development: the contribution of european archaeology. In: Proceedings of the International Workshop "Socio-Environmental Dynamics over the Last 12 000 Years: The Creation of Landscapes" Kiel, pp. 251–264 (2010)

Nakoinz, O.: Models of centrality. J. Ancient Stud. Spec. 3, 217–223 (2012)

Olševičová, K., Cimler, R., Machálek, T.: Agent-based model of celtic population growth: NetLogo and python. In: Nguyen NT, A., Trawiński B, B., katarzyniak, R., Jo, G.-S. (eds.) Advanced Methods for Computational Collective Intelligence, Studies in Computational Intelligence, pp. 135–143. Springer, Berlin (2012)

Östeborn, P., Gerding, H.: Network analysis of archaeological data: a systematic approach. J. Archaeol. Sci. 46, 75–88 (2014)

Powel, A.S., Shennan, S.J., Thomas, M.G.: Late pleistocene demography and the appearance of modern human behavior. Science 324, 1298–1301 (2009)

Premo, L.: Exploring behavioral terra incognita with archaeological agent-based models. Beyond Illustration: 2D and 3D Technologies as Tools of Discovery in Archaeology. BAR International Series 1805, 46–56 (2008)

Premo, L.: Equifinality and explanation: the role of agent-based modeling in postpositivist archaeology. In: Costopoulos, A., Lake, M.W. (eds.) Simulating the Change Archaeology into the Twenty-First Century, pp. 28–37. University of Utah Press, Salt Lake City (2010)

Salgado, M., Noguera, J.A., Miguel, F.: Modelling cooperation mechanisms: some conceptual issues. J. Archaeol. Method Theory **21**, 325–342 (2014)

Shennan, S.: The spread of farming into central europe ind its consequences: evolutionary models. In: Kohler, T.A., van der Leeuw, S.E. (eds.) The Model-Based Archaeology of Socionatural Systems, pp. 141–156. Santa Fe, New Mexico (2007)

Thér, R., Mangel, R.: Inovace a specializace v hrnčířském řemesle v době laténské: model vývoje forem organizace výroby. *Archeologické Rozhledy* LXVI, pp. 3–39 (2014)

van der Vaart, E., de Boer, B., Hankel, A., Verheij, B.: Agents Adopting Agriculture:Modeling the Agricultural Transition. In: Nolfi, Stefano, Baldassarre, Gianluca, Calabretta, Raffaele, Hallam, John C.T., Marocco, Davide, Meyer, Jean-Arcady, Miglino, Orazio, Parisi, Domenico (eds.) SAB 2006. LNCS (LNAI), vol. 4095, pp. 750–761. Springer, Heidelberg (2006)

Wainwright, J.: Can modelling enable us to understand the rôle of humans in landscape evolution? Geoforum **39**, 659–674 (2008)

Workshop on Intelligent Systems
for Context-Based Information Fusion

Costs of Protecting Privacy in Agent Trust Relationships

Mar Lopez$^{(\boxtimes)}$, Javier Carbo, and Jose M. Molina

Computer Science Department, Universidad Carlos III de Madrid,
Campus de Colmenarejo, Madrid, Spain
{mariamar.lopez,javier.carbo,jose.molina}@uc3m.es

Abstract. In this paper we remarked the relevance of using of privacy-protection measures in trust models, since them imply conscious exchanges of opinions about third parties. Additionally to the already published description of the extra message exchanges that would protect privacy in a agent-mediated trust domain as ART testbed, we evaluate (through estimated weights) the communication and computation cost of these additional message exchanges at the level of their interactions. Although the effects of introducing them on the accuracy of trust valuations could also be considered in future works, in this contribution we focus our attention in an approach based on the weight of the information brought by an interaction.

1 Introduction

While in closed traditional systems, a central trusting entity may ensure privacy through an exhaustive control of identities and information exchanges, in electronic, distributed and open systems this trusting responsibility lies with participants. These is the case of agent systems [12]. Trusting agent systems challenge privacy in two ways: agents are able to collect large and detailed information and they can integrate, interpret and classify it [14]. Since agents were created to provide personalized services, these features can not be removed but they have to be reviewed according to the data protection law, specifically under the light of the Directive of Data Protection 95/46 [17].

The aim of this article is to analyze the communication and computational cost of proposing privacy protecting measures that can be adopted, without significantly removing the benefits of the assumed autonomy of agents. Therefore, we look forward computer-based auto regulatory control instead of solutions based on law restriction and prohibition [18].

Trust is a relevant issue present in any social relationship, even when such relationship is distant and with electronic means. It is a fact the increasing interest to the computer scientist about how trust is acquired and maintained. Delegation of control in distributed and open systems needs that multiple and human agents collaborate and interact among themselves. Design of a trust model needs to deploy a privacy risk analysis considering social and organizational content. When human users are represented by autonomous agents that act on behalf of

J. Bajo et al. (Eds.): PAAMS 2015 Workshops, CCIS 524, pp. 179–190, 2015.
DOI: 10.1007/978-3-319-19033-4_15

them, the interests of these users have to be taken in consideration in the decisions and relationships held by these agents. In this case, a trust model is applied by autonomous agents in two ways: searching trustworthy partners and as an incentive/punishment mechanism to prevent dishonest behaviors. The reputational image of such agents could be computed in a centralized way as a global property by a sole entity (as many actual commercial applications do [6]), but it implies a loss in personalization and privacy.

Therefore we assume (as many researchers in Distributed AI) that each member of a society of agents is in charge of computing the reputation of all other agents that belong to this society. Many trust models have been proposed and they are very different among them [19]. Witness information can be considered the most complex one involved in trust models, specifically the way it is managed. Witness information is the information that an agent (we will call it in advance first agent) receives from a second agent about a third one. Witness information, also called indirect information or word-of-mouth, can be based on the direct experiences of the second agent or it can be based on indirect information from other agents (the so called referrals). In this case, in many trust models, second agents just share the reputational image (a joint computation of several direct experiences and witness information) of the third agent; this is the classic way to do it. But some models include in the witness information about the third agents also the referrals of this indirect information, forming then a chain of trust [7,21]. Therefore privacy of how third party agents behaved with second agents is involved in "classic" witness information but privacy problems become more extended in the case of trust models that include referrals identity. Both, third party agents and referrals, are then concerned by the disclosure of their behavior that could be violating the intention of those agents of exchanging its knowledge just to receptors (second agents) and not to any other agent (first agents). In this case, these agents do not share it freely and publicly, and the knowledge of these opinions may have future consequences over their acts in the society as we will show in the domain example of Sect. 3. Therefore it is necessary established privacy limitations when agents are sharing such information.

2   Adapting Trust Models to Protect Privacy

In order to define conditions of privacy protection for personal information in trust models, it is necessary to identify (according to the European Directive [17] which legal conditions trust models have to satisfy related to Privacy. The communications involved in the application of trust models must legally guarantee the exercise the compliance of the following rights:

1. Participating agents have to be informed that other agents will collect (trust opinions) personal data about them.
2. Participating agents have to know the name of other agents that will collect such personal data, what the processing is going to be used for, to whom your data may be transferred. They have to receive this information whether the data was obtained directly or indirectly.

3. Participating agents are entitled to ask other agents if these other agents are processing personal data about them;
4. Participating agents are entitled to receive a copy of this personal data in intelligible form;
5. Participating agents are entitled to ask for the deletion, blocking or erasing of the data.
6. Considering that decisions based on such personal data can significantly affect other agents, participating agents must adopt suitable safeguards, such as giving you the opportunity to discuss the thinking behind them, for instance claiming decisions based on inaccurate data.

To integrate these privacy rights, we propose to include additional message exchanges in the protocols of trusting relationships that would act as control mechanisms that allow trust model to satisfy these privacy rights derived from the European Directive. These additional message exchanges that we proposed in [3] are:

1. An only way communication: A single message informing to each third agent about the future collection of opinions about them (what are the opinions be used).
2. A pair of additional messages: corresponding to a negotiation protocol (a proposal followed by a counterproposal) on whom these opinions may be propagated (the potential first agents in our notation). Although agents collecting opinions (the role of second agents) send an initial proposal (to everyone, to a list of possible first agents, or to none) about the two types of possible opinion transmission (direct or indirect) the final decision has to correspond to the third agents, either considering or ignoring the proposal of second agents. We also define an additional privacy constraint to each possible first agent according to the similarity of security policies applied in the communication, in order to limit the possibility of unconscious disclosure of opinions. The corresponding final decision takes then the form of a privacy statement.
3. Third agents will request any other collecting agents (first agents) if they are already collecting information about them and what is this information. Two messages are then implicated: one requesting the information and the corresponding response.
4. An argumentative dialog between second and third agents about the reasons behind the collected and propagated opinions with arguments about the inaccuracy of such decisions. This sequence of messages may conclude into a final agreement or with a disagreement.
5. A single message ordering the deletion or blocking of the already collected opinions by a third agent will then be sent in case of disagreement.

3 Application of Privacy Protection to ART Testbed Domain

In the application of Agent Reputation and Trust (ART) in testbed domain [8], the agents act as painting appraisers. Each agent has high expertise appraising paintings on some given eras but not in the others. Each agent requires the cooperation of other agents to appraise paintings belonging to eras with own low expertise. The real goal of this ART game is the knowledge and cooperation of each agent with complementary agents who has high expertise in the eras with own low expertise. The criteria by which each agent decides what agents are interesting partners in this ART domain are: honest and cooperative attitude, valuable knowledge about others and a complementary expertise in the eras. A general incentive mechanism for providing truthful opinions by these agents is being honest and cooperative with the request from any other agent. In this ART game, we considered that a gaining strategy would be to limit the propagation of the knowledge about others to those agents that are of our interests (complementary expertise) while avoiding such knowledge to reach agents who are our natural competitors [11]. We obtain the roles, illocutions and relationships corresponding to ART interactions from previous works of some of the authors moving the adhoc ART testbed platform to JADE environment [15]. Such protocols correspond to those protocols involved in ART testbed which were formalized in a FIPA-compliant way in another previous publication from some of the authors [2].

We have used the ART application domain to define the additional messages required to comply the corresponding privacy requirements of the five types defined before in the previous section. These messages include the corresponding concepts, predicates and actions used to define the message contents. Therefore, we proposed and implemented in [3] the next five privacy-preserving (FIPA-compliant) protocols applied to ART-testbed that we have implemented in JADE [1]:

1. A message with INFORM as FIPA performative, and with an IsCollecting predicate as content. The properties of this predicate have the next concepts as values: Who (Appraiser Agent), On (Era), Value (Reputation).
2. A pair of messages: The first one with a PROPOSE performative and a StatesPrivacy action as content. The concepts as values of this predicate are: Who (Appraiser Agent), On (Era), Whom (None/All/Appraiser Agent), Type (Indirection Level), How (Security Policy). The values of Indirection Level concept are: Direct (direct experiences) and Indirect (witness information). In this case, Security Policy would describe the rules to be applied into cryptographic algorithms of communications. The corresponding response to this PROPOSE message is a second message that may be an ACCEPT PROPOSAL or an REJECT PROPOSAL (in this case the message will include a StatesPrivacy action as content in order to be considered a counterproposal).
3. A pair of messages: The first one with QUERY-REF as FIPA performative with an Is Collecting predicate as a content, where property Value has a void Concept associated. The second message is an INFORM-REF performative with the value property of "'Is Collecting"' predicate fulfilled with the actual Reputation collected.
4. A message with REQUEST as FIPA performative, and with Blocking or Deleting action as content. The properties of this predicate are: Who (Appraiser Agent), On (Era), Value (Reputation). In the response message, the other agent has to answer with an AGREE performative.

5. A sequence of messages: The first one from an initiator agent with QUERY-REF as FIPA performative with a '"Justification"' predicate as a content and with the next properties: Who (Appraiser Agent), On (Era), Value (Reputation), From (Appraiser Agent), Type (Indirection Level), Initial Value. The properties From, Type and Initial Value have a void Concept associated that the corresponding response (second message) INFORM-REF message would fulfill with the Agent source of such argued reputation value the way this reputation value was collected (direct vs. indirect) and the value originally sent by this source agent. An additional REQUEST message might take place from the initiator agent to suggest the other agent to rectify the reputation value collected from the source agent. This REQUEST message includes a Rectifying action that includes the real and appraised value of the painting corresponding to such interaction. To motivate such rectification, the initiator agent would include the details of the direct interactions (if it really took place) with such source agent. Finally, the other agent could answer with a REFUSE of either an AGREE performative in the response message.

Once the additional message exchanges to be applied in the ART application domain to protect legally privacy were defined by us in [3], we now have to evaluate how much extra cost these interactions add (the real contribution of this paper).

4   Evaluation of Interactions Cost in Alternative Agent Systems

The evaluation of alternative agent systems may be done through different ways, for instance using the architectural style [5]; or according to software engineering criteria applied into agent-oriented methodologies [10,16] or through the estimation of how much complex are the involved agent interactions [13]. This last approach is the one we chose to evaluate the privacy protection in trust agent systems. We follow the orientation defined in [13] who is based in the idea of estimating with a weight the effect of an interaction unit (message) in the receptor. As it is just an estimation has some limitations that can introduce some noise in the evaluation results: first, the effects of a given message in an agent system may not be equivalent in another agent system. Second protocols may include message that are received but cause no effect at all. Assuming both circumstances is a prerequisite to apply this evaluation method.

According to [13], we have to start classifying received messages into categories with an expected similar weight. Then, we have to decide a weight value which would correspond to a message according to its category. Next we will consider the effects of the message in the receptor. In other words, we estimate how many changes in the internal state of the agents were caused and the cost of computing the corresponding decisions (the actions that will be handled by the receptor agent as consequence of this received message). We have previously applied this evaluation method to compare two alternative agent architectures in an ambient intelligence domain [20].

In [9] four possible interaction types were considered: present, request, answer, and inform. But as we implemented in JADE the interactions that provide privacy between trusting agents in ART testbed, and since JADE is FIPA-compliant, we have an easily already-defined classification: messages are already classified into the categories corresponding to FIPA performatives.

Once a message classification is given, we have to define several functions:

– A function that gives a weight to the message according to its category in a domain-independent way. We will call such function $Weightingtypes$ 1.

$$Weightingtypes = Message_{type} \rightarrow \text{weight value} \qquad (1)$$

– A function that estimates the effects of a message in the receptor. This function evaluates the cost of managing such particular message. It is the sum of two subfunctions: one that evaluates the scope and complexity of the decision on the possible courses of action to take, $Decisions$ 3 and another one that evaluates the scope and complexity of the internal changes of state in the agent, $State$ 2. The function $State$ associates a value to the variation of the internal state (caused by message received), for instance in rule-based systems that could be: number of facts to be modified/included/excluded. We then consider that $State$ function has two parameters: So the set of original internal states for the agent while Sf is the set of final internal states. The quantification of the change in state characteristics is then domain dependent.

$$State = So \times Sf \rightarrow \# \text{of state characteristics that changed} \qquad (2)$$

Concerning $Decisions$, this function gives an estimated weight to the complexity of the actions triggered by the reception of the message. Again, as with $State$ function, quantifying the triggered actions depends on the application domain.

$$Decisions = Actions \rightarrow \sum \text{weights of triggered actions} \qquad (3)$$

Therefore the interaction costs is computed as the sum of these three elements: weights of received messages by category, number of of state characteristics that changed, and weights of the triggered actions taken. We have now to define the domain dependent function components and then to apply the corresponding computation in order to conclude a final estimation of the interaction costs.

4.1   Weights by Message FIPA Category: Function $WeightingTypes$

In order to decide adhoc numerical values to the message categories, as [9] did (for their proposed 4 categories: present, request, answer and inform) we focus for each message category (with domain independence) on the existence of an expected response, and on the existence of a possible change of state in the receiver. Assuming an interaction unit has at least a weight of 1, each one of these two circumstances would increase by 1 the corresponding weight of such message category. Now we proceed to give values to each FIPA performative involved in the ART testbed interactions. To do it we consider the usual chain of performatives that FIPA protocols suggested in its specifications [4]. We consider three possible values: No response (no), Posible response (maybe), Response (yes), and in order to quantify them we assign the corresponding values of 1, 2 and 3 to these labels.

- INFORM: no 1, since an informing message has not to generate any answer.
- PROPOSE: yes 3, since it has to generate an answer (ACCEPT or REJECT PROPOSAL).
- ACCEPT PROPOSAL: no 1, since it has not to generate any answer.
- REJECT PROPOSAL: maybe 2 since it probably has to generate an additional alternative PROPOSAL.
- QUERY: yes 3 since it has to generate a INFORM response message.
- REQUEST: yes 3 since it has to generate a REFUSE or AGREE response message.
- AGREE: yes 3 since it has to generate an informing response with the results of the requested action.
- REFUSE: maybe 2 since it probably has to generate an additional alternative REQUEST.

4.2   Weights by Changes in Internal States of ART Trusting Agents: Function *State*

Next we have to evaluate the function *State* that computes the variation of internal state caused by a received message. In our ART domain the consequences of the messages in terms of changes in the internal state depends in some level to the particular implementation of ART agents, and therefore we can only logically estimate it. Next we explain the justification of the given weight (low, medium and high) to each of them according to the logic of this particular trusting domain:

1. The first protecting privacy protocol consists of a message informing to each third agent about the future collection of opinions about them. The internal state of the receiver agent would just record that information. So it would be a low change of internal state.
2. The second protecting privacy protocol consists of a proposal of privacy statement to the receiver agent who wants to collect opinions about the sender agent and the corresponding acceptance/rejection response. The privacy statement to be recorded when the proposal becomes accepted should include a list of agents to share with them such opinions, the two types of possible opinion transmission (direct or indirect) and the security policies applied in the communication. Therefore we consider that such size of information justifies a high weight, so it would be a high change of internal state.
3. The third protecting privacy protocol consists of a sender agent querying the receiver agent if the receiver is already collecting information about the

sender (and what is this information) and the corresponding inform response. The informing response about the collected opinions should include a list of them, so we consider that such size of information justifies a medium weight, therefore it would be a medium change of internal state.

4. The forth protecting privacy protocol consists of a sender agent requesting to the receiver the deletion or blocking of the already collected opinions about the sender and the corresponding accept/refuse message. The request would involve a medium level of changes in the internal state of the receiver (the set of opinions to be deleted).

5. Finally the fifth protocol consists of a sender agent querying about the reasons behind the propagated opinions (in which opinions/direct interactions are they based) with the corresponding inform response. The first query and inform messages do not involve relevant changes of internal state, and the same applies to the afterward request message of rectification, but the final AGREE message accepting such modification in the opinions (to be propagated in the future) of the sender agent involves a medium level of changes.

In order to quantify such low, medium and high level of changes in the internal state of the agents we assign the corresponding values of 1, 2 and 3, which also is the range of values of function *Weightingtypes*.

Finally we need to define *Decisions* function that estimates the level of actions (number and complexity) triggered by the reception of the messages. Therefore each type of actions should have a weight. The set of actions involved in our agent system are internal since the communicative responses to the given message were already considered by function *Weightingtypes*. The internal actions are the internal computations required to take the decisions posed by the reception of the message. Again we classify the weight of them in three categories: low, medium and high with the same corresponding values of functions *State* and *Weightingtypes*. We are going to use domain information to quantify it although specific values would depend on the particular implementation of each ART agent. Next we evaluate each of the five privacy protecting protocols according to the internal and external actions caused by the received message:

1. The first protecting privacy protocol consists of a message informing to each third agent about the future collection of opinions about them. The internal reasoning of the receiver agent would be minimal. So, it would be a low change of internal reasoning.

2. The second protecting privacy protocol consists of a proposal of privacy statement to the receiver agent who wants to collect opinions about the sender agent and the corresponding acceptance/rejection response. The privacy statement includes a list of agents to share with them such opinions, the two types of possible opinion transmission (direct or indirect) and the security policies applied in the communication. Therefore we consider that the evaluation of such privacy agreement requires a high level of computation due to its complexity, so, evaluating it at the reception of the propose message would imply a high level of internal reasoning. Additionally since the reject

proposal message would include an alternative privacy statement that has to be interpreted and considered by the receiver of the reject proposal then the reception of the proposal message would imply a high level of internal reasoning.

3. The third protecting privacy protocol consists of a sender agent querying the receiver agent if the receiver is already collecting information about the sender (and what is this information) and the corresponding inform response. Addressing such query is a simple collection of the recorded opinions and has a low level of internal reasoning.

4. The forth protecting privacy protocol consists of a sender agent requesting to the receiver the deletion or blocking of the already collected opinions about the sender and the corresponding accept/refuse message. The corresponding decision to be taken (to accept the deletion or not) would involve a low level of internal reasoning of the receiver.

5. Finally the fifth protocol consists of a sender agent querying about the reasons behind the propagated opinions (in which opinions/direct interactions are they based) with the corresponding inform response. The first query message involve a medium reasoning, and the same applies to the request of rectification, but the final accepting/rejecting messages involve a low level of reasoning.

In order to aggregate all these weights, we have to consider the frequency of the protocols:

1. We consider that this informing message is often going to be sent to all participant agents (let it note it as n agents) at the beginning of each ART testbed game if the sender agent behaves in a (privacy-related) honest way. So, it would be n times.

2. This protocol to establish a privacy-agreement is going to be sent to all participant agents (let it note it as n agents) at the beginning of each ART testbed game.

3. The protocol to request the information collected about the initiator agent would take place occasionally (m times, where $m \ll n$) when an agent suspects that some misinformation about the initiator agent is been propagated by the other agent.

4. The protocol to request the blocking/deletion of opinions about an agent would take place rarely (o times, where $o \ll m$) since this message should be sent when a misuse or abuse was detected by the sender agent and we assume a extended (privacy-related) honest behaviour of a majority of the participant agents.

5. The protocol to argue about the reasons behind a propagated opinion about the initiator agent would take place rarely (o times), since we assume that considering a majority of honest behaviour, such number of opinions that have to be rectified would be just a few of them.

Now we can aggregate all these weights into the final values of extra costs of the privacy protecting interaction as it is shown in Table 1, where n m and

Table 1. Final weights of agents interactions corresponding to protecting privacy protocol 1

Message #	Message type	Answers	State	Decisions	Times	Final weight
1	INFORM	no (1)	low (1)	low (1)	n	$(1+1+2)$ n $= 4$ n
2a	PROPOSE	yes (3)	low (1)	high (3)	n	$(3+1+3)$ n $= 7$ n
2b	ACCEPT PROPOSAL	no (1)	high (3)	low (1)	n/2	$(1+3+1)$ n $/ 2 = 5$ n
2b	REJECT PROPOSAL	maybe (2)	low (1)	high (3)	n/2	$(2+1+3)$ n $/ 2 = 3$ n
3a	QUERY	yes (3)	low (1)	low (1)	m	$(3+1+1)$ m $= 5$ m
3b	INFORM	no(1)	medium (2)	low (1)	m	$(1+2+1)$ m $= 4$ m
4a	REQUEST	yes (3)	medium (2)	low (1)	o	$(3+2+1)$ o $= 6$ o
4b	AGREE	yes (3)	low (1)	low (1)	m	$(3+1+1)$ o $= 5$ o
5a	QUERY	yes (3)	low (1)	medium (2)	o	$(3+1+2)$ o $= 6$ o
5b	INFORM	no (1)	medium (2)	medium (2)	o	$(1+2+2)$ o $= 5$ o
5c	REQUEST	yes (3)	low (1)	low (1)	o	$(3+1+1)$ o $=) 5$ o
5d	AGREE	yes (3)	medium (2)	low (1)	o/2	$(3+2+1)$ o $/2 = 3$ o
5d	REFUSE	maybe (2)	low (1)	low (1)	o/2	$(2+1+1)$ o $/2 = 2$ o

o stands for the estimated times the protocols are expected to take place, and the number of the messages correspond to those of the five protocols mentioned before in alphabetical order according to the order of execution inside the protocol. The row entitled "'Answers"' corresponds to the *Weightingtypes* function.

We can observe relevant differences between the privacy protecting protocols, and the obvious dependance of the costs to the values of n, m and o, that logically if the behaviour of agents is not widely honest the values of m and o could be close to n, and the extra costs of protecting privacy would considerably increase.

5   Conclusions

In this paper we try to overcome part of the reticence to apply privacy protection measures in agent systems. According to the current European law requirement, we had previously defined five privacy protection protocols to be applied in agent-mediated trust systems such as the ART testbed domain. They were also implemented as interaction protocols with JADE in the ART testbed domain in our previous works. But since we think that the generalized no-use of them relies upon the perception of the high costs of using them (in terms of trust accuracy and of communication and computational costs), we propose in our research to address publicly both issues to promote privacy protection in trusting agent systems. A fair comparison and specific evaluation of agent systems is a difficult task due to the particular features of decentralization, parallelism and heterogeneity of these systems. From the research conducted to address this issue, we chose an evaluation method based on the estimation of interactions between agents. In this paper, we have defined the corresponding estimation functions to be applied in the ART testbed domain according to this evaluation method. Our approach allowed us to experience the problems of giving values to such weights that are obviously adhoc. With them we evaluate the extra costs (in terms of communications and computation overhead) of protecting privacy in the ART testbed games. Although as any estimated evaluation, the conclusions deduced from the results can not be conclusive, this approach opens a way to prove the viability of protecting privacy through the quantification of the high perceiving costs of applying privacy. As future work we would like to apply these same evaluation functions to all the communication protocols of ART testbed in order to estimate the relative cost of applying privacy related to the total costs of running an ART testbed game. Finally, it is also our future intention to address the cost of protecting privacy in terms of trust accuracy.

Acknowledgements. This work was supported in part by Projects MINECO TEC2012-37832-C02-01, CICYT TEC2011-28626-C02-02, CAM CONTEXTS (S2009/TIC-1485).

References

1. Bellifemine, F.L., Caire, G., Greenwood, D.: Developing Multi-Agent Systems with JADE (Wiley Series in Agent Technology). John Wiley & Sons (2007)
2. Carbo, J., Molina, J.M.: A jade-based art-inspired ontology and protocols for handling trust and reputation. In: Ninth International Conference on Intelligent Systems Design and Applications, ISDA. pp. 300–305 (2009)
3. Carbo, J., Pedraza, J., Lopez, M., Molina, J.M.: Privacy protection in trust models for agent societies. In: de la Puerta, J.G., Ferreira, I.G., Bringas, P.G., Klett, F., Abraham, A., de Carvalho, A.C.P.L.F., Herrero, A., Baruque, B., Quintián, H., Corchado, E. (eds.) International Joint Conference SOCO'14-CISIS'14-ICEUTE'14. AISC, vol. 299, pp. 135–144. Springer, Heidelberg (2014)
4. Committees, F.T.: Foundations for Intelligent Phisical Agents Specifications. Geneve, Switzerland (1997)
5. Davidsson, P., Johansson, S., Svahnberg, M.: Characterization and evaluation of multi-agent system architectural styles. In: Garcia, A., Choren, R., Lucena, C., Giorgini, P., Holvoet, T., Romanovsky, A. (eds.) SELMAS 2005. LNCS, vol. 3914, pp. 179–188. Springer, Heidelberg (2006)
6. Dellarocas, C.: The digitization of word of mouth: promise and challenges of online feedback mechanisms. Manag. Sci. **49**, 1407–1424 (2003)
7. Esfandiari, B., Chandrasekharan, S.: On how agents make friends: mechanisms for trust acquisition. In: Proceedings of the Fourth Workshop on Deception, Fraud and Trust in Agent Societies, pp. 27–34 (2001)
8. Fullam, K., Klos, T., Muller, G., Sabater, J., Schlosser, A., Topol, Z., Barber, K.S., Rosenschein, J., Vercouter, L., Voss, M.: A specification of the agent reputation and trust (art) testbed: experimentation and competition for trust in agent societies. In: The Fourth International Joint Conference on Autonomous Agents and Multiagent Systems (AAMAS-2005), pp. 512–518 (2005)
9. Gaspar, G.: Communication and belief changes in a society of agents: towards a formal model of autonomous agent, d.a.i. 2, 1991. In: Descentralized A. I. 2. pp. 245–255. Elsevier Science, Amsterdam (1991)
10. Giunchiglia, F., Mylopoulos, J., Perini, A.: The tropos software development methodology: processes, models and diagrams. In: Proceedings of the First International Joint Conference on Autonomous Agents and Multiagent Systems, pp. 63–74. ACM Press (2002)

11. Gómez, M., Carbo, J., Benac-Earle, C.: Honesty and trust revisited: the advantages of being neutral about other's cognitive models. Auton. Agents Multi-Agent Syst. **15**(3), 313–335 (2007)
12. Calvo-Rolle, J.L., Corchado, E.: A bio-inspired knowledge system for improving combined cycle plant control tuning. Neurocomputing **126**, 95–105 (2014)
13. Joumaa, H., Demazeau, Y., Vincent, J.: Evaluation of multi-agent systems: the case of interaction. In: 3rd International Conference on Information and Communication Technologies: From Theory to Applications, pp. 1–6. IEEE (2008)
14. Wozniak, M., Graa, M., Corchadob, E.: A survey of multiple classifier systems as hybrid systems. Inf. Fusion **16**, 3–17 (2014)
15. Moya, J., Carbo, J.: Distributing art agents with JADE. In: 10th European Workshop on Multi-Agent Systems, EUMAS (2012)
16. Bresciani, P., Giorgini, P., Giunchiglia, F., Mylopoulos, J., Perini, A.: TROPOS: an agent-oriented software development methodology. J. Auton. Agent. Multi-Agent Syst. **8**(3), 203–236 (2004)
17. Parliament, E.: Directive 95/46/ec of the european parliament and of the council of 24 october 1995 on the protection of individuals with regard to the processing of personal data and on the free movement of such data, October 1995. http://eur-lex.europa.eu/LexUriServ/LexUriServ.do?uri=CELEX:31995L0046:en:HTML
18. Pedraza, J., Patricio, M.A., de Ass, A., Molina, J.: Privacy-by-design rules in face recognition system. Neurocomputing **109**, 49–55 (2013)
19. Sabater-Mir, J., Sierra, C.: Review on computational trust and reputation models. Artif. Intel. Rev. **24**, 33–60 (2005)
20. Sanchez-Pi, N., Griol, D., Carbo, J., Molina, J.M.: Evaluating interaction of MAS providing context-aware services. In: O'Shea, J., Nguyen, N.T., Crockett, K., Howlett, R.J., Jain, L.C. (eds.) KES-AMSTA 2011. LNCS, vol. 6682, pp. 373–382. Springer, Heidelberg (2011)
21. Yu, B., Singh, M.P.: An evidential model of distributed reputation management. In: Proceedings of First International Joint Conference on Autonomous Agents and Multiagent Systems, pp. 294–301. ACM Press (2002)

Modeling Human-Machine Interaction
by Means of a Sample Selection Method

Ikram Chairi, David Griol[(✉)], and José Manuel Molina

Computer Science Department, Carlos III University of Madrid,
Avda. de la Universidad, 30, 28911 Leganés, Spain
{ikram.chairi,david.griol,josemanuel.molina}@uc3m.es

Abstract. This paper presents a practical application of Sample Selection techniques to model the process of selecting the next system response of a conversational agent. Our proposal deals with the important problem of imbalanced training data that is usually present in the selected application domain. This process is modeled as a classification task that takes the dialog history as input, and selects the next system response as output. **Our proposal improves the classifier's performance** by automatically selecting examples that are difficult to classify during the training phase, considering the criteria of proximity to the border and the typicality of the examples. We present a practical application of this technique for a conversational agent providing railway information. **Simulation results support the usefulness of the proposed approach to provide the better selection of the responses of the conversational agent.**

Keywords: Sample Selection · Imbalanced data · Clustering · Human-Machine interfaces · Conversational agents · Spoken interaction

1 Introduction

Classical learning algorithms generally use all the available training set to adjust their parameters without taking into account the contribution of every sample in the training, then considering that all the samples have the same contribution in the definition of the borders between the different classes. However, in practical cases, in which the training data is oversized, the use of all training set is computationally expensive, or can prevent the training to converge to an acceptable minimum.

At the end of 80's Sample Selection techniques (SS) emerged to deal with those problems [1, 2]. These techniques took as point of practices the capacity of the classifier to learn from examples, which was considered as a beginning of a line of works that gave fruitful results in several application fields [3].

The basis of these techniques is that the convergence of learning will be accelerated when a selected sample are presented in learning than a random one [4]. SS methods consist of, implicitly, dividing the training set into samples that contribute to the definition of the class borders (those that will be used to update the weights of the classifier during training), named "critical" samples, and other redundant ones that do not give any information during the training process.

© Springer International Publishing Switzerland 2015
J. Bajo et al. (Eds.): PAAMS 2015 Workshops, CCIS 524, pp. 191–200, 2015.
DOI: 10.1007/978-3-319-19033-4_16

However, SS techniques have some limitations. The most important one is related to the problem of selecting samples which are "critical". This choice will depend, in general, on the classifier used, and the data distribution [1].

Denker and Huyser show that for a carefully designed multilayer perceptron (MLP) architecture, a training set formed only by examples near the border is enough to ensure a good generalization [2, 3]. In [4] a criterion based on the nearest neighbor is used to distinguish examples that generate confusion (i.e., a sample that has a nearest neighbor belonging from other class is probably near to the border). Zhang proposed a SS method named Incremental Selection, in which the sample of training is growing by the learning [5, 6]. Cachin proposed another method of SS named "Pedagogical Pattern Selection Strategies" [7], based on selection of samples having high error.

Recent works has used SS techniques as a method of under-sampling to deal with the problem of imbalance between classes: The generalization of a classifier is then improved by eliminating the least contributed samples in majority class for the definition of the borderline, then obtaining balance between classes [8–10].

This paper presents an application of SS techniques for the selection of the next system response in conversational agents [11]. Our proposal considers the codification of the complete dialog history until the current moment as an input of a classification process, which decides the next system response of the conversational agent. The main benefits of our proposal are based on the very important problem of imbalance training data between classes (i.e., system responses) that is usually present in this application domain.

Thus, the main objective is to improve the prediction using a selected sample for the training of the classifier. Technically speaking, the proposed method applies a focused under-sampling on the training data, in order to adjust the parameters of a Multi-Layer Perceptron (MLP) so as to increase the accuracy. To properly evaluate the effectiveness of our study, we used the assessment metrics that are adapted to imbalanced data distribution such as the true positive rate.

The rest of the paper is organized as follows. In Sect. 2, we describe in details our proposed method. In Sect. 3, we present a practical application of the approach on a practical conversational agent providing railway information, and discuss the results. Finally, in Sect. 4, we conclude the paper and outline future work.

2 Proposed Method: Sample Selection Under Constraint of Distance from the Borderline

Most standard algorithms assumes that training sets are perfect, and do not take in consideration the common anomalies that can be founded in real world data [12, 13]. In our approach, we develop a classifier that provides a good generalization when applied on a data presenting a problem of imbalance between classes. For that, we used the principle of SS, as many works has shown that these techniques allows to accelerate the convergence of the learning [4, 9, 14, 15].

The objective is to construct a new training sample that contains the most difficult examples to learn, by applying a focused under-sampling of the majority class. Summing up, besides being small, a desirable training set must be constructed in a smart way: It must represent correctly the class boundaries and distribution.

Figure 1 shows a summary of the different steps of the proposed method.

Fig. 1. Diagram of steps of proposed method

Subsequently, we detail these four steps for getting a critical set of training.

Step1: Clustering of data using Vector quantization
In order to minimize the computational cost, we proceed to carry out a clustering of the data and use the centroids instead of all examples.

Firstly, clustering is realized using Vector Quantization algorithm (VQ). This method is based on the competitive learning paradigm. It works by dividing a large set data into groups having approximately the same number of points closest to them. Each group is represented by its centroïde point [16].

The main problem of this technique is related to the initialization: if a centroïde was initialized in an area where the distribution has a high density of probability, the process could ignore other centers, and the distribution of clusters will not be representative.

Thus, we apply frequency sensitive competitive learning (FSCL) [17], an efficient scheme that avoids initialization problems. In particular, we apply FSCL assigning a number of centroids to each class and using a reinforcing/anti-reinforcing training using the following equation:

$$c_j(k+1) = \begin{cases} c_j(k) + \beta_1(k)\big[x_k - c_j(k)\big] x_k \in C_j \\ c_j(k) - \beta_1(k)\big[x_k - c_j(k)\big] x_k \notin C_j \end{cases} \tag{1}$$

where $\beta_1(k)$ is a contractive learning parameter, C_j is the class of the centroids $c_j(k)$, and x_k is the winner sample, which is selected with the usual FSCL modified distance criterion presented in Eq. (2).

$$j = argmin_m\Big\{N_k\big\|x_k - c_j(k)\big\|^2\Big\} \tag{2}$$

N_k denotes the number of times in which the centroïde $c_j(k)$ was selected.

In order to better represent the distribution of the data, centroids are adjusted using the supervised learning Kohonen's LVQ3 [18].

- If the two closest centroids to a sample x_k are c_i and c_j where c_j correspond to x_k's class and c_j correspond to a different class, the adaptation of the centers are applied as:

$$c_i(k+1) = c_i(k) + \beta_2[x_k - c_i(k)] \tag{3}$$

$$c_j(k+1) = c_j(k) - \beta_2[x_k - c_i(k)] \tag{4}$$

- If the two closest centroids are from the same class than x_k, so the new centers are:

$$c_{i,j}(k+1) = c_{i,j}(k) + \beta_3[x_k - c_{i,j}(k)] \tag{5}$$

β_2 and β_3 are two weighting parameters.

Step 2: Selection of critical centroids

Critical centroids are determined using the principle of the closest opposing pairs [19]. All the centroids are visited, and, for each one, the nearest centroïde of the other class is determined. When two centroids of different classes are the nearest in both senses, both are included in the first group of critical centroids.

Considering C1 and C2 two sets formed by centers of positive and negative class respectively. To construct the set of nearest opposing pairs, we firstly determine P1, the set of nearest centers for C1, then we define P2 the set of nearest centers for C2. The final set of closest opposite pairs is the intersection between P1 and P2. The couple (c_1, c_2) is the closest opposing pairs if

$$D(c_1, c_2) = \min_{c_k \in C_1} D(c_1, c_k) = \min_{c_k \in C_2} D(c_2, c_k) \tag{6}$$

As it's illustrated in Fig. 2, the couple (C3, S3) is considered as a closest opposing pair.

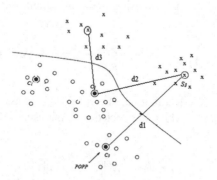

Fig. 2. Selection of the closest opposite pairs

Step 3: Selecting centroids with constraint of typicality

In principle, it seems that, proximity to the border is enough to consider a sample as critical, but it does not consider if the sample is "typical" or not. As Fig. 3 shows, this can be a problem when the closest opposing pairs are not sufficient to represent the distribution of data throughout the borderline [15, 20].

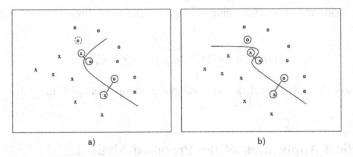

Fig. 3. The importance of typical centroids. (a)- The borderline using only proximity. (b)- Adapted borderline with typicality criterion

To apply this new concept of typicality, we define a new function that takes in consideration both criterion of proximity and typicality. This function is defined as

$$FI_c(x, \delta) = \|w^T x + b\| + \delta . exp(-\|x - x_0^p\|) \tag{7}$$

where x can be a centroïde, and x_0^p is the orthogonal projection of the centroïde c on the borderline. δ is a ponderation parameter of typicality criterion.

By minimizing the function presented in Eq. 7, we, simultaneously, reduce the distance between x and the borderline, and increase distance between x and x_0^p. Figure 4 illustrates the principle of proximity and typicality as calculated in the function FI.

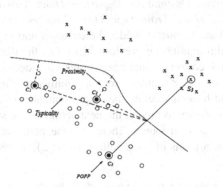

Fig. 4. Concept of proximity and typicality

Considering C_k the set of critical centers selected in the previous step, and C the set of all centers. For each critical centroïde c_k from C_k, the distance $FI_{c_k}(c, \delta)$ is calculated between c_k and each centroïde c from C. Lastly, the centroïde c that minimize $FI_{c_k}(c, \delta)$ will also be considered as critical.

Step 4: Construction of new training set
The final step of the proposed approach consists of applying a focused under-sampling of the imbalanced data. Concretely, the final training set will contains all examples

belonging from minority class and examples belonging from critical centroids of majority class.

$$Train\_set = \{Class_{minority} \cup \{x \in C_k\}\} \tag{8}$$

By this way, the training set is balanced and contains examples that are difficult to learn.

3   Practical Application of the Proposed Method

We have applied our proposal in a mixed-initiative spoken conversational agent providing railway information system using spontaneous speech in Spanish [21]. As in many other conversational agents, the semantic representation chosen for dialog acts of the Spoken Language Understanding module is based on the concept of frame [22]. This way, one or more concepts represent the intention of the utterance, and a sequence of attribute-value pairs contains the information about the values given by the user. For the task, we defined eight concepts and ten attributes. The eight concepts are divided into two groups:

- Task-dependent concepts: they represent the concepts the user can ask for (*Timetables, Fares, Train-Type, Trip-Time,* and *Services*).
- Task-independent concepts: they represent typical interactions in a dialog (*Acceptance, Rejection,* and *Not-Understood*).

The attributes are: *Origin, Destination, Departure-Date, Arrival-Date, Ticket-Class, Departure-Hour, Arrival-Hour, Train-Type, Order-Number,* and *Services*.

The conversational agent must consider the concepts and values for the attributes provided by the user throughout the previous history of the dialog to select the next system response. For the conversational agent to take this decision, we have assumed that the exact values of the attributes are not significant. They are important for accessing databases and for constructing the output sentences of the system. However, the only information necessary to predict the next action by the system is the presence or absence of concepts and attributes. Therefore, the codification we use for each concept and attribute is in terms of three values, $\{0; 1; 2\}$, according to the following criteria:

- (0): The concept is unknown or the value of the attribute is not given;
- (1): The concept or attribute is known with a confidence score that is higher than a given threshold;
- (2): The concept or attribute has a confidence score that is lower than the given threshold.

Using the previously described codification for the concepts and attributes, when a dialog starts (in the greeting turn) all the values are initialized to "0". The information provided by the users in each dialog turn is employed to update the previous values and obtain the current ones, as Fig. 5 shows.

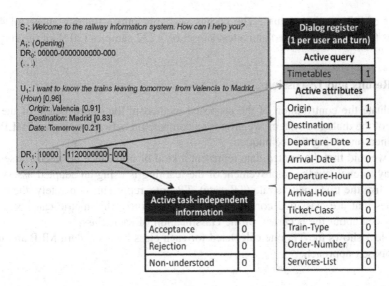

Fig. 5. Excerpt of a dialog with its correspondent representation of the task-dependent and active task-independent information for one of the dialog turns

This figure shows the semantic interpretation and confidence scores (in brackets) for a user's utterance provided by the SLU module. In this case, the confidence score assigned to the attribute Date is very low. Thus, a "2" value is added in the corresponding position for this attribute. The concept (*Hour*) and the attribute *Destination* are recognized with a high confidence score, adding a "1" value in the corresponding positions.

Taking into account the codification of the current state of the dialog, which is denoted in Fig. 5 by means of DR_1: 10000 – 1120000000-000, we propose the use of a classification process that receives this codification as input and provides the probabilities of selecting each one of the system responses as output.

The classification function can be defined in several ways. We have evaluated four different definitions of such a function: a multinomial naive Bayes classifier, n-gram based classifiers, a classifier based on grammatical inference techniques and a classifier based on neural networks [23]. The best results were obtained using a multilayer perceptron (MLP) [24] where the input layer holds the codification of the dialog state. The values of the output layer can be seen as an approximation of the a posteriori probability of belonging to the class associated to each one of the system responses.

A total of 14 system responses, i.e., system classes, were defined for the task (classified into confirmations of concepts and attributes, questions to require data from the user, and answers obtained after a query to the database).

An initial corpus of 900 dialogs (10.8 h) was acquired for the task by means of the Wizard of Oz technique with 225 real users, for which an initial dialog strategy was defined by experts [21]. A set of 20 scenarios was used to carry out the acquisition. Each scenario defined one or two objectives to be completed by the user and the set of attributes that they must provide. The corpus consists of 6,280 user turns, with an average number of 7.7 words per turn. The corpus was split into a training subset of 4,928 samples (80 % of the corpus) and a test subset of 1,232 samples (20 % of the corpus).

3.1   Results and Discussion

To evaluate the contribution of the proposed method in the improvement of the prediction of the dialogue system, we propose a comparison between a standard MLP, and a modified one using SS technique.

As we said that the treated data represent a kind of imbalance between classes, the best way to evaluate the improvement of the learning is using an adapted assessment metrics like the true positive rate (*TP_rate*). *TP_rate*, represents concretely, the rate of examples that are classified correctly. So in other words, this metric can gives us a precise idea about the accuracy of the classification of each class.

Table 1 shows the TP_rate calculated for each class by a standard MLP and using our proposed approach.

Table 1. Comparison of *TP_rate* class by class

Class	Standard MLP	MLP using SS
System response 1	87.82 %	90.62 %
System response 2	98.95 %	99.04 %
System response 3	91.52 %	95.92 %
System response 4	87.70 %	95.92 %
System response 5	89.66 %	94.38 %
System response 6	67.42 %	92.50 %
System response 7	91.48 %	91.36 %
System response 8	37.14 %	49.08 %
System response 9	83.70 %	92.50 %
System response 10	36.56 %	66.63 %
System response 11	88.24 %	90.00 %
System response 12	0.00 %	50.00 %
System response 13	73.17 %	64.10 %
System response 14	28.57 %	87.20 %

Note that we get better performance (TP_rate) using the proposed method than that given by the standard MLP. The increase of TP_rate is moderately around 17 %.

Thus we are getting very good results, and the general accuracy of learning is increasing.

By applying a focused under-sampling of the training set we provided a kind of balance between the classes, so the classifier will not ignore the minority class.

On the other hand, the way that the training set was constructed allows selecting the critical samples, and keeping the initial distribution of data near the borderline.

4 Conclusions and Future Work

In this paper we have proposed a practical application of SS methods for improving the selection of the system responses in conversational agents. We modeled the selection by mean of a classification process that considers the complete history of the dialogue. The application of our proposed SS-based technique to model this classification process provides very important benefits.

Firstly, the approach provides a solution for the problem of imbalanced distribution between classes. In fact, the set of data is balanced by a focused under-sampling, and the classifier takes in consideration the existence of the minority class. Also, the general accuracy of classification is improved by training the classifier using the critical samples. Finally, the computational cost of the proposed method is not high because of the use of clustering.

The application of the proposed method on a conversational agent's data provides very good results that allow concluding that the proposed approach does permit an eventual improvement in performance with respect to the standard classifier.

Following this line of work, many extensions of these methods can be studied, especially, use a combined classifier as boosting, also use the proposed method as a technique of automatic labeling and apply it on more complicated structures.

Acknowledgements. This work was supported in part by Projects MINECO TEC2012-37832-C02-01, CICYT TEC2011-28626-C02-02, and CAM CONTEXTS (S2009/TIC-1485).

References

1. Denker, J., Schwartz, D., Wittner, B., Solla, S., Howard, R., Jackel, L.: Large automatic learning, rule extraction, and generalization. Complex Syst. **1**, 877–922 (1987)
2. Huyser, K., Hororwitz, A.: Generalization in connectionist networks that realize boolean functions. In: Connectionist Models Summer School, pp. 191–200 (1988)
3. Munro, P.: Repeat until bored: a pattern selection strategy. Adv. Neural Inf. Proc. Syst. **4**, 1001–1008 (1992)
4. Ohnishi, N., Okamoto, A., Sugi, N.: Selective presentation of learning samples for efficient learning in multilayer perceptron. In: Proceedings of the IEEE International Conference on Neural Networks, vol. 1, pp. 688–690 (1991)
5. Zhang, B.T.: Accelerated learning by active example selection. Int. J. Neural Netw. **5**(1), 67–75 (1994)
6. Zhang, B.T.: An incremental learning algorithm that optimizes network size and sample size in one trial. In: Proceedings of the IEEE International Conference on Neural Networks, pp. 215–220 (1994)
7. Zhang, B.T., Veenker, G.: Neural networks that teach themselves through genetic discovery of novel examples. In: Proceedings of the International Joint Conference on Neural Networks, vol. 1, pp. 690–685 (1991)
8. Chairi, I., Alaoui, S., Lyhyaoui, A.: Intrusion detection based sample selection for imbalanced data distribution. In: IEEE Xplore. Second International Conference on Innovative Computing Technology, pp. 259–264 (2012)

9. Chairi, I., Alaoui, S., Lyhyaoui, A.: Learning from imbalanced data using methods of sample selection. In: IEEE Explore. International Conference on Multimedia Computing and Systems, pp. 254–257 (2012)

10. Chaïri, I., Alaoui, S., Lyhyaoui, A.: Balancing distribution of intrusion detection data using sample selection. J. Inf. Secur. Res. **3**, 153–163 (2012)

11. Pieraccini, R.: The Voice in the Machine: Building Computers that Understand Speech. The MIT Press, Cambridge (2012)

12. Chawla, N.V., Japkowicz, N., Kolcz, A.: Editorial: special issue on learning from imbalanced data sets. SIGKDD Explor. **6**(1), 1–6 (2004)

13. Williams, D., Myers, V., Silvious, M.: Mine classification with imbalanced data. IEEE Geosci. Remote Sens. Lett. **3**(6), 528–532 (2009)

14. El Jelali, S., Lyhyaoui, A., Anibal, R., Figueiras, V.: An emphasized target smoothing procedure to improve MLP classifiers performance. In: European symposium on artificial Neural Networks (2008)

15. Lyhyaoui, A., Martinez, M., Mora, I., Vázquez, M., Sancho, J.L., Figueiras-Vidal, A.R.: Sample selection via clustering to construct support vector-like classifiers. IEEE Trans. Neural Netw. **10**, 1474–1481 (1999)

16. Lyhyaoui, Tesis doctoral: Classificadores RBF via técnicas de agrupamiento y selecton de muestras. Universidad Carlos III de Madrid, Madrid (1999)

17. Ahalt, S., Stanley, C., Krishnamurthy, K., Chen, P., Douglas, M.E.: Competitive learning algorithms for vector quantization. Neural Netw. **3**, 277–290 (1990)

18. Kohonen, T.: The self-organizing map. Proc. IEEE **78**, 1464–1480 (1990)

19. Sklansky, J., Michelotti, L.: Locally trained piecewise linear classifiers. IEEE Trans. Pattern Anal. Mach. Intell. **2**, 101–111 (1980)

20. Yuhua, L., Maguire, L.: Selecting critical patterns based on local geometrical and statistical information. IEEE Trans. Pattern Anal. Mach. Intell. **33**, 1189–1201 (2011)

21. Griol, D., Hurtado, L., Segarra, E., Sanchis, E.: A statistical approach to spoken dialog systems design and evaluation. Speech Commun. **50**(8–9), 666–682 (2008)

22. Minsky, M.: A framework for representing knowledge. In: Winston, P. (ed.) The Psychology of Computer Vision, pp. 211–277. McGraw-Hill, New York (1975)

23. David, G., Zoraida, C., Ramón, L.-C., Giuseppe, R.: A domain independent statistical methodology for dialog management in spoken dialog systems. Comput. Speech Lang. **28** (3), 743–768 (2014)

24. Rumelhart, D.E., Hinton, G.E., Williams, R.J.: Learning internal representations by error propagation. In: Rumelhart, D.E., McClelland, J.L. (eds.) PDP: Computational Models of Cognition and Perception, pp. 319–362. MIT Press, Cambridge (1986)

25. Zhang, T., Mühlenbein, H.: Genetic programming of minimal neural nets using Occam's razor. In: Proceedings of the International Conference Genetic Algorithms, pp. 342–349 (1993)

SafeRoute: An Example of Multi-sensoring Tracking for the Elderly Using Mobiles on Ambient Intelligence

Javier Jiménez Alemán[1(✉)], Nayat Sanchez-Pi[2], and Ana Cristina Bicharra Garcia[2]

[1] Institute of Computing, IC, Fluminense Federal University, Rua Passo da Pátria,
São Domingos, Niterói, Rio de Janeiro, Brazil
jjimenezaleman@ic.uff.br
[2] ADDLabs, Documentation Active and Intelligent Design Laboratory of Institute of Computing,
Fluminense Federal University, Av. Gal. Milton Tavares de Souza, Boa Viagem, Niterói,
Rio de Janeiro, Brazil
{nayat,cristina}@addlabs.uff.br

Abstract. New technologies have become an important support for the monitoring of older people in outdoor environments by their caregivers. Smart phones equipped with a rich set of powerful sensors allowed the ubiquitous human activity recognition on mobile platforms at a low cost. Ambient Intelligence (AmI) is an emergent area that provides useful mechanisms that allows tracking elderly people through opportunistic sensing using smartphone devices. This paper aims to show the second version of *SafeRoute*, an AmI system that fusions geo-localization sensors data embedded in smartphone devices for the monitoring of elderly people. This version improves functionalities of the previous one with the inclusion of new ones in the two components of this system: the Android OS application *CareofMe* and the web system *SafeRoute*. The proposed system merges localization data from GPS and Wifi sensors data in Android OS and includes the use of GoogleMaps functionalities in Android OS and web environments for provide alerts for caregivers.

Keywords: Information fusion · Opportunistic sensing · Ambient intelligence · Elderly tracking

1 Introduction

There are a real problem with the increase of the average age of the population and life expectancy in all world. The Brazilian Institute of Geography and Statistics (IBGE) estimated that the Brazilian population over 65 years old will reach 29 % in 2050 and 36,1 % in 2075 [1] from its current status. The same study reveals that nowadays in Brazil live with this disease approximately 1 million 200 thousands people, with more than 70 % living in their own homes. Those facts implies an increase of the permanent attention to these people by his caregivers and relatives and a growing necessity to create mechanism to support this task [2].

The European Community's Information Society Technology (ISTAG) defined the concept of Ambient Intelligence (AmI) in 2001 as an emergent topic that proposes ways

© Springer International Publishing Switzerland 2015
J. Bajo et al. (Eds.): PAAMS 2015 Workshops, CCIS 524, pp. 201–212, 2015.
DOI: 10.1007/978-3-319-19033-4_17

to response the human necessities through digital and technological environments, allowing innovative ways of human-computer interactions [3]. Tools of Ambient Assisted Living (AAL) are the Ambient Intelligence based technologies for the support to daily activities and can be used in prevention of accidents and to improve the health conditions and comfort of the elderly people [4]. These technologies can supply security to the elderly, developing response systems for smartphone systems, falls detection systems and video surveillance systems. Furthermore, AAL technologies also allow best communication between those people that needs special cares with his relatives and friends [5].

Nowadays, most of smartphones not only work like communication devices, but also are equipped with several sensors like accelerometer, gyroscope, proximity sensors, microphones, GPS system and camera. All these sensors make possible a wide range of applications like the assistance to people with disabilities, intelligently detecting and recognizing the context.

Fusion data was defined by [6] as "*a process dealing with the association, correlation, and combination of data and information from single and multiple sources to achieve refined position and identity estimates, and complete and timely assessments of situations and threats, and their significance. The process is characterized by continuous refinements of its estimates and assessments, and the evaluation of the need for additional sources, or modification of the process itself, to achieve improved results*".

Information fusion focused in sensors [6] has become increasingly relevant during the last years due to its goal to combine observations from a number of different sensors to provide a solid and complete description of an environment or process of interest.

Traditionally, activity recognition system usually employs hard sensor, however, there are other user information sources available in the smartphones. Users daily share their personal information on social networks sites, Facebook, LinkedIn, Twitter, and so on. These type of sensors are called soft sensors in information fusion researches, which are referred as human observer that provides his/her point of view of something [7].

The information fusion systems are characterized by its robustness, increased confidence, reduced ambiguity and uncertainty, and improved resolution. There are many examples of applications of information fusion techniques [8] that use sensors in different environments such as remote sensing, surveillance, home care, and so forth [9], but there are few applications using smartphones devices. For that reason, taking advantage of information fusion techniques, in [8] for example, has been deployed an architecture of smart phones to collect user data and infer the user's context smartphones.

The Data Fusion Model maintained by the JDL Data Fusion Group is the most widely used method for categorizing data fusion-related functions [10]. They proposed a model of six levels (Fig. 1), of which the first is related to information extraction, and the last with the extraction of knowledge. Authors of [11] explained these levels in detail:

- Level 0 (Source Preprocessing/Subject Assessment): Estimation and prediction of observable states of the signal or object, based in the association and characterization of data at a signal level.
- Level 1 (Object Assessment): In this level, objects are identified and located. Hence, the object situation by fusing the attributes from diverse sources is reported.

- Level 2 (Situation Assessment): The goal of this level is construct a picture from incomplete information provided by level 1, that is, to relate the reconstructed entity with an observed event.
- Level 3 (Impact Assessment): Estimation and prediction of the effects that would have the actions provided by participants, taking into account the information extracted at lower levels.
- Level 4 (Process Refinement): Modification of data capture systems (sensors) and processing the same, to ensure the targets of the mission.
- Level 5 (User or Cognitive Refinement): Modification of the way that people react from the experience and knowledge gained.

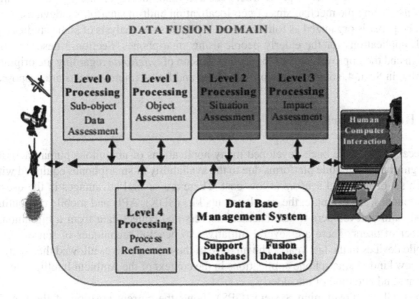

Fig. 1. JDL information fusion model (Taking from [12])

The JDL model was never intended to decide a concrete order on the data fusion levels. Levels are not alluded to be processed consecutively, and it can be executed concurrently [8].

Although the JD data fusion model has been criticized, still constitutes a reference to design and build systems to obtain information from the data in complex systems and generate knowledge from the extracted information.

Elderly people often suffer problems of aging such as memory loss, difficulty walking, etc. Many times, these people have to stay at home alone for long periods, but they normally do various activities outside the home (go to the market, visiting friends, etc.) during this time. Once they are in outdoor environments, elderly people are at risk of fall down or getting lost on the way. In these cases, it is very important that elderly people can communicate with their relatives for help and receive orientations in real time.

Taking these factors in consideration, *SafeRoute* was created as an AAL system for care elderly people in open-air environments and improving response time in emergencies. In our initial approach, we design two components (the Android application *CareofMe* and the web service *SafeRoute*). These two components work in a combined way as tools for tracking elderly people, using the sensors built-in in mobile devices to offer the current position and using a web server to show the route followed by users in a friendly way. After doing some tests of the original version of *SafeRoute* in real environments, was detected some deficiencies that made difficult the interaction with users.

This work aims to improve the SafeRoute system for assist elderly people in their day-to-day activities in outdoors environments. Our goal is to provide solutions to improve the communication process between users and carivegers, and try reducing time responses using the mechanisms of geo-localization built-in smartphone devices.

The paper is organized as follows: Sect. 2 presents the analysis of some studies and AAL applications for the elderly people using smartphones. Section 3 describes the design and the improvements of the second version of *SafeRoute* regarding the original. Finally, in Sect. 4, some conclusions are given and future improvements are proposed.

2   Related Work

In recent years have been developed many applications of ubiquitous human activity recognition with mobile platforms due to the availability of smartphones equipped with a rich set of powerful sensors at low cost. There are several advantages in the use of smartphones, for example, the developments kits (SDK), APIs and mobile computing clouds allow developers to use backend servers and collect data from a big amount number of users. There are several initiatives to develop techniques of sensoring in mobile devices in the last years. The mixture of these perspectives allowed the creation of a new kind of smartphone applications in the context of the Ambient Intelligence for the care and attention of the elderly.

The Global Positioning System (GPS) shows the current position of the user in almost every place in the Earth. It is recognized as a mature technology for the localization in outdoors environments and once that are built-in inside the smartphones, offers many opportunities to help even more to track and monitoring people with physics disabilities or health problems. The position of a smartphone phone can be provided in two dimensions (latitude, longitude) when the receptor is capable to receive signals at least of three satellites.

Systems that try to offer intelligent responses to the stimulus of the environment and be sensitive to the context can be implemented of different ways. There are different election criteria, like the sensors localization, the possible quantity of users or the available resources (PCs and mobile devices). In addition, data collection is very important in system design because it defines the architectural style. In this work were identified different perspectives in the architectural style of AAL systems: (1) Centralized architecture [13, 14]; (2) Distributed architecture [15–17]. There are not decisive criteria to determine which the best architectural style is, because that strongly depends of the project's characteristics. The centralized architectural style provide bigger security and protection because the information is mainly concentrated in a single place. In addition, improves the decision-making process and the system maintenance. On the other hand, this architectural style has disadvantages like slowness, product of the dependency of just one central connection. The distributed architectural style has some advantages, for example, the increase of the trustworthiness, since in case of defect in one system; the others can continue their work independently. In addition, the interface is friendlier and the response velocity faster. This architectural style has the problem that usually works with expensive technology and the work of maintenance is complex due to the amount of resources that involves. Moreover, the data integrity is most difficult to control. This last approach are of particular interest for our proposed system.

Regarding the use of multi-agent systems, [15] is a system that acts in real time to combat the problem of falls in older people using sensors embedded in mobile devices. The system emit responses to the old man's caregivers by means SMS or an automatic call in case to detect a fall.

There are different ways to AAL systems provide useful information in real time related users (older people and their carivegers). Many systems implement services to communicate with users because of the friendliness of the web interfaces for most users. The web services are very useful because the involved technologies (HTTP, XML) are independent of programming languages, platforms and operational systems. For example, [13] makes possible do the tracking of an old person's route through a web site that sends alert in case of distancing. On the other hand, in [18], authors implement a solution that provides the exact position of the old person in Google Maps using a social network and shows the user location through a radar when the map information is lost or disabled.

Some of the related works presented above are summarized in Table 1 attending their contributions and limitations.

The *SafeRoute* system (Fig. 2) was designed and implemented trying to summarize some of the good experiences presented above in the developing of AAL systems for the care of the elderly people in outdoors environments. It was composed by two components: the Android OS application *CareofMe* and the web system *RotaSegura*.

Firstly, the *CareofMe* application use a combination of *GPS* and *Wifi* technologies to show the current user localization in an outdoors environment. *CareofMe* uses *GoogleMap Android* v2 API for working with maps in mobile environments and starts to send the coordinates of the current position (Latitude, Longitude) to the web server installed in *RotaSegura*.

On the other hand, in this original *SafeRoute* system was conceived *RotaSegura* as a web service for the constantly monitoring of the user's position and the sending of alerts to the old person in case of distancing. The advantages mentioned above of using web technology influenced the choice for use in *SafeRoute*. For instance, the independence of this type of technology in relation to any programming language used for the access to this type of system.

Table 1. Works related according its architectural style

	Architectural style	Contributions	Limitations
[13]	Middleware (Centralized)	Original architectural style with the inclusion of *Smartshoe* and the integration with GPS and Bluetooth	The lack of details of the inference process position The system does not give feedback to users
[15]	Architectural style oriented to MAS (Distributed)	This is one of the first studies in the area of MAS for fall detection using smartphone devices. Authors made many successful simulations	Simulations were not made in real environments
[16]	Architectural style oriented to MAS (Distributed)	This solution optimizes the system functioning with limited resources, allowing agents to manage and control all the available sensors in the smart-phone devices	This work shows a static approach and the authors omit to describe the importance of each agent
[17]	Architectural style oriented to MAS (Distributed)	The authors achieved to combine a big quantity of diverse tech-nologies like federated data-bases, sensors environments, secure communications, etc.	The authors did not present related works and did not do simula-tions
[14]	Middleware (Centralized)	Original approach of an architec-tural design totally developed for Android OS smartphones with an opportunistic approach	The authors do not describe about how they did the reasoning with data

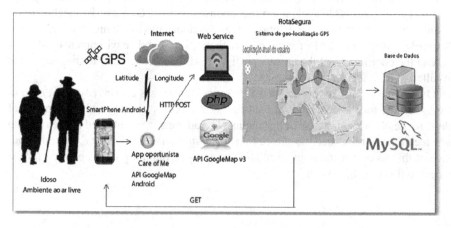

Fig. 2. Distributed architectural design of the *SafeRoute* project

In our approach, we try to include new features and to improve the existing ones in the two main components of the system (the Android OS application *CareofMe* and the web service *SafeRoute*). These two components work in a combined way and merge information from sensors embedded in mobiles devices for tracking elderly people, showing to carivegers of the elderly people the current position and the route followed by them in a friendly way. It is also presented as future work, a group of challenges to implement in our system to improve the quality of life of older people in outdoor environments.

3   SafeRoute2

Because of the advantages mentioned above of the distributed architecture, the original system followed this approach. The distributed system is composed by two components: the Android OS application *CareofMe* and the web system *SafeRoute*. However, the original version of *SafeRoute* presented some deficiencies that made difficult the interaction with users. The weaknesses identified were:

– The feedback mechanism proposed in the first version (Fig. 3) was considered poor because only reported to the old person about the distance of the predetermined route. In addition, *SafeRoute* could not inform to old people's caregivers about the position of the elderly person in case of distancing.

Fig. 3. Feedback in case of distance in *CareofMe*

– The web interface of *SafeRoute* was not enough intuitive considering all the potentialities of the web design. Example: The system could propose path to follow in case of distance of the old person.

In response to the deficiencies detected in the original version of *SafeRoute*, we decided to implement some improvements in the second version of our system.

Firstly, we improved the *CareofMe* system's feedback, adding to the information of distance in meters in case of distance, an image that indicate the nearby path to follow to successfully to end the route (Fig. 4).

Fig. 4. Feedback with proposed path in case of distance in *CareofMe*

Secondly, we tried to improve the feedback that *SafeRoute* offered to users that are following the old people's route. In this direction, we include an alert mechanism through emails to the old people's caregivers. The email contain an image with the localization of the old people in case of distance. This way, the old person caregivers can check the old person position in every moment.

In (Fig. 5), we describe the architecture of our system to obtain localization from a user who carries out a smartphone.

Firstly, the *CareofMe* application use a combination of *GPS* and *Wifi* sensors to find the current user localization in an outdoors environment. *GPSTracker* is the responsible class for managing position dates through the class *LocationManager*, belonging to the *GoogleMap Android* v2 API for working with maps in mobile environments. The class *LongOperation* receives information of routes to select and class *HttpAsyncTask* sends coordinates of the current position (Latitude, Longitude) to the web server installed in *SafeRoute*.

On the other hand, *SafeRoute* system was conceived as a web service for the constantly monitoring of the user's position and the sending of alerts to relatives and the elderly person in case of distancing. The Route Tracking functionality uses the *CoordDistanceAB* class to calculate distance between user locations received in real-time (*Localization*) and the locations of the predefined route (*Route*). *PHPMailer* sends an email to the cariveger with the exactly position of the elderly person in case of distancing.

Furthermore, Fig. 6 is shown the algorithm used to compute distance between two points in space, given the longitude and latitude. We implemented an algorithm based in the haversine formula to calculate distance.

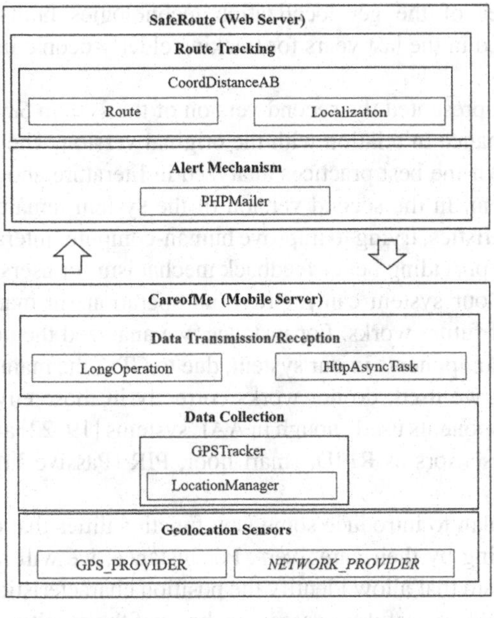

Fig. 5. Architecture of the *SafeRoute* project

```
$delta_lat = $this->lat_b - $this->lat_a ;

$delta_lon = $this->lon_b - $this->lon_a ;

$earth_radius = 6372.795477598;

$alpha = $delta_lat/2;

$beta = $delta_lon/2;

$a = sin(deg2rad($alpha)) * sin(deg2rad($alpha))
+ cos(deg2rad($this->lat_a)) * cos(deg2rad($this->lat_b)) * sin(deg2rad($beta)) * sin(deg2rad($beta)) ;

$c = asin(min(1, sqrt($a)));

$distance = 2*$earth_radius * $c;

$distance = round($distance, 4);

$this->measure = $distance;
```

Fig. 6. Distance calculation algorithm

4 Conclusions and Future Work

The use of smartphone devices is increasing gradually, making these devices a new source for developing solutions in various technologies. In AmI, AAL is gaining more prominence by providing mobile response systems, fall detection systems or video surveillance systems that can supply security to the elderly and to their caregivers.

The potentialities of the geo-localization technologies built-on in smartphone devices has been used in the last years for tracking elderly people in outdoors environments.

In this paper, we presented the second version of the system *SafeRoute*, looking to improve the performance in relation with the original version. The actual system tries to summarize some of the best practices analyzed in literature about the development of this kind of system. In the second version of the system remained the initial geo-localization characteristics, trying to improve human-computer interaction in *SafeRoute* web application and providing better feedback mechanism for users.

We believe that our system can improve its operations in many aspects and we identified a group of future works. For instance, we analyzed the necessity of include indoor localization components in our system, due to GPS, the main outdoors localization technology that we used, do not works correctly in those environments. Indoor mechanisms are components used enough in AAL systems [19–22] and there are studies that combine many sensors as RFID, smart floor, PIR (Passive Infrared Sensor) and ultrasonic technology.

In addition, we plan to introduce some new functionalities that could facilitate the elderly people tracking by their caregivers. For instance, we will introduce a context recognition mechanism that allow identify the position characteristics (water, etc.). We also believe that would be useful for caregivers know if the monitored elderly person is delayed for a certain control point. Attending that, in future version we will include a time control component that inform caregivers for delays in the route.

Although, we considered that our solution could to take advantages of all the sources of information that provides the sensors embedded inside smartphones (accelerometer, gyroscope, compass, magnetometer, proximity sensor, light sensor, etc.) in order to reach better results in activity recognition problem.

The JDL data fusion and information model, may be the reference model on which we could base our future work to generate knowledge from information extracted from the data of all these sensors. In addition, taking in count that in the last years, the interest in ontologies as symbolic models to acquire, represent, and exploit knowledge in data fusion, has increased considerably, we propose as future work the develop of a ontological model for tracking and activity recognition data for elderly people in outdoors and indoor environments. We will follow the level 2 (Situation Assessment) of the JDL model to associate entities with environmental and performance data in this context.

The proposed solution has demonstrated to be useful for the elderly care in outdoor environments, enabling effective monitoring mechanism for caregivers. Our work demonstrated the validity of merging a group of well-recognized technologies in the AAL context through the development of a simple application.

References

1. Instituto Brasileiro de Geografia e Estatística (IBGE). Sinopse dos Resultados do Censo (2010). http://www.censo2010.ibge.gov.br/sinopse/webservice/
2. Nealon, J.L., Moreno, A.: Applications of Software Agent Technology in the Health Care Domain. Birkhauser Verlag AG Whiteistein Series in Software Agents Technologies, Bases (2003)
3. Sadri, F.: Ambient intelligence: a survey. ACM Comput. Surv. **43**(4), 1–66 (2011). http://doi.acm.org/10.1145/1978802.1978815
4. Rashidi, P., Mihailidis, A.: A survey on ambient-assisted living tools for older adults. IEEE J. Biomed. Health Inform. **17**(3), 579–590 (2013)
5. Roussaki, I., et al.: Hybrid context modeling: a location-based scheme using ontologies. In: Proceedings of the 4th Annual IEEE International Conference on Pervasive Computing and Communications Workshop (2006)
6. White, F.: Data Fusion Lexicon, JDL, Technical Panel for C3, Data Fusion SubPanel. Naval Ocean Systems Center, San Diego (1987)
7. Hall, D.L., Llinas, J.: An introduction to multisensor data fusion. Proc. IEEE **85**(1), 6–23 (1997)
8. Blázquez, G., Berlanga, A., Molina, J.M.: InContexto: multisensor architecture to obtain people context from smartphones. Int. J. Distrib. Sens. Netw. **2012**, 1–15 (2012)
9. Sanchez-Pi, N., et al.: An information fusion framework for context-based accidents prevention. In: 2014 17th International Conference on Information Fusion (FUSION). IEEE (2014)
10. Steinber, A., Bowman, C., White, F.: Revisions to the JDL data fusion model. In: Sensor Fusion: Architectures, Algorithms, and Applications (1999)
11. Rosa, M.: El modelo JDL de fusión de datos. Transformación de la información en conocimiento en el entorno marítimo. Semana Naval de la Armada (2013). http://www.armada.mde.es/mardigital/biblioteca-digital/jornadas-tecnologicas-iii-snm/14_jornadas-tecnologicas-manuel-rosa-zurera.pdf
12. Salerno, J.: Where's Level 2/3 Fusion – a Look Back over the Past. Air Force Research Laboratory, Rome Research Site (2007)
13. Silva, B., Rodrigues, J., Simões, T., Sendra, S., Lloret, J.: An ambient assisted living framework for mobile environments. In: BHI 2014 (2014)
14. Meroni, P., et al.: An opportunistic platform for android-based mobile devices. In: Second International Workshop on Mobile Opportunistic Networking (2010)
15. Martín, P., Sánchez, M., Álvarez, L., Alonso, V., Bajo, J.: Multi-agent system for detecting elderly people falls through mobile devices. In: Novais, P., Preuveneers, D., Corchado, J.M. (eds.) ISAmI 2011. AISC, vol. 92, pp. 93–99. Springer, Heidelberg (2011)
16. Muldoon, C., O'Hare, G.M., O'Grady, M.J.: Collaborative agent tuning: performance enhancement on mobile devices. In: Dikenelli, O., Gleizes, M.-P., Ricci, A. (eds.) ESAW 2005. LNCS (LNAI), vol. 3963, pp. 241–258. Springer, Heidelberg (2006)
17. Camarinha-Matos, L., et al.: Telecare: Collaborative virtual elderly support communities. In: TELECARE 2004 (2004)
18. Calvo-Palomino, R., de las Heras-Quirós, P., Santos-Cadenas, J.A., Román-López, R., Izquierdo-Cortázar, D.: Outdoors monitoring of elderly people assisted by compass, gps and mobile social network. In: Omatu, S., Rocha, M.P., Bravo, J., Fernández, F., Corchado, E., Bustillo, A., Corchado, J.M. (eds.) IWANN 2009, Part II. LNCS, vol. 5518, pp. 808–811. Springer, Heidelberg (2009)

19. Hightower, J., et al.: Design and calibration of the spoton ad-hoc location sensing system. Technical report, University of Washington, Seattle, WA (2001)
20. Ni, L.M., et al.: Landmarc: indoor location sensing using active RFID. In: Proceedings of the First IEEE International Conference on Pervasive Computing and Communications (2003)
21. Bahl, P., Padmanabhan, V.: Radar: an in-building RF-based user location and tracking system. In: Proceedings of the Annual Joint Conference on Computer and Communications Societies (2000)
22. Priyantha, N.B., Chakraborty, A., Balakrishnan, H.: The cricket location-support system. In: Proceedings of the International Conference on Mobile Computing and Networking (2000)

Thresholding the Courtesy Amount of Brazilian Bank Checks Using a Local Methodology

Rafael Felix[✉], Leandro Augusto da Silva,
and Leandro Nunes de Castro

Natural Computing Laboratory, Mackenzie Presbyterian University,
Sao Paulo, SP, Brazil
rfelixmg@gmail.com,
{leandroaugusto.silva,lnunes}@mackenzie.br

Abstract. This paper presents a new thresholding methodology for complex background images with an application to the courtesy amount of Brazilian bank checks. Courtesy amount images present a complex background and the proposal of an automatic thresholding process brings benefits to other steps in bank check clearance, such as the Optical Character Recognition (OCR). Experimental results showed that the proposed methodology yields good results, with average accuracy over 95 %, superior to standard methods from the literature.

Keywords: Image binarization · Thresholding · Pattern recognition · Bank checks · Multi-layer perceptron · Support vector machines

1 Introduction

Automatic thresholding applications are aimed at finding either a global or several local threshold values capable of accurately separating an image into object or background. This is a challenging task because pixels with the same gray level within the same window of observation will always be attributed to the same class, even if they are spatially separated or do not belong to the same class.

The automatic thresholding process of Brazilian bank checks is an important task when developing check clearance applications [1, 2]. The automatic check clearance allows different financial institutions to settle debit and credit balances from their members and to check transactions accomplished by other institutions, making check clearance a critical financial task. When the check clearance process started using images, it eliminated check cloning, loss and theft [1, 2]. Thresholding methods define a value that segments an image into background and object. These methods are divided into two groups, one based on the number of threshold values (bi-level and multilevel); and another based on spatiality (global and local) [3]. Common thresholding methods that use a threshold value to split the image into background and object are named binarization approaches [3].

There are thresholding methods that use Pattern Recognition (PR) approaches to define either a local or a global threshold, which is then used to separate the image into

© Springer International Publishing Switzerland 2015
J. Bajo et al. (Eds.): PAAMS 2015 Workshops, CCIS 524, pp. 213–221, 2015.
DOI: 10.1007/978-3-319-19033-4_18

background and object [3]. This paper proposes an automatic bi-level thresholding methodology for complex background images based on local characteristics. This methodology uses pattern recognition techniques to classify each pixel as background or object. Differently from most approaches available in the literature that use the PR method to define a single global threshold, in the present proposal the proposed method is used to automatically and locally define the threshold based on a given neighborhood of the pixel to be thresholded. As such, the proposed methodology allows that pixels with the same intensity in a given image be classified differently either as background or as object, depending on their neighborhood. To illustrate such situation, consider two pixels $p(383, 67)$ and $p(537, 90)$, both with the same gray level $f = 125$. A standard thresholding method with a threshold value of 123 would classify both pixels as belonging to the object. However, the local analysis of the proposed methodology allows their suitable classification (see Fig. 1).

Fig. 1. Suitable thresholding based on local features.

In the experiments performed here to assess the proposed methodology, the courtesy amount area of 60 Brazilian bank checks and two classifiers (PR methods) were used: a Multi-Layer Perceptron neural network [4, 5]; and a Support Vector Machine (SVM) [4–6]. The experimental results showed the capability of the proposed methodology to segment background and object keeping relevant information and excluding noise to improve other processes, such as Optical Character Recognition (OCR) and Handwritten Recognition (HWR).

The paper is organized as follows. Section 2 describes the problem and provides a brief literature review. Section 3 introduces the proposed methodology and Sect. 4 brings some experimental evaluations. The paper is concluded in Sect. 5 with a general discussion and perspective for future research.

2 Problem Statement and Related Works

The distinction between background and object is not evident in complex background images [7, 8]. These images contain shadows, non-uniformity, low contrast, different colors, textures, fonts and dimensions, making it hard the use of thresholding methods [8].

Bank check images belong to the group of complex background images and represent a challenge for digital image processing applications, such as thresholding methods. This kind of image presents complex texture, colors and human interference, such as the insertion of noisy elements for security [8]. This paper focuses on the application of the proposed thresholding methodology to the courtesy amount images (Fig. 2). This is one of the hardest areas, since it is filled in by human and contains different handwritings, typed fonts, spatial positioning, and security elements, like '#' and '*' commonly used to hinder others actions [1].

The growing volume of image applications requires thresholding methods capable of automatically thresholding images [2, 3, 9]. In turn, these methods require algorithms capable of defining adaptive thresholding values among different types of images, including the complex background ones [8–10]. The thresholding algorithms can be divided into six categories based on the type of information used [9]: (1) histogram shape information; (2) measurement space clustering; (3) histogram entropy information; (4) image attribute information; (5) spatial information; and (6) local characteristics. The methodology to be presented in the sequence uses local characteristics to define if a pixel belongs to background or object considering its neighborhood.

Fig. 2. Region of Interest (*RoI*) samples: the courtesy amount area.

3   The Proposed Methodology

There is currently a growing interest in automatic thresholding methods for complex background images [3, 9, 11]. As the methodology to be proposed here uses local characteristics to define each pixel's class, it becomes more robust and generic to be applied to thresholding complex background images. The automatic thresholding methodology contains the following steps: image database construction; region of interest extraction; pattern matrix construction; pattern labelling; database sampling; and classifier training (Fig. 3). Each of these steps will be discussed in the following.

In the present proposal pattern recognition algorithms are used to threshold the images. Differently from most methods available in the literature that use intelligent algorithms to find the best threshold value, in the methodology proposed here such algorithms are used to define the class (object or background) of each pixel based on local characteristics. Thus, for each input pattern (pixel) presented to the algorithm a new pixel is constructed in the new thresholded image.

Fig. 3. The proposed methodology flowchart.

3.1 Image Database Construction

The image database is composed of a set of images that will be used to train and test the methodology. This set of images must contain the same type of image, such as images of documents, vehicles, portraits, maps, medical images, among others.

3.2 Extracting the Region of Interest

Let $RoI \in Z^{c \times r}$ denote the region of interest to be extracted from a specific image database, where d is the number of pixels in RoI ($d = c \times r$). Consider the example illustrated in Fig. 4 where the RoI is the courtesy amount area of Brazilian bank checks.

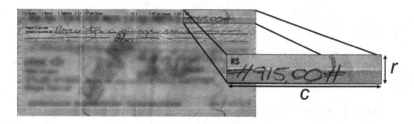

Fig. 4. The RoI is the courtesy amount area of size $c \times r$.

3.3 Pattern Matrix Construction

The following step aims to construct a matrix using patterns that contain the training and test sets for the classifiers. For each pixel in the region of interest, a pattern $s_i \in Z^V$, $i = 1, \ldots, d$, is constructed by taking the reference pixel, $p(x, y)$, and a square neighborhood, $V = v \times v$, around it, as illustrated in Fig. 5 for the reference pixel of value 108. The pattern matrix $S = [s_i]_{i=1 \cdots d}$ is built after passing through all d pixels in the RoI.

3.4 Pattern Labelling

The next step is to label the patterns, that is, to assign a class (background or object) for each pattern in the pattern matrix. Consider the example in Fig. 6 that presents the pattern labelling process. Each pattern constructed from the grayscale image is labelled assuming the label obtained by manually thresholding the original image. This labelling process is necessary for the algorithm to learn which pixels belong to the background or object. These patterns will be used to train the classifiers.

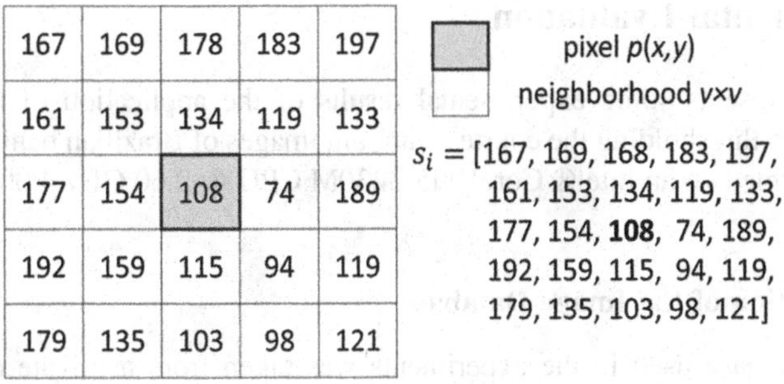

167	169	178	183	197
161	153	134	119	133
177	154	108	74	189
192	159	115	94	119
179	135	103	98	121

pixel $p(x,y)$

neighborhood $v \times v$

$s_i = [167, 169, 168, 183, 197,$
$161, 153, 134, 119, 133,$
$177, 154, \mathbf{108}, 74, 189,$
$192, 159, 115, 94, 119,$
$179, 135, 103, 98, 121]$

Fig. 5. Example of a representation of one pattern using a neighbourhood of size 5 × 5.

3.5 Database Sampling

As each pixel in an image becomes a pattern, even a set containing few images with low dimension generates a huge pattern matrix. A practical approach to optimize classifier training and study the feasibility and performance of a classifier is to sample the database. Two sampling approaches are used in this methodology:

- Random sampling (RAND), which randomly selects a portion of the database;
- Based on the standard deviation (STD) of the gray scale values of the patterns attributes (the patterns are sorted in descending order of their standard deviation and a number of the patterns with the highest std values are taken).

3.6 Classifier Training

Finally, the sampled patterns are used to train the classifiers. This step consists of selecting and training one or more classifiers using the sampled patterns. In principle, any classifier capable of dealing with numeric or discrete inputs can be used. The role of the classifier is to define if a given pixel will be classified as belonging to the object or to the background. Note that this is much different from defining a single threshold to all pixels, because in the proposed methodology the classifiers are responsible for making an analysis of each pixel and its neighborhood so as to decide to which class it belongs.

Fig. 6. Sample of manually thresholded image for labelling each pattern.

4 Experimental Evaluation

This section presents some experimental results of the application of the proposed methodology to thresholding the courtesy amount images of Brazilian bank checks. The test was performed on an Intel® Core™ i5-3230M CPU @ 2.60 GHz 4.00 GB (RAM).

4.1 Description of the Image Database

The image database used in the experiments was taken from a private database and contains 60 grayscale images of checks from six different Brazilian banks. Each image has a 200 dpi resolution and a dimensionality of 1575 × 600 pixels.

4.2 Extracting the Region of Interest

This paper uses the courtesy amount as the region of interest to be thresholded. The layout of Brazilian bank checks is defined by the Brazilian Federation of Banks (FEBRABAN) as illustrates Fig. 7 (Area 2) [1]. The layout defined contains four areas:

- Area 1: bank code, account number and other reserved numbers;
- Area 2: courtesy amount;
- Area 3: legal amount; and
- Area 4: magnetic code, known as CMC-7.

In the *RoI* extraction step, each courtesy amount was extracted automatically using a mask of 500 × 120 pixels taken from the top-right corner of each check image, as defined by FEBRABAM [1].

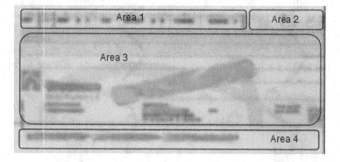

Fig. 7. Layout of Brazilian bank checks.

4.3 Pattern Matrix Construction

The parameters used to build the pattern matrix are $c = 120$ pixels, $r = 500$ pixels and the square neighborhood size, V, equal 25. Thus, the pattern matrix building steps results in a matrix $\mathbf{S} \in Z^{(120 \times 500) \times 25}$.

4.4 Pattern Labelling

For each image it was created an equivalent image thresholded using a global method, where the threshold value was the average value of its pixels. The resulting image was manually enhanced in order to extract noise. Each pattern constructed from the gray-scale image is labeled assuming the value obtained by manually thresholding the original image.

4.5 Database Sampling and Classifier Training

For each sampling method (RAND and STD) 10^3 patterns were chosen. Two classifiers were used with the following configuration:

- A Multi-Layer Perceptron (MLP) trained with the Scaled Conjugate Gradient algorithm [12], one hidden layer with 10 neurons, hyperbolic tangent transfer function, 5×10^3 training epochs and two output neurons [12]; and
- A Support Vector Machine (SVM) with linear kernel and implementation from LIBSVM [6].

4.6 Experimental Results

The measures used to analyse the proposed methodology are: (1) Accuracy (Acc); (2) Precision (Pr); and (3) Recall (Re) [2, 3, 9]. Table 1 shows the mean ± standard deviation of each classifier performance for a 10-fold cross-validation and the sampled database to train and test each classifier.

Table 1. Accuracy (Acc), Precision (Pr) and Recall (Re) for the sampled training data.

Sampling method	Classifier	Acc	Pr	Re
RAND	MLP	0.95 ± 0.004	0.94 ± 0.004	0.94 ± 0.006
	SVM	0.94 ± 0.001	0.93 ± 0.002	0.95 ± 0.002
STD	MLP	0.97 ± 0.002	0.96 ± 0.003	0.98 ± 0.003
	SVM	0.96 ± 0.002	0.95 ± 0.002	0.97 ± 0.002

The trained classifiers were then applied to binarize the courtesy amount of the 60 images from the database and their performance were compared to that of OTSU [13], NIBLACK [14] and SAUVOLA [15] (Table 2). OTSU consists of a thresholding methodology that selects a global threshold [13], NIBLACK is a methodology that defines multiple local thresholds [14], and SAUVOLA consist of a hybrid method to improve the NIBLACK algorithm by using filters to enhance the final result [15].

Figure 8 illustrates some visual results of the thresholding methods applied to the courtesy amount of bank checks. It can be observed that the proposed methodology is more robust and generic than the standard techniques in terms of accuracy. By comparing the results of Table 2 and Fig. 8 it is possible to note that the precision is more

Table 2. Thresholding performance of 60 images of the courtesy amount area.

Sampling method	Classifier	Acc	Pr	Re
RAND	MLP	**0.96**	0.71	0.95
	SVM	**0.96**	0.73	0.96
STD	MLP	0.94	0.67	0.97
	SVM	0.90	0.44	0.98
-	OTSU [13]	0.89	0.56	0.98
-	NIBLACK [14]	0.54	0.51	**0.99**
-	SAUVOLA [15]	0.94	**0.98**	0.95

related with the impact of false positive pixels in the background of the images, as can be observed in Fig. 8(c), in which the background appears quite dark. On the other hand, it is possible to note that recall is more related with the false negative pixels in the foreground of the images, as can be observed in Fig. 8(d) where the foreground of the images is not properly fulfilled. The proposed methodology presented a highest accuracy when compared with the other methodologies from the literature and Fig. 8, what seems to be related with enhanced images for human visualization.

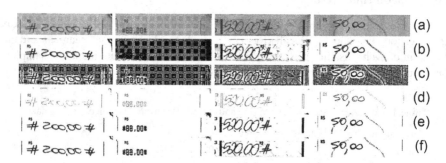

Fig. 8. Sample images of the courtesy amount and results after thresholding. (a) Grayscale image. (b) OTSU [13]. (c) NIBLACK [14]. (d) SAUVOLA [15]. (e) MLP RAND. (f) SVM RAND.

5 Discussion and Future Trends

This paper proposed a new thresholding methodology for complex background images with an application to the courtesy amount images of Brazilian bank checks. The main steps of the proposed methodology are: image database construction; extraction of the region of interest; pattern matrix construction; pattern labelling; database sampling; and classifier training. This methodology presents the capability of adapting to specificities of the courtesy amount of Brazilian bank checks. The experimental results performed with images of 60 different checks showed that the methodology is robust and presents an average accuracy over 95 % of selecting the correct class of each pixel, a performance superior to the one presented by the OTSU method [13], NIBLACK [14] and SAU-VOLA [15] that defines global and multiple local thresholds, respectively.

Future researches include the use of the proposed methodology in other image databases, the comparison of this methodology with other methods from the literature, including other pattern recognition and local approaches.

Acknowledgments. The authors thank Capes, Fapesp (Proc. 2013/05757-2) and Sincronica Sistemas Integrados LTDA for the financial support.

References

1. FEBRABAN: "FEBRABAN," Federação Brasileira de Bancos, 24 September 2014. www.febraban.org.br. Accessed 24 Sept 2014
2. Jayadevan, R., Kolhe, S., Patil, P., Pal, U.: Automatic processing of handwritten bank cheque images: a survey. Int. J. Doc. Anal. Recogn. (IJDAR) **15**(4), 267–296 (2012)
3. Sahoo, P.K., Soltani, A.K.W.S., Chen, Y.C.: A survey of thresholding techniques. Comput. Vision Graph. Image Process. **41**, 233–260 (1988)
4. de Castro, L.: Fundamentals of natural computing: an overview. Phys. Life Rev. **4**(1), 1–36 (2006)
5. Duda, R.O., Hart, P.E., Stork, D.G.: Pattern Classification, 2nd edn. Wiley-Interscience, New York (2000)
6. Chang, C.-C., Lin, C.-J.: LIBSVM: a library for support vector machines. ACM Trans. Intell. Syst. Technol. **2**, 1–27 (2011)
7. Chen, Y.-L.: A robust technique for character string extraction from complex document images. In: International Symposium on Information Technology, 2008, ITSim 2008, Kuala Lumpur, (2008)
8. Rabelo, J.C., Zanchettin, C., Mello, C.A., Bezerra, B.L.: A multi-layer perceptron approach to threshold documents with complex background. In: 2011 IEEE International Conference on Systems, Man, and Cybernetics (SMC), Chicago (2011)
9. Sezgin, M., Sankur, B.: Survey over image thresholding techniques and quantitative performance evaluation. J. Electron. Imaging **131**(1), 146–168 (2004)
10. Ahmad, I., Mahmoud, S.A.: Arabic bank check analysis and zone extraction. In: Campilho, A., Kamel, M. (eds.) ICIAR 2012, Part I. LNCS, vol. 7324, pp. 141–148. Springer, Heidelberg (2012)
11. Alginahi, Y., Sid-Ahmed, M., Ahmadi, M.: Local thresholding of composite documents using multi-layer perceptron neural network. In: The 2004 47th Midwest Symposium on Circuits and Systems, 2004, MWSCAS 2004 (2004)
12. de Castro, L.N., Von Zuben, F.J.: Optimised training techniques for feedforward neural networks. DCA-RT (1998)
13. Otsu, N.: A threshold selection method from gray-level histograms. IEEE Trans. Syst. Man Cybern. **SMC-9**(1), 62–66 (1979)
14. Niblack, W.: An Introduction to Digital Image Processing. Prentice Hall, Englewood Cliffs (1986)
15. Sauvola, J., Matti, P.: Adaptive document image binarization. Pattern Recogn. **33**(2), 225–236 (2000)

Workshop on Multi-agent Based Applications for Smart Grids and Sustainable Energy Systems

An Agent-Based Approach for Energy Management in Smart-Grids

Joelle Klaimi[1,2]([✉]), Rana Rahim-Amoud[1], Leila Merghem-Boulahia[2], and Akil Jrad[1]

[1] EDST, Centre-Azm, Laboratoire des Systèmes électroniques, Télécommunications Et Réseaux (LaSTRe), Lebanese University, Beirut, Lebanon
{rana.rahim,ajrad}@ul.edu.lb
[2] ICD/ERA (UMR CNRS 6281), Troyes University of Technology, Troyes, France
{joelle.klaimi,leila.merghem_boulahia}@utt.fr

Abstract. The advances in Information and Communication Technologies (ICT) permits interactions among the computational and the physical elements of the smart-grid, and provide opportunities for novel energy management techniques allowing thus renewable energy integration and energy price minimization. Few of the current energy management schemes integrate storage aspects. In this paper, we propose an agent-based algorithm for better energy management in the smart-grid using a storage system. Furthermore, we propose a negotiation algorithm to help consumer choose the appropriate producer which provides him the needed energy at the lowest price. Simulation results show that our proposal minimizes the energy costs for each energy demand and reduces conventional energy utilization.

Keywords: Smart-grids · Energy management · Renewable resources · Storage systems · Multi-agent systems

1 Introduction

The power grid is evolving to a new generation called "Smart-Grid" which introduces several technologies such as ICT to guarantee reliability, demand management, storage, distribution and transport of electrical energy [1,2]. Smart-grid is expected to incorporate distributed renewable resources such as wind or solar energy to offer a greener solution compared to traditional energy sources such as fossil. Although renewable energy is inexhaustible, it is however intermittent and irregular which makes it difficult to balance supply and demand. In this context and facing to the necessity of integration of renewable sources, energy management algorithms are of great importance to meet energy needs, to minimize energy loss and to reduce consumers' energy bill.

The term "energy management" is defined as the essential functions needed to increase energy efficiency and to optimally coordinate several energy sources. It is the process of observing, controlling and conserving electricity usage in a

© Springer International Publishing Switzerland 2015
J. Bajo et al. (Eds.): PAAMS 2015 Workshops, CCIS 524, pp. 225–236, 2015.
DOI: 10.1007/978-3-319-19033-4_19

building, a neighborhood, etc. It should find a solution that optimizes costs and minimizes the risk of loss of production excess.

In the other hand, in certain hours of the day or periods of the year the produced energy can exceed the consumption needs. This energy excess justifies the use of a storage system that allows short-term balance [3].

To be able to make intelligent decisions about energy management a multi-agent approach has been used by several researchers. Because of its distributed nature, a multi-agent system (MAS) represents an excellent tool for self control in widely distributed systems whose characteristics are very dynamic [4]. In this paper, we propose a negotiation algorithm to help consumer choose the appropriate producer that provides the energy he needs at the lowest price.

The remainder of the paper is organized as follows. In Sect. 2, we describe some of the existing approaches that are related to our work. We present in Sect. 3 our proposal and we explain our model and its characteristics, the agents' algorithms and the chosen scenarios. We describe in Sect. 4 the simulation results. We conclude our paper and give the future research directions in the Sect. 5.

2   Related Work

Several researchers have paid attention to the use of multi-agent systems and/or storage systems for energy management in smart-grids or microgrids. Microgrids can be defined as a cluster of energy sources, fuel cells and load serviced by a distributed system which may be integrated to the main grid or can be operated as a standalone system.

Some approaches have used storage systems in order to help in smart-grid energy management [5,6] while others introduced storage systems and microgids in order to enable an electricity market for the operation of a microgrid in both islanded and grid-connected modes [7]. Furthermore, an algorithm for energy management in smart-grid using a multi-agent system was proposed by Nagata et al. [8]. In this algorithm, there is a smart-grid controller unit that aims to negotiate and optimize the buying prices for consumers. This energy management algorithm aims to reduce the energy costs. Colson et al. [9] proposed an energy management algorithm for microgrid, using an MAS. In this algorithm, consumer agents use negotiation to get the energy at the lowest price. Finally, an agent-based approach was proposed in [10]. In this work, the authors proposed an agent-based algorithm allowing more efficient use of energy while minimizing cost and taking into account the integration of distributed renewable energy resources.

Some approaches summarized in this section have a common drawback which is lack of the integration of a storage system [8–10]. The approach proposed in [7] uses a storage system but without introducing intelligence to the storage management. In addition, the approaches presented in [5,6] consider only storage agents in their system. In our proposed approach which will be explained in the following section, we aim to ensure energy demand to consumers at the lowest price by introducing a storage system and negotiation algorithms.

3   ANEMAS: The Proposed Approach

This section describes our proposal "ANEMAS" (Agent-based eNErgy MAnagement in Smart-grids) which aims to resolve the problem of generation intermittency and to optimize in real time the consumer bill by integrating a storage system and using multi-agent algorithms (including negotiation).

3.1   The Proposed Multi-agent Model

The Agents are integrated in the different components of the smart-grid. They must control generation, load, and storage assets primarily from the standpoint of power flows. In our proposal, we define four agents:

1. Grid Agent: satisfies the energy lack and buys the excess of energy produced.
2. Storage Agent: controls the energy storage and are introduced in batteries.
3. Prosumer Agent: controls the distribution of the energy he produces.
4. Consumption Agent: negotiates the energy purchase with other consumers and prosumers.

The energy management system in our approach is divided into two layers: the proactive layer and the reactive layer. The proactive layer is responsible for the prediction of energy production and consumption. We choose the period as $\Delta t =$ 24 h. In this layer, the predicted values of consumption and production are those adopted by EDF (Electicité de France) and defined in [11]. The reactive layer is responsible for planning and negotiating consumption at shorter periods $\Delta t' =$ 1 h [10] and helps to buy energy with a minimal cost.

A priority P will be assigned for each user demand according to the user's preferences and the required quantity of energy. A demand's priority can be High, Medium, or Low, and the energy grid prices, at each period, are fixed by the grid. The agent satisfies the highest priority demands at the beginning, then it will satisfy the medium priority demands and finally the lowest priority ones. The agent can delay the medium priority for a given time, that we call Medium Delay (MD), and the low priority for a Low Delay (LD), such as $LD > MD$. Moreover, the consumption periods are divided during the day as follows: the Off-Peak period (OP), the Low-Peak period (LP) and the High-Peak period (HP). In the Off-Peak period, the energy use and the cost are minimal while in the Low-Peak period, the energy consumption and the purchase of energy start to increase. Finally, in the High-Peak period, the energy use reaches its maximum and the purchase price of energy becomes very high [10].

Within the constraints listed above, an algorithm is proposed for each agent for the purpose of energy management.

3.2   Agents Algorithms

Each agent has its own algorithm that we will describe in the following.

Grid Agent

The grid agent provides the lack of energy to consumers when the production of renewable energy does not meet their demands. Furthermore, in case of an excess of production, this agent can arrange to purchase energy in excess. This agent receives requests from consumers to meet the demands unsatisfied by the renewable resources and from producers to sell him their excess.

Storage Agent

The storage agent is responsible for providing energy to consumers during peak hours or in case of lack of energy. In case of production excess, these agents store energy. This stored energy may be used later in order to reduce energy cost. The storage agent has to respect multiple constraints, presented hereafter, concerning the amount of energy to store in order to meet the users needs:

- SOC_{min}: minimum state of charge.
- SOC_{max}: maximum state of charge.
- PR: grid price.
- PR_{min}: minimum grid price.
- Peak = sum of peak demands predicted for all consumers.
- SOC(t) = instantaneous state of battery charge.
- D_j = requested demand for period j.
- RE_j = renewable energy produced on period j.
- EN_{st} = energy to be stored.
- $tpeak$ = time corresponding to the maximum consumption during a day.

The steps of the storage agent algorithm are presented in the Algorithm 1. In Table 1, we show an example to explain how we calculate EN_{st}. We suppose that $Peak - SOC(tpeak) - RE_{tpeak} = Peak - \sum_{j=0}^{tpeak-1}(RE_j - D_j) - RE_{tpeak}$ and we consider that at period 0 the energy price is minimal so the storage agent will calculate the energy to store. For sake of clarity, we will present only 3 periods. As shown in the example, the High-peak period is the period 1. Normally, the battery should store the lack of energy that can occur, which is 3 in this example but in the peak period the consumers may have a lack of energy that the storage cannot satisfy. In this period (High-peak) the demand may be greater than the total lack, in this example it is 5 which is greater than 3 so the storage system should store 5 KW (max(5,3)) at period 0.

Consumption Agent

We consider that consumption agents are deployed in smart homes. At each period, the consumption agent divides its demands into three priorities: (1) the priority 1 is the higher priority and its demands should not be delayed or dropped, (2) the priority 2 is the medium priority and its demands can be delayed for a short time, (3) and finally the priority 3 is the lowest one and its needs can be delayed for a time higher than the delay time for the priority 2.

Algorithm 1

$EN_{st} \leftarrow max(Peak - SOC(tpeak) - RE_{tpeak}, \sum_{j=i}^{23} D_j - \sum_{j=i}^{23}(RE_j) - SOC(t));$
//Amount of energy to store in order to complement the RE produced and satisfy
all the demands (from the current period (i) to period 23)
if $PR = PR_{min}$ then
  if $EN_{st} \leq SOC_{max}$ then
    RequestCharge(EN_{st}); //The storage agent requests an amount of energy equal
    to EN_{st} from the grid
  else
    RequestCharge(SOC_{max}); //The storage agent requests an amount of energy
    equal to SOC_{max} from the grid
  end if
else //PR is not equal to PR_{min}
  if $SOC(t) < EN_{st}$ and $PR_i < PR_{i+1}$ then //If the storage cannot meet all the
  demands and the energy price at period i+1 is greater than the energy price at
  period i
    if $RE_{i+1} < D_{i+1}$ and $D_{i+1} - RE_{i+1} \geq SOC_{max} - SOC(t)$ then
    RequestCharge($D_{i+1} - RE_{i+1}$); //If there is a space in the storage system
    ($SOC_{max} - SOC(t)$) to charge the energy needed ($D_{i+1} - RE_{i+1}$), then the
    storage agent requests an amount of energy equal to $D_{i+1} - RE_{i+1}$ from the
    grid
    end if
  end if
  GoToNextPeriod();
end if

Table 1. Example of EN_{st}

Period (i)	0	1	2
$D_i(KW)$	3	12	8
$RE_i(KW)$	2	8	10
$\sum_{j=0}^{2} D_j - \sum_{j=0}^{2}(RE_j) - SOC(t)$	(3+12+8)-(2+8+10)-0 = 3	-	-
$Peak - SOC(tpeak) - RE_{tpeak}$	12-(2-3)-(8)=5	-	-

The activities with priority 2 or 3 can be delayed without causing any inconvenience. The priority 2 activities delay is called Medium Delay (MD) and the priority 3 activities delay is called Low Delay (LD). The MD and the LD will be chosen so that the consumer does not lose in comfort. In other words, the MD and the LD have a maximum that will be selected so that the activity will be satisfied. This maximum will be set by the system administrator.

Case 1: Decision for Highest Priority Data. Data with Priority 1 are satisfied at the beginning. The consumption agent negotiates the purchase of renewable energy (Fig. 1, (1)) by using the negotiation strategy explained below:

1. Consumption agent receives at each period the production and the consumption data from each prosumer and consumption agent.

2. Consumption agent j calculates the utility function f(j) defined in the Algorithm 2 Where:

Algorithm 2

$f(j) = 0$; //initialize the utility function
if $RE_j < E_j$ then //The production of prosumer can not meet its demands
    while $E_j > 0$ do //while demand is not satisfied the consumer or prosumer chooses to buy its demands from sources which have the cheapest price
        for all $0 < i \leq NbProsumers$ and $i \neq j$ do
        ChooseMinimal($min(C_{ji} * P_{ji} * E_{ji})$)
        $f(j) += C_{ji} * P_{ji} * E_{ji}$;
        $E_j = E_j - E_{ji}$
        end for
    end while
end if
for all $0 < i \leq NbConsumers$ and $i \neq j$ do //after satisfying its demands a consumer uses to meet the demands of other consumers with a minimum price
    if $RE_i < E_i$ then //The production of prosumer can not meet its demands
        while $E_i > 0$ do
        for all $0 < k \leq NbProsumers$ and $k \neq i$ do
        ChooseMinimal($min(C_{ki} * P_{ki} * E_{ki})$)
        $f(j) += C_{ki} * P_{ki} * E_{ki}$;
        $E_i = E_i - E_{ki}$
        end for
        end while
    end if
end for

- f(j)= utility funtion for agent j.
- NbProsumers = prosumers total number.
- NbConsumers = prosumers total number.
- P_{ji} = priority that increases if the resource is closer to the consumer, we consider $P_{ii} = 1$ and $P_{ij} = P_{ji}$.
- E_{ji} = maximum energy that can be bought from prosumer i to consumer j.
- C_{ji} = renewable energy cost, we consider $C_{ii} = 0$.

3. Consumption agent sends its proposition to all consumption agents.
4. When consumption agent receives all the proposals, it chooses the one with the highest utility function and purchases energy according to this proposal.

When the negotiation ends (Fig. 1, (2)), and after buying energy from the renewable resources, the consumer agent follows these steps:

- If there is a demand that cannot be satisfied by renewable resources (Fig. 1, (3)), then the consumption agent compares the storage cost and the grid cost to choose the minimum between them (Fig. 1, (5)).
- If the grid has the minimum cost and can provide energy (Fig. 1, (7)) a request will be sent to the grid (Fig. 1, (8)).

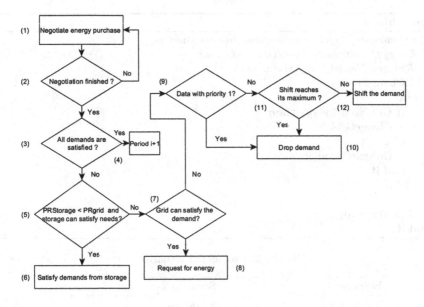

Fig. 1. Consumption agent algorithm

- If the storage cost is less than the grid cost and the available storage energy can meet the demands (Fig. 1, (5)), so a request will be sent to the storage system to satisfy user demands (Fig. 1, (6)).
- If the grid and the storage cannot satisfy the demands so the activity will be dropped (Fig. 1, (10)). In fact, this situation is very rare and should be avoided.

Case 2: Decision for Medium or Low Priority Data. Data with Priority 2 or 3 are satisfied after the data with priority 1. In this case, if the grid and the storage cannot satisfy the demands, so the activity will be delayed for MD for priority 2 demands and for LD for priority 3 demands (Fig. 1, (12)). This activity will be dropped if the maximum which is 1 h for priority 2 and 3 h for priority 3 of delayed periods is reached (Fig. 1, (10)).

Prosumer Agent

Prosumer agents are introduced in production units renewable (photovoltaics, wind turbines, etc.). For each period i, the prosumer agent aims to satisfy firstly its demands, and if the energy it produced exceeds its needs, it will satisfy other consumers demands and buy the energy to the grid or to the storage system. The steps of the prosumer agent algorithm is presented in the Algorithm 3.

3.3 Description of the Considered Scenarios

We choose to implement in our system an agent for the grid, an agent for each consumer, an agent for the storage system and an agent for each prosumer. For our simulation, we consider two scenarios. Table 2 presents the chosen scenarios.

Algorithm 3

MeetDemands(); //satisfies requests from consumers
if $EnergyProduced > UsersDemands$ then
  if StorageNeedsEnergy then
    ChargeStorage();
  else
    if GridNeedsEnergy then
      ChargeGrid();
    else
      GoNextPeriod();
    end if
  end if
else
  GoNextPeriod();
end if

Table 2. Considered scenarios

Scenario 1	Scenario 2
1 grid agent	1 grid agent
5 consumption agents:	10 consumption agents:
3 Prosumers + 2 consumers	7 Prosumers + 3 consumers
1 storage agent	1 storage agent

The Scenario 1 is a simplified one with 1 grid agent, 2 consumer agents, 3 prosumer agents and 1 storage agent that has a large charge state to serve all the system. Some complexity is introduced in scenario 2 to test the performance of our proposal when we increase agents number. This scenario has 1 grid agent, 3 consumer agents, 7 prosumer agents and 1 storage agent that has a large charge state to serve all the system. Simulation results are presented in the following section.

4   ANEMAS Performance Evaluation

In order to evaluate the performance of our scheme, we simulate the agent behaviors with JADE (Java Agent Development Framework) [12]. It is one of the most popular MAS simulators used for the development of distributed applications.

4.1   Simulation Parameters

The consumption periods during the day are splitted into: the Off-Peak period (OP), the Low-Peak period (LP) and the High-Peak period (HP). Moreover, the day is divided into 24 periods and grid prices vary between 10 cents and 22 cents and wind turbine energy (our renewable energy) prices vary between 14 cents and 7 cents [11]. The peak hours are represented in Table 3.

Table 3. Day peak

Period	OP	LP	HP
Hour	00:00 to 12:59	13:00 to 19:59	20:00 to 23:59

4.2   Results

After showing the different scenarios that can take place in a negotiation for energy purchase, the efficiency of ANEMAS will be shown by comparing it to a typical billing scheme used in most electric power systems where some or all consumers pay a fixed price per unit of electricity independently of the cost of production at the time of consumption, this scheme is referred Conventional-case in the following. In addition, we compare our algorithm to a system that uses the renewable resources but do not use storage systems, the scheme used in this case is called RE-case.

Firstly, we illustrate the simulation results for one day of operation. The first simulation test is carried out by using scenario 1 and the results are given in Figs. 2 and 3. Figure 2 shows consumers buying prices with the three defined schemes. During the day, the reduction in consumer bills is caused by the use of renewable energy or by the use of renewable energy and storage systems.

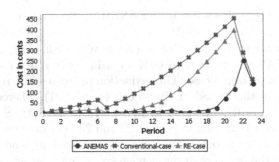

Fig. 2. Consumer bills for Scenario 1

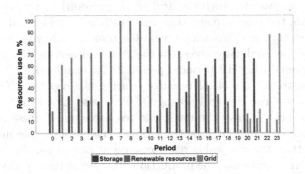

Fig. 3. Resources use for ANEMAS (Scenario 1)

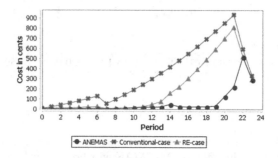

Fig. 4. Consumer bills Scenario 2

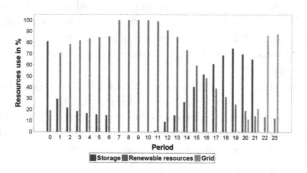

Fig. 5. Resources use for ANEMAS (Scenario 2)

During Off-Peak hours the reduction of cost is very high, it is more than 90 % by using ANEMAS and more than 60 % by using only renewable resources in comparison to conventional-case. This reduction decreases and reaches 75 % by using ANEMAS in the period of High-Peak (period 21), whereas during this period the decrease in RE-case is 16 %. In both cases (ANEMAS and RE-case), there is no more cost reduction at periods 22 and 23. The decrease in bills is due to the use of renewable resources for RE-case. Increased demand and decreased production cause the decrease in the percentage of price reduction in Low-peak and High-peak hours. Therefore by switching from Off-Peak to the High-Peak, consumer bills increase to reach the grid costs. In addition, we notice that, by using ANEMAS, the costs are less than costs in RE-case. This reduction is due to the use of storage systems with renewable resources, buying stored energy when costs are low, reducing access to the grid and serving the users with a minimal cost even during HP periods (period 21 for example).

Figure 3 shows the use of all resources during the day by ANEMAS. Our algorithm does not use the grid during Off-Peak and Low-Peak periods (grid use is equal to zero). It uses the renewable resources and if these resources do not meet all the demands, it uses the storage. The storage use increases and will be higher than the renewable resources use at period 15, this is caused by the consumption increase and the production decrease at these periods. Furthermore, the use of the grid increases in High-Peak hours and after period 21 the storage use is equal to 0 and the grid use increases. This change is due to the storage charge which reached its minimal value during High-Peak hours.

The results for scenario 2 are shown in Figs. 4 and 5 respectively. When we analyze the results shown in these two figures we can conclude that these results have not much differences from the results of Scenario 1. Figure 4 gives the consumers bill for scenario 2, and shows that minimization of costs is the same as that in scenario 1 in both cases (ANEMAS and RE-case). In High-Peak (period 21), the cost minimization reaches 75 % for ANEMAS and 16 % for RE-case.

Furthermore, resources use shown in Fig. 5 demonstrates that the use of the grid increases in high-peak (period 21) when we use our algorithm (Fig. 5).

These results of our proposed algorithm ANEMAS show that when the number of consumers increases, the cost reduction and the grid use remain the same.

5   Conclusion

Introducing renewable energy sources into smart-grids has some inconvenience due to the weather and time dependencies. The use of energy storage systems and multi-agent approach are good solutions to ensure the energy management, to reduce the consumers' bills and to minimize the access to the grid. Our proposal introduces four agent types into the system: the grid agent, the storage agent, the prosumer agent and the consumption agent. It aims to lead to more responsible energy consumption while establishing lower contract prices. After simulating the proposed approach using JADE, we noticed that the use of a storage system reduces the energy cost and the grid utilization which will reduce the CO_2 emissions. As a future work we plan to consider more storage systems which may be in competition. Furthermore, we will compare our approach with other approaches in the literature and will study other negotiation algorithms.

References

1. Petinrin, J.O., Shaaban, M.: Smart power grid: technologies and applications. In: 2012 IEEE International Conference on Power and Energy (PECon), pp. 892–897. December 2012
2. Mets, K., Strobbe, M., Verschueren, T., Roelens, T., De Turck, F., Develder, C.: Distributed multi-agent algorithm for residential energy management in smart grids. In: 2012 IEEE Network Operations and Management Symposium (NOMS), pp. 435–443. April 2012
3. Guo, Y., Pan, M., Fang, Y.: Optimal power management of residential customers in the smart grid. IEEE Trans. Parallel Distrib. Syst. **23**(9), 1593–1606 (2012)
4. Belkacemi, R., Bababola, A.: Experimental implementation of multi-agent system algorithm for distributed restoration of a smart grid system. In: IEEE SOUTH-EASTCON 2014, pp. 1–4. March 2014
5. Alberola, J.M., Julián, V., García-Fornes, A.: A self-configurable agent-based system for intelligent storage in smart grid. In: Corchado, J.M., Bajo, J., Kozlak, J., Pawlewski, P., Molina, J.M., Julian, V., Silveira, R.A., Unland, R., Giroux, S. (eds.) PAAMS 2013. CCIS, vol. 365, pp. 240–250. Springer, Heidelberg (2013)

6. Vytelingum, P., Voice, T.D., Ramchurn, S.D., Rogers, A., Jennings, N.R.: Theoretical and practical foundations of large-scale agent-based micro-storage in the smart grid. J. Artif. Int. Res. **42**, 765–813 (2011)

7. Logenthiran, T., Srinivasan, D.: Multi-agent system for market based microgrid operation in smart grid environment. Department of Electronics and Computer Science, National University of Singapore (2011)

8. Nagata, T., Ueda, Y., Utatani, M.: A multi-agent approach to smart grid energy management. In: IPEC, 2012 Conference on Power Energy, pp. 327–331. December 2012

9. Colson, C.M., Nehrir, M.H.: Algorithms for distributed decision-making for multi-agent microgrid power management. In: 2011 IEEE Power and Energy Society General Meeting, pp. 1–8. July 2011

10. El Nabouch, D., Matta, N., Rahim-Amoud, R., Merghem-Boulahia, L.: An agent-based approach for efficient energy management in the context of smart houses. In: Corchado, J.M., Bajo, J., Kozlak, J., Pawlewski, P., Molina, J.M., Julian, V., Silveira, R.A., Unland, R., Giroux, S. (eds.) PAAMS 2013. CCIS, vol. 365, pp. 375–386. Springer, Heidelberg (2013)

11. EDF (2013). http://france.edf.com/france-45634.html

12. JADE (2015). http://jade.tilab.com/

Forming Coalitions of Electric Vehicles in Constrained Scenarios

Ana L.C. Bazzan[⊠] and Gabriel de O. Ramos

Instituto de Informática, Universidade Federal do Rio Grande do Sul,
Porto Alegre, Brazil
{bazzan,goramos}@inf.ufrgs.br

Abstract. Finding an optimal coalition structure is a hard problem. In order to simplify this process, it is possible to explore some characteristics of the agents organization. In this paper we propose an algorithm that deals with a particular family of games in characteristic function, but is able to search in a much smaller space by considering organizational issues such as constraints in the number of participants. We apply this approach to the domain of smart grids, in which the aim is to form coalitions of electric vehicles in order to increase their reliability when supplying energy to the grid.

1 Introduction

A coalition can be defined as a group of agents that decide to cooperate in order to achieve a common goal. An outcome of a coalitional game is a partition of the set of all players into coalitions, together with an action for each coalition. However, partitioning agents in coalitions is not a trivial problem. In multiagent systems (MASs), there has been an increasing interest in coalition formation involving cooperative agents in order to deal with problems such as task allocation [1]. In general, the research on CGs tackles one or more of these activities: coalition structure generation (CSG hereafter); solving the joint problem; dividing the value among the members of the coalition. The former and the latter have been extensively studied in game-theory, while the second is tackled by the MASs community. This paper focuses on the first (as other works mentioned in the next section) since this is a key aspect for effective organizations in MASs. The bad news is that this problem is equivalent to the set partitioning one, which is NP-complete [2]. In the general case, the number of coalition structures is so large ($O(a^a)$, where a is the number of agents) that it cannot be enumerated for more than a few agents.

The first algorithm to establish a bound with a minimal amount of search was given in [2] (henceforth S99). In 2004, [3] (henceforth DJ04) provided a faster algorithm that is within a finite bound from the optimum and is faster than the S99. Then, Rahwan *et al.* have proposed further algorithms [4–6]. The former (henceforth IP) introduced a near-optimal anytime algorithm for coalition structure generation, which partitions the space in terms of coalitions of

© Springer International Publishing Switzerland 2015
J. Bajo et al. (Eds.): PAAMS 2015 Workshops, CCIS 524, pp. 237–248, 2015.
DOI: 10.1007/978-3-319-19033-4_20

particular sizes. In [5] (henceforth IDP) an algorithm was proposed, which is based on dynamic programming as was the case in [7]. The hybrid of IDP and IP (IDP-IP) was a breakthrough, but it is still in $O(3^a)$. In [6], the quality guarantees provided by [2] were improved. Specifically, it was shown that there is a minimum search required to establish any bound in any subset of the search space. However, a new question has emerged, which regards how to identify the coalition structures that belong to such subsets. These and other works are based on a search in a coalition structure graph (see [2] for an explanation). In these graphs, each node corresponds to a coalition structure. Nodes are grouped in levels according to the number of partitions they have (e.g., coalition structures comprising two coalitions appear in the second level of the graph, and so on). An arc between two nodes represent (i) a splitting of one coalition of the CS into two, or (ii) a merging of two coalitions into a single one. Based on such representation of the search space, [2] showed that searching the two lowest levels of the graph is enough to establish a bound a on the solution quality.

Despite the fact that a bound can be established in linear time in the size of the input, the bad news is that 2^{a-1} nodes of the coalition structure graph have to be searched in order to guarantee the worst case bound from optimum. This prevents the use of that kind of algorithm for a high number of agents. Even if some researchers have shown that it is possible to lower the bound with further and/or smarter search, due to the aforementioned complexity problem, this road is unlike to lead to efficiency when it comes to real-world applications with more than 30 agents. Rather, it is necessary to count on something for which AI is well known, namely exploitation of domain knowledge.

Thus, in the present paper we rely on domain knowledge to define a particular class of CSG in which coalitions are constrained in their size. The knowledge employed here comes from the domain of smart grids[1]. Specifically, we take advantage of the fact that, in order to increase the robustness of providing energy to the grid, eletric vehicles (EVs) must work together in so-called virtual power plants (VPPs). However, to this aim, EVs cannot be arbitrarily located (due to energy transmission constraints), nor can the VPP be arbitrarily large. Thus coalitions of EVs are constrained with respect to their size and distance. Besides, in the game structure proposed here, searching in the two lowest levels of the coalition structure graph, as in S99, is not necessarily the best strategy. For example, electrical vehicles are likely to be partitioned in more than two coalitions so that it seems illogical to start looking at partitions of size two.

We consider games that are neither superadditive nor subadditive (same as in S99, DJ04, IP, IDP, and others) but whose characteristic function has the property of being monotonically increasing in a certain interval. This property allow us to direct the search to levels other than those proposed previously. As we show, for particular characteristic functions, the coalition structure (CS) with maximum value can be located by visiting one single level of the CS graph.

---

[1] We remark that the CSG class defined here is general, and it is not restricted to the smart grid problem.

This paper is organized as follows. In the next section we give a motivation for forming coalitions in the smart grid domain. We also discuss the background of generation of CSs as well as some of the algorithms already mentioned. Following, in Sect. 3 we formalize our approach and discuss some of its variants. Examples of its utilization in the smart grid domain are also discussed. In Sect. 4 we show experimental results, which are then followed by a conclusion (Sect. 5).

2   Smart Grids: The Example of Electric Vehicles

In most countries, electric power generation strongly depends on non-renewable, polluting energy sources whose availability is becoming scarce. Furthermore, environmental and economic impacts resulting from the use of non-renewable energy sources have become an issue in our society. In order to reverse this scenario, many governments have been focusing on the transition to a low carbon economy. One of the major challenges arising from this transition refers to the modernization of the energy infrastructure (the grid). Electricity grids have evolved very little over the years. In this context, the concept of smart grids emerges, which is described by the U. S. Department of Energy [8] as "a fully automated power delivery network that monitors and controls every customer and node, ensuring a *two-way flow* of electricity and information between the power plant and the appliance [. . .]". The smart grid concept is closely related to computing, and in particular, given its essentially distributed nature, smart grids represent a large field of research for MASs [9,10].

In addition to the concept of smart grids, recently the concept of vehicle-to-grid (V2G) has drawn attention, in which electric vehicles (EVs) can provide part of the energy stored in their batteries back to the grid when needed. This mechanism becomes important in situations where the grid relies on intermittent renewable energy, as it is the case of energy provided by wind turbines and solar panels. In such cases, the energy stored in the EVs' batteries can be provided back to the grid when production is not able to meet the demand.

The use of V2G mechanisms has received great attention of many researchers who associate agents and smart grids, as in [11–16]. In essence, the concept of V2G can be seen as a distributed energy storage system. However, EVs are unable to operate alone in a reliable and cost-effective way due to insufficient energy capacity and due to lack of full availability (EVs can supply energy back to the grid just when they are not in use). Therefore, coalition formation is an efficient way to increase the reliability on EVs' supply of energy.

Regarding other works, many of these address coalition formation between distributed energy resources (DERs) to form VPPs. DERs are renewable energy generators with small to medium energy capacity, like wind turbines, solar panels etc. Taking into account that renewable energy sources are intermittent due to weather conditions, many approaches suggest grouping DERs to promote reliability and efficiency on production predictions. Examples are [11–14]. The former focuses on mechanism design rather than in coalition structure generation, disregarding how far the solution is from the optimal one; in the others, coalition structure generation is made in an ad hoc fashion, without necessarily concerning the optimal solution.

It is then clear that most existing works have given greater importance to applications of smart grids than to coalition formation itself. A more concrete step into this direction was given in [15,16], where the coalition formation process was extended to dynamic scenarios. In these works, coalition formation is locally negotiated by the agents. However, despite promising experimental results, no quality guarantees were provided.

3   Finding Optimal Coalition Structures for a Sub-class of CFGs: Smart Grid Problems

3.1   Coalition of Electric Vehicles

As mentioned, the motivation for forming coalitions of EVs is that they cannot operate alone in a reliable way [17]. Basically, the capacity/effectiveness of a VPP on supplying energy to the grid is proportional to its size (number of EVs). On the other hand, it is known that the energy loss is proportional to the distance of transmission. Thus, the size of coalitions must be restricted to, for instance, EVs that are within a certain radius. An example could be all EVs parked in a given building. Finally, in some circumstances, VPPs may be able to include not only EVs but also other DERs such as wind turbines. In this case, it is clear that a coalition that includes such a turbine shall have a higher value, since a turbine is a more valuable player in the coalition. The reason for this is the fact that turbines have a higher availability.

Grounded on these facts, we introduce a particular class of CFGs, where coalitions are restricted in their sizes, and show how the optimal CS can be found by searching a single level of the CS graph. The rest of this section first introduces the notation and shows how to find the level l where the CS with maximal value is located (for the particular class of CFGs we tackle here). It then discusses a case in which the CFG is modified to include agents that bring more value to the coalition, and presents special configurations and constraints that allows us to find level l in a straightforward way.

3.2   Definitions

The notation used in this paper is the following:

- A: the set of agents (here EVs), with cardinality $a = |A|$;
- $K \subseteq A$: a coalition of size $|K|$;
- $v(K)$: value of coalition K, given by a characteristic function (CFG) defined on the set of all coalitions (2^a). In the general case, the CFG is defined as $v : 2^a \to \mathbb{R}$ with $v(\emptyset) = 0$.
- CS is a coalition structure, i.e., a particular partition of A into disjoint and exhaustive sets; the value of the structure $V(CS)$ is given by $V(CS) = \sum_{K \in CS} v(K)$;

- $CS^\star$ is the optimal CS, i.e., the one with maximal value;
- l is a level in the CS graph, meaning that the l-th level has l subsets in each coalition structure (for example, in level $l = 2$ all coalition structures have two coalitions each).

We consider a subclass of CG's which has CFG's with the following structure[2]:

- $v(\emptyset) = 0$
- $v(K) = 0$ if $|K| = 1$
- $v(K) = 0$ if $|K| \geq \alpha$ with $\alpha = \lfloor \frac{a}{\rho} \rfloor$, $\rho = \{1, 2, ..., \frac{a}{3}\}$
- $v(K) = \varphi(K)$ if $2 \leq |K| < \alpha$

This means that coalitions of size one, α, or bigger than α have $v = 0$, and that we wish to partition A in at least two coalitions. Note that this value (two coalitions) can easily be changed, as well as the fact that in what follows we use $\varphi(K) = |K|$.

We show here that, for CFG's as above, the coalition structure with maximum value can be located by visiting one single level of the CS graph. This is similar to the algorithm S99 (which visits levels 1 and 2 of the CS graph) but by visiting level l we guarantee finding the $CS^\star$ while they found a bound. It is important to notice that more than one CS may have the same maximum value. If this is the case, the maximum value may occur in other levels as well, but visiting the level our algorithm computes, it is guaranteed to find at least one of the CSs with maximum value.

After the level containing $CS^\star$ is found, a search must be performed in order to find the $CS^\star$ itself. The size of this search space is given by the Stirling number of the second kind $S(a, l)$, which gives the number of partitions of a set A into l non empty sets: $S(a, l) = \frac{1}{l!} \sum_{i=0}^{l-1} (-1)^i \binom{l}{i} (l - i)^a$.

3.3   General Structure of the Algorithm

The level l that has the CS with maximum value $(CS^\star)$ is computed by Eq. 1, where:

- $1 \leq j \leq (\alpha - 1)$
- $v(K_j)$ is the value of the coalition of size j
- $i = \lfloor \frac{a}{j} \rfloor$
- $\gamma = \begin{cases} 0 \text{ if } \mod(a,j)=0 \\ 1 \text{ otherwise} \end{cases}$

$$l = \arg \max_i [i \times v(K_j)] + \gamma \tag{1}$$

---

[2] As in previous algorithms, we also assume that $v(K) \geq 0$ for any K (or at least those CSs visited by the algorithm), which is not a restrictive assumption given that the CFG can be normalized.

The rationale behind Eq. 1 is that the level l where $V(CS^\star)$ is to be found is the one where it is possible to put the highest number of coalitions with high value, with the least remainder (zero if possible). To do this, it is necessary to test $(\alpha - 1)$ values for $(i \times v(K_j))$ in order to find the maximum value for this product[3]. This maximum corresponds to one or more values of i. When more than one exists, one must use some domain dependent heuristic, or select the i that implies the smallest search space (easily computed by the Stirling number of the second kind) for the actual determination of the $CS^\star$.

Notice that Eq. 1 returns the *level* where $CS^\star$ is to be found, not necessarily the $CS^\star$ itself. This only happens if i is a factor of a. In this case, $V(CS^\star)$ is found after $(\alpha - 1)$ computations of $(i \times v(K_j))$, without further search in the space spanned by the Stirling number of the second kind. Here the algorithm finds $V(CS^\star)$ linearly in the number of agents. However, this is not always the case: among the $(\alpha - 1)$ values for $(i \times v(K_j))$, it is not necessarily the case that we find $V(CS^\star)$ because i might not be a factor of a. Thus, in the most general case, level l (but only this level) must be searched completely to find $CS^\star$.

Proposition 1. $CS^\star$ is located in level l given by Eq. 1.

Proof. Call $(i^\star, j^\star)$ the pair (i, j) that maximizes $(i \times v(K_j))$. When $i^\star$ is a factor of a, the proof is trivial because consequently $j^\star$ is also a factor and there is no better way to partition a (remember that the maximum $(i \times v(K_j))$ was selected). Other partitions can have at most the same value, but never exceed the one given by $(i^\star, j^\star)$.

If i is not a factor of a, then there are $i^\star$ coalitions (of size $j^\star$ each) plus a remainder. These are:

$$\{1, ..., j^\star\}\{j^\star + 1, ..., 2j^\star\}...\{(i^\star - 1)j^\star + 1, ..., i^\star j^\star\} \; \{i^\star j^\star + 1, ..., a\}$$

When $a = i^\star j^\star + 1$, then the last set has only one element and hence value zero. Therefore, the whole CS has value smaller than a (in fact $a - 1$). If we take one element out of any of the $i^\star$ sets (say, the first), then this one will have value $(j^\star - 1)$ and the last set will have value 2. The total value of the CS is then: $(j^\star - 1) + (i^\star - 1)j^\star + 2 = i^\star j^\star + 1 = a$.

When $a > i^\star j^\star + 1$, then the last set has a non zero value and thus all sets sum to a. $\qquad \square$

Next we give examples of how to compute l. In the tables, hatched rows represent those l's where $CS^\star$'s can be found.

Example 1. $a = 20$ EVs, $\alpha = 5$.

j	i	$(i \times v(K_j))$	l
1	20	0	
2	10	20	10
3	6	18	
4	5	20	5

---

[3] This comes from the fact that, for $j \geq \alpha$ coalitions of size j have value zero and hence $(i \times v(K_j))$ has value zero as well. Thus it makes no sense to compute i's for $j \geq \alpha$.

In this case the least search space refers to $i = 5$, thus Eq. 1 returns $l = 5$. As here i is a factor of a, $V(CS^*)$ is found directly.

Example 2. $a = 20$ EVs, $\alpha = 4$.

The table is the same as in Example 1, without the last line. In this case, Eq. 1 returns $l = 10$.

Example 3. $a = 13$ EVs, $\alpha = 4$.

j	i	$(i \times v(K_j))$	l
1	13	0	
2	6	12	7
3	4	12	5

In this case, $l = 5$ yields less search than $l = 7$. Thus $i = 4$, and i is not a factor of a. This value for i corresponds to $l = 5$ (see table). In this level, there are partitions like this: 4 coalitions of size 3 and one of size 1, which is not optimal. However, as proven above, level $l = 5$ has also the CS^*: it has 3 coalitions of size 3 and 2 of size 2.

3.4 Coalitions with More Valuable Players

The games with CFG's as in the given examples do not distinguish between individual values of agents (here, DERs). In some cases, more valuable DERs aggregate an additional value $\delta > 1$ to the coalitions they are in.

Games with more valuable agents require slight modifications in the CFG previously defined. We define $G \subset A$ as the set of more valuable agents, and:

- $v(\emptyset) = 0$
- $v(K) = 0$ if $|K| = 1$
- $v(K) = 0$ if $|K| \geq \alpha$ with $\alpha = \lfloor \frac{a}{\rho} \rfloor$, $\rho \in \{1, 2, ..., \frac{a}{3}\}$
- $v(K) = \varphi(K)$ if $2 \leq |K| < \alpha$ and $G \cap K = \emptyset$
- $v(K) = \varphi(K) \times \delta$ if $2 \leq |K| < \alpha$ and $G \cap K \neq \emptyset$

We now show that when $G \neq \emptyset$, the level where the value of CS is maximum can still be found by Eq. 1. However, because $\delta > 1$, bigger coalitions have more value and hence l should be as low as possible. The modification is given in Eq. 2.

$$l = min[\arg \max_i [i \times v(K_j)] + \gamma] \qquad (2)$$

For the sketches of the proofs, we assume (without loss of generality) that the coalitions with additional values are the first ones. Each of these have value $j^* \times \delta$.

We first show that no other level below l contains CSs with higher value than that found in level l. In the level $(l - 1)$, there are $(i^* - 1)$ coalitions. In respect to level l, this means that some coalitions somehow join to form this additional set. The highest possible value for the CSs in level $(l-1)$ occurs when the agent(s) that bring additional value remain partitioned as in level l. Any two other coalitions that join together would have size higher than $(\alpha - 1)$ and hence value zero. Thus no CS would have higher value in level $(l - 1)$. This holds for lower levels as well due to the same reason.

We now look at level $l + 1$, where one coalition splits into two. If this split yields one coalition of size exactly one (e.g., splitting of a coalition of size 3), then this has value zero and hence the total value is reduced. If the split yields two coalitions of size greater than one, then the two coalitions together will have no more value than when they were together, so the value increases in no case.

Example 4. Consider that there are 2 wind turbines and 14 EVs, thus $a = 16$, $A = \{A1, A2, ..., A16\}$, $G = \{A1, A2\}$. Assuming $\alpha = 5$:

j	i	$(i \times v(K_j))$	l
1	16	0	
2	8	16	8
3	5	15	
4	4	16	4

Here $l = 4$ is better than $l = 8$, thus one of the CS^*s returned after searching this level is given by: $\{\mathbf{A1}, A3, A4, A5\}, \{\mathbf{A2}, A6, A7, A8\}, \{...\}, \{A13, ..., A16\}$ (value $4\delta + 4\delta + 4 + 4 = 8\delta + 8$). In level $l = 3$ one of the CS's that has the highest value is formed by merging coalitions that do not contain A1 or A2 (otherwise these players would find themselves in a coalition of value zero because it has a cardinality higher than α): $\{\mathbf{A1}, A3, A4, A5\}, \{\mathbf{A2}, A6, A7, A8\}, \{A9, .., A16\}$ (value is only 8δ). In level $l = 5$, splitting coalitions with agents A1 or A2 makes no sense, so the best case is when one of the others split (say, the last): $\{\mathbf{A1}, A3, A4, A5\}, \{\mathbf{A2}, A6, A7, A8\}, \{...\}, \{A13, A14\}, \{A15, A16\}$ (value $8\delta + 8$). Thus in level $l = 4 + 1$, there is no increase in the value.

This example illustrates the above proof that the level where the value of CS is maximum remains as given by Eq. 1 when some agents aggregate an additional value of δ to the coalition they join.

3.5 Heuristics for Finding Level l

Equation 1 is general and computes the level where the CS of maximum value is in any case (provided the CFG has the structure presented). However, the algorithm to perform the calculation still has to be performed $\alpha - 1$ times in order to find the i for which the product $(i \times v(K_j))$ is maximum. In some special cases, we can compute the level l without using Eq. 1.

Case one. α is a factor of a, and $\rho < \alpha$. For this case, the following holds:

Proposition 2. $l = \alpha$.

Lemma 1. If α is a factor of a (and thus ρ is also a factor of a), then dividing A in ρ subsets of size α yields $v(CS) = 0$.

Proof. If A is equally partitioned into ρ sets, then each set has $\frac{a}{\rho} = \alpha$ elements as follows:

$\{1, ..., \alpha\}\{\alpha + 1, ..., 2\alpha\}\{2\alpha + 1, ...3\alpha\}...$ ...$\{(\rho - 1)\alpha + 1...a\}$. Clearly, each has value zero because its size is $\frac{a}{\rho}$. $\qquad\square$

Lemma 2. If α is a factor of a, and $\rho < \alpha$, then dividing A in α subsets yields $v(CS) = a$.

Proof. Dividing A in α subsets (each of size $\frac{a}{\alpha} = \rho$):

$\{1, ..., \rho\}\{\rho + 1, ..., 2\rho\}\{2\rho + 1, ..., 3\rho\}...\{(a - \rho) - 1, ...a\}$

Because $\rho < \alpha$, the value of this CS is $\frac{a}{\rho} \neq 0$ (number of subsets) multiplied by ρ (value of each subset), which yields the value a. $\qquad\square$

We can now prove Proposition 2 ($l = \alpha$) by showing that, since we cannot divide A in ρ subsets (Lemma 1), we divide it in α subsets and this coalition structure has value a. This is trivial because, since $\alpha > \rho$, this means that dividing A in α subsets yields more subsets of *smaller* size. Lemma 2 shows that the CS so formed has value a.

Case two. A similar case happens when ρ is a factor of a but α is not. Then, $l = \frac{a}{\rho}$ because ρ is a factor of a and so A can be partitioned into $\frac{a}{\rho}$ subsets. Since $\rho < \alpha$, this means that sets of size ρ do have a value that is not zero (Lemma 2). Hence the value of all $\frac{a}{\rho}$ sets of individual value ρ are $\frac{a}{\rho} \times \rho = a$.

Case three. $\rho \geq \alpha$. Then, the following holds:

Proposition 3. $l = \lfloor \frac{a}{\alpha - 1} \rfloor + \beta$ where $\alpha \geq 2$ and $\beta = 0$ if $\mod(a, \alpha - 1) = 0$ and $\beta = 1$ otherwise.

Proof. According to Lemma 1, dividing A in ρ subsets yields $v(CS) = 0$. Since $\rho \geq \alpha$, dividing A in ρ subsets would result in less subsets which would have even bigger sizes and hence value zero as well. Therefore, the solution is to divide A in more subsets of smaller sizes (but as big as possible as those have higher values). This means dividing A in a number of sets having size $(\alpha - 1)$ each. There are at least $\lfloor \frac{a}{\alpha - 1} \rfloor$ of these subsets. If $(\alpha - 1)$ is a factor of a, then there are exactly $\frac{a}{\alpha - 1}$ of them; otherwise there is an additional subset which has the remainder of the division of a by $(\alpha - 1)$, i.e. there are $\lfloor \frac{a}{\alpha - 1} \rfloor + 1$ subsets.

We first handle the case $(\alpha - 1)$ is a factor of a.

Let $\lfloor \frac{a}{\alpha - 1} \rfloor = \lambda$. Because $(\alpha - 1)$ is a factor of a, we can also write $\lambda = \frac{a}{\alpha - 1}$. The λ subsets of A that have size $(\alpha - 1)$ each are: $\{1, ..., \alpha - 1\}\{\alpha, ..., 2(\alpha - 1)\}...\{(\lambda - 1)(\alpha - 1) + 1, ..., a\}$, where each subset has a value $(\alpha - 1)$. Since there are $\frac{a}{\alpha - 1}$ of them, the value is a. In case $(\alpha - 1)$ is *not* a factor of a (remember that here $\lambda = \lfloor \frac{a}{\alpha - 1} \rfloor$), the subsets of A in this case are: $\{1, ..., \alpha - 1\}\{\alpha, ..., 2(\alpha - 1)\}...\{(\lambda - 1)(\alpha - 1) + 1, ..., \lambda(\alpha - 1)\}\{\lambda(\alpha - 1) + 1, ...a\}$. The λ first subsets of A have size $(\alpha - 1)$ each and this is the maximum value possible (as sets of size α have no value). As already mentioned, there are at least $\lfloor \frac{a}{\alpha - 1} \rfloor$ of these subsets. Thus the total value is at least $\lfloor \frac{a}{\alpha - 1} \rfloor \times (\alpha - 1)$ which is smaller than a because $(\alpha - 1)$ is not a factor of a. The last subset has all the remaining elements and hence the maximum value possible (as there will never be α of them). The size (and hence value) of this last subset is $a - [\lambda(\alpha - 1)] = a - [\lfloor \frac{a}{\alpha - 1} \rfloor \times (\alpha - 1)]$. This is equivalent to $a - [a - (\mod(a, (\alpha - 1)))]$ and this is always at least 1. $\qquad\square$

Table 1. Percentage of the space searched by S99, IP, and our algorithm

	Algorithms		
a	S99	IP	Our
10	0.5×10^{-7}	$\approx 100\%$	4×10^{-6}
20	10^{-21}	$\approx 50\%$	10^{-15}
50	10^{-70}	–	10^{-40}
50			10^{-52}
100	10^{-170}	–	10^{-89}
100			10^{-107}

4   Evaluation of the Algorithm

In order to evaluate the proposed algorithm, we compare the percentage of the effectively searched space to the size of the whole space ($O(a^a)$). This is done using our algorithm, IP, and S99. The algorithm DJ04 could be used (instead of S99) but it would make very little difference since it also searches more than two levels of the CS graph. Please notice that both S99 and DJ04 just find a bound for $CS^\star$. However, they are general in the sense that they work for any CFG. IP also works for any CFG but the time taken to find $CS^\star$ is an issue if the number of agents is high. Contrarily to this, we are able to find $CS^\star$ (for games within the class of CFG defined before). This must be taken into account in the comparison. Due to complexity issues, experiments with IP are reported only up to 20 agents.

Table 1 shows the percentage of the space searched by each algorithm. Our algorithm performs a search in level l, where l depends on α. Therefore we show here examples with different values for α. When $a = 10$ we use $\alpha \in \{3, 4, 5\}$, all yielding $l = 5$ and hence a search space of $S(10, 5) = 4.2 \times 10^4$ that corresponds to $\approx 10^{-6}\%$ of the search space. Similarly, we use: $\alpha = 5$ ($l = 5$) when $a = 20$; $\alpha = 5$ (third line in table) and $\alpha = 16$ (fourth line) when $a = 50$; $\alpha \in \{6, 12\}$ (fifth line), and $\alpha = 20$ (sixth line) when $a = 100$.

It is clear that both our algorithm and S99 search only a very small portion of the space while IP searches much more because here we compare with the situation when their algorithm is run until it finds the optimum. Thus the first conclusion is a consequence of IP's complexity: their algorithm is the best for a small number of agents.

For a high number of agents, [2] searches less than our algorithm but finds a bound from optimum, while we find the optimum value (again, for a particular family of CFG). Moreover, the bound they found is $a = |A|$ (from optimum) which means that, for 10 agents the value found is only 10% of $V(CS^\star)$. For more agents the bound is much farther from $V(CS^\star)$. Therefore our algorithm is a good compromise between performance, generality, and number of agents.

Table 2. Running time (milliseconds) for finding CS^*

	Algorithms		
a	IP	Our	
13	477	416	$(\alpha = 4,\ G = \emptyset)$
16	1,391,534	125,955	$(\alpha = 5,\ G = \{1,2\})$
20	28,820,231	2,328,965	$(\alpha = 4,\ G = \emptyset)$

Finally, Table 2 shows the running times for IP compared to our approach, for different number of agents. A machine running Linux Ubuntu 12.04 with processor Intel(R) Core(TM) i7-2600 3.40 GHz and 16 GB of RAM was used.

5   Concluding Remarks

We presented an algorithm for finding the optimal coalition structure that works for a family of CFGs related to several games of practical interest. In particular, we have illustrated the example of DERs in smart grids. In these applications, coalitions must respect some constraints as for instance on the minimum and maximum number of agents, and/or value of agents that contribute more to the coalition.

The proposed algorithm is efficient, searching only a small portion of the space (a single level of the CS graph). The search is directed by domain knowledge in the sense that this knowledge is used in the CFG to valuate the coalitions according to restrictions they have (e.g., number of participants). We remark that, in spite of not being general, the CSG class proposed in this work is not restricted to the smart grids scenarios used here.

Two related issues will be tackled next: the modification necessary to accommodate more agents having different values, and how to distribute the payoff among them. Because the game is neither subadditive nor superadditive, the core is empty for the resulting coalitions. Thus other solution concepts must be used, such as the Shapley value.

Acknowledgments. This research was partially supported by CNPq.

References

1. Shehory, O., Kraus, S.: Methods for task allocation via agent coalition formation. Artif. Intell. **101**, 165–200 (1998)
2. Sandholm, T., Larson, K., Andersson, M., Shehory, O., Tohmé, F.: Coalition structure generation with worst case guarantees. Artif. Intell. **111**, 209–238 (1999)
3. Dang, V.D., Jennings, N.R.: Generating coalition structures with finite bound from the optimal guarantees. In: 3rd International Joint Conference on Autonomous Agents and Multiagent Systems (AAMAS 2004), pp. 564–571. IEEE Computer Society, New York (2004)

4. Rahwan, T., Ramchurn, S.D., Dang, V.D., Jennings, N.R.: Near-optimal anytime coalition structure generation. In: Proceedings of the International Joint Conference on Artificial Intelligence (IJCAI 2007), pp. 2365–2371 (2007). http://ijcai.org/proceedings07.php

5. Rahwan, T., Jennings, N.R.: An improved dynamic programming algorithm for coalition structure generation. In: Proceedings of the Seventh International Conference on Autonomous Agents and Multiagent Systems (AAMAS 2008), Estoril, Portugal, pp. 1417–1420 (2008)

6. Rahwan, T., Michalak, T., Jennings, N.R.: Minimum search to establish worst-case guarantees in coalition structure generation. In: Walsh, T. (ed.) Proceedings of the Twenty-Second International Joint Conference on Artificial Intelligence, IJCAI 2011, pp. 338–343. AAAI Press, Barcelona (2011)

7. Yeh, D.Y.: A dynamic programming approach to the complete set partitioning problem. BIT Numer. Math. **26**, 467–474 (1986)

8. U.S. Department of Energy: Grid 2030: A national vision for electricity's second 100 years (2003)

9. Ramchurn, S., Vytelingum, P., Rogers, A., Jennings, N.: Putting the "smarts" into the smart grid: a grand challenge for artificial intelligence. Commun. ACM **55**, 86–97 (2012)

10. Rigas, E., Ramchurn, S., Bassiliades, N.: Managing electric vehicles in the smart grid using artificial intelligence: a survey. IEEE Trans. Intell. Transp. Syst. (2015, to appear)

11. Chalkiadakis, G., Robu, V., Kota, R., Rogers, A., Jennings, N.R.: Cooperatives of distributed energy resources for efficient virtual power plants. In: Proceedings of 10th International Conference on Autonomous Agents and Multiagent Systems, Taipei, Taiwan, pp. 787–794 (2011)

12. Vasirani, M., Kota, R., Cavalcante, R., Ossowski, S., Jennings, N.: An agent-based approach to virtual power plants of wind power generators and electric vehicles. IEEE Trans. Smart Grid **4**, 1314–1322 (2013)

13. Kamboj, S., Kempton, W., Decker, K.S.: Deploying power grid-integrated electric vehicles as a multi-agent system. In: Proceedings of 10th International Conference on Autonomous Agents and Multiagent Systems, Taipei, Taiwan, pp. 13–20 (2011)

14. Mihailescu, R.-C., Vasirani, M., Ossowski, S.: Dynamic coalition adaptation for efficient agent-based virtual power plants. In: Klügl, F., Ossowski, S. (eds.) MATES 2011. LNCS, vol. 6973, pp. 101–112. Springer, Heidelberg (2011)

15. de O. Ramos, G., Burguillo, J.C., Bazzan, A.L.C.: Self-adapting coalition formation among electric vehicles in smart grids. In: 2013 IEEE Seventh International Conference on Self-Adaptive and Self-Organizing Systems (SASO), pp. 11–20. IEEE, Philadelphia (2013)

16. de O. Ramos, G., Burguillo, J.C., Bazzan, A.L.C.: Dynamic constrained coalition formation among electric vehicles. J. Braz. Comput. Soc. **20**, 1–15 (2014)

17. Pudjianto, D., Ramsay, C., Strbac, G.: Virtual power plant and system integration of distributed energy resources. IET Renew. Power Gener. **1**, 10–16 (2007)

Electricity Usage Efficiency in Large Buildings: DSM Measures and Preliminary Simulations of DR Programs in a Public Library

Hugo Algarvio[1]([X]), Joaquim Viegas[2], Fernando Lopes[1], Diogo Amaro[3], Anabela Pronto[3], and Susana M. Vieira[2]

[1] LNEG–National Research Institute, Est. Paço do Lumiar 22, Lisboa, Portugal
{hugo.algarvio,fernando.lopes}@lneg.pt
[2] IDMEC, LAETA, Instituto Superior Técnico,
Universidade de Lisboa, Lisboa, Portugal
{joaquim.viegas,susana.vieira}@tecnico.ulisboa.pt
[3] Faculdade de Ciências e Tecnologia, Universidade Nova de Lisboa, Lisboa, Portugal
{diogo.amaro,amg1}@fct.unl.pt

Abstract. The programs and actions to rationalize energy consumption and increase energy efficiency, such as demand-side management (DSM) and demand response (DR), are receiving increasing attention. DSM involves the selection, planning, and implementation of measures intended to have an influence on the demand or customer-side of the electric meter. DR includes programs designed to encourage end-users to make short-term reductions in energy demand in response to price signals from the market or triggers initiated by electricity grid operators. This paper aims at studying DSM actions and DR programs to improve electricity efficiency in a public library (large building), taking into account a time of use (TOU) tariff. It presents a model of the library developed with the software DesignBuilder and using real data. It also proposes DSM actions to improve efficiency and reduce energy costs. Specifically, the analysis of the building equipment and their usage constraints lead to the development of load shifting and peak clipping mechanisms. Regarding DR programs, the library manager adopts a load direct control program proposed by a retailer and involving a reduction in consumption in the peak period of the day. The agents negotiate the terms and conditions of a bilateral contract, notably energy prices and contract duration. The DSM actions, the DR program and the negotiated rate allow the library manager to reduce consumption by 4 % and lead to savings of about 7 % in total annual costs.

Keywords: Demand-side management · Demand response · Commercial buildings · Efficient operation · Agent-based modeling and simulation

H. Algarvio, J. Viegas and F. Lopes—This work was performed under the project MAN-REM (FCOMP-01-0124-FEDER-020397) and PD/BD/105863/2014 (H. Algarvio) and SFRH/BDE/95414/2013 (J. Viegas), supported by FEDER Funds through the program "COMPETE–Programa Operacional Temático Factores de Competividade" and National Funds through "FCT–Fundação para a Ciência e a Tecnologia".

© Springer International Publishing Switzerland 2015
J. Bajo et al. (Eds.): PAAMS 2015 Workshops, CCIS 524, pp. 249–259, 2015.
DOI: 10.1007/978-3-319-19033-4_21

1   Introduction

The electricity sector has experienced several changes during the past few years, including the restructuring process that resulted from the liberalization of electricity markets, which led to several changes in the system operating paradigm. The traditional approach was mainly to meet all energy demand requirements whenever they occur. However, the new philosophy states that the system will be more efficient if fluctuations in demand are kept to minimal.

The reliable operation of the electric system needs a perfect real time balancing between supply and demand. This balancing is not easy to achieve, since both supply and demand levels can quickly and unexpectedly change, due to numerous reasons, including forced interruptions in generation units, interruptions in transmission lines and distribution, and sudden load changes [1]. In addition, for economic reasons, electricity can only be stored in very limited quantities. In this way, it is important to study management actions on both the supply and demand sides, which is one of the major concerns of the world's societies.

Regarding the supply of energy, several solutions to reduce the power generation dependence on fossil fuels were implemented, particularly as more renewable energies are produced and traded. On the demand side, however, there have been several obstacles to rationalize energy consumption. Accordingly, there is a pressing need to study measures directly related to consumption efficiency. One of the most well-known group of measures is referred to as demand-side management (DSM), involving actions linked to conservation concepts, management and rational use of energy. Many of the actions are performed by consumers and seek to reduce their electricity costs. Typically, consumers prefer two-rate or three-rate tariffs and adopt DSM measures to reduce their final costs.

Besides DSM, there are also demand response (DR) programs, such as priced-based and incentive-based programs. DR involves changes in electric usage by end-use customers from their normal consumption patterns in response to changes in the price of electricity over time, or to incentive payments designed to induce lower electricity use at times of high wholesale market prices or when system reliability is jeopardized [2]. Price-based programs refer to changes in usage by customers in response to changes in the prices they pay and include real-time pricing, critical-peak pricing, and time-of-use rates. Incentive-based programs are established by utilities, load-serving entities, or regional grid operators. These programs give customers load-reduction incentives that are separated from, or additional to, their retail electricity rates, which may be fixed (based on average costs) or time-varying [1,2].

The concept of DR can be traced back to the US electric power industry during the mid-1890s, where systems engineers and production companies discussed an optimal method to define energy prices and also the first DR programs based on rates fluctuating hourly. The initial interest in energy load management was driven, in part, by the growing penetration of air conditioning, which resulted in significant power peaks [3]. The situation of DR in the world was briefly discussed in [4]. Several implementations of DR in wholesale markets have occurred in Europe [5], China [6] and elsewhere [7].

This paper focuses on a public library composed by several electrical equipment, notably a ventilating and air conditioning (HVAC) system. Specifically, it presents a model of the library developed with DesignBuilder (Sect. 2). This is followed by the description of key DSM measures and their application to the library (Sect. 3). Next, several DR programs are described (Sect. 4) and a simplified case study on bilateral contracting with DR is presented (Sect. 5). Finally, concluding remarks and future work are described in Sect. 6.

2   Public Library: Data and Model

The library consists of an auditorium, two large reading rooms, individual and group working rooms, an informal reading room, an exhibition zone, and a laboratory of design and innovation. Some of the general numbers that characterize the building are as follows:

- $6500\,m^2$;
- 5 floors;
- 6 reading spaces;
- more than 400 sitting places;
- more than 40 computers;
- 40 working rooms.

DesignBuilder was used to develop a detailed model of the building, which involves the building geometry, the external structure, openings, materials, the detailed HVAC system, occupancy and equipments. The real data considered is related to the following: CAD drawings, construction materials, characteristics of the central heating and cooling system, building project details (such as planned occupancy), detailed information on lighting equipment, and number and characteristics of other equipment (such as computers, copying machines, projectors and bathroom dryers). The projected occupancy of the building is 824.

The HVAC system is partially auto-sized by the software and is controlled by air temperature. All spaces are connected to the central heating and cooling system, except the bathrooms. The construction characteristics of both the exterior and interior walls were considered and U-values of 0.592 and $1.688\,W/m^2K$ were obtained. For the windows, the default project double windows with a small air gap were used. Details of the electricity tariff are presented in Tables 1 and 2.

2.1   Equipment

The heating and cooling needs of the building are satisfied by a central HVAC system composed of an electric chiller with a chilling power of 293 kW and CoP of 2.7, and a natural gas boiler with a nominal efficiency of 93 %, which generates a maximum of 265 kW of heat. The heating setpoint temperature is equal to 20°C and the cooling setpoint temperature to 24°C.

Th lighting equipment includes a mix of halogen, fluorescent, incandescent and lighting projector lamps, with a total power of 71.242 kW. Also, the library

Table 1. Electricity pricing periods (Winter)

Winter Schedules - October to March				
	Cost [€/kWh]	Working day	Saturday	Sunday
Peak	0.0712	17.00 - 20.00		
Mid-Peak	0.0684	00.00 - 00.30	10.30 - 12.30	
		07.30 - 17.00	17.30 - 22.30	
		22.00 - 24.00		
Off-Peak	0.0571	00.30 - 02.00	00.00 - 03.00	00.00 - 04.00
		06.00 - 07.30	07.00 - 10.30	08.00 - 24.00
			12.30 - 17.30	
			22.30 - 24.00	
Super Off-Peak	0.0566	02.00 - 06.00	03.00 - 07.00	04.00 - 08.00

Table 2. Electricity pricing periods (Summer)

Summer Schedules - April to September				
	Cost [€/kWh]	Working day	Saturday	Sunday
Peak	0.0712	14.00 - 17.00		
Mid-Peak	0.0684	00.00 - 00.30	10.00 - 13.30	
		07.30 - 14.00	19.30 - 23.00	
		17.00 - 24.00		
Off-Peak	0.0571	00.30 - 02.00	00.00 - 03.30	00.00 - 04.00
		06.00 - 07.30	07.30 - 10.00	08.00 - 24.00
			13.30 - 19.30	
			23.00 - 24.00	
Super Off-Peak	0.0566	02.00 - 06.00	03.30 - 07.30	04.00 - 08.00

includes a large number of computers reaching a total of 25.26 kW. Other relevant equipment includes projectors, copying machines and bathroom dryers, with a power of 18.02 kW (although they have a low usage rate).

2.2 Scheduling

The library is located in Lisbon and thus follows the Portuguese academic scheduling and holidays, although we consider that it is opened on all working days (except in August), to simplify the modelling and simulation processes. The library is open from 9h00 to 20h00. The central heating system works in the months of January, February, November and December. The cooling system works every working day of the year. The HVAC system starts working at 7h00 and stops at 19h00.

The lighting equipment is on when the library is open (except the emergency lights that are always on). The computers are assumed to work 7 h every day, with consumption distributed between 10h00 and 17h00, which are typically the hours with the highest occupation rate. Two of the computers are always working due to the library's needs. The projectors are assumed to be used 3 h every day and the consumption is distributed through a 24 h day. The copying machines are assumed to work 1 h every day and the consumption is also distributed throughout the day. Bathroom dryers are also considered to run 1 h every day with consumption distributed throughout the day.

2.3   Energy Efficiency in the Library

Practicing energy efficiency is important to generate energy and economic savings in buildings. Energy efficiency is related to doing more work with the same unit of energy. In buildings, the concept of practicing energy efficiency can be described as using less energy or using energy in periods of higher availability (e.g. using electricity in periods of reduced demand) to provide the same outcome on a long term basis. Energy efficiency improvement from the point of view of good progress in energy end-use efficiency is an outcome of technological, behavioural and/or economic changes.

Energy savings are equal to the amount of energy consumption saved before and after implementing energy efficiency improvement measures, whilst considering consistent environmental conditions. If one wishes to achieve optimum energy savings, the reliance is not just on efficient devices, but also on a better use of these devices. Practicing energy efficiency will not only reduce energy usage in buildings, but also reduce energy costs, improve environmental problems, and reduce carbon dioxide emissions [8].

As mentioned before, the central cooling system is turned on throughout the year. This may be a major source of inefficiency due to the verified usage of cooling in cold days with high temperature variability, when the heating system is turned on during the morning. Based on this information, the first efficiency improving measure that was considered was the improvement of the scheduling of the cooling system, shutting it off for the months for which it was found that it was not needed. Following this, DSM methods and DR programs were studied and simulated to further increase energy savings and reduce associated costs.

3   Demand-Side Management

Demand-side management can be defined as the selection, planning, and implementation of measures intended to have an influence on the demand or customer-side of the electric meter, either caused directly or stimulated indirectly by the utility [9]. The most common rationale for DSM in the power sector is the belief that it is often more cost effective and socially beneficial to reduce or manage electricity demand through investments in efficiency and other demand side measures than to increase power supply or transmission capacity.

DSM programs are used to eliminate or reduce the need for additional peak or base load generating capacity and/or distribution facilities. DSM also permits existing generation to meet the needs of a larger number of consumers or defers or reduces the need for new capacity. DSM programs encourage end-users to be more efficient when using energy. Typical DSM actions include lighting retrofits, building automation upgrades, re-commissioning, HVAC improvements, and variable frequency drives.

3.1   DSM Programs: Planning and Implementation

Several important questions to planning and implementing DSM programs are as follows [9]:

- Should the program target peak loads or encourage a general reduction in electricity consumption?
- Is a market transformation program needed or is the objective to reduce demand in a particular sector or area?
- Should the program target existing stock or new equipment?
- Are the targeted participants communities and consumers in low income situations or those which can more easily afford to participate?

The answers to these questions help to decide on specific types of programs. Each program should be long enough to ensure complete market transformation or to achieve other program goals. Also, each program should ensure that improvements in efficiency continue after its end. DSM includes several major programs, notably [9]:

1. *Load research:* undertake load/market research to identify end-use patterns and market barriers;
2. *Define load-shape objectives:* based on the results of the load research in the utility, DSM engineers define the load;
3. *Assess program implementation strategies:* identify target sectors, end-uses, and measures;
4. *Implementation:* DSM engineers design and promote the program;
5. *Monitoring and evaluation:* involves tracking the program design and implementation, and comparing it with the proposed DSM objectives.

In this work, special attention is devoted to step 2 (see Fig. 1 and the load-shape changes below).

- Peak clipping: the reduction of load during periods of peak demand;
- Valley filling: building load in off-peak periods;
- Load shifting: demand shifting to non peak;
- Strategic conservation: the reduction of utility load, more or less equally, during all or most hours of the day;
- Strategic load building: the increase of utility loads;
- Flexible load shape: interruptible agreements by utilities to alter customer energy consumption on an as-needed basis.

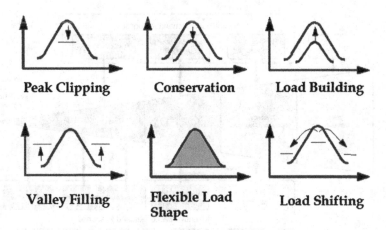

Fig. 1. Load-shape objectives [9]

3.2   DSM Actions for the Library

For the typical days of winter and summer, we consider that the most appropriate DSM actions are peak clipping of the load-shape in summer and load shifting in winter. In summer, the outside temperature θ_o in peak periods is higher than in other periods, leading to larger cooling needs in peak periods, and thus the most appropriate solution is to consider the cooling set back temperature $\theta_{c_{SB}}$ for peak periods and the reference temperature $\theta_{c_{ref}}$ for other periods. The adoption of the cooling set back temperature automatically reduces the cooling consumption at peak hours resulting in a peak clipping load shape. By performing these DSM actions, we reduce the total electricity cost and consumption, and additionally the electrical system becomes more efficient (by reducing consumption during peak periods).

4   Demand Response Programs

Demand Response (DR) is a term used for programs designed to encourage end-users to make short-term reductions in energy demand in response to price signals from the market or triggers initiated by electricity grid operators. Typical DR actions are related to shutting down part of a manufacturing process or adjusting HVAC levels.

In general, DR programs can be divided into two categories [1,2]: incentive-based programs (IBP) and price-based programs (PBP) (see Fig. 2). Incentive-based programs provide fixed or time variable incentives to consumers, in addition to their electrical charges. These incentives are presented to consumers, regardless of the tariff plan where they are inserted, to carry out a reduction of the load in situations where the operator considers that security conditions are compromised, or in situations where the cost of energy is very high.

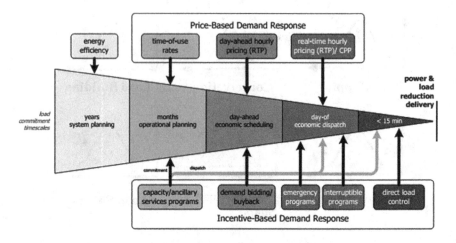

Fig. 2. Types of DR programs [2]

IBPs are further divided into classical and market-based programs. Classical programs include direct load control and interruptible/curtailable service programs. Market-based programs include emergency DR, demand bidding/buyback, capacity market programs, and ancillary services market programs. In classical IBPs, participating customers receive participation payments, usually as a bill credit or discount rate, for their participation in the programs. In market-based IBPs, participants are rewarded with money for their performance, depending on the amount of load reduction during critical conditions.

In price-based programs, consumers adjust their consumption level in response to tariff changes. These programs are based on dynamic pricing rates, where electricity rates are not constant. The goal of price-based programs is to distribute demand to smooth consumption peaks, typically considering high prices during peak periods and reduced prices in off-peak periods [1,2]. Price-based programs include the following main types of rates: time of use (TOU), critical peak pricing (CPP), extreme day pricing programs (EDP), extreme day CPP and real time pricing (RTP).

5   Case Study

In spot markets, all parties who wish to either sell or buy electricity submit their price and quantity bids. The resulting hourly prices are usually determined by considering an algorithm known as locational marginal pricing. Also, bilateral contracts are agreements between buyers and sellers for the purchase and sale of electricity at negotiated terms, including price, duration, and any other terms which may be deemed applicable. In this case study we focus primarily on bilateral contracting and adopt the agent-based system outlined in [10].

The major components of the system include a graphical user interface, a simulation engine, and a number of domain-specific agents. The following two types of agents are of particular importance to this paper: retailer or suppliers (representing business units that sell electricity to consumers) and customer or consumer agents (including commercial, industrial and other electricity consumers). Specifically, we consider a seller agent a_s representing a retailer company and a buyer agent a_b representing the library manager. The agents are equipped with a generic model of individual behavior [11]. In short, each agent has a set of beliefs (representing information about the agent itself, other existing agents, and the market), a set of goals (representing world states to be achieved), a library of plan templates (representing simple procedures for achieving goals), and a set of plans for execution, either immediately or in the near future.

The library manager agent is willing to adopt either a price-based or an incentive-based demand response program, although the preference is for a price-based program (e.g., critical peak pricing). The retailer agent, however, places greater emphasis on an incentive-based program, namely a direct load control (DLC) program, to get access to heating and cooling equipment. DLC is a demand response program primarily offered to small commercial customers and by which a program operator remotely shuts down or cycles customers electrical equipment (e.g. air conditioner, water heater) on short notice [2]. Accordingly, and mainly for economic reasons, we consider a DLC program with cutting limitations in terms of amplitude and periods. Specifically, the retailer may shut down the library's equipment for a limited number of days (set to 20) and for a specific block of each day only. Also, the maximum energy cut takes into account the following: the temperature inside the library and the reference temperature of the heating/cooling system should not differ more than $3^{\circ}C$.

The agents negotiate the terms and conditions of a four-rate tariff. To this end, they are equipped with a bilateral negotiation framework [12–14]. They interact according to the rules of an alternating offers protocol [15]. Negotiation starts with an agent, say a_s, submitting a proposal $p_{s \to b}^1$ to the opponent a_b in period $t = 1$. The opponent a_b receives $p_{s \to b}^1$ and can either accept the offer, reject it and opt out of the negotiation, or reject it and continue bargaining. In the first two cases the negotiation ends. Specifically, if $p_{s \to b}^1$ is accepted, negotiation ends successfully and the agreement is implemented. Conversely, if $p_{s \to b}^1$ is rejected and a_b decides to opt out, negotiation terminates with no agreement. In the last case, negotiation proceeds to the next time period $t = 2$, in which a_b makes a counter-proposal $p_{b \to s}^2$. The tasks just described are then repeated.

The agents make decisions according to negotiation strategies. The retailer agent a_s pursues a low-priority concession making strategy [13]: a_s reduces the demands by yielding on less important or low-priority prices. Worthy of mention are also concession making strategies: agents reduce demands to (partially) accommodate the opponent. In particular, the library manager a_b pursues a concession strategy based on the quantity of energy traded in a given period of the day [16]. That is, changes in prices are computed by using an exponential function of the amount of energy that a_b is willing to trade in each period.

As noted, negotiation involves an iterative exchange of offers and counter-offers. The retailer's prices decrease monotonically and the customer's prices increase monotonically. The acceptability of a proposal is determined by a nego-tiation threshold: an agent a_i (either a buyer or a seller) accepts a proposal $p_{j\rightarrow i}^{t-1}$, submitted by the opponent a_j at $t-1$, when the difference between the benefit provided by the proposal $p_{i\rightarrow j}^t$ that a_i is ready to send in the next time period t is lower than or equal to the negotiation threshold. The agents are allowed to exchange only a maximum number of proposals, denoted by p_{max} (set to 10).

The agent reached agreement after exchanging six proposals (the retailer and the library manager submitted 3 proposals each). There are several similarities between the retailer's first offer and the final agreement. The main differences are related to the price of the mid-peak period. Specifically, the retailer reduces this price by 3€/MWh, thus making the corresponding offer more attractive to the library manager. This price reduction can be considered a compensation or incentive payment to the library manager for adhering to the direct load control program.

6   Conclusion

This paper has focused on a public library composed by several electrical equip-ment, notably a ventilating and air conditioning (HVAC) system. Specifically, it has presented a model of the library, described the application of DSM measures to improve energy efficiency, and introduced a simplified case study on bilateral contracting with DR.

The actual operation of the library was not considered efficient, since there are several days during the year when the heating system is operating in the morning, and the cooling system is on during the afternoon. By optimizing the temperature control system, we defined working hours for the heating and cooling system that avoid both systems working on the same day. Also, by applying specific DSM measures, namely load shifting in winter to take advantage of periods where rates are lower, and peak clipping in summer placing the cooling system operating at the set back temperature, we reduced the costs of electricity. Additionally, by adopting a DLC program and negotiating a bilateral contract with a retailer, the library manager obtained a reduction of about 5 % in the mid-peak rate.

In short, by applying DSM measures and adopting a DR program, the library manager reduced the electricity consumption by 4 % and negotiated a better rate, leading to a saving of about 7 % in total annual costs.

References

1. Albadi, M., El-Saadany, E.: A summary of demand response in electricity markets. Electr. Power Syst. Res. **78**, 1989–1996 (2008)
2. Benefits of demand response in electricity markets and recommendations for achieving them. Report to the United States Congress, US Department of Energy (2006)
3. Cappers, P., Goldman, C., Kathan, D.: Demand response in U.S. electricity mar-kets: empirical evidence. Energy **35**, 1526–1535 (2010)

4. Woo, C., Greening, L.: Guest editors' introduction. Energy **35**, 1515–1517 (2010)
5. Torriti, J., Hassan, M., Leach, M.: Demand response experience in Europe: policies, programmes and implementation. Energy **35**, 1575–1583 (2010)
6. Wang, J., Bloyd, C., Hu, Z., Tan, Z.: Demand response in China. Energy **35**, 1592–1597 (2010)
7. Charles River Associates: Primer on demand-side management with an emphasis on price-responsive programs. Report for The World Bank, Washington, DC (2005)
8. Bakar, N., Hassan, M., Abdullah, H., Rahman, H., Abdullah, M., Hussin, F., Bandi, M.: Energy efficiency index as an indicator for measuring building energy performance: a review. Renew. Sustain. Energy Rev. **44**, 1–11 (2015)
9. Demand Side Management Best Practices Guidebook for Pacific Island Power Utilities. International Institute for Energy Conservation (IIEC) (2006)
10. Lopes, F., Algarvio, H., Coelho, H.: Agent-based simulation of retail electricity markets: bilateral trading players. In: 24th International Workshop on Database and Expert Systems Applications (DEXA), pp. 189–193. IEEE Computer Society (2013)
11. Lopes, F., Mamede, N., Novais, A.Q., Coelho, H.: Towards a generic negotiation model for intentional agents. In: 11th International Workshop on Database and Expert Systems Applications, pp. 433–439. IEEE (2000)
12. Lopes, F., Mamede, N., Novais, A.Q., Coelho, H.: Negotiation among autonomous agents: experimental evaluation of integrative strategies. In: 12th Portuguese Conference on Artificial Intelligence, pp. 280–288. IEEE Computer Society Press (2005)
13. Lopes, F., Coelho, H.: Concession behaviour in automated negotiation. In: Buccafurri, F., Semeraro, G. (eds.) EC-Web 2010. LNBIP, vol. 61, pp. 184–194. Springer, Heidelberg (2010)
14. Lopes, F., Coelho, H. (eds.): Negotiation and Argumentation in Multi-agent Systems. Bentham Science, The Netherlands (2014)
15. Osborne, M., Rubinstein, A.: Bargaining and Markets. Academic Press, London (1990)
16. Lopes, F., Algarvio, H., Coelho, H.: Bilateral contracting in multi-agent electricity markets: negotiation strategies and a case study. In: International Conference on the European Energy Market (EEM-2013), pp. 1–8. IEEE (2013)

Bilateral Contracting in Multi-agent Energy Markets: Forward Contracts and Risk Management

Hugo Algarvio[1(✉)], Fernando Lopes[1], and João Santana[2]

[1] LNEG – National Research Institute, Est. Paço do Lumiar 22, Lisbon, Portugal
{hugo.algarvio,fernando.lopes}@lneg.pt
[2] Instituto Superior Técnico, Universidade de Lisboa, INESC-ID, Lisbon, Portugal
jsantana@ist.utl.pt

Abstract. Electricity markets are systems for effecting the purchase and sale of electricity using supply and demand to set energy prices. Pool prices tend to change quickly and variations are usually highly unpredictable. Bilateral contracts allow market participants to set the terms and conditions of agreements independent of a market operator. This paper describes on-going work that uses the potential of agent-based technology to help addressing several important issues related to market models. Specifically, the paper is devoted to risk management in bilateral contracting of electricity. Two agents interact and trade according to the rules of an alternating offers protocol. The paper focuses on both risk attitude and risk asymmetry and how they can influence price negotiation. In particular, it describes the trading process, introduces strategies that model typical patterns of concessions, and presents several concession tactics. The article also presents a case study on forward bilateral contracting involving risk management: a producer agent and a retailer agent negotiate a three-rate tariff.

Keywords: Electricity markets · Bilateral contracts · Risk attitude · Risk asymmetry · Trading strategies · Autonomous agents

1   Introduction

The electricity industry throughout the world, which has long been dominated by vertically integrated utilities, has experienced major changes. In particular, liberalization has led to the establishment of a wholesale market for electricity generation and a retail market for electricity retailing [1].

H. Algarvio and F. Lopes—This work was performed under the project MAN-REM (FCOMP-01-0124-FEDER-020397) and PD/BD/105863/2014 (H. Algarvio), supported by FEDER Funds through the program "COMPETE−Programa Operacional Temático Factores de Competividade" and National Funds through "FCT−Fundação para a Ciência e a Tecnologia".

J. Bajo et al. (Eds.): PAAMS 2015 Workshops, CCIS 524, pp. 260–269, 2015.
DOI: 10.1007/978-3-319-19033-4_22

Spot markets provide supply for a specific period, typically one day, and involves no negotiation between the participants. In these markets, all parties who wish to either sell or buy electricity submit their price and quantity offers and bids. Each market settles simultaneously by selecting the lowest priced resources (based on the owners' bids) needed to meet load, given transmission constraints, usually following an algorithm known as locational marginal pricing (LMP). The resulting hourly locational market prices are determined by the price bid by the marginal supplier selected through this process.

Bilateral contracts are agreements between willing buyers and willing sellers for the purchase and sale of electricity-related products at negotiated terms, including duration, price, delivery location, times of performance, and any other terms which may be deemed applicable. Electricity-related products may be electric energy, capacity (including demand response), ancillary services or some combination of those. In this work we focus primarily on bilateral contracts for electrical energy.

Most market participants and analysts agree that bilateral contracts are crucial to the functioning of electricity markets, because they allow both parties to have the price stability and certainty necessary to perform long-term planning and to make rational and socially optimal investments. The revenue and cost certainty associated with bilateral contracts presents a number of benefits to sellers and buyers. Ranked roughly from near-term to longer-term, these benefits include [2]: less volatile retail prices, mitigation of market power, support for development of new resources, and more cost-effective, environmentally attractive resources in the long-term.

Short- or medium-term contracts, with durations up to a few years, are often used to supply standard offer service, and may help stabilize short-term fluctuations in prices and counteract market power. However, they are unlikely to provide much benefit in terms of supporting the development of new resources. Long-term contracts are crucial for supporting new resources, but they may be perceived as a potential source of stranded costs should market prices ultimately fall below contract prices for a prolonged period. Healthy markets, therefore, should support a range of bilateral contracts of varying durations, enabling market participants to readily hedge their obligations, giving producers opportunities to ensure long term revenue stability, and generally offering the most flexibility for all parties in mitigating risks [2].

However, while bilateral contracts are widely recognized as crucial to the functioning of truly competitive electricity markets, there are several obstacles to a vigorous, competitive, long-term bilateral contracting in energy markets. Chief among these is risk asymmetry: buyers and sellers face typically different risks in waiting to transact in spot markets, so some of them can charge risk premiums for bilateral contracts. Accordingly, for the existence of a robust bilateral market, there has to be sufficient incentives for both parties to transact in it, leading to symmetrical risks and comparable judgments of acceptable prices at which to transact.

This article presents several key features of software agents able to negotiate forward bilateral contracts, paying special attention to risk management, notably risk attitude and risk asymmetry, and introducing trading tactics based on risk parameters. The work presented here builds on our previous work in the areas of automated negotiation [3–6] and bilateral contracting [7]. It also refines and extends our previous work in the area of risk management in electricity markets [8]. The remainder of the paper is structured as follows. Section 2 introduces forward bilateral contracts and addresses the key issue of risk management during contract negotiation. Section 3 presents a case study on forward bilateral contracting involving risk management. Finally, concluding remarks are presented in Sect. 4.

2 Bilateral Contracting and Risk Management

Either physical or financial, bilateral contracts are typically negotiated weeks or months prior to their delivery and can include the following specifications: (i) starting date and time, (ii) ending date and time, (iii) price per hour over the length of the contract, (iv) variable megawatt amount over the length of the contract, and (v) range of hours when the contract is to be delivered.

Software agents are computer systems capable of flexible, autonomous action and able to communicate, when appropriate, with other agents to meet their design objectives. Specifically, each agent has the following key features [3]:

- A set of *beliefs* representing information about the agent itself, the market, and other agents trading in the market.
- A set of *goals* representing world states to be achieved.
- A library of *plan templates* representing simple procedures for achieving goals. A plan template *pt* has an header and a body. The header defines a name for *pt*. The body specifies either the decomposition of a goal into more detailed subgoals or some numerical computation.
- A set of *plans* for execution, either immediately or in the near future. A plan is a collection of plan templates structured into a hierarchical and temporally constrained And-tree. The nodes of the tree are instantiated plan templates retrieved from the library. The header of each instantiated plan template is referred to as *intention*.

The generation of a plan *p* from the simpler plan templates stored in the library is performed through an iterative procedure involving four main tasks: (i) plan retrieval, (ii) plan selection, (iii) plan addition, and (iv) plan interpretation. In brief, plan retrieval consists of searching the library for any plan template whose header unifies with the description of a goal. Plan selection consists of selecting the preferred plan template (from the set of retrieved plan templates). Plan addition consists of adding the preferred plan template to *p*. Plan interpretation consists of selecting a composite plan template from *p*, establishing a temporal order for the elements of its body, and picking the first ordered element (which is interpreted as a new goal).

The agents are broadly classified into risk-averse ($\lambda > 0$), risk neutral ($\lambda = 0$), and risk-seeking ($\lambda < 0$), where λ is a risk preference parameter. They interact and trade according to an alternating offers protocol [9]. In particular, they bargain over $n \geq 2$ issues by alternately submitting offers at times in $\mathcal{T} = \{1, 2, \dots\}$. This means that one offer is made per time period $t \in \mathcal{T}$, with an agent offering in odd periods and the other agent offering in even periods. An offer (or proposal) is a vector specifying a division of the surplus of all the issues. After receiving an offer, an agent can either accept it, reject it and opt out of the negotiation, or reject it and continue bargaining. In the first two cases, negotiation ends. In the last case, negotiation proceeds to the next time period, in which the other agent makes a counter-proposal. The tasks just described are then repeated.

The agents are equipped with an additive function for rating offers and comparing counter-offers [10]. They pursue negotiation strategies that model typical patterns of concessions. Generally speaking, concession making involves reducing negotiators' demands to accommodate the opponent. This behaviour can take several different forms. For instance, negotiators can start with ambitious demands, well in excess of limits and aspirations, and concede slowly. High demands and slow concessions, also referred to as starting high and conceding slowly, are often motivated by concern about position loss and image loss [11]. A formal definition of a negotiation strategy that models this and other existing forms of concession making is presented elsewhere [7].

Furthermore, negotiation strategies are computationally tractable functions that define the negotiation tactics to be used during the course of negotiation. In particular, concession tactics model the concessions to be made throughout negotiation. A formal definition of a generic concession tactic follows (without loss of generality, we consider that an agent a_i wants to maximize an issue x).

Definition 1 (Concession Tactic [7]). Let $\mathcal{A} = \{a_b, a_s\}$ be the set of negotiating agents, $\mathcal{I} = \{x_1, \dots, x_n\}$ the negotiating agenda (i.e., the set of issues under discussion), and $\mathcal{D} = \{D_1, \dots, D_n\}$ the set of issue domains. A concession tactic $Y_i \colon D \times [0, 1] \to D$ of an agent $a_i \in \mathcal{A}$ for an issue $x \in \mathcal{I}$ is a function with the following general form:

$$Y_i(x, C_f) = x - C_f(x - lim) \tag{1}$$

where $C_f \in [0, 1]$ is the concession factor of a_i for issue x and lim is the limit of a_i for x (i.e., the fallback position).

The following three levels of concession magnitude are commonly discussed in the negotiation literature [12]: large, substantial, and small. To this we would add two other levels: null and complete. Accordingly, we consider the following five concession tactics: (i) stalemate (models a null concession on an issue x), tough (models a small concession), moderate (models a substantial concession), soft (models a large concession), and accommodate (models a complete concession on x). These and other similar tactics can be defined by considering specific values for the concession factor C_f.

Now, concession tactics can generate new values for each issue at stake by considering specific criteria. Typical criteria include [13]: the time elapsed since the beginning of negotiation, the quantity of resources available, and the previous behavior of the opponent. In this work, we consider two different criteria directly related to risk management, namely risk attitude (modelled by $\lambda \in [-1, 1]$) and risk asymmetry (modelled by $\beta \in [0, 1]$).

Specifically, the concession factor is modeled as a function of the attitude towards risk, taking into account the following: greater negotiation flexibility means more concessions, and a greater chance to reach agreement. As noted earlier, market participants have several choices to transact power and manage risk, including the spot market and forward bilateral contracts. The price stability and certainty associated with bilateral contracts have positive effects on the functioning of electricity markets, and can benefit both producers and consumers. In particular, these contracts are important to hedge against short-term price fluctuations.

Risk-averse agents show typically more flexibility to secure a deal, and therefore, concede more to avoid that negotiation ends prematurely without agreement. If an agreement is reached, these agents will probably buy (sell) energy at a higher (lower) price compared to agents that are not averse to risk. Conversely, risk-seeking agents are more willing to be firm and rigid, tending to win negotiation without great regard to its success or failure, and thus conceding less to get a deal. Despite this, if negotiation ends successfully with agreement, risk-seeking agents will probably benefit more than risk-averse agents in similar situations. Hence, considering "success/failure to agree" as the key concern of the negotiating parties, we postulate that risk-averse agents tend to adopt higher concession factors than risk-seeking agents.

Furthermore, the concession factor is also modeled as a function of risk asymmetry: buyers and sellers typically face disproportionate risks by waiting to transact in the spot market and also bear different risks by entering into bilateral contracts. Sellers typically face bid-based clearing prices and the potential for windfall profits. Buyers also face substantial risks in waiting to trade in the spot market, since they must procure energy to meet their obligations to serve load (to avoid severe sanctions). Also, buyers bear the risk of being held to account for misjudgment in making contracts than in failing to do so when it would have been prudent. If they enter into contracts that later turn out to be "out of the market" they risk being left without cost recovery for the excess [2].

The terms and conditions of bilateral contracts can vary significantly, leading to a myriad of potential categories, although the following two are of particular importance: contract duration and contract pricing terms. There is no standard definition of short-, medium- or long-term with respect to bilateral contracts. However, contracts of five years or more are often referred to as long-term contracts. They are required to provide the level of revenue guarantee that developers need to finance new resources. Short- and medium-term contracts (five years or less) also have an important role to play in electricity markets. Their primary function is to smooth out year-to-year and shorter-term price volatility.

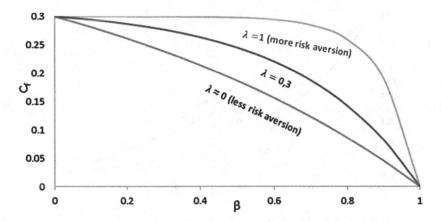

Fig. 1. Risk-averse seller: concession factor vs. risk asymmetry

Regarding contract price, an important distinction is between fixed-price and indexed price contracts [2]. In particular, some contracts (often referred to as "tolling" contracts) provide agents with the right to convert fuel into electricity, but no protection from variations in fuel prices, unless load-serving entities (LSEs) procure all or a portion of their fuel supply through contracts as well. This can still have benefits, including protecting purchasers from scarcity rents in times of very high prices, supporting needed resources with a guaranteed stream of revenue, and providing some protection from market power as purchase prices are based on a formula instead of supply offers. Further, an emerging issue of importance for bilateral contracts is the treatment of future carbon emissions costs: will these be the responsibility of generators, or flowed through to buyers?

Against this background, this work considers a parameter β to model risk asymmetry, placing emphasis on price risk (mainly related to high price volatility at times of peak demand and supply shortages). The concession factor $C_f(\lambda, \beta)$ is, therefore, modeled as a function of both risk attitude and risk asymmetry.

In situations where sellers face less risks than buyers (e.g., $\beta = 0.30$), risk-averse sellers are willing to be flexible to secure a deal, typically making substantial concessions to avoid ending negotiation prematurely without agreement. Also, in situations where sellers face more risks than buyers (e.g., $\beta = 0.80$), risk-averse sellers can work hard toward an effective agreement, but tend to adopt a more moderate stance, making smaller concessions during the course of negotiation. Simply put, as risk asymmetry increases, the likelihood of risk-averse sellers adopting small concession factors increases (but see Fig. 1).

Risk-seeking sellers tend to be more rigid and firm than risk-averse sellers, typically adopting a tougher, more competitive stance, and thus conceding less throughout negotiation. They are more willing to show a weak concern for negotiation success. For these agents, the willingness to make substantial concessions decreases with risk asymmetry, increasing the likelihood of adopting small concession factors (but see Fig. 2).

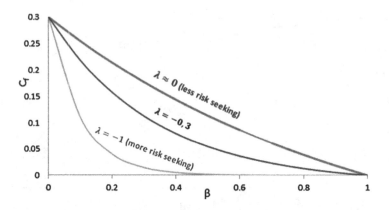

Fig. 2. Risk-seeking seller: concession factor vs. risk asymmetry

Buyers exhibit a negotiation behavior similar to the aforementioned behavior of sellers. For a reasonable value of β, say 0.45, meaning reduced risk asymmetry, risk-averse buyers are willing to adopt a position of moderateness and understanding, to secure profits. Also, for larger levels of risk asymmetry, say $\beta = 0.20$, meaning that buyers expect to face more risks than sellers, risk-averse buyers are willing to adopt a tougher, more competitive bargaining position.

Risk-seeking buyers are more willing to show a strong interest in substantive outcomes—winning this negotiation, getting this deal—with little regard for the success or failure of negotiation. For a reduced level of risk asymmetry, they can make a few substantial concessions that typically seek reciprocal concessions. Higher levels of risk asymmetry typically mean smaller concessions throughout negotiation, i.e., the adoption of smaller concession factors.

The concession factor can be represented by considering either a polynomial or an exponential function. In this work, we consider an exponential function. A formal definition of $C_f(\lambda, \beta)$ for a seller agent follows (the definition of $C_f(\lambda, \beta)$ for a buyer agent is essentially identical, and details are therefore omitted).

Definition 2 (Risk dependent concession factor). Let $a_i \in \mathcal{A}$ be a negotiating agent (i.e., a buyer or seller agent) and $x \in \mathcal{I}$ an issue at stake. The concession factor $C_f : [-1,1] \times [0,1] \to [0,1]$ of a_i for x is modelled as a function depending on both risk attitude and risk asymmetry as follows:

$$C_f(\lambda, \beta) = \begin{cases} \dfrac{C_{f_n} - e^{ln(C_{f_n}) + k\lambda(1-\beta)}}{1 - e^\lambda}, & \text{for } \lambda \neq 0 \\ C_{f_n} & \text{for } \lambda = 0 \end{cases} \tag{2}$$

where $\lambda \in [-1,1]$ is the value of a_i's risk aversion, $\beta \in [0,1]$ is the level of risk asymmetry, $C_{f_n} \in [0,1]$ is the concession factor of a risk-neutral agent ($\lambda = 0$), and k is a constant that shapes the function's curvature.

Figures 1 and 2 depict several exponential functions for the computation of the concession factor. For each Figure, the ordinate represents the concession

Table 1. Initial offers and price limits (€/MWh)

	Producer		Retailer	
Period	Price	Limit	Price	Limit
peak	50.99	47.99	49.48	52.48
mid-peak	44.43	42.04	42.62	45.05
off-peak	40.99	38.16	40.06	41.74

factor and the abscissa the risk asymmetry. The solid lines correspond to different levels of risk aversion. To keep multi-agent negotiation as close as possible to real-world negotiations, functions that give values for C_f larger than 30 % were not considered, as these values do not represent reasonable negotiation stances.

3 Case Study

A multi-agent energy market system, involving a wholesale market and a retail market, is currently being developed. Market participants are able to exhibit goal-directed behavior and interact, when appropriate, with other agents to meet their design objectives. In particular, buyer and seller agents can negotiate the terms and conditions of forward bilateral contracts. This sections presents a case study to illustrate the behavior of concession strategies and tactics, particularly tactics based on the aforementioned exponential function for computing the concession factor. The case study has several similarities with the case study presented in [8], and thus we emphasize the differences below (rather than the commonalities).

A producer or seller agent (a_s) and a retailer or buyer agent (a_b) negotiate a three-rate tariff. The agents are moderately risk-averse (λ is set to 0.5). Also, they face slightly different risks (β is set to 0.6, meaning that the buyer faces greater risks than the seller). The initial prices and the limits of both agents are shown in Table 1. The energy quantities are set as follows: 2.47 for peak-load, 2.64 MWh for medium-load, and 1.99 MWh for off-peak. These quantities remain fixed during the course of negotiation.

The agents iteratively exchange offers and counter-offers over energy prices. They pursue starting reasonable and conceding moderately strategies [4]. The producer's offers decrease monotonically and the retailer's offers increase monotonically. Also, the agents employ concession tactics based on functions 1 and 2 (see above). The parameter C_{f_n} (i.e., the concession factor of a risk-neutral agent) is set to 0.15.

The acceptability of a proposal is determined by a negotiation threshold: an agent $a_i \in \mathcal{A}$ accepts a proposal $p_{j \to i}^{t-1}$, submitted by $a_j \in \mathcal{A}$ at $t-1$, when the difference between the benefit provided by the proposal $p_{i \to j}^t$ that a_i is ready to send in the next time period t is lower than or equal to the negotiation threshold. The agents are allowed to exchange only a maximum number of offers denoted by p_{max}.

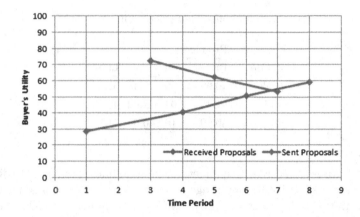

Fig. 3. Utility of the exchanged offers to the retailer agent

Agreement is reached after the exchange of 7 proposals. The agents agree on the following prices: 49.87 €/MWh for peak-load, 43.54 €/MWh for medium-load, and 39.94 €/MWh for off-peak. Figure 3 depicts the proposals sent and received by the retailer agent (i.e., the negotiation dance). The abscissa represents the utility of each proposal to this agent, and the ordinate the time when the proposals were submitted or received. The benefit of the agreement to the agents are as follows: 53.30 for the producer and 59.16 for the retailer.

4   Conclusion

This article has presented several key features of software agents able to negotiate bilateral contracts in energy markets, paying special attention to risk management. In particular, it has described several concession tactics that generate values for each issue at stake by considering two criteria directly related to risk management, namely risk attitude (modelled by $\lambda \in [-1, 1]$) and risk asymmetry (modelled by $\beta \in [0, 1]$). The article has also presented a case study on forward bilateral contracting involving risk management: a producer and a retailer negotiate a three-rate tariff.

In the future, we intend to perform a number of inter-related experiments to to empirically evaluate the concession tactics in different negotiation situations. Also, we intend to refine and extend the framework for contract negotiation with risk management. Specifically, to associate risk asymmetry with the main risks faced by buyers and sellers of electrical energy.

References

1. Kirschen, D., Strbac, G.: Fundamentals of Power System Economics. Wiley, Chichester (2004)
2. Hausman, E., Hornby, R., Smith, A.: Bilateral Contracting in Deregulated Electricity Markets. Report to the American Public Power Association, Synapse Energy Economics, April 2008

3. Lopes, F., Mamede, N., Novais, A.Q., Coelho, H.: Towards a generic negotiation model for intentional agents. In: 11th International Workshop on Database and Expert Systems Applications, IEEE, pp. 433–439 (2000)
4. Lopes, F., Coelho, H.: Strategic and tactical behaviour in automated negotiation. Int. J. Artif. Intell. 4(S10), 35–63 (2010)
5. Lopes, F., Coelho, H.: Concession behaviour in automated negotiation. In: Buccafurri, F., Semeraro, G. (eds.) EC-Web 2010. LNBIP, vol. 61, pp. 184–194. Springer, Heidelberg (2010)
6. Lopes, F., Coelho, H. (eds.): Negotiation and Argumentation in Multi-agent Systems. Bentham Science, The Netherlands (2014)
7. Lopes, F., Coelho, H.: Concession strategies for negotiating bilateral contracts in multi-agent electricity markets. In: 23rd International Workshop on Database and Expert Systems Applications (DEXA), IEEE, pp. 321–325 (2012)
8. Algarvio, H., Lopes, F.: Risk management and bilateral contracts in multi-agent electricity markets. In: Corchado, J.M., et al. (eds.) PAAMS 2014. CCIS, vol. 430, pp. 297–308. Springer, Heidelberg (2014)
9. Osborne, M., Rubinstein, A.: Bargaining and Markets. Academic Press, London (1990)
10. Raiffa, H.: The Art and Science of Negotiation. Harvard University Press, Cambridge (1982)
11. Pruitt, D.: Negotiation Behavior. Academic Press, New York (1981)
12. Lewicki, R., Barry, B., Saunders, D.: Negotiation. McGraw Hill, New York (2010)
13. Faratin, P., Sierra, C., Jennings, N.: Negotiation decision functions for autonomous agents. Robot. Auton. Syst. 24, 59–182 (1998)

Dynamic Fuzzy Estimation of Contracts Historic Information Using an Automatic Clustering Methodology

Ricardo Faia, Tiago Pinto[(✉)], and Zita Vale

GECAD – Knowledge Engineering and Decision-Support Research Center,
Institute of Engineering – Polytechnic of Porto (ISEP/IPP), Porto, Portugal
{rfmfa, tmcfp, zav}@isep.ipp.pt

Abstract. With the recent liberalization of electricity markets, market players need to decide whether to and how to participate in each electricity market type that is available to them. The search for the best opportunities to sell or buy the required energy is, however, not an easy task. Moreover, the changes that electricity markets are constantly suffering make this an highly dynamic environment, with huge associated unpredictability. Decision support tools become, therefore, essential for market players to be able to take the best advantage from market participation. This paper proposes a methodology to estimate the expected prices of bilateral contracts based on the analysis of contracts' historic log. The proposed method is based on the application of a clustering methodology that groups the historic contracts according to their prices' similarity. The optimal number of groups is automatically calculated taking into account the preference for the balance between the estimation error and the number of groups. The centroids of each cluster are used to define a dynamic fuzzy variable that approximates the tendency of contracts' history. The resulting fuzzy variable allows estimating expected prices for contracts instantaneously and approximating missing values in the historic contracts log.

Keywords: Clustering · Electricity markets · Fuzzy logic · Portfolio optimization

1 Introduction

The restructuring of electricity markets has increased the competitiveness of this sector, which has led to relevant changes and new problems to be addressed, namely physical constraints, market operation rules and financial issues [1, 2]. Electricity markets have become complex and challenging environments, involving a considerable number of participating entities, operating dynamically trying to obtain the best possible advantages and profits [2]. Potential benefits, however, depend on the efficient operation of

This work is supported by FEDER Funds through COMPETE program and by National Funds through FCT under the projects FCOMP-01-0124-FEDER: PEst-OE/EEI/UI0760/2015, PTDC/ EEA-EEL/122988/2010 and SFRH/BD/80632/2011 (Tiago Pinto PhD).

© Springer International Publishing Switzerland 2015
J. Bajo et al. (Eds.): PAAMS 2015 Workshops, CCIS 524, pp. 270–282, 2015.
DOI: 10.1007/978-3-319-19033-4_23

the market. Market players and regulators are very interested in foreseeing market behavior, as it is essential for them to fully understand the market's principles and learn how to evaluate their investments in such a competitive environment [1]. The development of simulation platforms based in Multi-Agent Systems (MAS) is increasing as a good option to simulate real systems in which stakeholders have different and often conflicting objectives. These systems allow simulating scenarios and strategies, providing users with decision support according to their profile of activity. Several modeling tools can be fruitfully applied to study and explore restructured power markets, such as AMES Wholesale Power Market Test Bed [3] and EMCAS (Electricity Market Complex Adaptive System) [4].

MASCEM - Multi-Agent Simulator for Electricity Markets [5, 6] is also a simulation tool to study and explore restructured electricity markets. Its purpose is to simulate as many market models and player types as possible. The learning process of its agents is undertaken using MASCEM's connection with ALBidS (Adaptive Learning strategic Bidding System) [6]. ALBidS provides decision support to electricity market players, allowing them to automatically adapt their strategic behavior to different contexts of negotiation. Additionally, the intelligent use of multiple market opportunities as they arise is supported by a portfolio optimization mechanism for electricity market participation [7]. With the use of a large number of algorithms, an adequate balance between the efficiency and effectiveness (2E) of the several algorithms is essential. For this, a 2E management methodology is used to suit the execution time of the decision support to the purposes of each simulation [8].

The requirement for fast responses and the need to deal with data that often contains missing values are the main incentives for the development of the presented work. This paper proposes a methodology that estimates expected bilateral contract prices by analyzing the historic log of established contracts. Each bilateral contract is characterized by a specific amount of power and an associated price. However, predictions of expected prices for different amounts of power than those contained in the historic log are often required. Hence, an adequate estimative is essential. Moreover, so that a suitable portfolio optimization can be executed, the expected return prices for each possible amount of power are required. This, however, is impracticable due to the number of possible amounts (which tends to infinite when increasing the number of decimal places of the power amount value). For these reasons, the development a dynamic fuzzy variable that approximates the values of contract prices for different negotiated power amounts is proposed. Dynamic fuzzy membership functions are defined accordingly to the output of a clustering process, which groups the historical contracts depending on their similarity. The optimal number of clusters, which defines the number of fuzzy intervals, is calculated automatically, taking into account the preference for the balance between the estimation error and the number of fuzzy intervals. The proposed methodology allows estimating the large number of historic contract prices by means of a single fuzzy variable, hence reducing drastically the amount of variables to be considered by the portfolio optimization algorithm, and consequently contributing to the decrease of the optimization execution time. Additionally, the adaptation of the number of fuzzy intervals allows considering more or less fuzzy functions in the problem, hence adapting the balance between the execution time and quality of the estimation, depending on the requirements of each execution. The 2E balance management methodology of ALBidS is responsible for making the decision on the degradation of the results' quality that is necessary in each moment in order to guarantee the desired execution time. This requirement provided by the 2E mechanism indicates if the proposed method should consider more or less clusters in its analysis, and so, if it is allowed to perform estimates of more or less quality.

2 Decision Support in Electricity Markets Negotiation

Electricity market simulators must be able to cope with this complex dynamic reality and provide market players with adequate tools to adapt themselves to the new reality, gaining experience to act in the frame of a changing economic, financial, and regulatory environment. With a multiagent simulation tool the model may be easily enlarged and future evolution of markets may be accomplished. Multiagent simulation combined with other artificial intelligence techniques may result in sophisticated tools, namely in what concerns players modelling and simulation, strategic bidding and decision-support. There are several experiences that sustain that a MAS with adequate simulation abilities is suitable to simulate electricity markets [3–6], considering the complex interactions between the involved players.

MASCEM [5, 6] aims to facilitate the study of complex electricity markets. It represents the entities that typically participate in electricity markets as software agents, namely: market operator agent, independent system operator agent (ISO), market facilitator agent, buyer agents, seller agents, Virtual Power Player (VPP) agents and VPP facilitators. MASCEM allows the simulation of the main market models: day-ahead pool (asymmetric or symmetric, with or without complex conditions), bilateral contracts, balancing market, forward markets and ancillary services. Hybrid simulations are also possible by combining the market models mentioned above. Also, the possibility of defining different specifications for the market mechanisms, such as multiple offers per period per agent, block offers and flexible offers, as part of some countries' market models, is also provided.

In order to allow players to automatically adapt their strategic behaviour according to their current situation, a new decision support system has been integrated with MASCEM. This platform is ALBidS [6, 8], and provides agents with the capability of analysing contexts of negotiation, allowing players to automatically adapt their strategic behaviour according to the current situation. To choose the most adequate technique, ALBidS uses reinforcement learning algorithms and the Bayes theorem. ALBidS is as a MAS itself, in which each agent is responsible for an algorithm, allowing the execution of several algorithms simultaneously, increasing the performance of the platform. It was also necessary to build a suitable mechanism to manage the algorithms efficiency in order to guarantee the minimum degradation of MASCEM's execution time. For this purpose, a methodology to manage the 2E balance of ALBidS has been developed [8]. The 2E balance methodology analyses the quality of results that each algorithm is achieving at each moment, and the time needed to achieve such results. Algorithms that are taking too long to achieve not so good results, given the requirements of each simulation, can be excluded from the system, or asked to reduce their execution time by adapting themselves internally.

Additionally, ALBidS is equipped with a portfolio optimization methodology, which enables players to decide the participation investment that should be made in each available type of market, in order to optimize the potential profits from selling their power, or minimize the costs of buying the required amounts of power [7]. The portfolio optimization methodology considers the forecasted market prices that are expected to be found in each alternative market or market session that the supported player is allowed to participate in (e.g. day-ahead spot market, each session of the intraday market, bilateral contracts, forward markets).

3 Proposed Methodology

Due to the need for fast responses in the decision making process and the necessity to deal with often incomplete data, adequate estimates on data are essential. The proposed methodology estimates the expected prices in markets based on bilateral contracting (e.g. bilateral contract markets or forward markets). The proposed method is based on the development a dynamic fuzzy variable that approximates the values of contract prices for different negotiated power amounts. Dynamic fuzzy membership functions are defined accordingly to the output of a clustering process, which groups the historical contracts depending on their similarity. The optimal number of clusters, which defines the number of fuzzy intervals, is calculated automatically, taking into account the 2E preference, i.e. the balance between the estimation error and the number of fuzzy intervals. A higher preference for the optimization of the estimation error results in a fuzzy variable with an extended number of intervals, which causes an increase in execution time when using the fuzzy variable as estimation for decision support purposes. On the other hand, when requiring a faster execution time, the number of fuzzy intervals will be smaller, resulting in a faster response, yet with an higher associated error. Figure 1 presents the flowchart of the proposed methodology.

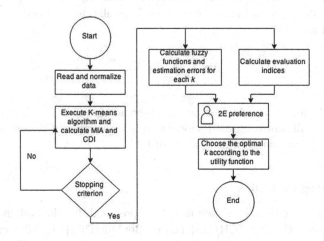

Fig. 1. Proposed methodology flowchart.

Figure 1 depicts the flow of the proposed methodology. At first, data is loaded and normalized, so that the K-Means clustering algorithm [9] can be executed (see Sect. 3.1). The K-Means algorithm is repeated successively for different numbers of clusters (k), until the stopping criterion, which is presented in Sect. 3.2, is reached. With this, a set of possible k is defined, accordingly to the clustering evaluation performed by different evaluation indices (as presented in Sect. 3.2). Each of these k represents a potential final solution to be used to define the dynamic fuzzy variable (as in Sect. 3.3). In order to test the estimation capability of the dynamic fuzzy variable, this variable is constructed taking into account the different potential k, and the estimation errors are calculated, as presented in Sect. 3.4. Finally, using the 2E preference for the balance between the execution time and the estimation quality, the final k is chosen, accordingly to the utility function that is presented in Sect. 3.4. The results of the clustering process using the optimal k are then used to define the final dynamic fuzzy variable; where the *centroid* of each cluster corresponds to the maximum membership value of each fuzzy function, as detailed in Sect. 3.3.

3.1 Clustering Process

A cluster is a collection of data objects that are similar to one another within the same group and are dissimilar to the objects in other clusters. A good cluster partition must present objects with high similarity among them and low similarity among objects that belong to other clusters [10]. In [11] an extensive discussion on data clustering theory is provided, as well as several algorithms and applications. Many different algorithms can be used for clustering analysis; however, the most popular and widely used is the K-Means algorithm, despite the many years since its first appearance [9].

The K-Means algorithm requires a single user-defined input parameter: the number of clusters (k). Firstly, it randomly selects k objects, where each initially represents a cluster mean or *centroid*. Each of the remaining objects is assigned to the cluster to which it is the most similar, based on the distance between the object and the cluster *centroid*. It then computes the new *centroid* for each cluster [12]. This process is iterative until the criterion function converges. Typically, the square-error criterion is used, defined as in (1).

$$\min \sum_{i=1}^{k} \sum_{x \in C_i} ||x - \mu_i||^2 \tag{1}$$

This methodology considers a set of observations ($x_1, x_2, ..., x_n$), where each observation is a dimensional real vector, and n is the number of considered observations, C_i is a cluster and μ_i is the *centroid* of C_i.

3.2 Clustering Evaluation

Several indices for cluster validation have been proposed. In this work the following are used: Calinski–Harabasz (CH) [13], Davies–Bouldin (DB) [14], Silhouette (S) [15], the Mean Index Adequacy (MIA) and Cluster Dispersion Indicator (CDI) [12].

The distance between two points x_i and x_j, is calculated using the Euclidian distance (d), as defined in (2).

$$d(xi, xj) = \sqrt{\sum_{k=1}^{d}(x_{i,k} - x_{j,k})^2} \qquad (2)$$

The CH index is a ratio type index where the cohesion is estimated based on the distances from the points in a cluster to its *centroid*. The separation is based on the distance from the centroids to the global *centroid* [13]. It can be defined as in (3).

$$CH = \frac{SS_B}{SS_W} \times \frac{(N-k)}{(k-1)} \qquad (3)$$

where SS_B (4) is the sum of between-cluster variance, and SS_W (5) represents the sum of within-cluster variance.

$$SS_B = \sum_{i=1}^{k} ni\, d^2(C_i, \mu) \qquad (4)$$

$$SS_W = \sum_{i=1}^{k}\sum_{x \in C_i} d^2(x, C_i) \qquad (5)$$

where μ is the sum mean of the sample data, and x is an object in cluster C_i.

The DB index estimates the cohesion based on the distance from the points in a cluster to its *centroid* and the separation based on the distance between *centroids* [14]. It is defined as in (6).

$$DB = \frac{1}{k}\sum_{i=1}^{k} max_{J \neq i}\{D_{ij}\} \qquad (6)$$

where D_{ij} is the within-to-between cluster distance ratio for the ith and the jth clusters, as defined in (7).

$$D_{ij} = \frac{(\bar{d}_i + \bar{d}_j)}{d_{ij}} \qquad (7)$$

where $\bar{d}_i$ is the average distance between each point in the ith cluster and the *centroid* of the *same* cluster. $\bar{d}_j$ is the average distance between each point in the ith cluster and the *centroid* of the jth cluster. d_{ij} is the distance between the *centroids* of the ith and jth clusters.

The S index is a normalized summation-type index. The cohesion is measured based on the distance between all the points in the same cluster and the separation is based on the nearest neighbor distance [15]. It is defined as in (8).

$$S = \frac{(b_i - a_i)}{max(b_i, a_i)} \tag{8}$$

where a_i is the average distance from ith point to other points in the same cluster, and b_i is the minimum average distance from the ith point to points in a different cluster.

MIA uses the Euclidian distance (2) method to determine the value that reflects the quality of a cluster partition. MIA gives a value which relies on the amount by which each is compact, if the members in the cluster are close together the MIA value is low. This index is calculated as in (9).

$$MIA = \sqrt{\frac{1}{K} \times \sum_{k=1}^{K} d^2(x^{(k)}, \mu^{(k)})} \tag{9}$$

CDI also depends on the distance between the members of the same cluster, but also incorporates the evaluation of the distances between the *centroids* for different clusters. Hence, this index assesses both the compactness of the clusters and the amount by which each cluster differs from the others.

$$CDI = \frac{\sqrt{\frac{1}{K} \sum_{k=1}^{K} \left[\frac{1}{2.n^{(k)}} \sum_{m=1}^{n^k} \hat{d}^2(x^m, \mu^k) \right]}}{\sqrt{\frac{1}{2.K} \sum_{K=1}^{K} d^2(x^{(K)}, R)}} \tag{10}$$

In order to automatically define the optimal k, a set of potential best k is defined. This is done by executing the K-Means algorithm iteratively for an incremental number of k (starting from a value of 1) and calculating the MIA and CDI values for each k. The iterative process is finished when the stopping criterion is reached. The stopping criterion is obtained by analyzing the behavior of MIA and CDI. The value of these indices tends for zero when the value of k increases, since they represent the variance of the clustering process. When comparing the variance values provided by MIA and CDI that each k originates, the first clusters will add much information (explain a lot of variance), but at some point the marginal gain will drop; i.e. from this point the gain (in variance reduction) of adding another cluster is not as significant as before. In order to capture this point, the variance between each two consecutive variance values of MIA and CDI is calculated. The slope of the achieved variance (of variances) value indicates if the gain of information is increasing (slope with a positive value) or decreasing (negative slope value). When the slope value reverses, indicating that variances provided by MIA and CDI are stabilizing, the stopping criterion is triggered, defining the set of potential best k, which ranges from the "elbow" point minus 3 to plus 3.

3.3   Dynamic Fuzzy Variable

Fuzzy logic [16] is used to estimate the contract pricing values. Historic contract information is limited, i.e. the information concerns only prices for certain values of contracted power amounts. When it is necessary to achieve an expected price for a contract based on an amount of power that has never been negotiated before, this value has to be estimated. Using fuzzy logic, the estimative is done by defining power intervals, for which the expected price is similar. The fuzzy process allows smoothing the interval transition values. E.g. when negotiating 50 MW in a certain market (part of one power interval) the expected price is X; when negotiating 51 MW in the same market, amount of a different power interval, the expected price is Y. However, the difference from 50 to 51 MW is minimal, and not enough to represent a large difference in the expected price. The fuzzy process allows these transition values between different intervals to be smoother, avoiding abrupt price changes. Figure 2 shows the fuzzy variable that represents the different intervals.

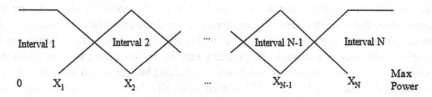

Fig. 2. Dynamic fuzzy variable

The lower limit of the function variable is zero and the upper limit is the maximum power in the input data. Intervals are constructed according to the cluster *centroids*. Each cluster *centroid* defines the maximum membership value of each fuzzy function, i.e. X_1 to X_N of Fig. 2 are the power amounts defined in each of the k clusters' *centroids*, hence $N = k$. The limits of each function assume the value of the preceding and following cluster *centroids*, which assume membership values of zero. All membership functions are triangular, except from the first and last.

The fuzzy variable is, therefore, dynamic, since its definition in done at runtime, depending on the number of clusters, since these vary with different data. The algorithm is prepared to receive different data series, and arrive at a good value of clusters to define the most adequate fuzzy function, which is able to make the best estimation of the input data. With a dynamic fuzzy definition, the data estimation problem becomes easy to implement since the user does not need to have knowledge of the data; the user simply needs to specify the 2E preference for the utility function.

3.4 Utility Function

Automatically determining the number of clusters has been one of the most difficult problems in data clustering. Usually, clustering algorithms are executed for different values of k, and the best value of k is chosen based on a predefined criterion. Once the range of possible k values is defined, the fuzzy variables for each k are defined, and the correspondent estimation error value is calculated. The error measure used is the Mean Absolute Deviation Percent (MADP) [17] as defined in (11):

$$MADP = \frac{\sum_{x=1}^{N} ||F_x - A_x||}{\sum_{x=1}^{N} ||A_x||} \tag{11}$$

where F_x represents the fuzzy estimated value, and A_x the real value.

After the calculation of the errors for each k in the set, they are normalized and scaled, as in (12) The values of k suffer the same process, so that the scale of both variables is identical.

$$x_{inorm} = \frac{x_i - \min(x)}{\max(x) - \min(x)} \tag{12}$$

The choice of the minimum number of k that best reduces the error is a multi-objective problem, where there are two goals that are divergent, i.e. when trying to improve one, the other worsens (the estimation error decreases when k increases, and vice versa). In choosing the cluster number by the mechanism used, the solution space where he will seek not always all of them can be chosen. Because the result of mechanism is one number integer and in set of solutions integer not all are dominant in two objectives. The K_{best} function (13) is used to specify the utility, by considering the minimization of both variables.

$$K_{best} = \min(wc \times K_{norm} + we \times MADP_{norm}) \tag{13}$$

where K_{norm} and $MADP_{norm}$ represent the normalized k and the error value, and wc and we are weights for the preference between k and the error value, according to the specification of the 2E balance The value of both weights ranges from 0 to 1.

4 Experimental Findings

This case study considers a data sample of 50 observations, concerning the contract prices for different negotiated power amounts (ranging from 1 to 50 MW). The used data sample can be visualized in Fig. 5. The objective, using the proposed methodology, is to approximate the data sample values by means of a dynamically defined fuzzy variable. Figure 3 presents the values of the several evaluation indices for the K-Means clustering process with different values of k.

From Fig. 3 it is visible that the MIA and CDI values have a decreasing trend, which is softened (the decrease stabilizes) when $k = 5$. As defined in Sect. 3.2., this "elbow" is the point that is captured by the stopping criterion, defining the range of potential best k from $k = 2$ to $k = 8$. The CH and S indices present the maximum gain value for $k = 7$, while the DB index has the maximum value in $k = 2$. Hence, the considered indices have resulted in several options for selecting the best value of k, i.e. there is no consensus on the best k, which supports the need for an adequate evaluation depending on the user's preference for 2E balance.

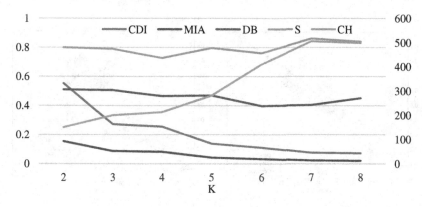

Fig. 3. Evolution of indices.

As explained in Sect. 3.3, the dynamic fuzzy variable is defined for each different k of the set of potential best options. Figure 4 presents the evolution of the estimation error, using the MADP, for each fuzzy function created using each k.

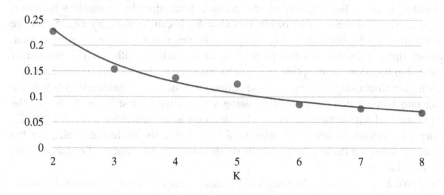

Fig. 4. MADP estimation error.

The plot of Fig. 4 represents the two objectives: the Y-axis represents the value of estimation error (MADP) and the X-axis defined the number of clusters (k). As mentioned before, this multi-objective problem has two objectives. This means that there is a set of solutions possible to accept. The name of set solution is the Pareto front, which has one set of solutions that are discrete and finite [18]. As has already been explained, with the objective of improving the solution from the standpoint of one objective, the other is deteriorated. This is visible from the graph of Fig. 4, where a solution with a small error has a high k; on the other hand, with a small k, the error is higher. For this reason, in order to achieve a unique response, a weight value has to be attributed to each of the two objectives, indicating the importance that each has for the final solution. Figure 5 illustrates the estimation results of two different simulations, using two different dynamic fuzzy variables, which are defined from the clustering data of different optimal k that results from the attribution of with different weights.

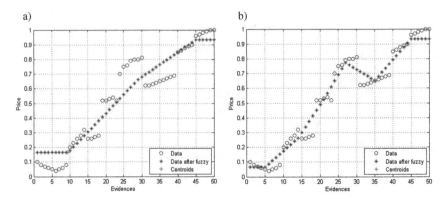

Fig. 5. Dynamic fuzzy estimation values for the optimal k resulting from; a), $wc = 0.7$ $we = 0.3$; b), $wc = 0.3$ $we = 0.7$.

In Fig. 5(a) results are shown for a case with a higher weight for the number of clusters, which, as expected, results in a solution with a small number of clusters, which in this case is three. In the case of Fig. 5(b), where the higher weight is given to the estimation error, the proposed model presents a solution that minimizes the error, with an increase of the number of clusters ($k = 6$). It can be seen, by Fig. 5 that the estimation with a higher value of k, as in b) achieves much better estimation results; however, the computational effort of using a fuzzy variable with a larger number of membership functions in an optimization problem, such as the portfolio optimization, is much higher than using a fuzzy variable defined by only three membership functions, taking into account that the estimation using a very small k is still able to follow the trend of the real data sample, as in a). This decision is, nevertheless, a result of the 2E balance mechanism, in which the user is able to define the preference value for the execution time or for the quality of results (in the case, for the number of clusters, or for the estimation error).

In Table 1 are expressed the values of the utility function for different combinations of weights for the minimization of the two objectives: k and estimation error. The shaded

Table 1. Different weights for different number of cluster

we	K							wc
	2	3	4	5	6	7	8	
0,1	0,1	0,2036347	0,3430273	0,4854827	0,6104469	0,7550376	0,9	0,9
0,2	0,2	0,2406027	0,3527213	0,4709654	0,5542271	0,6767419	0,8	0,8
0,3	0,3	0,2775707	0,3624153	0,4564481	0,4980074	0,5984462	0,7	0,7
0,4	0,4	0,3145387	0,3721093	0,4419308	0,4417876	0,5201505	0,6	0,6
0,5	0,5	0,3515067	0,3818032	0,4274136	0,3855678	0,4418548	0,5	0,5
0,6	0,6	0,3884746	0,3914972	0,4128963	0,3293481	0,3635591	0,4	0,4
0,7	0,7	0,4254426	0,4011912	0,398379	0,2731283	0,2852633	0,3	0,3
0,8	0,8	0,4624106	0,4108852	0,3838617	0,2169085	0,2069676	0,2	0,2
0,9	0,9	0,4993786	0,4205792	0,3693444	0,1606888	0,1286719	0,1	0,1

values represent the optimal solution of the utility function (as represented by the Pareto front in Fig. 4), taking into account the weighing criteria.

From Table 1 it is visible that attributing a small value of weight for the error, and high for k results in achieving a solution with a small k (where the minimization of the two objectives reaches its smaller value). On the other hand, a high weight for the error minimization objective results in the choice of larger k. Since the proposed method can only choose an integer value of k (as it represents an integer number of clusters), the set of solutions is discrete and finite $k \in [2, \ldots, 8]$. Solutions $k = 4$, $k = 5$ and $k = 7$ are not selected in any of the considered weight combinations because the gain in estimation error when comparing to the previous k is very small, which means that is almost always preferable to use $k = 3$ where the error is very similar, and the k objective is better, than $k = 4$ or $k = 5$, where the gain in error is minimal, and the degradation of the k objective is not compensated. The same is observable for $k = 7$ (see Fig. 4, where the gain in error can be compared when increasing the value of k).

5   Conclusions

The problem of choosing the optimal k in clustering is very popular, and a consensual approach has not yet been discovered. This paper proposes a methodology to automatically achieve the optimal k, depending on the objective preference of the user. In this case, the optimal k is used to estimate bilateral contract prices though the application of a dynamic fuzzy variable, which is defined automatically depending on the clustering results, taking into account the clustering evaluation process, in order to reach the best estimative for the specific objectives of the user (faster execution time, i.e. least number of clusters, or better estimation error, i.e. larger k).

The proposed methodology includes the use of the K-means clustering algorithm, whose results are evaluated automatically so that a dynamic fuzzy variable can be defined automatically using these clustering data. The price estimation of the fuzzy variable is also evaluated automatically, taking into account the preference weight for both objectives (2E), and the final result is achieved.

The presented experimental findings results show that the proposed methodology is able to adapt itself to the input data, being capable of providing adequate results for when the user requests a better estimation accuracy (less error), and also for when a faster execution time is required. The estimation performed by the dynamic fuzzy variable is able to follow the real data series' trend in all cases, being the quality of the estimation a result of the user's preference.

As future work, the proposed methodology will be included in the portfolio optimization problem, as a way to estimate bilateral contracts' prices. The influence of using different numbers of k to define the fuzzy variable will then be evaluated, so that conclusions can be taken on the advantages of using more or less k, depending on the influence on the objective function value and on the optimization execution time.

References

1. Shahidehpour, M., et al.: Market Operations in Electric Power Systems: Forecasting, Scheduling, and Risk Management, pp. 233–274. Wiley-IEEE Press, New York (2002)
2. Meeus, L., et al.: Development of the internal electricity market in Europe. Electr. J. **18**(6), 25–35 (2005)
3. Li, H., Tesfatsion, L.: Development of open source software for power market research: the AMES test bed. J. Energy Markets **2**(2), 111–128 (2009)
4. Koritarov, V.: Real-world market representation with agents: modeling the electricity market as a complex adaptive system with an agent-based approach. IEEE Power Energy Mag. **2**, 39–46 (2004)
5. Praça, I., et al.: MASCEM: a multi-agent system that simulates competitive electricity markets. IEEE Intell. Syst. **18**(6), 54–60 (2003)
6. Pinto, T., et al.: Adaptive learning in agents behaviour: a framework for electricity markets simulation. Integr. Comput. Aided Eng. **21**(4), 399–415 (2014)
7. Pinto, T., Vale, Z., Sousa, T.M., Sousa, T., Morais, H., Praça, I.: Particle swarm optimization of electricity market negotiating players portfolio. In: Corchado, J.M., et al. (eds.) PAAMS 2014. CCIS, vol. 430, pp. 273–284. Springer, Heidelberg (2014)
8. Pinto, T.: Bid definition method for electricity markets based on an adaptive multiagent system. In: Demazeau, Y., Pěchouček, M., Corchado, J.M., Pérez, J.B. (eds.) PAAMS 2014. AISC, vol. 88, pp. 309–316. Springer, Heidelberg (2011)
9. Jain, A.K.: Data clustering: 50 years beyond K-means. Pattern Recognit. Lett. **31**(8), 651–666 (2010)
10. Jiawei, H., Kamber, M.: Data Mining: Concepts and Techniques, p. 800. Morgan Kaufmann, San Francisco (2006)
11. Jain, A.K., Murty, M.N., Flynn, P.J.: Data clustering: a review. ACM Comput. Surv. **31**(3), 264–323 (1999)
12. Dent, I., Craig, T., Aickelin, U., Rodden, T.: Variability of behaviour in electricity load profile clustering; who does things at the same time each day? In: Perner, P. (ed.) ICDM 2014. LNCS, vol. 8557, pp. 70–84. Springer, Heidelberg (2014)
13. Calinski, T., Harabasz, J.: A dendrite method for cluster analysis. Commun. Stat. **3**(1), 1–27 (1974)
14. Davies, D.L., Bouldin, D.W.: A cluster separation measure. IEEE Trans. Pattern Anal. Mach. Intell. (PAMI) **1**(2), 224–227 (1979)
15. Kaufman, L., Rouseeuw, P.J.: Finding Groups in Data: An Introduction to Cluster Analysis. Wiley, Hoboken (1990)
16. Dianhui, W., Tapan, S.: A robust elicitation algorithm for discovering DNA motifs using fuzzy self-organizing maps. IEEE Trans. Neural Netw. Learn. Sys. **24**(10), 1677–1688 (2013)
17. Gladun, V., Yadid-pecht, O.: Information technologies and knowledge. Int. J. **5**(1), 2 (2011)
18. Hu, X.B., Wang, M., Di Paolo, E.: Calculating complete and exact pareto front for multiobjective optimization: a new deterministic approach for discrete problems. IEEE Trans. Cybern. **43**(3), 1088–1101 (2013)

Agent-Based Smart Grid Market Simulation with Connection to Real Infrastructures

Gabriel Santos[1], Tiago Pinto[1(✉)], Luís Gomes[1], Marco Silva[1], Hugo Morais[2], Zita Vale[1], and Isabel Praça[1]

[1] GECAD – Knowledge Engineering and Decision-Support Research Center, Institute of Engineering – Polytechnic of Porto (ISEP/IPP), Porto, Portugal
{gajls,tmcfp,lufog,marsi,zav,icp}@isep.ipp.pt
[2] Automation and Control Group, Technical University of Denmark, Kongens Lyngby, Denmark
morais@elektro.dtu.dk

Abstract. The consensus behind Smart Grids (SG) as one of the most promising solutions for the massive integration of renewable energy sources in power systems has led to the practical implementation of several prototypes and pilots that aim at testing and validating SG methodologies. The urgent need to accommodate such resources of distributed and intermittent nature and the impact that a deficient management of energy sources has on the global population require that alternative solutions are experimented. This paper presents a multi-agent based SG simulation platform that is connected to physical resources, so that realistic scenarios with palpable influence on real resources can be simulated. The SG simulator is also connected to the Multi-Agent Simulator of Competitive Electricity Markets (MASCEM), which provides a solid framework for the simulation of restructured electricity markets. Taking advantage on the complementarities between the simulators, a SG market is proposed, and a realistic simulation scenario, using two real buildings acting in a simulated SG is presented.

Keywords: Electricity markets · Multi-agent simulation · Smart grids

1 Introduction

The increasing shortage in the reserves of fossil fuels and the resulting rising of prices, backed up by environmental concerns with this type of fuel consumption, led to a growth of distributed generation (DG). However, this brings several problems, such as the dispatch ability, the participation of small producers in the market, and the high cost of maintenance. Such issues must be solved in order to make DG a real advantage [1]. Yet to enable the potential of DG, the creation of subsystems of the main network is evolving

This work is supported by FEDER Funds through COMPETE program and by National Funds through FCT under the projects FCOMP-01-0124-FEDER: PEst-OE/EEI/UI0760/2015 and PTDC/EEA-EEL/122988/2010; and by the SASGER-MeC project no. NORTE-07-0162-FEDER-000101, co-funded by COMPETE under FEDER Programme.

© Springer International Publishing Switzerland 2015
J. Bajo et al. (Eds.): PAAMS 2015 Workshops, CCIS 524, pp. 283–295, 2015.
DOI: 10.1007/978-3-319-19033-4_24

quickly into reality. These subsystems are composed by generation units and the associated loads. This limits the greenhouse gas emissions, reduces power losses in the transmission of energy and delays the construction of new network infrastructures. Coordination of this type of subsystem is the most challenging task and requires the implementation of distributed artificial intelligence, giving birth to the concept of Smart Grid (SG) [2].

The use of distributed energy resources (DER) is increasing significantly, and SG are rapidly evolving to a practical reality [3]. Today, Electricity Markets (EM) are a reality based on more complex and much stronger models than the ones that were on their basis [4]. However, the two concepts do not seem to be converging towards common goals and technical and economic relationships are addressed in an over simplistic way. Present operation methods and market organization do not take the most advantage of installed DG, yielding to inefficient resource management that should be overcome by adequate optimization methods [5]. EM do not allow integrating the required amount and diversity of DG and put serious limitations to the participation of small and medium size resources [6], putting at risk SG success and limiting competitiveness.

Simulation combined with distributed artificial intelligence techniques is growing as an adequate form to study the evolution of electricity markets and the coordination with SG, in order to accommodate the integration of the growing DG penetration. Modelling the SG environment with multi-agent systems enables model enlargements to include new players and allows studying and analyzing both the individual and internal performance of each distinct player; as well the global and specific interactions between all the involved players.

MASGriP - Multi-Agent Smart Grid simulation Platform [7] is a multi-agent system that models the internal operation of SGs. This system considers all the typically involved players, which are modeled by software agents with the capability of representing and simulating their actions. Additionally, some agents, namely the ones representing small players, are directly connected to physical installations, providing the means for an automatic management of the associated resources.

The Multi-Agent Simulator of Competitive Electricity Markets (MASCEM) [8] is a modeling and simulation tool that was developed for studying complex restructured electricity markets. It provides market players with simulation and decision-support resources, being able to provide them competitive advantage in the market.

This paper presents the integration between MASCEM and MASGriP, providing the means for a joint simulation of EM and SG. The dispatch of energy resources in a SG scope is proposed by means of a SG market, where SG players can benefit from a competitive environment, aiming at a reduction of the price of electricity. The SG competitive environment opposes to the usual approach, where energy resources are managed by a single controlling entity, such as a SG operator or a Virtual Power Player (VPP) [5, 9]. The competitive negotiation of the transacted power inside a SG comes to complement the centralized approach that has been assumed is previous work, namely in [5], considering the energy resource scheduling by means of a VPP, and in [9] where the internal SG dispatch is also done in a centralized form, and only afterwards is the negotiation performed with external entities, such as other VPPs with nearby SG control areas. A case study is presented, in which two real buildings, controlled by software agents, acting in the frame of a simulated SG, participate in a SG market environment with the purpose of negotiating the required power.

2   Multi-agent Simulation

Electricity market and power system simulators must be able to cope with an evolving complex dynamic reality in order to provide players with adequate tools to adapt themselves to the new reality, gaining experience to act in the frame of a changing economic, financial, and regulatory environment. With a multi-agent simulation tool the model may be easily enlarged and future evolution of markets may be accomplished. The integration of different models and the interconnection with other systems, with their own social environment are some of the best advantages of multiagent based platforms.

This section presents an overview of two multiagent systems that are directed to study of electricity markets. MASCEM detains the capability of simulating electricity markets, while MASGriP simulates the SG environment, with connection to real physical resources. The connection between these systems is highly advantageous in order to achieve a realistic and coherent representation of a broader environment.

2.1   MASCEM Overview

MASCEM [9–11] is a multi-agent based simulator of competitive electricity markets aiming to the study and comprehension of complex and restructured electricity markets. Software agents in MASCEM represent the main entities and players involved in electricity markets, such as the market and system operators, buyer and seller agents (consumers and producers), and VPPs (aggregators). The user defines each scenario by inputting the market type to simulate, the number of participating players and their strategies considering each type of agent, with their own decision-support resources, assuring them competitive advantage in the market.

MASCEM allows the simulation of the main market models: day-ahead pool (asymmetric or symmetric, with or without complex conditions), bilateral contracts, balancing market, forward markets and ancillary services. By selecting a combination of these market models, it's also possible to perform hybrid simulations.

Since electricity market players are complex and independent entities with distinct behaviors, goals and purposes, taking their own decisions while interacting with each other; MASCEM was developed as a multi-agent simulator that modulates the complexity of dynamic market players, their interaction and medium/long-term gathering of information (data and experience in the market).

All communications between agents are carried out through the exchange of messages [12]. FIPA suggests Agent Communication Language (ACL) as a standard for communications between agents. Its content includes the content language, specifying the syntax, and the ontology which provides the semantics of the message assuring the correct interpretation [13]. MASCEM agents use ontologies to allow the interoperability with other systems that intend to participate in the available electricity markets, as is the case of MASGriP.

2.2 MASGriP: Connection to Physical Resources

MASGriP [7] is a multi-agent system that supports the simulation and management of SG. It models the distribution network and the involved players, such as Domestic Customers (DM), Small (SC), Medium (MC) and Large Commerce (LC), Small (SI), Medium (MI) and Large Industrial (LI) and Rural Consumers (RC), all of them may consider Demand Response (DR) and/or micro/mini-generation and/or Electric Vehicles (EVs), as well as different sizes of DG and EV Parks. Each player is represented by a software agent with the ability of simulating its actions and behaviors. Each agent, with the exception of the facilitator, represents a physical player or part of it, detaining all the information concerning the physical installation, including its geographic coordinates and the electric characteristics. Concerning the type of player, the business model and the contracts being used, each agent has the necessary information to share with the other agents. The sharing rules can be modified according to negotiations between the players and the aggregators, making MASGriP a dynamic system.

MASGriP is also used to control real physical installations (namely two buildings in GECAD) through its integration with the SCADA (Supervisory Control and Data Acquisition) Office Intelligent Context Awareness Management (SOICAM). SOICAM was developed in GECAD under GID-Microrede project. It is implemented in two buildings (building N and building I) covering more than 30 researchers. SOICAM was implemented in June, 2014. The system monitors all the consumption and generation of GECAD. The generation data (namely solar and wind based) is stored individually every 10 s. The consumption data is divided by three main types (Fig. 1): Illumination; Heating, Ventilation and Air Conditioning (HVAC); and electrical sockets. The consumption data is also stored every 10 s. All data is stored in a SQL Server database, allowing the study of consumption and generation in GECAD, as well as its management by MASGriP's software agents.

SOICAM is also able to control HVAC systems. This functionality is only available for one building, affecting 19 researchers. The possible control is only on/off for now. New hardware is being developed and implemented to allow individual load management and control. Using refined control over the load and not only on/off control, the SOICAM performance and utility is increased.

SOICAM uses five switchboards to incorporate the energy analysers and the HVAC control system. These switchboards communicate with two main communication switchboards (one for each building) via RS485. The main communication switchboards aggregate the energy analysers' information. The information can be accessed by MODBUS/TCP.

The data acquired by SOICAM is used to test and validate the participation of SOICAM as a SG player. Additionally, the use of MASGriP for real-time control enables the simulation of real scenarios with visible outcomes on the loads.

3   Smart Grid Market

The simulation of a competitive SG market is proposed, by using the common market mechanisms that are usually implemented in worldwide electricity markets. The larger

Fig. 1. Monitored loads (blue: illumination; red: HVAC; green: electrical sockets) (Color figure online)

amount of electricity that is transacted in European electricity markets is negotiated in auction based day-ahead pool markets. These mechanisms have shown to be solid and adequate for electricity negotiation, and for this reason they are the main resource that should be experimented in a SG environment.

The most common type of pool negotiations is a standard uniform auction [14, 15]. If both buyers and sellers can compete, it is called symmetric market. If only sellers compete in the pool, than it is asymmetrical market. Figure 2 presents both market types.

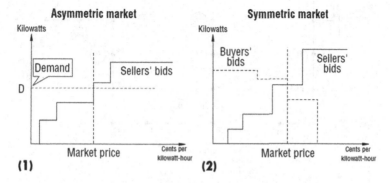

Fig. 2. Market types: (1) asymmetric; (2) symmetric [16].

In the symmetric market, both buyer and seller agents submit bids. The market operator sorts the selling bids from the lowest price to the highest, and the demand bids from the highest price to the lowest. The proposed bids form the supply and demand step curves, and the market price paid to all accepted supplier is determined by the point where both curves intersect. Every seller bids offering prices lower than the established market price and buyer bids offering prices higher than the market price will be accepted.

In the case of the asymmetric market, only seller agents present their bids. Buyer agents only reveal their needs to set up the demand. The market operator sorts the selling bids from the lowest price to the highest, and once he knows the demand, it accepts the supply until the required demand is fulfilled. The market price is set by the last accepted bid.

4   Case Study

The presented case study was tested using a MV (Medium-Voltage) distribution network at the level of 12.66 kV. This is an existing test network published in the scientific literature [17] with radial operating system, including 15 DG units, consisting of 32 lines and 32 buses and is connected to the rest of the electric power system through an interconnection point, substation (bus 33).

Based on the studies provided by [18], the energy resources penetration in this network for 2020 has been projected. Figure 3 presents the projection of energy resources for the year 2020 in the 32 buses distribution network.

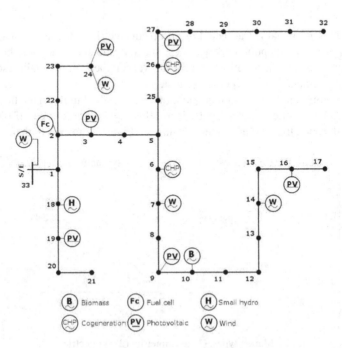

Fig. 3.   Projection of energy resources for the year 2020 in the 32 buses distribution network.

Each bus is represented by a SG agent in the SG market. Buildings I and N of GECAD (as presented in Sect. 2.2) are located in bus 23 and 24 respectively. Building N, as mentioned in Sect. 2.2, includes wind and solar based generation. Each of the two buildings is also represented by a software agent in the SG market. Figure 4 discriminates the consumption of Buildings I and N for the 24 h of the considered simulation day. Figure 5 presents the total wind and solar based generation of Building N during the 24 h of the considered simulation day.

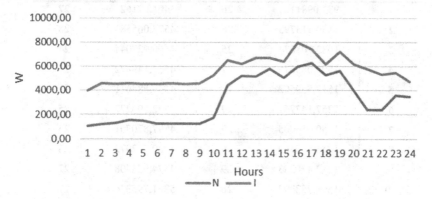

Fig. 4. Total Consumption of Buildings I and N during the 24 h of the considered simulation day.

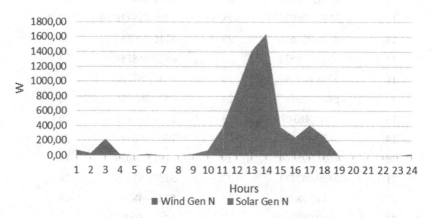

Fig. 5. Total Solar and Wind Generation of Building N during the 24 h of the considered simulation day.

Since the total generated energy of building N is not enough to meet the required consumption, this SG player needs to buy the fault energy in the grid in order to fulfill its requirements. Building I, without generation, needs to buy the full amount of its consumption as well. Table 1 shows the required energy and prices offered by both buildings, i.e., the bids they presented in the SG market. The bid prices of the players that represent both buildings are defined accordingly to the cost values that have been defined in previous work [19], which represent the cost that buildings have in a SG simulated environment for their purchase of power.

Table 1. Bids of buildings I and N in the SG market.

Hours	Building N		Building I	
	W	€/MWh	W	€/MWh
1	974,0981122	26	4012,7162	27
2	1150,913793	26	4577,065583	28
3	1083,708074	25	4560,927044	24
4	1509,085676	27	4567,149872	25
5	1512,559502	24	4549,584611	27
6	1257,147761	29	4532,596227	25
7	1250,450005	29	4597,870701	25
8	1256,576369	26	4520,732972	28
9	1212,470293	29	4574,923408	27
10	1699,752397	26	5261,795346	27
11	4076,451011	29	6550,343609	28
12	4371,724113	26	6227,917769	26
13	3797,528936	28	6709,418378	27
14	4186,982675	29	6716,740835	25
15	4695,796523	26	6428,068751	24
16	5748,607191	24	7951,967265	29
17	5865,485199	24	7433,502956	25
18	5014,46319	28	6204,044345	29
19	5639,493148	25	7237,960291	24
20	4001,995764	29	6197,874025	28
21	2409,567551	27	5757,792413	24
22	2414,558784	24	5321,448589	29
23	3569,059502	27	5488,750062	26
24	3494,575701	25	4744,456081	27

As mentioned above, the aim of this study is to test different market algorithms that could be applied to the internal negotiation of smart grids, in order to verify if they would be more beneficial to the SG players than the usual centralized management approach. For that purpose the SG market has been simulated both with the symmetrical and asymmetrical algorithms. The results for each of the algorithms are presented in the following sections (symmetrical market in Sect. 4.1, and asymmetrical market in Sect. 4.2).

4.1 Symmetrical Algorithm

After running the simulation, the results are provided in data files and also in graphics mode for a more immediate analysis. Figures 6 and 7 present the results obtained by the players representing Building I and Building N respectively. In these figures, the bars represent the amount of power that has been purchased in each business opportunity, namely by means of aggregation with a VPP, in negotiations with other SG, through bilateral contracts (BC), or in the SG market. The lines represent the established market price and the bid price offered by the player (Building I and Building N respectively).

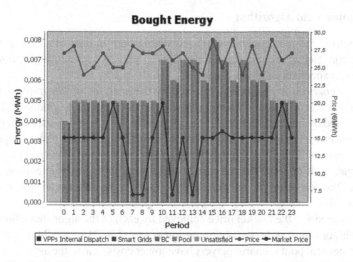

Fig. 6. Building I results when running the symmetrical pool algorithm.

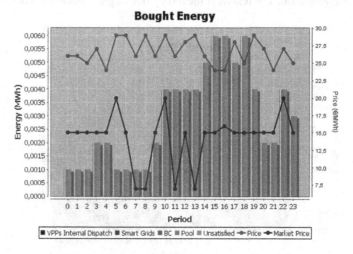

Fig. 7. Building N results when running the symmetrical pool algorithm.

By analyzing both graphics it is possible to see that using the symmetrical algorithms both players fulfill all their needs in the SG market, and for this reason no power is allocated to other negotiations. It is also visible that the prices offered by both players are significantly higher than the established market price. Hence, the symmetrical algorithm allows players to achieve better results in the market (lower prices) due to its competitiveness. While some players need to buy at any cost (e.g. players representing Building I and Building N), others try to minimize their costs using strategies for prices definition, trying to influence the market price outcome.

4.2   Asymmetrical Algorithm

As seen before, the results achieved are available both in data files and in graphical representation. Below are presented the results of players representing Building I and Building N, respectively in Figs. 8 and 9.

In this scenario it is also possible to see by the analyses of the graphics that both buyers bought all the required energy in the SG market. In the asymmetrical pool the price presented by buyers is ignored, as explained in Sect. 3, which means that the bids presented by buyer agents is sorted by order of arrival. In this case, players representing Building I and Building N submitted their offers in time and managed to get all the required energy. If that was not the case, if there were not enough generation in the SG to fulfill all the consumption, they could have failed to buy energy in one, some or all trading periods.

When comparing the market price achieved by each of the algorithms, the symmetrical pool algorithm stands out, obtaining lower prices in 21 of the 24 hourly periods. In the symmetrical pool scenario players have lower costs than in the asymmetrical pool scenario. However this does not mean that the symmetric algorithm always gets better results than asymmetric. The results achieved by both algorithms always depend on the

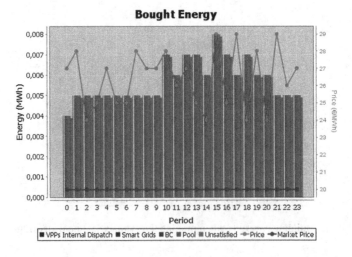

Fig. 8. Building I results when running the asymmetrical pool algorithm.

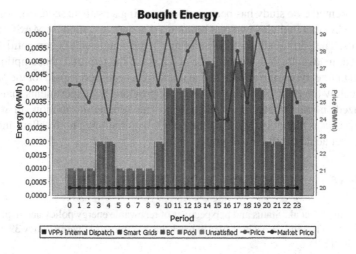

Fig. 9. Building N results when running the asymmetrical pool algorithm.

prices proposed by seller agents, but in the case of symmetrical pool they also depend on the bids presented by buyer agents. Therefore, the symmetrical pool algorithm is more competitive and has the potential of achieving lower market prices, as buyer agents also influence the price definition with their bids.

The use of market negotiation models provided by MASCEM have allowed the SG participating players to negotiate the available SG power internally, improving the competitiveness inside the SG, and with this decreasing the energy transaction prices.

5   Conclusions

The practical implementation of SG is, nowadays, a reality. Several pilot implementations have been experimented and full scale tests and validations are being conducted in order to draw conclusions and refine the used methods, so that the replication and consequent spread of SG implementation can be performed safely.

With the worldwide implementation of SG, management and negotiation mechanisms need to be robust in order to take full advantage of the potential of DG and local control of demand.

This paper has presented the integration between two complementary multiagent simulators, which together provide the means to create realistic simulation environments, involving the SG and electricity markets. Taking advantage on this integration it is possible to simulate the participation of SG players in electricity markets, in order to reach conclusions on the steps that are necessary to enable the full participation of DG in the markets; and also to validate potential alternatives for a competitive SG market environment. With this purpose, the use of two of the most widely used market mechanisms (symmetric and asymmetric auction pools) is proposed in a SG scope.

The presented case study has been performed using a realistic scenario, considering a simulated SG that includes two real buildings that are controlled by MASGriP's software agents. The participation of the buildings in the simulated SG competitive market has resulted in advantageous deals in the purchase of the required consumption power. In both SG market types, the established market price, i.e. the price paid for the purchased power is below the price paid for consumers in previous SG experiments that consider a centralized, non-competitive, management. The symmetric auction, in which the competitiveness is higher by allowing the prices' negotiation of both sellers and buyers, is the one that achieved the lower prices.

References

1. Klessmann, C., et al.: Status and perspectives of renewable energy policy and deployment in the European Union—What is needed to reach the 2020 targets? Energy Policy **39**(12), 7637–7657 (2011)
2. Blumsack, S., Fernandez, A.: Ready or not, here comes the smart grid! Energy **37**(1), 61–68 (2012)
3. Bo, Z., Xuesong, Z., Jian, C.: Integrated microgrid laboratory system. IEEE Trans. Power Syst. **27**, 2175–2185 (2012)
4. Meeus, L., et al.: Development of the internal electricity market in Europe. Electr. J. **18**(6), 25–35 (2005)
5. Sousa, T., et al.: Intelligent energy resource management considering vehicle-to-grid: a simulated annealing approach. IEEE Trans. Smart Grid **3**, 535–542 (2012)
6. Shahidehpour, M., et al.: Market Operations in Electric Power Systems: Forecasting, Scheduling, and Risk Management, pp. 233–274. Wiley-IEEE Press, New York (2002)
7. Oliveira, P., et al.: MASGriP - a multi-agent smart grid simulation plataform. In: IEEE Power and Energy Society General Meeting, San Diego, California, USA, pp. 1–10 (2012)
8. Pinto, T., et al.: Strategic bidding in electricity markets: an agent-based simulator with game theory for scenario analysis. Integr. Comput. Aided Eng. **20**(4), 335–346 (2013). IOS Press
9. Pinto, T., et al.: A new approach for multi-agent coalition formation and management in the scope of electricity markets. Energy **36**(8), 5004–5015 (2011)
10. Praça, I., et al.: MASCEM: a multi-agent system that simulates competitive electricity markets. IEEE Intell. Syst. **18**(6), 54–60 (2003). Special Issue on Agents and Markets
11. Vale, Z., et al.: MASCEM: electricity markets simulation with strategic agents. IEEE Intell. Syst. **26**(2), 9–17 (2011)
12. Foundation for Intelligent Physical Agents (FIPA), Agent Management Specification (2002) http://www.fipa.org/specs/fipa00023/SC00023J.html. Accessed on January 2015
13. Foundation for Intelligent Physical Agents (FIPA), FIPA ACL Message Structure Specification (2002). http://www.fipa.org/specs/fipa00061/SC00061G.html. Accessed on January 2015
14. Sheblé, G.: Computational Auction Mechanisms for Restructured Power Industry Operation. Kluwer Academic Publishers, Boston (1999)
15. Klemperer, P.: Auction theory: a guide to the literature. J. Econ. Surv. **13**(3), 227–286 (1999). www.nuff.ox.ac.uk/economics/people/klemperer.htm
16. Praça, I., et al.: MASCEM: a multiagent system that simulates competitive electricity markets. IEEE Intell. Syst. **18**(6), 54–60 (2003)
17. Baran, M.E., Wu, F.F.: Network reconfiguration in distribution-systems for loss reduction and load balancing. IEEE Trans. Power Deliv. **4**, 1401–1407 (1989)

18. World Energy Council: Energy Scenario Development Analysis: WEC Policy to 2050, press office, 20th world energy congress (2007)
19. Silva, M., et al.: Real-time energy resource scheduling considering a real Portuguese scenario. In: 19th World Congress of the International Federation of Automatic Control (IFAC 2014), Cape Town, South Africa, 24–29 August, 2014

Workshop on Multiagent System Based Learning Environments

Dynamic e-Learning Content Selection
with BDI Agents

João de Amorim Jr.[✉], Thiago Ângelo Gelaim,
and Ricardo Azambuja Silveira

PPGCC – UFSC, Florianópolis, Brazil
{joao.amorim,thiago}@iate.ufsc.br,
ricardo.silveira@ufsc.br

Abstract. This paper presents an e-learning content selection model, based on multi-agent paradigm, aiming to facilitate the learning material reuse and adaptability on Learning Management Systems. The proposed model was developed according to a BDI multi-agent architecture, as an improvement of the Intelligent Learning Objects approach, allowing the dynamic selection of Learning Objects. A prototype was implemented to validate the proposed model, using the JADEX BDI V3 platform, and allowing to build improved learning experiences.

Keywords: Dynamic learning experience · Intelligent Learning Objects · Intelligent learning environments

1 Introduction

The distance learning plays an important role on the educational process worldwide. Several learning institutions have adopted e-learning as one of their acting strategies, and new ways of online learning are becoming more and more common [1].

Teaching aid systems must be geared to enhance the educational experience. Two aspects contribute to it: adaptability and reuse. The former is related to different students' needs and styles. An adaptable system increases the student understanding, in a personalized way [2–4]. The latter avoids the need of developing a new resource if exists another one with the same learning intention [3, 5].

Intelligent Tutoring Systems (ITS), Learning Management Systems (LMS) and Learning Objects (LO) are some computational tools that enrich the learning process. ITS are applications created for a specific educational domain, usually with some few adaptability and interoperability resources [6]. Thus, if a change in the learning domain is needed, the ITS must be reconfigured. Following, LMS are learning environments used to build online courses (or publishing material), to monitor the student progress and to manage educational data [1, 7, 8]. Finally, LO are digital artifacts for supporting the teaching-learning process, promoting reuse and adaptability [9].

Although LO and LMS allow reusability, they have a limited level of adaptability. The kind of adaptation they offer needs to be pre-programmed by the instructional designer or teacher, that is, this systems usually are no dynamic adaptable [8, 9].

© Springer International Publishing Switzerland 2015
J. Bajo et al. (Eds.): PAAMS 2015 Workshops, CCIS 524, pp. 299–308, 2015.
DOI: 10.1007/978-3-319-19033-4_25

This article presents the first results of our research that seeks the convergence of these three different paradigms for the development of intelligent learning environments. The first step, presented in this paper, was to develop a search engine, delivery and presentation systems to get learning objects obtained from repositories.

1.1   Related Work

There are several similar studies developed to provide adaptability to educational systems. Some of them are built as an extension of a LMS using conditional jumps [8], Bayesian networks [4] or data mining technics [7] as their adaptive strategy. Other researches are not integrated with a LMS, and use distinct ways to adapt the learning to the students' style, such as ITS [6], Recommender System [2], etc. [10, 11].

In addition, there are also some works based on the Multi-Agent System (MAS) approach to produce smarter applications. MAS are composed by autonomous entities (agents) which percept the environment they are situated in and act on it to achieve their objectives. The communication and cooperation of individual agents make possible to solve complex problems, which they cannot solve individually [12, 13].

An important MAS architecture for intelligent agents is the BDI model. BDI agents are composed of mental attitudes (Belief, Desire, Intention), and act following the practical reasoning process (goal deliberation and means-end reasoning) [12, 14].

Some analyzed works combine LMS and MAS to make the former more adaptive. An example is the use of data obtained from a MOODLE [15] forum to show resources and activities to the students [16]. There is also an intelligent, dynamic and adaptive environment, based on agents that are able to identify the student cognitive profile [17].

However, all this related studies have two features that can be improved. The former is the way as the student's learning style is determined. The analyzed works use questionnaires in the beginning of the course to do it. This extra step can be considered intrusive and distracting [2]. The exception is the work that clusters students in profiles based on their assessments performance (grades) [17]. The latter is the possibility of coupling new learning resources (LO) dynamically to the environment. The teacher (or instructional designer) need to configure previously all the possible course paths for each student style, what could be hard and take so much time [4, 18]. Further, the attaching of a new LO to the course involves modifying the course structure.

To produce more intelligent LO, previous researches proposed the convergence between the LO and MAS technologies, called Intelligent Learning Objects (ILO) [19, 20]. This approach makes possible to offer more adaptive, reusable and complete learning experiences. An ILO is an agent capable to play the role of a LO, which can acquire new knowledge by the interaction with students and other ILO (agents information exchange), raising the potential of student's understanding.

The LO metadata permits the identification of what educational topic is related to the LO [9]. Hence, the ILO (agents) are able to find out what is the subject associated with the learning experience shown to the student, and then to show complementary information (another ILO) to solve the student's lack of knowledge in that subject.

The next section presents a different model to handle the two issues pointed out in the analyzed works, and to improve the ILO model as well.

2   ILOMAS

The new proposed model is based on MAS approach integrated to a LMS, resulting on the improvement of the analyzed related works, allowing that LO can be included to the learning experience dynamically, adding intelligent behavior to the system. The solution's adaptability is based on the possibility of new LO be attached to the LMS without previous course configuration, as soon as the system finds out that the student needs to reinforce its understanding on a specific concept. This is automatically identified through the verification of the student assessment performance (grade), on each instructional unit, or by student choice, when interacting with the LO. Moreover, the course structure becomes more flexible, since it is unnecessary to configure all the possible sets of learning paths for each student profile.

The proposed model achieves reuse by the combination of pre-existed and validated LO whose concept (subject) is the same of that the student needs to learn more about, avoiding that teachers or instructional designers need to build new materials.

The objective of the new model called Intelligent Learning Object Multi-Agent System (ILOMAS) is to enhance the framework developed to create ILO based on MAS with BDI architecture [21], extending this model to allow the production of adaptive and reusable learning experiences. The idea is to select dynamically ILO in the LMS according to the student performance, without previous specific configuration on the course structure. The ILOMAS is composed by agents with specific goals, and capable of communicating and offering learning experiences to students in a LMS course, according to the interaction with these students.

3   Analysis and Design

The modeling of the ILOMAS framework uses an Agent-Oriented Software Engineering methodology. The Prometheus methodology defines a detailed process to specify, design and implement intelligent agent systems based on goals, plans and beliefs (BDI) [22]. It is composed of several activities and phases to generate specification and design documents. Another reason to choose this methodology is the existence of Prometheus Design Tool (PDT), an Eclipse IDE plug-in that supplies an iterative development of the Prometheus diagrams [23].

Following the Prometheus methodology, on the system specification phase, it was identified the goals, roles, agents and their respective interfaces with the environment (perceptions, actions and external data). It was detected two kinds of agents (Fig. 1):

- LMSAgent – Represents the LMS. It is responsible for: (1) receiving the student learning experience request (*Learning Experience Request* perception); (2) finding out the subject that the student must learn about (*Learning Experience Subject Identifier* role), according to the information provided from the LMS data base (external data); and (3) for passing the control of the interaction with the student to a new agent of the kind ILOAgent (*Inform Learning Object Subject* message).

Its beliefs are information provided from the LMS database, such as the students, the courses and the respective subject related to the current learning experience (that is, the topic that the student must learn about), for each student enrolled on the LMS's courses. The communication between the agent and the LMS can be made through the calling to data base access API functions (such as Java JDBC, PHP PDO, etc.) or Web Services. The LMSAgent goals are *GetStudentCourseGoal* and *GetStudentSubjectGoal* (sub-goals of *IdentifyLearningExperienceSubject* goal), which allow the agent to identify the information of the current learning experience associated with a specific student.

- ILOAgent – Agent responsible for showing the learning experience to the student. This is made through the presentation of a LO related to the subject that the student needs to learn about, as determined by the LMSAgent. The function of an ILO-Agent agent is to search a correspondent LO on the LO repository (*Learning Object Searcher* role) and show it to the student (*Learning Experience Show* action), furthermore, this kind of agent must keep itself aware to the interaction between the student and the system (*Learning Object Player* role).

The beliefs of this agent are the information about the current learning experience (obtained from LMSAgent), the chosen LO, and the status of the interaction with the student. The goals are *GetLORepositoryGoal*, *GetRelatedLOGoal*, and *SelectLOGoal* (sub-goals of *SearchLearningObject* goal), which enable the agent to search for a LO (related to the specific subject) in the repository.

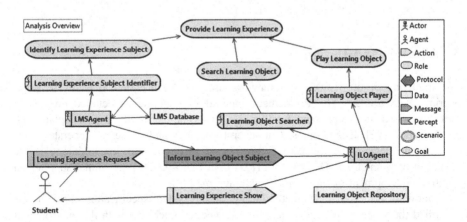

Fig. 1. Analysis overview diagram

The Agent Overview diagram (Fig. 2) presents the agent's plans (the concrete way to achieve the agent's goals [12]), perceptions, actions, internal messages, and capabilities. The idea of using capabilities is to module the agent features, allowing the reuse of commons characteristics (such as plans, goals, etc.) among distinct agents [22].

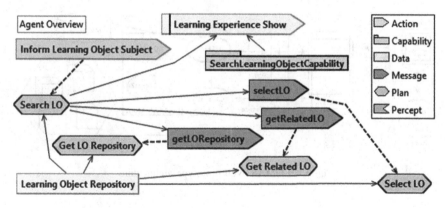

Fig. 2. Agent overview diagram (i.e.: ILOAgent)

4 Implementation

After the modeling phase, the ILOMAS framework and a prototype instance were implemented to validate the proposed model. The JADEX framework [24, 25] – an extension to JADE platform (FIPA compliant) with support to develop intelligent agent systems – was chosen to implement the agents based on the BDI architecture [12, 14].

The JADEX platform permits the creation of active components, an approach that gets benefits from the association of two distinct technologies: Agents and SCA. The SCA model was proposed by IT companies (i.e.: IBM, ORACLE) with the intention of promoting the interoperability among distributed applications, according to concepts of components and service oriented architecture (SOA) [24, 25].

The newest JADEX platform version is JADEX BDI V3 (V3). Before V3, the agents were built in ADF files (XML tags for beliefs, desires, etc.) and Java classes (plans) [26]. However, on V3 the agents are developed with pure Java classes (without XML files) and the annotations mechanism (beliefs, plans, etc.) [14, 25]. Further, on V3 the recommended way of agent communication is through service invocation. The BDI agents can be service providers (declaring specific annotations and implementing specific interfaces) and can request services of other agents, components, etc. [24, 25].

It is necessary to point out the implementation limitations. Instead of putting emphasis on visualization issues (such as formats, rich graphical user interfaces, etc.), it was emphasized the MAS development (with the agents and their interactions).

The interaction interface between the student and the agents' environment was implemented based on the Java Servlets and JSP technologies, getting benefits of the JADEX BDI V3 services communication structure. The Servlets technology allows the execution of services and Java classes at the server side from Web requests.

On the prototype, the servlet layer delegates the handle of the student's browser request to a class (non-agent) based on the Facade design pattern. This pattern provides a unified and simplified interface to a sub-system, promoting low coupling [27]. The ILOMASFacade class offers to the servlet classes the access to agents' services (the agents' capabilities, plans, etc.) keeping the separation between the MAS layer and the external items (front-end and servlets), avoiding unnecessary coupling (Fig. 3).

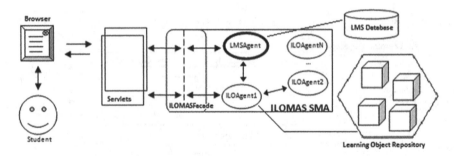

Fig. 3. ILOMAS Web prototype architecture

4.1   Developed Classes

Following JADEX BDI V3 framework structure, the developed agents were declared with the @Agent annotation and with the BDI suffix in their class name. Besides, it was required to specify a BDIAgent type attribute (annotated with @Agent). This attribute type provides the necessary methods to execute the reasoning and behaviors on the BDI model, such as dispatch an agent goal (leading to plan execution).

Other annotations can be used in agent classes to declare BDI attributes (@Belief, @Capability, etc.) and methods. The method annotations define agent behavior to specific states of the agent's life cycle, such as @AgentCreated (after agent start up), @AgentKilled (before agent die), and @AgentBody (agent run) [14, 25, 28], i.e.: when the ILOAgentBDI starts running, its goal of search what LO will be shown to the student is dispatched, according to the subject identified by the LMSAgentBDI. Additionally, the agents were specified as service providers, using the annotations @Service and @ProvidedService, and implementing the methods of the Java Interface corresponding to each respective service, whose return is asynchronous [25, 28].

The BDI elements (beliefs, goals and plans) related to the functionality of determining the subject associated with the learning experience were grouped on the IdentifyLearningExperienceCapability class. This capability class has beliefs that are instances of another class, which keeps information obtained from the LMS database (annotated with @Belief).

The IdentifyLearningExperienceCapability has also the goal *IdentifyLearningExperienceGoal* (and its sub-goals *GetStudentCourseGoal* and *GetStudentSubjectGoal*), declared with the @Goal annotation. The execution of a goal is made through the triggering of a specific plan represented by a method, using the @Plan and @Trigger annotations, (i.e.: *identifyLearningExperienceSubject* method).

Another developed capability was SearchLearningObjectCapability, whose main goal *SearchLOGoal* is composed of sub-goals: (1) find out the repository, (2) get the list of LO associated with the subject within the repository, and (3) choose one LO. Some metadata elements declared in IEEE-LOM [9] are used in this process. The ILOAgentBDI has the SearchLearningObjectCapability, which uses the element "keywords" of the LOM metadata to define the list of related LO.

The SearchLearningObjectCapability class declares one belief which references the LO repository found. The dispatching of the main goal *SearchLOGoal* results in the execution of the *searchLearningObject* plan method (annotated with @Plan and @Trigger).

4.2 ILOMAS Validation

The prototype was deployed to an Apache Tomcat Server (7.0.57) to test the proposed model. On the test beginning, a student accessed the system and the LMSAgent has identified that the student needed to learn about photosynthesis (Biology course). After, the student asked for the learning experience, leading to a new servlet requesting. This servlet has forwarded it to ILOMASFacade, which has waited for the end of ILOAgentBDI's deliberation. Then, this agent has discovered a LO related to the subject within the repository. Finally, this LO was shown to the student successfully.

Besides, it was simulated a student's request for a complementary learning experience (by pressing the corresponding button). As result, a new ILOAgentBDI was created on the system, which searched for and found a different LO related to the same subject (photosynthesis) within the repository. It was not explicitly defined in the database that the student should have watched this new LO (only the subject was required, no specific LO), so the MAS obtained the related LO dynamically (Fig. 4).

Fig. 4. ILOMAS Web prototype

5 Conclusions and Future Work

This paper presented a model to build more adaptive and reusable educational experiences, compared to related works. The ILOMAS framework was designed to allow the dynamic LO selection on LMS courses, as an improvement of ILO's previous approach. The agents are modeled based on the practical reasoning paradigm (towards goal achievement). The MAS was developed following the JADEX BDI V3 framework, which permits that the agents' functionalities can be accessed as services. The use of Servlet technology provides the integration of front-end and intelligent layer.

A prototype was implemented to verify the proposed model, and some evaluation tests were executed. As result, the ILOMAS has received the learning experience requested by the student, and has identified dynamically a LO associated with the subject that the student must have learned about (according to the LMS database).

As future work, the ILOMAS framework will be extended to supply the integration with SCORM [29] in order to raise reuse, dynamic sequencing, and interoperability. This improvement on the system will make possible to identify accurately the need of reinforcement by the student, according to the information about the interaction between the student and the object, provided by the messages received from and sent to the SCORM API (the data model elements, such as success, fail, latency, weighting, objectives, etc.) [30].

Another enhancement on the framework would be the use of some recommendation mechanism, made by specialized agents, to better choosing a LO among the list of objects associated with the specific subject within the repository. Currently, when there are more than one LO related to the desired subject within the repository, a random choice is made to select the next LO to be presented to the student, considering only the objects not shown. The overall process can be smarter by using a multiagent based recommender system for indexing and retrieving LO [31, 32]. The ILOMAS framework can consult this system before accessing the repository.

Finally, future works involve also the testing of the model with different learning situations and real students.

References

1. Allison, C., Miller, A., Oliver, I., Michaelson, R., Tiropanis, T.: The Web in education. Comput. Netw. **56**, 3811–3824 (2012). Elsevier
2. Vesin, B., Klasnja-Milicevic, A., Ivanovic, M., Budimac, Z.: Applying recommender systems and adaptive hypermedia for e-learning personalization. Comput. Inform. **32**, 629–659 (2013). Institute of Informatics
3. Mahkameh, Y., Bahreininejad, A.: A context-aware adaptive learning system using agents. Expert Syst. Appl. **38**, 3280–3286 (2011). Elsevier
4. Bachari, E., Abelwahed, E., Adnani, M.: E-learning personalization based on dynamic learners' preference. Int. J. Comput. Sci. Inf. Technol. (IJCSIT) **3**(3), 200–216 (2011)
5. Caeiro, M., Llamas, M., Anido, L.: PoEML: modeling learning units through perspectives. Comput. Standards Interfaces **36**(2), 380–396 (2014). Elsevier

6. Santos, G., Jorge, J.: Interoperable intelligent tutoring systems as open educational resources. IEEE Trans. Learn. Technol. **6**(3), 271–282 (2013). IEEE CS & ES
7. Despotovic-Zrakic, M., Markovic, A., Bogdanovic, Z., Barac, D., Krco, S.: Providing adaptivity in moodle LMS courses. Int. Forum Educ. Tech. Soc. **15**(1), 326–338 (2012). International Forum of Educational Technology & Society
8. Komlenov, Z., Budimac, Z., Ivanovic, M.: Introducing adaptivity features to a regular learning management system to support creation of advanced eLessons. Inform. Educ. **9**(1), 63–80 (2010). Institute of Mathematics and Informatics
9. Barak, M., Ziv, S.: Wandering: A web-based platform for the creation of location-based interactive learning objects. Comput. Educ. **62**, 159–170 (2013). Elsevier
10. Chen, C.: Intelligent web-based learning system with personalized learning path guidance. Comput. Educ. **51**, 787–814 (2008). Elsevier
11. Kurilovas, E., Zilinskiene, I., Dagiene, V.: Recommending suitable scenarios according to learners' preferences: An improved swarm based approach. Comput. Hum. Behav. **30**, 550–557 (2014). Elsevier
12. Wooldridge, M.: An Introduction to MultiAgent Systems, 2nd edn. Wiley, New York (2009)
13. Weiss, G. (ed.): Multiagent Systems: A Modern Approach to Distributed Artificial Intelligence. The MIT Press, Cambridge (1999)
14. Pokahr, A., Braubach, L., Haubeck, C., Ladiges, J.: Programming BDI agents with pure Java. In: Müller, J.P., Weyrich, M., Bazzan, A.L. (eds.) MATES 2014. LNCS, vol. 8732, pp. 216–233. Springer, Heidelberg (2014)
15. MOODLE – Modular Oriented-Object Dynamic Learning Environment. http://moodle.org
16. Alencar, M., Netto, J.: Improving cooperation in virtual learning environments using multi-agent systems and AIML. In: 41st ASEE/IEEE Frontiers in Education Conference, Session F4C, pp. 1–6. IEEE (2011)
17. Giuffra, P., Silveira, R.: A multi-agent system model to integrate virtual learning environments and intelligent tutoring systems. International Journal of Interactive Multimedia and Artificial Intelligence (IJIMAI) **2**(1), 51–58 (2013)
18. Brown, E., Cristea, A., Stewart, C., Brailsford, T.: Patterns in authoring of adaptive educational hypermedia: a taxonomy of learning styles. Edu. Technol. Soc. **8**(3), 77–90 (2005). International Forum of Educational Technology & Society
19. Silveira, R., Gomes, E., Vicari, R.: Intelligent learning objects: an agent-based approach of learning objects. In: van Weert, T., Tatnall, A. (eds.) Information and Communication Technologies and Real-Life Learning. IFIP, vol. 182, pp. 103–110. Springer, Boston (2006)
20. Silva, J., Silveira, R.: The development of intelligent learning objects with an ontology based on SCORM standard. In: Seventh International Conference on Intelligent Systems Design and Applications, pp. 211–216. IEEE (2007)
21. Bavaresco, N., Silveira, R.: Proposal of an architecture to build intelligent learning objects based on BDI agents. In: XX Informatics in Education Brazilian Symposium (2009)
22. Padgham, L., Winikoff, M.: Developing Intelligent Agent Systems – A practical guide. Wiley, New York (2004)
23. Prometheus Design Tool (Eclipse Plug-in). https://code.google.com/p/pdt-plugin/
24. Pokahr, A., Braubach, L., Jander, K.: The jadex project: programming model. In: Distributed Systems and Information Systems, Chap. 1, pp. 1–34. University of Hamburg (2012)
25. JADEX Active Components. http://www.activecomponents.org/
26. Braubach, L., Pokahr, A.: Jadex Active Components Framework – BDI Agents for Disaster Rescue Coordination. University of Hamburg (2011)
27. Gamma, E., Helm, R., Johnson, R., Vlissides, J.: Design Patterns: Elements of Reusable Object-Oriented Software. Addison-Wesley, New York (1995)

28. Braubach, L., Pokahr, A.: Developing Distributed Systems with Active Components and JADEX. University of Hamburg (2012)
29. SCORM 2004. Advanced Distributed Learning. http://www.adlnet.org/scorm
30. SCORM Run-Time Reference. Rustici Software. http://scorm.com/scorm-explained/technical-scorm/run-time/run-time-reference/
31. Vian, J., Campos, R., Palomino, C., Silveira, R.: A multiagent model for searching learning objects in heterogeneous set of repositories. In: 2011 11th IEEE International Conference on Advanced Learning Technologies (ICALT), pp. 48–52. IEEE (2011)
32. Campos, R.L.R., Comarella, R.L., Silveira, R.A.: Multiagent based recommendation system model for indexing and retrieving learning objects. In: Corchado, J.M., Bajo, J., Kozlak, J., Pawlewski, P., Molina, J.M., Julian, V., Silveira, R.A., Unland, R., Giroux, S. (eds.) PAAMS 2013. CCIS, vol. 365, pp. 328–339. Springer, Heidelberg (2013)

Multi-plataform Interface to an ITS
of Proposicional Logic Teaching

Fabiane F.P. Galafassi[1(✉)], Alan Velasques Santos[1],
Rafael Koch Peres[1], Rosa Maria Vicari[1], and João Carlos Gluz[2]

[1] Instituto de Informática, Universidade Federal do Rio Grande do Sul,
Porto Alegre, RS 91501-970, Brazil
{fabiane.penteado,alanvelasques,
rafaelkperes}@gmail.com, rosa@inf.ufrgs.br
[2] Programa Interdisciplinar de Pós Graduação em Computação Aplicada
(PIPCA), Universidade do Vale do Rio dos Sinos (UNISINOS),
275-93.022-000, São Leopoldo, RS, Brazil
jcgluz@unisinos.br

Abstract. The present article has the objective to show some preliminary results of new Web interface developed to multi-agent system named Heraclito. The Heraclito is one Intelligent Tutoring System (ITS) who has as objective teach propositional logic to undergraduate students of Computer. This version was developed with Test Driven Development (TDD) technique. This approach allowed us to create an interface more friendly and, the access by Web Browser, turned the tool adaptive, may now been available to work on computers, tablets, smartphones and also on Smart TVs.

1 Introduction

In accord with the official grade of Education Ministry on Brazil, the Logic, on the undergraduate schools on computer and informatics, is essential and non-elective subject for all courses. A statistic research[1] realized in the last eight years, shows high levels of failure and dropout in this subject [1]. The dropout, in particular, starts to appear on the beginning of the subject, usually when the Natural Deduction contents begin to deal with Propositional Logic context. In practice, the difficulties starts when subjects as formula, deduction rule and formal proof begin to be shown by the teacher. In a way to contribute to improve the present rates, was used one dialectic method to teach Logic, grounded in one social historical pedagogy and in one mediation model by computer modeled on multi-agent system, who was named Heraclito.

The Heraclito system [1] has for objective, help students of Logic subject. Your editor interface helps in the proof elaboration of formal arguments as a primary functionality by the Natural Deduction rules and, in its actual composition, shows two versions: Desktop/Laptop (computer) and Mobile (tablet and smartphones). The

---

[1] The compiled data for this article who justify the development of this teach system for Logic can be founded on: http://biblioteca.asav.org.br/vinculos/000003/00000335.pdf, page 15, item 2.1 Justification.

© Springer International Publishing Switzerland 2015
J. Bajo et al. (Eds.): PAAMS 2015 Workshops, CCIS 524, pp. 309–319, 2015.
DOI: 10.1007/978-3-319-19033-4_26

Heraclito is part of OBAAMILOS [2] project and its software architecture is compatible with MILOS[2] agents infrastructure. To facilitate Heraclito interoperability between devices and the reusability, the Heraclito is encapsulated in Learning Objects (LO) and is part of Repository of educational contents OBAA, at UFRGS.[3]

With this architecture base and the OBAA[4] standard functionalities, the Heraclito system was projected to cover the adaptability requirement. In this approach, it just will be needed one Web Browser to the user access the tools of this resource, without need a specific requirements for any platform used, it can be accessed on computers, tablets, smartphones and even on Smart TVs, independent of the operational system and the size of the screen. The aggregation of this functionality also does effect on the technological independency requirement, since the Web Browser is a basic resource and available on almost all platforms, and provides easy adaptation to new versions.

The present paper was distributed on this way: Sect. 2 shows the Natural Deduction on Propositional Logic. Section 3 addresses the Heraclito system and OBAAMILOS infrastructure. Section 4 presents a survey on the state of the art with respect to tools designed for teaching logic. Section 5 is presented to the proposed new development of Heraclitus interface to the Web. In Sect. 6 presents the integration of the Heraclitus system and its tests editor with the new Web Interface. And in Sect. 7 the findings are presented and future work of this work.

2 The Natural Deduction on Propositional Logic

Natural Deduction is one of the systems which we use to build formal demonstrations in Logic of the logic proposition (or just one proposition). One proposition is one phrase or sentence that can assume only one truth value: or the sentence is true (it says the truth) or it is false (it says falsehood) [3].

To occur one formal derivation, is necessary formalize the expression which we want demonstrate. Formalize means translate from the usual linguistic way to one logic notation, in other words, one way that is understandable for anyone, independent to the natural language used.

Among these notations, the prepositions are usually symbolized (represented) by capitalized letters of the start of the alphabet: A, B, C, ... The logical values of the prepositions are represented by short way using V to true and F to false. The prepositions can be simple or compounds. Formal logic deals also with a particular type of argument, called deductive argument, which allow us deduce a conclusion Q, based on a set of prepositions P_i, where $i = \{1, ..., n\}$, where Q and P_i represent full formulas

---

[2] The infrastructure MILOS agents is an agent infrastructure that supports authoring, management, search and provision of learning objects compatible with the OBAA (Learning Object Based Artificial Agents), and is more general objective of the project Infrastructure OBAA-MILOS create the technological foundation that can perform the adoption of the proposed metadata OBAA learning objects. More information at: http://www.portalobaa.org/padrao-obaa/relatorios-tecnicos/copy_of_ 1o-relatorio-parcial-obaa-milos-comunidade-finep/AnexoA-EspecArqMILOSV10.pdf/view.

[3] The Heraclito system can be accessed in: http://gia.inf.ufrgs.br/heraclito_web/. Information and documentation in: http://obaa.unisinos.br/heraclito.htm.

[4] More information about the OBAA project in: http://www.portalobaa.org/.

well-formed of the propositional logic. One deductive argument can be represented in symbolic form as follows: $P_1 \wedge P_2 \wedge P_3 \wedge \ldots \wedge P_n \rightarrow Q$. The prepositions P_i are denominated assumptions or premises of the argument. The preposition is denominated conclusion of the argument. This method is based on application rules of natural deduction (or inference rules) that modify formulas to preserve your logical value [3].

3 Heraclito System and MILOS Infrastructure

The Heraclito system [1] is one ITS focused to teaching of propositional logic. It consists of one proof editor, with dialogic features, that can offer support to elaborate formal statements about Natural Deduction rules of Propositional Logic. Still in this context, Heraclito was built through the use of the pedagogical agents' technology (student profile, mediator, expert), which are responsible by the iteration with student and system and, yet as an intelligent tutor that helps on proof development indicating correct, incorrect and not recommended paths during the proof [5]. This architecture features differentiate Heraclito from a theorem prover and the transforms it into ITS.

Its current interface was developed in Java language and designed in two versions: Desktop/Laptop and mobile devices (Tablets e Smartphones). The Desktop/Laptop version consisting of one file in .jar format (java applet) and mobile version consisting of one file in .apk format (Android Package).[5]

3.1 MILOS Infrastructure

The MILOS infrastructure gives support of the authorship process, manage, search and providing learning objects according to the proposal of the OBAA standard proposal metadata [4].

The software architecture defined to the Heraclito system is integrated to the agents infrastructure. The Fig. 1 shows that integration between the MILOS and the Heraclito passing by agent layer on pedagogical level.

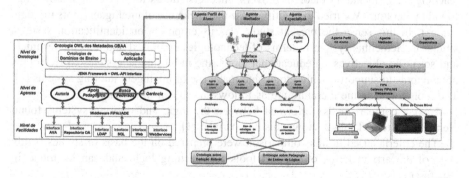

Fig. 1. MILOS architecture, detailed layer to Pedagogical support and Heraclito system architecture.

---

[5] The latest versions can be downloaded in: http://obaa.unisinos.br/heraclito.htm.

As can be seen in Fig. 1, the MILOS is projected in three big abstraction levels: (a) Ontology Level: responsible for specification of the knowledge that will be shared between the infrastructure agents; (b) Agents Level: responsible for implementing the support to the adaptability, interoperability and accessibility requirements in the OBAA proposal [4]; (c) Interface Facilities Level: responsible for the MILOS agents communication with the Web servers, virtual environments, LO repositories, databases, directory services and other types of educational applications. It is in ontology level which is specified, besides the OBAA metadata ontology, all of other ontologies about the learning domain and educational or multimedia applications are all defined in OWL.

Still in the Fig. 1, we have the agent level layer that implements the support of activities of LO life cycle, including authorship support, adaptation, management, publication, localization and use of the OBAA compatible LOs. This support was distributed in four big multi-agents systems: (1) Federated Search System, which support the location activities of the OAs, (2) Pedagogical Support System, who gives support to the use of LOs on the learning environments, (3) Authorship System, responsible for give support to the authorship activities of LOs, including support to multiplatform adaptation, and (4) Management System, responsible to storage activities, management, publication/distribution multiplatform of Los [4]. Thus, the Pedagogical Support System is related directly to the Heraclito system. The objective of this system is offer intelligent support to the use of LOs. This includes from the available of search mechanisms of LO with support of the semantic search context, as was defined by specific ontology of the teaching domain, until the availability of the mechanisms that help or facilitate in the application of strategies and tactics of learning appropriate to the LO, like adopted by ITS. In practice, the Heraclito system is the initial prototype of the Pedagogical Support System of the MILOS infrastructure [5].

4 Tools Support Logic Education

The development of Heraclitus took from a study by means of support tools for teaching logic, including theorem provers, checkers/editors formal tasks and systems, found in literature. We tried to identify those that make use of intelligent tutors in Logic context. In this sense the present study was its emphasis on identification systems similar to Heraclitus system in terms of technologies employed and also the technical and scientific objectives. In educational terms, the most similar systems to Heraclitus are the tools to support teaching logic and make use of intelligent tutoring systems [1]. The tools found in the literature are as follows, as shown in the table.

Next a comparison is performed between the logic and tutoring systems found Heráclito system. Table 2 shows this comparison [1].

The criteria[6] used in this comparison were prepared on the basis of studies (study state of the art) in terms of support tools for teaching logic and can be found in Galafassi [1].

---

[6] The tools found and used in Table 1 for comparison between Logic tutoring systems surveyed and Heraclitus system, the latest systems dating from 2005, which leads us to believe that this issue stopped being studied and addressed in the middle research academic (at least temporarily).

Table 1. Tools for teaching logic

Tools	Description
Proofs tutorial	It is considered a learning tool aided by computer and has been used for the practice of evidence in upper-level courses that include discrete mathematics discipline [15]
Logic-ITA	It is a teaching assistant /learning propositional logic with intelligent system [16]
Intelligent tutoring system based on Web	Intelligent tutoring system based on Web This article reports on the efforts to develop an intelligent tutoring system for the construction of proof in propositional logic [17]
KRRT	The junction has as its acronym meaning: KR Logic First Order (LPO) and KRRT (Knowledge Representation and Reasoning Tutor). KRRT is a Web-based system whose main goal is to help students to learn natural language formulas (FOL) and how to construct formal proofs [18]
Mathematical Logic Tutor – Propositional Calculus (MLT-PC)	Mathematical Logic Tutor - Propositional Calculus (MLT-PC). This program is designed to help students in Introduction to Logic (ILO) and aims to provide students with a software tool able to assist them in the study of the first part of the course, dedicated to propositional logic [19]
P-Logic Tutor	The main objective of P-Logic Tutor is to teach students fundamental concepts of propositional logic and theorems of trial techniques [20]

In Logic tutors for teaching this subject (content) can also be used as automatic tools tasters, evidence and proof checkers editors. The tools found in the literature are: Assistant Coq evidence [7], evidence Wizard HOL [8], theorem prover Otter [10], Theorem Prover Prover9/Mace4 [12], Theorem Prover EProver [14] Taster Spass [13] theorem JAPE [9] and the testing editor Pandora [11].

In our analysis, despite the existence of various systems, all showed significant shortcomings that prevent their direct use in Heraclitus project. The Coq and HOL should be used through very complex programming languages which makes it unfeasible its application in courses of initial semesters of a course in Computing. The aforementioned automatic tasters (plus many others) use advanced systems test (typically based on Hyper-Resolution) that are completely inappropriate for teaching, untranslatable and are substantially (at least a didactic manner that is acceptable) in Natural Deduction for demonstrations. The JAPE and Pandora editors are particularly complex to be customized and reused in unforeseen ways by its authors, at least if one considers that this customization should be made by a professor of logic and not by an expert in programming.

These editors also have automatic test capabilities that are required for an automatic system of pedagogical support, one of the main features introduced by Heráclito.

Table 2. Comparison of Logic tutoring systems surveyed and Heraclitus system

		Tools for Teaching Logic - Tutoring Systems						
		Proofs Tutorial	Logic-ITA	ITS based on Web (Java applets)	KRRT	Mathematical Logic Tutor	P-Logic Tutor	System Heráclito
1	Support the concept of OA	DO NOT	DO NOT	DO NOT	DO NOT	DO NOT	DO NOT	YES
2	Demonstration Use as a student model	YES	YES	YES	YES	YES	YES	YES
3	Generates Result of the test automatically	DO NOT	DO NOT	DO NOT	DO NOT	YES	DO NOT	YES
4	Full partial evidence	DO NOT	DO NOT	DO NOT	DO NOT	DO NOT	DO NOT	YES
5	Possibility of generating the next step	DO NOT	DO NOT	DO NOT	DO NOT	DO NOT	DO NOT	YES
6	Allows the student to reflect on the error	DO NOT	DO NOT	DO NOT	DO NOT	DO NOT	DO NOT	YES
7	AVA Support	DO NOT	DO NOT	YES	DO NOT	DO NOT	DO NOT	YES

5 Heraclito System Interface to Web

The new interface to the Heraclito System was developed to be used on Web Browsers and have responsive features. It had its development from the combination of several technologies like HTML5, CSS3 and also JavaScript.

Aimed at increasing safety, hardiness, compatibility with several systems and screen sizes, was used to the development of the system the Framework Bootstrap [6]. This framework provides a range of ready elements in HTML5, CSS3 and JavaScript that when are used on the correct way, help us on the site adaptation to the several systems and screen sizes, making the site responsive and that, the learning object can, with only one version, be distributed to several platforms reaching a bigger number of users.

How can we see in the next figures, the Heraclito interface, now Web, was tested, on its main functionalities, in three different systems with three different screen sizes. In Figs. 2 and 3, we can see the interface working on one computer desktop.

In Fig. 2 we have the initial screen with the access login in the right top corner, the system description and also the registration screen to the new users (required option to use tutors features). If the tutors features are not desirable, the user can download the offline version and use only the proof editor. In the Fig. 3 we have the proof screen (after do the login) in easy presentation to use the interface through the mouse. We have the rules buttons of inference basic and derived with different colors to facilitate the visual contact between user and tool. The white background makes the context clean providing a more friendly layout.

The Figs. 4 and 5 shows the Heraclito Interface on an iPad.

Fig. 2. Initial screen of Heraclito system accessed by desktop/laptop.

Fig. 3. Edition proof screen of Heraclito system accessed by desktop/laptop.

In the Figs. 4 and 5, where the interface is presented on one tablet, we can evidence the same elements that appeared in the interface working on computer but with more fluid presentation which facilitate use in the smaller screen, which are used with two hands ordinarily.

Lastly, in the Figs. 6 and 7, we can visualize the interface working on one smartphone. We can evidence that, like on the tablet and the computer, the main elements of system are still present, but the interface set for easily use of the system, presenting all the content in the smaller screen to the use with the only one finger touch, common on smartphones.

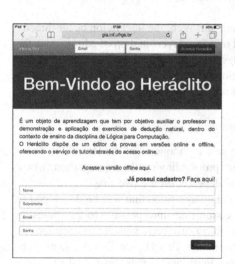

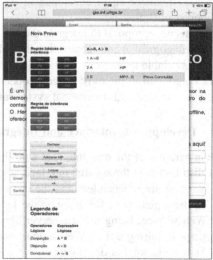

Fig. 4. Initial screen of Heraclito system accessed by iPad.

Fig. 5. Edition proof screen of Heraclito system accessed by iPad.

Fig. 6. Initial screen of Heraclito system accessed by smartphone.

Fig. 7. Edition proof screen of Heraclito system accessed by smartphone.

6   Integration Between Heraclito System and Web Interface

The Heraclito system is composed by one interface and one proof editor, both developed in Java, and by its pedagogical agents, student profile that was developed in Java too, mediator agent developed in AgentSpeak(L) and specialist agent that was developed in Prolog.

In this new proposal to integrate the system and Web, the integration occur directly in the pedagogical agents, abstracting the old interface layers and proof editor, since the current available technology is possible to develop just one version of the system that work on content in the most different operational environments and devices, adapting to the screen size and operational system as we can see in this chapter.

6.1   Development, Interface and Integration

The integration of the new interface with the new components of the Heraclito system was distributed on three parts: interface, logic (proof editor) and the integration, where the two first are independent and the last one depends on the two first.

To the logical part, we maintain the Java language since that will be developed to the Web service, being a client-server application and unresponsive to the choosing language, requiring only a Web support and object oriented language to organize.

As a basis for the development, we adopted the Test-Driven Development technique (TDD), where we define tests for every unity and that is developed to satisfy these tests, ensuring its functionality and avoiding errors in your future integration to the system.

To help in these tests, we used the JUnit framework. In that framework, to test the implementation of a rule, first we verify if the method of the application accept only the correct number of lines to this rule; then, we test a series of valid and invalid inputs ignoring the output, just evaluating the accept or reject to the entrance; Lastly we evaluate the outputs according the inputs, checking if the implementation is correct and if the result line was defined as result of the correct rule (than this line will show in the proof).

So that the interface binds to the logical part was used JavaServer Pages (JSP), which is likely to another back-end languages that help to develop web applications and use that to the Java language which can speak directly with the pedagogical agents already developed to the old version of Heraclito.

The choice of the client-server architecture for the development of new interface Heráclito was due to the safety and performance that this methodology, together with prepared programming languages, the system can offer, in order that the new system interface Heraclitus was developed in order to be portable to different devices with different capabilities, screen sizes and different performances.

In Fig. 8 you can see that there are two critical points in performance and safety are: the java language where the program logic, and the agents themselves who will contact the user. By using client server architecture, you can send to the user only for the answer in HTML, CSS and Javascript leaving all the logical part of the dressing room and everywhere agents being processed entirely within the server, which makes the system extremely lightweight and portable to any device that has a web browser.

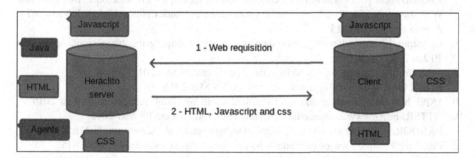

Fig. 8. Representation of the architecture client server of the new Heraclito

7 Conclusion and Future Work

Adapting to Web interface provided a unique implementation to meet all desired platforms, which is the main advantage of the developer's point of view, easy maintenance and adding new features. It also released an easy implementation of responsive interface elements, ensuring a great interface for any platform provided. These and other factors already mentioned generate a better user experience, which can access the Heraclito without much depending on the type or performance of its platform, also dispensing with the installation of the feature itself.

As future work we intend to complete the implementation of the new version integrating the html interface/css/js with logic (Java) already implemented, thus providing only what already existed in functionality previously. As new features will be add the option to save the current proof and continue it later; the internationalization of

Heraclito, allowing the page display in multiple languages; and the option to access Heraclito with offline resources, requiring internet connection only to access the home page.

Usability tests with the new interface are planned for the beginning of the semester of 2015/1 with undergraduate classes in: Federal University of Rio Grande do Sul and University of Vale do Rio dos Sinos. For 2015/2 we intend to integrate Heraclito with SAAPIENS system.[7]

References

1. Galafassi, F.F.P.: Agente Pedagógico para Mediação do Processo de Ensino-Aprendizagem da Dedução Natural na Lógica Proposicional. Dissertação de Mestrado. UNISINOS 2012. http://biblioteca.asav.org.br/vinculos/000003/00000335.pdf. Acesso em 9 January 2015
2. Vicari, R., Gluz, J., Passerino, L., et al.: The OBAA proposal for learning objects supported by agents. In: Procs. of MASEIE Workshop – AAMAS 2010, Toronto, Canadá (2010)
3. Gluz, J.C., Py, M.: Lógica para Computação. Coleção EAD. Editora Unisinos (2010)
4. Gluz, J.C., Vicari, R.M.: MILOS: Infraestrutura de Agentes para Suporte a Objetos de Aprendizagem OBAA. Anais do XXI SBIE (2010)
5. Galafassi, F.F.P., Gluz, J.C., Gomes, L., Mossmann, M.: Sistema Heráclito: Objeto de Aprendizagem para o Ensino da Dedução Natural na Lógica Proposicional. In: Anais dos Workshops do CBIE 2013. http://www.br-ie.org/pub/index.php/wcbie/article/view/2674. Acesso em 10 Jan 2015
6. Bootstrap: Framework web gratuito da empresa twitter. http://getbootstrap.com/. Acesso em 10 Jan 2015
7. COQ Proof Assistent. http://coq.inria.fr/. Acesso em 08 Mar 2015
8. HOL4. http://hol.sourceforge.net/. Acesso em 08 Mar 2015
9. JAPE. http://www.cs.ox.ac.uk/people/bernard.sufrin/jape.html. Acesso em 08 Mar 2015
10. OTTER. http://www.cs.unm.edu/~mccune/otter/. Acesso em 08 Mar 2015
11. PANDORA. http://www.doc.ic.ac.uk/pandora/newpandora/. Acesso em 08 Mar 2015
12. PROVER9. http://www.cs.unm.edu/~mccune/prover9/. Acesso em 08 Mar 2015
13. SPASS: An Automated Theorem Prover for First-Order Logic with Equality. http://www.spass-prover.org/. Acesso em 08 Mar 2015
14. The E Theorem Prover. http://www4.informatik.tu-muenchen.de/~schulz/E/E.html. Acesso em 08 Mar 2015
15. Barnes, T.; Stamper, J.: Automatic hint generation for logic proof tutoring using historical data. J. Educ. Technol. Soc., Special issue on Intelligent Tutoring Systems. 13(1), 3–15 (2010). http://www.academia.edu/442299/Automatic_Hint_Generation_for_Logic_Proof_Tutoring_Using_Historical_Data. Acesso em 08 Mar 2015
16. Lesta, L., Yacef, K.: An intelligent teaching assistant system for logic. In: 12th International Conference on Artificial Intelligence in Education. http://sydney.edu.au/engineering/it/~kalina/publis/lesta_yacef_its02.pdf. Acesso em 08 Mar 2015
17. Croy, M., Barnes, T., Stamper, J.: *Towards an Intelligent Tutoring System for Propositional Proof Construction*. University of North Carolina, Charlotte. http://www.philosophy.uncc.edu/mjcroy/croy_pubs/Croy_Barnes_Stamper_ECAP.pdf. Acesso em 08 Mar 2015

---

[7] More information about the SAAPIENS in: systemhttp://www.br-ie.org/pub/index.php/sbie/article/view/3041/2552.

18. Alonso, J.A; Aranda, Gonzalo A.; Martin-Mateos, F.J.: KRRT: Knowledge Representation and Reasoning Tutor System. http://150.214.140.135/~jalonso/publicaciones/2007-EUROCAST.pdf. Acesso em 08 Mar 2015
19. Moreno, A.: Mathematical Logic Tutor - Propositional Calculus. http://aracne.usal.es/congress/PDF/AntonioMoreno.pdf. Acesso em 08 Mar 2015
20. Lukins, S., Levicki, A., Burg, J.A.: Tutorial Program for Propositional Logic with Human/Computer Interactive Learning. Department of Computer Science Wake Forest University. Winston-Salem, NC. http://csweb.cs.wfu.edu/~burg/BurgMain/public/media/PropLogic.pdf. Acesso em 08 Mar 2015

Multi-agent System for Expert Evaluation of Learning Objects from Repository

Valentina Tabares[1(✉)], Néstor Duque[1], and Demetrio A. Ovalle[2]

[1] Universidad Nacional de Colombia Sede Manizales, Manizales, Colombia
{vtabaresm, ndduqueme}@unal.edu.co
[2] Universidad Nacional de Colombia Sede Medellín, Medellín, Colombia
dovalle@unal.edu.co

Abstract. Regarding the educational contexts based on e-learning, Learning Objects (LOs) have arisen as a new conceptual model to organize the content. Thus, it is necessary to analyze the potential impact of LOs on knowledge appropriation processes using the quality concept. In this case, quality is understood as the level of relevance of the educational resources in the teaching-learning process, associated to educational goal and other characteristics. The level of significance can be determined by evaluating the characteristics of the object by a group of experts; however, this process is not an easy task because different criteria should be considered, such as teaching, interoperability, scalability and reusability. On the other hand, a factor to solve is the selection of experts. This paper presents different dimensions and metrics to evaluate, and an automatic mechanism for the correct selection of the experts. The validation is done through the development a multi-agent system.

Keywords: Learning objects · Expert evaluation · Quality evaluation · Metrics · Multi-agent systems

1 Introduction

E-learning today has become one of the major schemes of education, changing the traditional teaching-learning process and providing numerous pedagogical and access advantages. This scheme generates new needs such as the development and improvement of educational materials, where Learning Objects (LOs) are distinguished from other resources by their possibility to be reused in multiple contexts, in addition to their availability in different environments. LOs are stored in digital libraries that are accessible via a network without prior knowledge of the structure to facilitate its search and retrieval, called Learning Objects Repositories (LORs) [1].

Due to the large number of LOs that are stored in the LORs which do not meet minimum quality according to the context where they are intended to be used, it is necessary to generate initiatives to evaluate LOs in a dynamic way, considering different aspects in order to provide the user only with the best resources [2].

The evaluation of LOs can be approached from different perspectives and considering different dimensions. In this paper, we present a model based on expert's evaluation and the developed tool for the allocation of the experts and for assessment of LOs.

© Springer International Publishing Switzerland 2015
J. Bajo et al. (Eds.): PAAMS 2015 Workshops, CCIS 524, pp. 320–330, 2015.
DOI: 10.1007/978-3-319-19033-4_27

For any evaluation by experts, it is essential to define the dimensions to evaluate, the metrics to qualify the object, and the instrument used to obtain such qualification, but it is also very important the proper selection of the experts who will conduct the assessment. The definition of the category of experts and their classification is a subject that attracts attention in different areas, as of this choice depends the quality of the evaluation.

Exploiting the advantages of Multi-Agent Systems (MAS), this paper proposes a system that supports the evaluation of LOs from the point of view of expert's review. The system covers the process of evaluation by experts, defining the necessary conditions to evaluate LOs, capturing information of LOs to be evaluated, and defining the profiles of experts that perform the evaluations. Based on this information, the system automatically assigns the LOs to experts. Evaluations are followed by the use of the collected information in order to apply previously established metrics.

The paper is organized as follows: Sect. 2 presents de basic concepts and Sect. 3 shows some works related. Section 4 presents the MAS proposed model, which allows review of LOs by experts. Section 5 shows prototype evaluation with a case study, and finally, Sect. 6 presents conclusions and future work.

2 Basic Concepts

Learning Objects (LOs): Wiley (2000) defines a LO as "any digital resource that can be reused to support learning". People who incorporate LOs can collaborate and benefit immediately from new versions. The potential impact of LOs is highlighted by Hodgins: They represent a completely new conceptual model for the mass of content used in the context of learning. LOs are destined to change permanently the form of learning, and in so doing, it is anticipated that they will also usher in an unprecedented efficiency of learning content design, development, and delivery. However, their most significant promise is to increase and improve human learning and performance [3]. Moreover, a remarcable feature of LOs is the possibility to be described by metadata, facilitating search and retrieval; they must also meet the needs of students for which they were designed.

Learning Objects Repositories (LORs): A digital repository is "any collection of resources that are accessible without prior knowledge of the structure" [4]. LORs are electronic databases that accommodate a collection of small units of educational information or activities that can be accessed for retrieval and use. LORs enable the organization of LOs, improve efficiencies, enhance LO reuse and collaboration, and support learning opportunities [5]. A further aspect of great importance is the fact that many people can contribute to the content to be shared with a community [6]. However, this creates the need for assessment processes that ensure the quality of the content to be delivered to users.

Quality of LOs: The Oxford dictionary defines quality as the standard of something as measured against other things of a similar kind. For Williams (2000), evaluation must assemble all the standards associated with objects, learners, instructional theories, and other stakeholder values. He also emphasizes the need to include evaluation as an integral part of any design process [7]. In the domain of LOs, quality is understood as a set of criteria for assessing the educational resources and determining their level of relevance in the teaching-learning process [1]. This degree of relevance of LO is measured in educational and technical terms. There are several criteria to evaluate the quality of LOs through metrics -some of them take advantage of product-centric approach and other in the process [8]. Despite its recognized importance, currently no consensus has been reached of all the elements involved in measuring quality of LOs.

3   Related Work

Today, LO evaluation is understood as a necessity that aims at solving problems caused by the growth of LORs and seeks to ensure the effective use of these resources designed to support teaching-learning processes. In this section, some jobs that have to do with the issues addressed are collected: Approaches, dimensions and metrics to qualify the object to be evaluated, and how the experts that undertake the assessment are selected. Several authors agree that concerns about quality normally focus on different criteria: accuracy, appropriateness to intended audience, effective design, aesthetics, functionality and quality of metadata [9–13].

Cechinel, in his doctoral thesis, recognizes that the creators of objects have a cumbersome task, which leads to the time of publication and the digital resource metadata not being incorporated or being done carelessly, which results in bad description and leads to difficulties for its recovery. To avoid this, the evaluation is required to be done manually or automatically [11].

For Cechinel and Ochoa, assessing quality of LOs is a difficult and complex task that normally revolves around multiple and different aspects that need to be addressed. Nowadays, quality assessment of LOs inside repositories is based on the information provided by the same community of users and experts that use such platforms [14].

The work [8] presents a proposal for implementation of a quality model for LOs based on ISO 9126 international standard for the evaluation of software quality. The proposed implementation is based on tools for gathering expert's opinion and analysis of metadata using Semantic Web technologies.

In [1], a methodology is suggested to assess the quality of the LOs considering pedagogical and usability issues. These criteria are formalized in a tool that guides experts during the review of LOs and the allocation of a numeric value to each element within a predefined range, which will be averaged to obtain a single value that reflects the quality of the resource. A MAS for searching and cataloging LOs is proposed, which provides the user with the resources according to specific characteristics.

The work presented in [15] defines a recognized instrument, called Learning Object Review Instrument (LORI), for the evaluation of LOs by experts, individually or collaboratively, allowing the assessment of nine dimensions. Each criterion is evaluated on a scale of five levels. Leacock and Nesbit provide some explanations about each one of the nine dimensions of LORI and how they should be interpreted to evaluate LOs. In addition to defining what should be evaluated, in the specific case of this work, it is necessary to determine the experts to evaluate the resources and how LOs are assigned to each expert. For Farrel and Nielsen, "how do I get a user experience career?" is the key question in the assessment process [16].

Botella et al. propose a classification of evaluators based on the university degree obtained or the number of hours of practice gathered in this field. This is why it is important to collect other attributes of each user such as domains, skills or projects to determine their expertise [17].

Returning to these elements, a model is proposed using a Multi-agent system that determines the dimensions and metrics to evaluate and also relies on an expert system for the selection of experts, the allocation of LOs that can be evaluated and presented according to their specific expertise.

4 Proposal of Multi-agent Architecture for LO Evaluation

To ensure the quality of the LOs and enhance the experience of users in the use of these resources, different evaluation strategies have been proposed. In previous works, we proposed strategies for automatic metadata evaluation calculating metrics [18, 19], using these metrics to support the processes of management repositories [20], and taking advantage of user perception can set the level of LOs quality [21]. In this article is presented a proposal that allows quality evaluation of LOs according to reviews by experts with different profiles. The evaluation is based on a set of metrics to determine the quality of resources and whether they can be published or continue visible to users, or require revisions and corrections.

The proposal supports the peer-review of LOs, similarly to assessing a scientific paper by critical examination of third parties that are experts in the area, and requests a group of experts to review it in order to obtain advice about whether or not the article must be accepted for publishing.

Specifically, this proposal uses MAS in the process of quality evaluation of LOs by experts, taking advantages that allow the disintegration into functional blocks, without losing the systemic point of view, which leads to distributing the solution in diverse entities that require specific knowledge, processing and communication between each other.

The architecture presented in Fig. 1 is proposed from the analysis and design made of MAS, where are the agents that interact within the system and the communication established among them. The system manages the evaluation process, which begins with the registration of each repository. The LOR administrator must select the metrics to be used, the weights for each metric, and the update mechanism of the information of the LOs. After the process of building the profile of experts is done, and using this information, a set of LOs is assigned to the experts for them to evaluate. Finally, using the answers given by the experts, metrics that will define the level of overall compliance with the quality indicators are calculated.

Repository Agent: This agent knows all the information associated with the repository to provide LOs to be evaluated and represents the LOR within the system. This agent is in charge of the initial configuration of the evaluation process, defining what metrics will be used to evaluate the LOs and their respective weights. This agent will also define the communication mechanism between the system and the LOR. They must

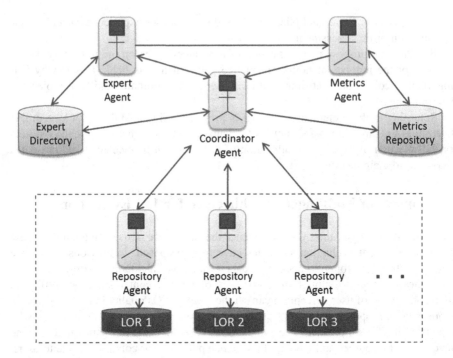

Fig. 1. Multi-agent system architecture diagram

continually update the metadata of LOs to be evaluated, so update mechanisms are available through the OAI-PMH protocol or XML files. Each Repository Agent sends this information to the Coordinator Agent.

Expert Agent: An expert is a person who has a set of skills and a level of experience that allows performing analysis of LOs and making judgments about them. The evaluation process should be realized confidentially, objectively and consensually. As not all experts have the same degree of expertise and knowledge, a process of defining the profile for each expert is performed. This process is based on information requested through questions to identify characteristics of each expert.

The dimensions and information sets in which the profile is based are presented below:

Personal Information: This is the basic information of the expert; it is used to identify and locate the expert. ***Preferences Information:*** In this part, the expert must specify topics and areas of academic and research interest. This information allows an association between the themes of LOs and the expert. ***Educational Dimension:*** This dimension allows identifying the level of expertise on issues related to the teaching-learning process. This experience allows the expert to analyze whether the material actually has an educational orientation, it is well constructed pedagogically and is of interest to prospective students. ***Content Dimension:*** The expert is asked their level of education, field of education and interest to establish the possibility of analyzing thematic and disciplinary aspects. ***Aesthetic Dimension:*** It defines whether the expert has training related to aspects of visual design. *Functional Dimension:* **It** determines whether the expert is familiar with technical aspects related with performance, availability and access of LOs. *Metadata Dimension:* Due to the great importance of metadata, it is necessary to determine knowledge about appropriate use of metadata and standards-compliance. *Relation Information:* To ensure that the evaluation process is objective, this information allows determining whether the expert is part of a group of managers of a specific LOR, thus preventing the allocation process to deliver LOs from this repository. *Experience Information:* This information is updated as the expert interacts with the system, as having a history of evaluations made is essential in the process of resource allocation.

When an expert is registered in the system, several questions for each dimension are carried out. The answers are processed by the agent to determine a Level of Expertise (LE) of each dimension. These numeric values are used in the metrics calculation. All expert profile information is stored in the Experts Directory, which will be consulted by the Coordinator Agent for assigning LOs evaluated. This Agent also receives assignment news and is responsible for returning response of acceptance or rejection. He also handles the subsequent capture of evaluations provided by human experts and provide this information to the Metrics Agent.

Metrics Agent: This agent is responsible for calculating the metrics to determine the quality of each LO. An assessment instrument with questions that can determine the level of compliance with desirable characteristics of LOs is proposed. For processing the answers given by the expert a set of 8 metric which belong to one of the dimensions are defined. These metrics are defined based on the review of the state of art and previous work experience. These are presented in Table 1.

A questionnaire with questions related to each metric is presented to each expert. The answers given by the experts and Expertise Levels (LE) defined in the profiles correspond to a numeric value between 0–5 and 1–5 respectively. An equation is usued to calculate each metric (1), where: n is the number of questions associated with the metric, k is the number of responses to question i, E_{ij} is the answer to the question i given by the expert j, and LE_j is the level of expertise in the dimension associated to the expert's profile j. After the metrics are calculated, they are stored in the Repository Metrics, which are reviewed by the Coordinator Agent.

$$Metric = \left(\sum_{i=1}^{n} \frac{\sum_{j=1}^{k} (E_{ij} \times LE_j)}{\sum_{j=1}^{k} LE_j} \right) \qquad (1)$$

Coordinator Agent: This is the agent responsible for making major decisions in the process of evaluation by experts. It is the agent with greater responsibilities within the system. The Coordinator Agent receives information from the Repository Agent related to the LOs to be evaluated and the metrics to be calculated, that are of interest by the LOR administrator. One of the main roles of this agent is the process of assigning LOs to be evaluated by each expert. This behavior is based on Expert System that executes rules from associated experts profile information and LO metadata to be assigned.

Table 1. Metrics description

Dimension	Metric	Description
Educational	Potential effectiveness	It determines the level of validity that can have an OA as a tool for teaching and learning
Content	Relevance and rigor	It analyzes whether the LO has problems with content that may confuse the student or any discriminatory information is presented
Aesthetic	Visual design	It evaluates that the resource presents an appearance that does not interfere with the learning process and comes to potentiate this
Functional	Reusability	It determines whether it can be used in different contexts, analyzing whether it may be independent or requires changes to be reused
	Facility of use	It analyzes whether the presentation of the contents is given so that students can navigate it intuitively
	Facility of access	It defines the facility to open and use the LO, or if it requires specialized software for viewing
Metadata	Completeness	It analyzes whether the metadata have valid values and the information presented is sufficient to understand the content of the object
	Precision	A comparison is made to determine whether the metadata describes the associated content accurately

In the Expert System, the role of Coordinator Agent has the following guidelines or rules:

1. Discarding experts who have some relationship with the repository that owns the LO.
2. Performing a comparison of similarity between the themes selected for the expert (Preferences Information) and title, description and keywords fields. These values are arranged in descending order and 6 with a higher similarity are selected.
3. The Ranking experts selected according to the amount of LOs evaluated (Experience Information).
4. Executing rules to compare the LE of the three experts with more experience and the three with less experience. The goal is to select the two experts (one from each sub-group) with higher LE in different dimensions.

If the execution of the rules of paragraph 4 do not generate difference between the experts, it is proceeded to conflict with a resolution algorithm inference engine. The strategy is to select those experts in each sub-group having the highest level of similarity to the object. If this value coincides with experts who have already evaluated some objects of that repository, and if ultimately there is no difference, they are selected randomly.

After selecting the experts to assign the LO, the Coordinator Agent sends the Expert Agent a notification that needs to be answered by indicating that the expert accepts the evaluation of the resource. Once the experts have performed the evaluation of LOs and the Metric Agent has calculated the values of the metrics, the Coordinator Agent calculates a final value for each LO following the Eq. (2). Where: n is the number of experts that evaluated this LO, k is the number of metrics evaluated by expert i, M_j is the metric value j by expert i, and W_j is the weigh by metric j.

$$LO\_Index = \sum_{i=1}^{n} \left(\sum_{j=1}^{k} (M_j * W_j) \right) \Big/ n \qquad (2)$$

The Coordinator Agent is responsible for analyzing whether the allocation of an expert is needed to make a new evaluation of LOs. If the LO gets a weight equal to or greater than 4 points, it means that the resource is approved for publication, if the result is between 3 and 3.9 a new evaluator is assigned and if the weight is less than or equal to 2.9, it is reported that the LO must go through a process of improvement and is not suitable for publication.

Repository, Expert an Metrics Agents are mainly used by the possibility that the tasks may have to be divided into functional blocks, while the coordinator agent uses an expert system based on rules for the process of decision making regarding the allocation of experts for each LO.

5 Experimental Work

The proposed MAS was implemented using the JADE platform (Java Agent Development Framework). The experimental work aims to validate the possibility of implementation and use of the system, and this is not directed to evaluate system performance.

A case study was conducted in which the proposed model was used to evaluate 46 LOs of FROAC for issues related to software, algorithm, and system audit. FROAC is a model used in Colombia for the establishment of a set of LORs that allow sharing these resources through the definition of policies, methodological foundations and processes of construction and administration of LOs [22].

For this case study, the work was carried out with a group of 15 experts, professors and postgradu-ate students of the Universidad Nacional de Colombia-Sede Manizales. This group had specific expertise in the subject of LOs, in the area of education, and in issues related to metadata and functionality of LOs. The allocation process was done following the rules of the Coordinator Agent and, on average, each expert reviewed 6 LOs. The results of the evaluation process are shown in Fig. 2.

As observed in Fig. 2, it was possible through the proposed system to establish what resources met the conditions defined and may be published, the resources that needed substantial changes were rejected and the objects that required placement in a new expert's area to enrich the results of the evaluation. The figure above shows the average score for each object and the graph below shows the summary; in our case, 43 % approved, 22 % rejected, and 35 % for review.

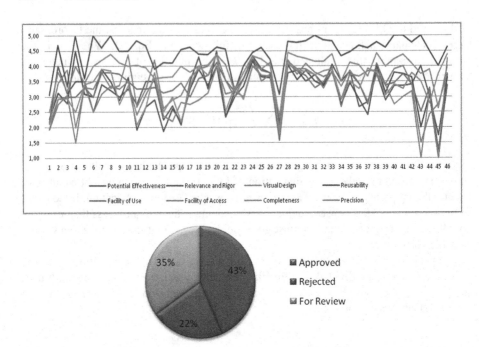

Fig. 2. Results of the case study

6   Conclusions and Future Work

The main purpose of this paper is to introduce our research for the evaluation process of LOs from the vision of the expert, as well as the modeling by means of MAS.

Our approach includes the definition of the expert profiles, the selection of experts for an specific LO to evaluate, the definition of our metrics for diverse dimensions and the integration of values calculated in the assessment of each LO.

An expert system is proposed for the automatic selection of experts to evaluate the different objects. The rules and inferences are related to their level of expertise and previous work performed. Other tools allow manual assignment of experts for evaluation, which would mean extra work for Repository Managers.

The development of a dimensional model and MAS approach allows organizing the assessment, conditionally determining the assigning of the experts and calculating the metrics independently and obtaining the result for each learning object. This proposal is versatile, as it is possible to determine what metrics are evaluated, as well as to add new ones.

Currently, our research interest is focused on some of the different open issues identified in our research: Integration of previous works in evaluation of Learning Objects in a single model, validation of the metrics proposed and the improved process of assigning LOs to experts. We also hope expects to make a full assessment of system performance.

Acknowledgements. The research reported in this paper was funded in part by the COL-CIENCIAS project entitled "RAIM: Implementación de un framework apoyado en tecnologías móviles y de realidad aumentada para entornos educativos ubicuos, adaptativos, accesibles e interactivos para todos".

References

1. Morales, E., Gil, A., García, F.: Arquitectura para la Recuperación de Objetos de Aprendizaje de calidad en Repositorios Distribuidos. In: SCHA Sist. Hipermedia Colab. y Adapt. II Congr. Español Informática CEDI 2007, vol. 1, pp. 31–38 (2007)
2. Kay, R.H., Knaack, L., Vaidehi, V.: A Multi-component model for assessing learning objects: the earning Object Evaluation Metric (LOEM). Australas. J. Educ. Technol. **24**, 574–591 (2008)
3. Hodgins, H.W.: The future of learning objects. In: Wiley, D.A. (ed.) The Instructional Use of Learning Objects: Online Version, pp. 1–24 (2000)
4. IMS Global Learning Consortium: The IMS digital repositories specification. http://www.imsglobal.org/digitalrepositories/
5. Lehman, R.: Learning object repositories. New Dir. Adult Contin. Educ. **113**, 57–66 (2007)
6. Frango, S.I., Nizam, O., Notargiacomo, P.: Architecture of learning objects repositories. In: Harman, K., Koohang, A. (eds.) Learning Objects: Standards, Metadata, Repositories, and LCMS, pp. 131–156. Informing Science Press, Santa Rosa (2007)
7. Williams, D.D.: Evaluation of learning objects and instruction using learning objects. In: Wiley, A. (ed.) The Instructional Use of Learning Objects: Online Version (2000)
8. Vidal, C., Segura, A., Campos, P., Sánchez-Alonso, S.: Quality in learning objects: evaluating compliance with metadata standards. Metadata Semant. Res. Commun. Comput. Inf. Sci. **108**, 342–353 (2010)
9. Custard, M., Sumner, T.: Using machine learning to support quality judgments. D-Lib Mag. **11** (2005)
10. Nesbit, J., Belfer, K., Leacock, T.: Learning Object Review Instrument (LORI) - User Manual (2003)
11. Cechinel, C.: Empirical Foundations For Automated Quality Assessment of Learning Objects Inside Repositories (2012)
12. Ochoa, X.: Learnometrics: Metrics for Learning Objects - Tesis Doctoral (2008)
13. Wetzler, P., Bethard, S., Butcher, K.: Automatically assessing resource quality for educational digital libraries. In: Proceedings of the 3rd Workshop on Information Credibility on the Web, pp. 3–10 (2009)
14. Cechinel, C., Ochoa, X.: A brief overview of quality inside learning object repositories. In: XV Congreso Internacional de Interacción Persona-Ordenador, Tenerife (2014)
15. Leacock, T.L., Nesbit, J.C.: A framework for evaluating the quality of multimedia learning resources. Educ. Technol. Soc. **10**, 44–59 (2007)
16. Farrel, S., Nielsen, J.: Users experience Careers, How to Become a UX Pro, and How to hire One (2013)
17. Botella, F., Hernandez, M., Alarcon, E., Peñalver, A.: How to classify to experts in usability evaluation. In: XV Congreso Internacional de Interacción Persona-Ordenador, Tenerife (2014)
18. Tabares, V., Duque, M.N., Moreno, J., Ovalle, D.A., Vicari, R.: Evaluación de la calidad de metadatos en repositorios digitales de objetos de aprendizaje. Rev. Interam. Bibl. **36**, 183–195 (2013)

19. Tabares, V., Rodríguez, P., Duque, N., Vicari, R., Moreno, J.: Multi-agent model for evaluation of learning objects from repository federations - ELO-index. Rev. Respuestas **17**, 48–54 (2012)
20. Tabares, V., Duque, N., Ovalle, D., Rodríguez, P.: Learning objects repository management using an adaptive quality evaluation multi-agent system. In: PAAMS 2013 – Work, MASLE, pp. 351–362 (2013)
21. Tabares, V., Duque, N., Baldiris, S.: Calidad de Objetos de Aprendizaje en FROAC desde la Percepción del Usuario. In: Congr. Int. en Ambient. Virtuales Aprendizajes Accesibles y Adapt. - CAVA 2013, En Evaluac (2013)
22. Tabares, V., Rodríguez, P.A., Duque, N.D., Moreno, J.: Modelo Integral de Federación de Objetos de Aprendizaje en Colombia - más que búsquedas centralizadas. Séptima Conferencia Latinoamericana de Objetos y Tecnologías de Aprendizaje - LACLO 2012, pp. 410–418 (2012)

Incorporating Context-Awareness Services in Adaptive U-MAS Learning Environments

Oscar M. Salazar[1], Demetrio A. Ovalle[1(✉)], and Néstor D. Duque[2]

[1] Universidad Nacional de Colombia - Sede Medellín, Medellín, Colombia
{omsalazaro,dovalle}@unal.edu.co
[2] Universidad Nacional de Colombia - Sede Manizales, Manizales, Colombia
ndduqueme@unal.edu.co

Abstract. The context-awareness concept, which is inherent to humans when performing any learning activity, becomes the main component for monitoring activities in virtual learning environments. The aim of this paper is to incorporate context-awareness services within an adaptive ubiquitous Multi-Agent System (U-MAS) learning environment intended for instructional planning and educational resource recommendation. The awareness agent developed that composes the system architecture provides the functionality that involves several context-awareness services. This characteristic allows both students and teachers at a given time be aware of their learning progress status during U-MAS execution. In order to validate the incorporation of context-aware services a prototype was built and tested through a case study. Results obtained demonstrate the effectiveness of using this kind of approaches in virtual learning environments which constitutes an attempt to improve learning processes.

Keywords: U-MAS · Context-awareness services · Adaptive virtual courses · Mobile devices

1 Introduction

Currently, learning-teaching methods used in virtual courses are not personalized i.e., they do not consider the student's needs, interests, and learning styles thus generating a lack of students' personal interest and significantly slows down their learning process. Consequently new learning-teaching mechanisms should be considered to be applied on virtual environments such as adaptive virtual courses (AVC) allowing the personalized monitoring of the students and creating awareness on them about their learning process performance.

The context-awareness concept, which is inherent to humans when performing any learning activity, becomes the main component for monitoring activities in virtual learning environments. Through context-awareness, students become conscious of all the changes produced within the learning environment by the action of their activities while performing learning tasks. Thus, it is easier for them to direct their behavior and acquire new knowledge [1]. The awareness provided by virtual learning environments allows students to generate a context of their own activity, i.e., the information regarding

© Springer International Publishing Switzerland 2015
J. Bajo et al. (Eds.): PAAMS 2015 Workshops, CCIS 524, pp. 331–339, 2015.
DOI: 10.1007/978-3-319-19033-4_28

their learning activities is constantly updated and thus improving the performance on their learning process.

Context-awareness services should also been used in collaborative learning environments the reason is that if two students are using distributed schemes of computer-supported collaborative work (CSCW) they generally cannot see or hear, and neither feel the presence and perceive each other actions. In this kind of CSCW environments, these awareness skills are quite limited. The context-awareness has thus become one of major issues when designing pedagogical computer systems in order to reduce the need of meta-cognitive efforts for collaborating on distributed computer environments [2]. Gaver highlights the importance of providing context-awareness information with the purpose of help people to change the individually work role to work in groups [3]. In this fashion, Dourish and Bellotti [4] apply this characteristic within shared learning environments and define the awareness as a shared understanding of each other activities, thus providing a context for their own activity.

The aim of this paper is to incorporate context-awareness services within adaptive U-MAS intended for instructional planning and educational resources recommendation. The recommendation process is performed through local and remote learning object repositories (LOR), and considers the students' preferences, needs, and weaknesses during their learning-teaching activities.

The rest of the paper is organized as follows: While Sect. 2 examines some related works Sect. 3 describes the model proposed, detailing the main components of the U-MAS (ubiquitous Multi-Agent System). Section 4 provides the prototype implementation and validation of integrated context-awareness services. Finally, Sect. 5 presents conclusions and future work.

2 Related Works

This section presents some related works to the research field, and compares them in order to identify their strengths and weaknesses.

Ovalle et al. use awareness services to support collaborative activities in the classroom assisted by a knowledge management system named KnowCat built at Universidad Autonoma de Madrid [1]. The proposed awareness services in this research are the following: (1) registered-students, (2) online-students, (3) radar-view, (4) historical-view, (5) participation-level, and (6) annotation-graph.

A context-aware learning environment was developed by Hwang et al. to guide the beginner researchers through practical experiments concerning single-crystal X-ray diffraction processes [5]. The application domain of this research regards to scientific experiments and therefore, when a student arrives at the laboratory and is in front of an instrument, sensors are able to detect the student location and thus transfer this information to server. The system performs real-time analysis using the following parameters concerning students: (1) environmental and personal context, (2) student's profile, and (3) online portfolio. The learning system is able to guide students in the laboratory, showing relevant information at the appropriate time such as processes able to be applied, the laboratory rules, as well as the emergency management procedures. Experimental results showed the benefits of applying the ubiquitous learning and context-aware approach in learning sciences as well as taking advantage of the manpower savings to assist and monitor students.

Considering the research works previously reviewed one of the improvements proposed in this paper in order to enhance current ubiquitous computing and ontological learning-teaching models is the integration of awareness services along with the personalized resources recommendation. These features regarding context-awareness and alerts offered by learning environments allow students to become conscious of the advancement status of their own learning activities and to interact with adaptive and personalized educational resources. In this way, the system gives the student the opportunity to maintain updated information that helps them to improve their performance during their learning process.

3   Model Proposed

Two main functionalities exhibit the proposed model. The first one offers context-awareness services and the second provides adapted educational resources. We seek to extend an existing virtual learning environment U-MAS-based for virtual course planning and educational resource recommendation.

Figure 1 presents main agents and interactions defined in the system showing a highly distributed topology of interconnected agents. The architecture is composed of three different modules: in the first module, we can find the agent main container that is a server on which the multi-agent platform is deployed. The second module is the BROA system—considered as a foreign module—that provides services such as LOs recovery, filtering, and recommendation [6]. The third and last module comprises all secondary containers concerning to each mobile device connected to the platform. In addition, a domain specific ontology is associated with the AVC planning functionality through which the adaptive and personalized virtual course structure can be inferred and accessed by students. It is important to highlight that the ontological modeling does not correspond to the aim of this paper; more details can be found in [7].

3.1   Agent Model and Functionalities

According to the requirements and objectives of the system 7 agents were considered. These agents are interconnected without any hierarchy and have common goals to achieve. Main functionalities of these agents are the following:

- AVC planner agent: this agent is responsible for the AVC automatic planning. To do so, the agent interacts with the recommender agent in order to recover educational resources regarding course topics. Subsequently, the student's profile is recovered from the system database and so this information is mapped into the ontology that involves the AVC knowledge semantic description [8].
- Evaluator agent: this agent is responsible for generating automatic assessments when the student completes a topic or wish to exonerate of it. Questions within tests are selected from a previously formed question bank and associated with a specific AVC

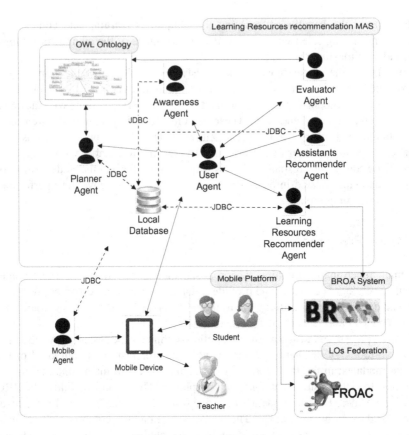

Fig. 1. Agent model overview.

topic [9]. An important issue is the average response time that the student spent to answer a question and the kind of question, i.e. multiple choice, single choice, true-false response, etc.

- Assistants recommender agent: this agent aims to find and recommend learning assistants for students who have deficiencies in the topics associated with the AVC or students who request advices. To carry out this objective, the agent must know the knowledge areas required by the student, as well the schedules handled by both students and assistants.

- Educational resource recommender agent: the main objective of this agent is to recommend educational resources such as LOs, books, experts, conferences, and seminars. In order to recommend LOs, this agent uses the service offered by the BROA system that require the student's profile and search parameters, and consequently returns a personalized list of LOs from different repositories. On the other hand, to recommend other resources the recommender agent uses the system local database wherein all the information related to books, experts, conferences, and seminars is stored.

- Awareness agent: this agent is in charge of offering different context-awareness services considered by the system, either at the request of students or for proactivity purposes always offering useful information. Some awareness services offered by this agent are participation-level, progress-graph, learning-assistant-student-interaction-graph, historical-learning-activity-view, alarms, among others.
- User agent: this agent is responsible for representing both students and teachers within the multi-agent platform, i.e., handling the user's profile by allowing the creation and modification of user's features and preferences. Also, this agent is responsible for managing every communication channel required by the user's mobile device, in this way, the user agent plays the role of the interface between users and the U-MAS. Finally, this agent has to request awareness services and receive useful information in order to subsequently deploy it to the user.
- Mobile agent: the main task of this agent is to gather the student's profile and his/her context features, and subsequently store them in the system database. To achieve this, it is necessary to adapt the specifications of the student's mobile device using the mobile agent typology along with the mobile device features.

3.2 Context-Awareness Services

The awareness agent provides this main functionality that considers several context-awareness services allowing both students and teachers at a given time be aware of their status during U-MAS execution. It is important to highlight that the information regarding students' learning activities is constantly updated and thus the fact to be aware of these changes might surely improve the performance on their learning process. Main context-awareness services are the following:

- Participation-level. It is a statistical view that allows identifying a student's participation level within the AVC topics, getting well an activity level measure associated with LOs.
- Progress-graph. It presents a student's state overview within the AVC and pending topics to be reviewed by the student, keeping in this way the teacher informed about the progress and the difficulties of the student in his/her learning process.
- Learning-assistant-student-interaction-graph: This graph exhibits the interaction between the student and learning assistants, showing if the student has received learning advice sessions. In addition, the graph detects the learning assistants that are the best recommended by students.
- Historical-learning-activity-view: it presents to both teachers and students recent learning activities that have been performed within a AVC, in this fashion, the teacher has the ability to continuously monitor the student learning process.
- Alarms: this service exhibits proactivity features since it is on charge of generating learning activity expiration alarms concerning AVC without student intervention. This fact can generate an awareness state in students of the activities that need to be performed and prevents the desertion of students in registered AVC.
- Online-assistants: this service deploys online learning assistants associated with each AVC. In addition, it presents the contact details and features of each learning assistant

such as knowledge areas, previous grades, proximity, and availability. As an additional functionality the U-MAS allows the student to contact in real time the assistant and to know its schedule availability.

- Accessed-educational-resources: this service enumerates the educational resources that the U-MAS has recommended to the student and emphasizes on previous resources that have been accessed by him/her.
- Practice-community: Given that the practice community is a space for sharing ideas and resources among registered students in the AVC, this service deploys it to students. The community idea is that teachers and students may raise issues about topics of the AVC, in order to generate a feedback from other students.
- Brainstorming wall: This service provides a space that allows the development of new ideas by students associated with the specific domain of the AVC.

4   Model Implementation and Validation

The U-MAS was implemented using JADE, a FIPA compliant framework [10]. This feature provides interoperability to the platform, what is needed for interconnect platforms and repositories. JADE was developed using JAVA language, this feature allows to integrate the ontology through JENA framework that was developed for JAVA environments as well.

Concerning the connection between the platform and user's mobile devices it was necessary to use Android platform, which allows the integration of mobile devices with the JADE Main Container hosted on the server. It is important to highlight that the platform which offers support to each AVC is self-authorship, and it was developed in the same server that deploys the U-MAS. The platform has access to a specific MySQL relational database that contains all AVC information.

In order to validate the proposed model, a study case that assesses the behavior of each of the proposed context-awareness services was raised. To achieve this, a student's profile was recovered wherein all features needed by the system are found.

Figure 2 presents three awareness services. The first one is the participation-level which presents the interaction percentage that the student has with the AVC topics, showing the interest of the student in the AVC. The second context-awareness service in Fig. 2 shows the recommended learning assistant interface for given course topics. This service provides in real time the assistants availability and location (considering the spatial and temporal context recorded in the ontology). In addition, the interface offers mechanisms like e-mail or chat to contact learning assistants. This service may be requested by the student or can be deployed proactively according to the deficiencies identified by the system in the student learning process. The third awareness service presents the educational resources recommended by the U-MAS to the student classified according to topic activities. The green color represents resources that were accessed by the student, whereas the red color represents recommended resources that the student did not use despite being made by the system.

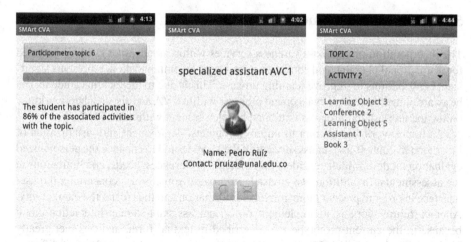

Fig. 2. Awareness services (participation-level, recommended-learning-assistants, and accessed-educational-resources)

Figure 3 exhibits three context-awareness services. The first one concerns to the student progress-graph. In this graph both students and teachers have the ability to visualize the student progress level within the AVC, the percentage of completion is presented in terms of learning activities for given topics. In this same interface, the alarm service can also be observed. This service enables to remember the activities that are going to expire. The second service presents the historical-learning-activity presenting a list of recent activities that the student has done within the CVA. The third service deploys a brainstorming-wall wherein students develop and publish new ideas related to AVC topics.

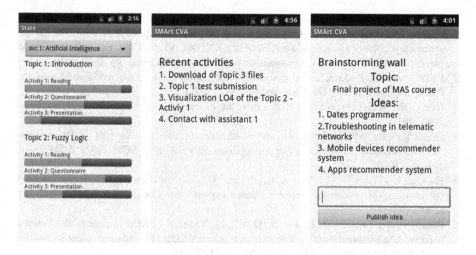

Fig. 3. Context-awareness services (progress-graph, historical-learning-activity-view and brainstorming-wall)

5 Conclusions and Future Works

The incorporation of context-awareness services within an adaptive U-MAS intended for instructional planning and educational resources recommendation, represents significant contributions to improve learning process. This is due to the fact that students can be aware of their learning advancement progress within CVA and also teachers can know online the interest and progress exhibited by each student within the CVA.

As future work, we attempt to improve contents, deployment and visualization of incorporated context-awareness services in the U-MAS and to enhance the personalized evaluation module, which considers the student's preferences, needs, and limitations in the assessments. In addition, we envisage improving some issues concerning the user interface in order to present more graphical information and thus foster the interactivity. Another future work is to implement the visual assistant-student-interaction-graph because in the current prototype it is described in textual form, and this fact greatly hinders its understanding. Finally, we expect to improve the testing phase of different U-MAS modules using new case studies.

Acknowledgments. The research presented in this paper was partially funded by the COLCIENCIAS project entitled: "RAIM: Implementación de un framework apoyado en tecnologías móviles y de realidad aumentada para entornos educativos ubicuos, adaptativos, accesibles e interactivos para todos" from the Universidad Nacional de Colombia, with code 1119-569-34172. This research was also developed with the aid of the master grant offered to Oscar M. Salazar by COLCIENCIAS through "Convocatoria 617 de 2013. Capítulo 1 Semilleros-Jóvenes Investigadores".

References

1. Ovalle, D., Jiménez, J., Collazos, C., Claros, I., Pantoja, L., Cobos, R., Moreno-Llorena, J., Pifarré, M., Argelagos, E.: Guía metodológica para el seguimiento y evaluación de aprendizaje colaborativo asistido por el sistema KNOWCAT. In: Congreso de Facultades de Ingeniería, ACOFI – Asoc. Colombiana de Facultades de Ingeniería, pp. 1–9 (2009)
2. Palfreyman, K., Rodden, T.: A protocol for users awareness on the world wide web. In: Proceedings of CSCW 1996, USA, pp. 130–139 (1996)
3. Gaver, W.: Sound support for collaboration. In: Proceedings of the ESCW 1991, pp. 293–308 (1991)
4. Dourish, P., Bellotti, V.: Awareness and coordination in shared workspaces. In: Proceedings ACM Conference on Computer Supported Cooperative Work (CSCW 1992). ACM Press, Toronto (1992)
5. Hwang, G., Yang, T.C., Tsai, C.C., Yang, S.: A context-aware ubiquitous learning environment for conducting complex science experiments. Comput. Educ. J. **53**, 402–413 (2009)
6. Rodríguez, P., Tabares, V., Duque, N., Ovalle, D., Vicari, R.: BROA: an agent-based model to recommend relevant learning objects from repository federations adapted to learner profile. Int. J. Artif. Intell. Interact. Multimedia **2**(1), 6–11 (2013)

7. Rodríguez, P., Salazar, O., Ovalle, D., Duque, N., Moreno, J.: Using ontological modeling for multi-agent recommendation of learning objects. In: Workshop MASLE - Multiagent System Based Learning Environments in ITS Conference, Hawaii (2014)

8. Arias, F.J.: Modelo multi-agente para la planificación instruccional y selección de contenidos en cursos virtuales adaptativos. In: Tesis de Maestría en Ingeniería de Sistemas. Universidad Nacional de Colombia – Sede Medellín (2009)

9. Moreno, J., Ovalle, D., Jimenez, J.: CIA: framework for the creation and management of adaptive intelligent courses. In: Proceedings of 9th World Conference on Computers in Education – WCCE, BentoGonçales, Brazil (2009)

10. Bordini, R., Braubach, L., Dastani, M., Seghrouchni, E.F., Gomez-Sanz, J., Leite, J., O'Hare, G., Pokahrand, A., Ricci, A.: A survey of programming languages and platforms for multi-agent systems. Informatica **30**(33), 33–44 (2006)

Design of an Educational Videogame to Transform Citizens into Agents of Change Considering a Colombian Post-Conflict Scenario

Julián Moreno(✉) and Santiago Alvarez

Universidad Nacional de Colombia, Facultad de Minas, Medellín, Colombia
{jmoreno1,saalvarezva}@unal.edu.co

Abstract. The project described in this paper proposes a model in which, through a videogame, players will become agents of change in a virtual world considering a Colombian post-conflict scenario. First we briefly describe a sample of games with similar approaches and later present the proposal making emphasis in explaining how the interaction between players is made, as well as the use of animated agents to provide narrative aspects. We also focus in one of the most important aspects of our proposal: a mechanism through which individual actions of each player, represented by an avatar, contribute to a collective construction. The metaphor used here is that, in the same way that players are able to collectively achieve the restauration of certain damaged zones within the virtual world, they would be able to contribute to peace in a Colombian post-conflict scenario.

Keywords: Serious game · Storytelling · Animated pedagogical agents · Colombian post-conflict · Games for change

1 Introduction

As is shown at the *Anuario de Procesos de Paz 2014* (Peace Process Yearbook 2014), Colombia is the only Latin-American country at present with an armed conflict. Guerillas with more than 50 years of formation participates and there is also a lot of violence generated by paramilitary structures linked with drug dealing [1]. Considering this scenario, the proposal in this paper is to use these capabilities of videogames to show the point of view in an armed conflict of the different parts involved: guerilla, militaries and citizens, and how a common person can become an agent of change in a post-conflict. This is made through a massive multiplayer online videogame called *EnTusZapatos* (InYourShoes), an instance of a bigger platform in development called *PLACCO* for its acronym in Spanish: *Plataforma Ludica de Aprendizaje y Construcción Colectiva Online* (Ludic Online Platform of Collective Learning and Construction). In this platform teachers can set courses and follow their students' progress through the use of funny mini-games and educative material. Everything gripped together into a collective construction of an alive changing virtual world in which it develops.

It is important to mention that videogames counts with a great versatility in narrative terms, can be engaging, and have the capacity to get to a lot of audience. Only in United

J. Bajo et al. (Eds.): PAAMS 2015 Workshops, CCIS 524, pp. 340–347, 2015.
DOI: 10.1007/978-3-319-19033-4_29

Stated, 67 % of the households plays videogames [2] and they can become to be great communication mediums of influence for their audience [3] and be used as effective vehicles of persuasion [4].

2 Related Works

Lately, videogames have started to get involved into social topics from different points of view. Topics as armed conflict, starvation and different social problems have been addressed by videogames. This is done in a well-structurated way searching for solutions, not only in ludic terms, but in educational terms as well.

Games like *September 12th: A Toy World* [5] and *The Best Amendment* [6] present critics towards society, showing how violence triggers more violence. Games like *Food Force* for example looks for fighting hunger, having a big success, reaching over 10 million of players around the world [7].

Some studies have used games as *PeaceMaker* and *Global Conflicts* to show how simulation games of the Israeli-Palestinian and Guatemalan scenarios can deal with political issues while making the player understand a conflict and start changing their attitudes about these scenarios [8,9,10].

Another example, developed by the same research group that developed *EnTusZapatos* is *Erudito,* an authoring tool that allows the creation and control of educational massive multiplayer online games [11]. Nowadays, it counts with more than 300 courses in mathematics, biology, computers, and other subjects, and has more than 10,000 users.

These games, with similar approaches as *EnTusZapatos,* shown how through different ludic mechanics may empower awareness about different issues. What differentiates *EnTusZapatos* from others is that it presents a virtual world in which players can interact between them, accessing educative content and more importantly, making a collective, positive change in that world.

3 Proposal for Collective Learning and Construction

The model proposed at *EnTusZapatos* aims to transform players into main agents of change in an online virtual world, through collective learning and construction. What they must learn through the game is the point of view of the different actors in the Colombian armed conflict, more specifically why they are there, what they wish have done different and finally, how they would like to contribute for building a better country once the conflict finishes as seen in Fig. 1.

As an overview, *EnTusZapatos* is a massive multiplayer videogame established in a 3D world in which the players interact with each other through a built-in chat and a graphical visualization as 3D avatars. Each player is able to accept and complete different missions which have a background history told by a Non-Playable Character (NPC) developed as an animated pedagogical agent into the game. Depending on the missions, these can be completed accessing some educative material or winning a mini-game and, is the completion of these missions, which produces the reconstruction of certain zones in the world.

Fig. 1. NPC dialog

3.1 Virtual World and Avatars

EnTusZapatos has been built mainly using Unity 3D, a game development software that allows for using different kind of assets (content), scripts (code) and physics. A preview of the virtual world is shown in Fig. 2.

Fig. 2. General game world view

The players can choose from a set of available avatars that represent the player in the virtual world and allow them to interact with others (Fig. 3).

Fig. 3. Player's avatars

The missions that players must accomplish are of two types: learning missions and action missions. The main goal of learning missions is allowing the player to accesses educative material in several formats like videos audios or text documents. Action missions put the player into mini-games that he/she accomplishes not only through the abilities required in each mechanic but also through what he/she has previously learned from learning missions.

For example there is a mini-game, as shown in Fig. 4, called "Trash recollection" where several trash bags are thrown during a running circuit. Each bag has a color and only those related to the color of the correct answer must be recollected without crashing the several obstacles of the circuit. Another example is presented in the Fig. 5 in a mini-game called "Reforestation" where the player must water some trees offspring in order to allow them to grow, but at the same time must use a weed-killer, the one that with the color corresponding to the correct answer, in order to kill the weed.

Fig. 4. Trash recollection mini-game

Fig. 5. Reforestation mini-game

Once an action mission is completed successfully, the corresponding contribution to the collective construction of the virtual world is presented to the player accordingly. For example, each time a player completes a trash collection mini-game a zone of the virtual world that is very polluted gets cleaned in a certain percentage and then is used to build a park. In a similar way, each time a player completes a reforestation mini-game a zone of the virtual world that is depleted of trees and arid gets reforested in a certain percentage until becomes a forest near the city.

3.2   Collective Construction Calculation

Considering that the main goal of the game is the collective construction of the virtual world, and in fact big part of the fun is being developed around this, the system must ensure that such "damaged" zones never reach a full reconstruction state. If that situation would happen, the player action would not have any repercussion in the game and therefore there would be no motivation to keep playing. It is because of this, that a mathematician calculation has been developed to determine, in a given moment, the total percentage of a zone reconstruction, obtained as the sum of the individual contributions of every player.

More specifically, the reconstruction rate of every zone must oscillate between 0 % and 100 %, but it must not be linear but decreasing over time. One way for doing that is using a logarithmic function as presented on Eq. 1.

$$10\log_{2.512}(c + 1) \tag{1}$$

Where c corresponds to the quantity of times that a mini-game has been completed successfully with a maximum of 20 for each player. The base of the logarithm was selected in a way that when c reaches a value close to 10,000, the restauration rate gets close to 99.99 %. This logarithmic shape allows for, the fewer players, the more individual effort contributes to the collective construction. On the contrary, the more players, the less individual effort contributes to the collective construction. A plot of such a function is presented on Fig. 6 for values of c between 1 and 2000.

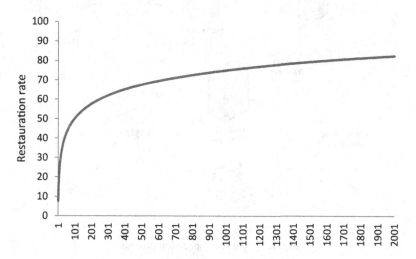

Fig. 6. Plot for the collective construction

3.3 Back-End Infrastructure Details

Unity allows the interconnectivity between players through the establishment of servers that work as hosts to which the players can connect. Being an online multiplayer game, *EnTusZapatos* counts with several hosts, one for each zone in the virtual world. Unity requires that such hosts must be registered to a Master Server that contains a list with every active host for the game. This Master Server automatically manages the incoming connections searching for active hosts and provides them the information required to perform a direct connection between hosts and players.

Another important aspect of the infrastructure is the database where all player information is stored. In this case, we use MySQL which is accessed to through PHP files that contain all the necessary queries.

A scheme of the whole proposal structure is presented in Fig. 7.

4 Concluding Remarks

Videogames can be used in many forms, not only ludic, but also pedagogically, even with social purposes, looking for transforming the way that players perceives local and foreign conflict scenarios. This is exactly what the project discussed in this paper aims for in the particular case of the Colombian armed conflict.

What differentiates this proposal from other works is that it does not only allow players to turn themselves into agents of change in a virtual world but, throughout their actions, contribute to a greater, collective, good. With such a feature, this proposal tries

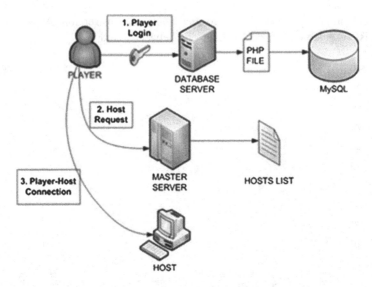

Fig. 7. Login and connection process

to empower motivation among players and show them how everyone can provide with their own 'molehill' in a peace construction scenario.

In the technical aspect, it is important to highlight that videogame engines like Unity facilitates the construction of huge virtual spaces as well as the communication between players and NPCs. The management of virtual worlds as a distributed host system, in which every zone of the world can be hosted in the same or different servers no matter the physical space where is being placed implies a reduce in the computational charge. Besides that, in case of a great amount of users, new hosts of the same virtual zone can be opened in which the players can play without lag troubles.

References

1. Escola de cultura de pau, Anuario de procesos de paz 2014 (2014). http://escolapau.uab.es/img/programas/procesos/14anuarie.pdf
2. ESRB - Entertainment Software Rating Board, Video Game Industry Statistics, Infographic List (2014). http://www.esrb.org/about/video-game-industry-statistics.jsp
3. Bogost, I.: Persuasive Games: The Expressive Power of Videogames. Mit Press, Cambridge (2007)
4. Khaled, R., Barr, P., Boyland, J., Fischer, R., Biddle, R.: Fine tuning the persuasion in persuasive games. In: de Kort, Y.A., IJsselsteijn, W.A., Midden, C., Eggen, B., Fogg, B.J. (eds.) PERSUASIVE 2007. LNCS, vol. 4744, pp. 36–47. Springer, Heidelberg (2007)
5. Games For Change, September 12th: A Toy World (2003). http://www.gamesforchange.org/play/september-12th-a-toy-world/
6. Games For Change, The Best Amendment (2013). http://www.gamesforchange.org/play/the-best-amendment/

7. WFP - World Food Programme, Online Game 'Food Force' Puts Players On Front Lines Of Hunger (2011). https://www.wfp.org/stories/online-game-food-force-puts-players-front-lines-hunger
8. Burak, A., Keylor, E., Sweeney, T.: Peacemaker: a video game to teach peace. In: Maybury, M., Stock, O., Wahlster, W. (eds.) INTETAIN 2005. LNCS (LNAI), vol. 3814, pp. 307–310. Springer, Heidelberg (2005)
9. Gonzalez, C., Saner, L.D., Eisenberg, L.Z.: Learning to stand in the other's shoes: a computer video game experience of the Israeli-Palestinian conflict. Soc. Sci. Comput. Rev. 31(2), 236–243 (2012)
10. Kampf, R., Cuhadar, E.: Do computer games enhance learning about conflicts? a cross-national inquiry into proximate and distant scenarios in Global Conflicts. Comput. Human Behav. (2014, in press)
11. Moreno, J., Zapata, F.A.: Towards the design of an educational agent within a game-based learning environment. In: 12th International Conference on Intelligent Tutoring Systems - ITS, Workshop on Multiagent System Based Learning Environments - MASLE (2014)

A Proposal to Integrate a Learning Companion Agent Within Claroline LMS

Demetrio A. Ovalle[✉], Mateo Hernández, and Julián Moreno

Universidad Nacional de Colombia–Sede Medellín, Medellín, Colombia
{dovalle,mahernandezsa,jmorenol}@unal.edu.co

Abstract. During the last decade, learning management systems (LMS) have become a useful tool for students and teachers seeking to assist virtual learning processes. The aim of this paper is to present a proposal for the design and integration of a learning companion agent within the Claroline LMS intended to foster collaboration, assistance, support, and motivation of students. Using a role-based design method a learning companion agent was built having three main roles: Competitor, Fault Detector, and Collaborator. Through these roles the platform provides student-centered responses, educational resources, and the possibility to interact within a healthy competition learning environment. The companion agent was implemented and validated through a case study that includes a test virtual course and assessments for several registered students. It can be concluded that using a companion agent students become aware of their learning failures and overall performance of the virtual course.

Keywords: Claroline · Learning companion agent · LMS · Competitor · Collaborator · Fault detector

1 Introduction

During the last decade, learning management systems (LMS) have become a useful tool for students and teachers seeking to assist virtual learning processes. They are mainly characterized by having a structure that facilitates the organization of learning information concerning virtual courses. Thus, LMS define a section for each of the following issues: agenda, announcement, document, learning path, assignments, forums, groups, users, wiki, chat, etc. In addition, LMS encapsulate tools for handling and managing learning resources useful for administrators and teachers who assist virtual learning processes. However, the majority of LMS are characterized by lack of functionalities intended to provide assistance, support, motivation, collaboration to students who have difficulties in their learning process. These functionalities should simulate a personalized teacher or even more a learning companion that help them for achieving the learning goals or also support any activity that students are not able to perform for themselves. In addition, the fact to incorporate competitiveness in students' learning processes while they are using a LMS is another good practice that might be considered.

The design and implementation of a learning companion agent can perform such functionalities that lack in LMS [1]. Thus, several roles could be assumed by the

© Springer International Publishing Switzerland 2015
J. Bajo et al. (Eds.): PAAMS 2015 Workshops, CCIS 524, pp. 348–355, 2015.
DOI: 10.1007/978-3-319-19033-4_30

companion agent such as competitor, in charge of motivating students to improve their performance themselves, fault detector, in charge of informing students on their failures during the learning process, and collaborator, to support the learning activities that the student is not able to do alone and also to assist those learning tasks that require reinforcement [2].

This paper aims to present the integration of a learning companion agent within the LMS Claroline that exhibits three roles: Competitor, Collaborator, and Fault Detector. These roles attempt to encourage healthy competition among students, detect learning failures after performing assessment exercises, and provide students with educational resources to enhance their learning processes.

The rest of the paper is organized as follows: Sect. 2 provides the conceptual framework of this research. While Sect. 3 presents related works, Sect. 4 describes in detail the model proposed. Section 5 offers the implementation and validation of the prototype developed using a case study. Finally, Sect. 6 presents main conclusions and future research work.

2 Conceptual Framework

There are two main elements involved in this research: learning companion agents and Claroline LMS. For one side, and according to Chou et al. [3] a learning companion agent is defined—as its name suggests—as a learning peer which acts as a fellow student during learning activities. To this purpose, the learning companion agent learns from a teacher, and collaborates or competes against human student.

Among the major roles that can assume a learning companion agent are the following [4]:

- Collaborator: this agent might be considered in the same position as the student, i.e. like a classmate, and as its name implies, its main function is to help the student for achieving the learning goals.
- Competitor: this agent is similar to the previous one in the sense that might be considered as a student classmate; however its role is quite different. Instead of collaborating, this agent serves as a reference point of someone to surpass. Even if this concept may seem not very "educational", truth is that competition is one of the most engaging forces in learning environments.
- Fault Detector: this agent is responsible for informing the student about the learning concepts or themes in which he/she presents failures after performing assessment tasks.
- Troublemaker: this agent is responsible for delivering misconceptions in order to generate reflection and questioning the student.
- Clone: this agent simulates to be a virtual actor similar to a specific student who represents him/her within the learning environment and whose main function is to show the student's performance during the learning process.
- Peer tutor: this agent is equivalent to a tutor who in turn is a study partner that helps and supports the student.
- Tutee: this agent is in charge of supporting any activity that the student is not able to perform for himself.

For the other side, and according to its Consortium [5], the Claroline LMS is an open source software that lets teachers and administrators to easily create an online platform dedicated to learning processes and collaborative work. It is available in multiple languages and is currently used in more than 100 countries around the world, especially in countries of the European Union. The learning approach used in Claroline is based on a flexible learning model according to which the information becomes knowledge through learning activities and productions of educational resources in a system mainly driven by interaction. Several tools are encapsulated in the Claroline LMS —similar to the vast majority of LMS—such as documents, forums, exercises, assessments, wikis, collaborative work groups, etc. The platform has also different kinds of users, such as administrators, teachers, and students.

3 Related Works

Butakov and Smolin [6] propose the integration of a multi-agent system and a learning environment intended to improve user learning. The platform is composed of 8 agents having specific functionalities. Some of the implemented agents are the following: Plagiarism Detection Agent (PDA), in charge of detecting plagiarism in tasks assigned to students, Syllabus Management Agent (SMA), responsible for controlling the content and structure of the syllabus of a course, User Management Agent (UMA), responsible for the management and authentication of users and their sessions, Course Material Management Agent (CMMA), in charge of defining the sequence of learning objects to be delivered to the user, and many more that provide assistance and resource management to teachers and administrators of virtual courses. Although this multi-agent platform provides good support in handling educational resources, however, a learning companion is not presented who can assist students in their learning process.

On the other hand, Bokhari and Ahmad [7] review characteristics of different multi-agent e-learning systems by making comparisons among them. From this comparison the ALLEGRO system is the closest to ours except for competitiveness issue providing flexibility, autonomy, and adaptability to learning environments. Agents defined in ALLEGRO are: tutor, interface, expert, diagnostic, and collaborator that are intended to guide the learning process of students by improving the human-computer interaction. In addition, the system manages educational contents, classifies students' learning level, and looks for synchronization with other students who are studying similar topics.

Bhaskaran and Swaminathan [8] build an intelligent adaptive e-learning model that is able to classify students using agents. This model is implemented based on three agents: Learners Agent, Classifier Agent and Collaborative Agent. The first agent is in charge of supporting students' learning process both online and offline. In addition, this agent provides interaction between the student and the system as well as registration or login; access to details of student's profile; recovery of learning materials, reading notes, quizzes responses, etc. The second agent classifies students according to their performance in novice, intermediate, advanced or expert. Finally, the last agent works along with the other two agents in order to check that the student's profile matches with similar profiles both locally and remotely.

Related works previously described are characterized by supporting not only students but teachers during learning processes; however, they do not match the competitive factor as well as the failure detection based on assessments. Our work attempts to gather competitiveness, failure detection, and educational contents recommendation within a role-based learning companion agent that is incorporated into the Claroline LMS.

4 Model Proposed

Our model is mainly composed of the Claroline LMS and a role-based learning companion agent. These two components work together to achieve the following functionalities:

Support and collaboration on learning processes: This functionality aims to support and collaborate students using adaptive educational contents such as links, learning objects, documents, books, etc. that enrich their knowledge provided by the learning companion agent.

Healthy competition encouragement: This functionality attempts to motivate students to healthily compete with their fellow students, because it has been demonstrated that competition plays a very important role in students which establish learning-level reference points that they try to overcome by themselves [9].

Learning process assessment: This functionality intends to have a track on the student's progress in a particular course and then to congratulate, advice, recommend or other action that is appropriate for a continuous support of the student.

Fault detection in learning process: After finishing, the assessment stage of learning process, this functionality serves to gather all the information concerning the learning tests failed by the student and so to tell him/her on faults and possible aid to overcome identified difficulties.

Student motivation for learning: This functionality consists of unconditional and motivational messages attempting that students never faint to learn and improve the results obtained in tests for a specific virtual course.

All these functionalities were mapped or assigned to the following roles: Collaborator, Competitor and Fault Detector. The three roles are integrated within a learning companion agent that extends the basic Claroline LMS functionalities.

Figure 1 shows the model structure firstly composed of the Claroline LMS that exhibits every tool provided (see at the left in the Fig. 1): agenda, announcements, documents, learning paths, assignments, etc. that cover basic functionalities of any LMS. The learning companion agent is the second component of our model who plays three exchangeable roles wherein each one has access to the system database in order to obtain all necessary information of the course and registered students to adequately perform its tasks. At right in the Fig. 1, the component of LO (learning objects) supports the Collaborator role whose main goal is to recover educational resources from LO federations such as FROAC, FEB, etc., adapted to student's profile. Students and teachers are the actors in charge of interacting with the platform both the student in the learning process supported by the learning companion agent, as well as the teacher in charge of supplying to the platform the educational resources or LO metadata required for the Collaborator role.

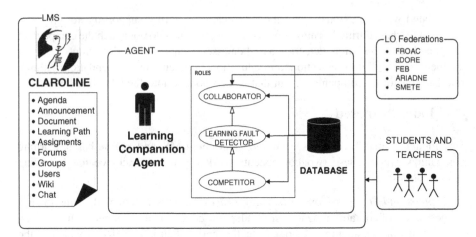

Fig. 1. Model structure incorporating a learning companion agent within Claroline LMS.

The sequence diagram in Fig. 2 shows the possible role changes that can occur in the behavior of the learning companion agent. A motivational message is used by the Competitor role to perform a role change to Fault Detector in order that the student be questioned by himself about assessments results. When lost exams or failures are detected a new change of role to Collaborator is generated to search and recover adaptive educational resources to be reviewed by the student to overcome its difficulties. Otherwise, the student is congratulated for his/her excellent performance.

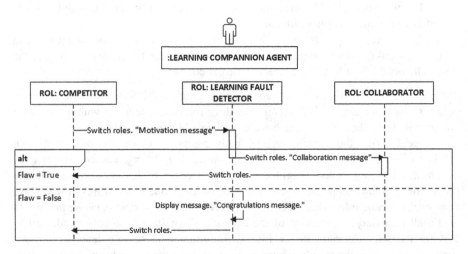

Fig. 2. Sequence diagram of the learning companion agent.

5   Implementation and Validation

The implementation of the model proposed is conducted within the Claroline LMS using several Web programming languages such as PHP, HTML and JavaScript. As a server-side programming language, PHP is thus employed for dynamic Web development. HTML is mainly composed of a series of labels that are enabling the development of templates interpreted by the browser. It contains labels for images, hyperlinks that allow us to address other pages, styles, fonts, tables, etc. Finally, JavaScript was useful to create actions in the platform, for example, database queries. In addition, the system has a database called "Claroline" created using MySQL DBMS. The database stores all the information of the courses and students, exercises, questions, documents, working groups, assessment results, and additional information required for both Claroline LMS as well as the learning companion agent.

All these components are located in XAMPP, a web server that meets the necessary requirements having an Apache server, the MySQL DBMS, and a language interpreter like PHP. These tools provide to the platform and specifically to the learning companion agent important characteristics such as dynamism, reactivity, graphical interface, and behavior changing required for a successful implementation.

Using tools previously described the following roles were developed in the learning companion agent:

Role 1: Collaborator. This role attempts to help, support and reinforce students on concepts involved in learning tasks. It is programmed in such a way that offers to students files, links, documents, books and other educational resources regarding to concepts on which he/she should reinforce. When the learning companion agent has detected failures, using student's assessment results, the Collaborator role is activated. In addition, educational resources—regarding the concepts in which the student has learning difficulties—adapted to student's profile are recovered from federations of learning objects such as FROAC, FEB, etc.

Role 2: Competitor. This role attempts to encourage healthy competition among students that directly relates to the increase of their learning as described in [8]. The companion agent presents to students a ranking table where are located all students wherein points are obtained calculating assigned weights by each question correctly answered. Besides, the companion agent shows general statistics about the performance of each attempt performed by students in different examinations. The fields that compose statistics are test name, average time, number of attempts, and the best and worst score, allowing the student to assess by itself on his/her academic performance. Also and within this role, the companion agent is always presenting motivational or encouragement messages in order that the student feels support, assistance, and desire to compete enhancing in this way its knowledge and learning level. At this stage and from this role, the student can request a change of role to the learning fault detector. This behavior is performed using a motivational message to the student to make the change, for example: "Come on, if you want to move up in the rankings detects your faults and retry the exercises for a best score, if you want to change give me click here". By clicking, the companion agent immediately changes to Role 3: Fault Detector (see Fig. 3).

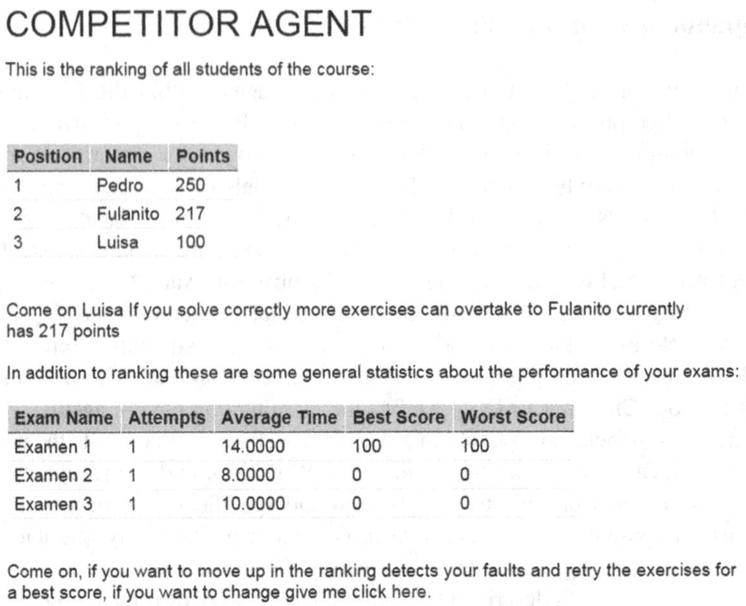

COMPETITOR AGENT

This is the ranking of all students of the course:

Position	Name	Points
1	Pedro	250
2	Fulanito	217
3	Luisa	100

Come on Luisa If you solve correctly more exercises can overtake to Fulanito currently has 217 points

In addition to ranking these are some general statistics about the performance of your exams:

Exam Name	Attempts	Average Time	Best Score	Worst Score
Examen 1	1	14.0000	100	100
Examen 2	1	8.0000	0	0
Examen 3	1	10.0000	0	0

Come on, if you want to move up in the ranking detects your faults and retry the exercises for a best score, if you want to change give me click here.

Fig. 3. Competitor role of the learning companion agent.

Role 3: Fault Detector. This role is in charge of presenting the student learning failures that has detected during the course, i.e. lost examinations. This role was programmed by performing a query on the database regarding examinations in which the student has obtained minor results under a threshold, e.g. 60/100. After presenting lost exams to the student immediately suggests a role changing to collaborator-role using motivational messages. To achieve this, the companion agent informs him/her that in a few minutes—determined by the system—the role will change from fault detector to collaborator. Consequently, educational resources will be proposed to the student by the learning companion agent in order to overcome poor performance.

6 Conclusions and Future Work

The student accompaniment during learning processes is of crucial importance since can achieve better learning performance of students as well as foster in them the interest in acquiring new knowledge. Collaboration is an extremely important issue in this process since students that have learning difficulties by using the companion agent can reinforce concepts through recommended educational resources adapted to student's profile. The collaboration intervenes when a student is unable to individually perform an activity, so that together with the companion agent can overcome these difficulties. The competitor role encourages students to improve themselves and their companions since when students directly perform this task of overcoming, their learning capacity increases, as previously mentioned, the competition is one of the best practices on learning environments. On the other hand, the criticism of the Fault Detector role is a very important issue because it allows students to know in which concepts should reinforce. It is important to mention that also motivation, monitoring, and assessment issues positively influence students' learning process. By using a companion agent students become aware of their learning failures and overall performance of the virtual course.

As future research work, we pretend to implement avatars for different roles attempting the learning companion agent become into something much more user-friendly to students. In addition, it is planned the development of a MAS based on learning companion agents using many more roles that were raised in the conceptual framework such as the troublemaker, the peer tutor or tutee, etc. Finally, a possible integration of this platform with a ubiquitous e-learning MAS based on mobile devices is also envisaged.

References

1. Kim, Y., Wei, Q.: The impact of learner attributes and learner choice in an agent-based environment. Comput. Educ. **56**(2), 505–514 (2011)
2. Cheng, B., Wang, M., Yang, S.J.H., Kinshuk, Peng, J.: Acceptance of competency-based workplace e-learning systems: effects of individual and peer learning support. Comput. Educ. **57**(1), 1317–1333 (2011)
3. Chou, C., Chan, T., Lin, C.: Redefining the learning companion: the past, present, and future of educational agents. Comput. Educ. **40**(3), 255–269 (2003)
4. Moreno, J., Zapata, F.A., Duque, N.D.: Towards the design of an educational agent within a game-based learning environment. In: Workshop MASLE - Multiagent System Based Learning Environments in ITS Conference, Hawaii (2014)
5. Consortium Claroline, Claroline, http://claroline.net/type/clarolinev (January 2014)
6. Butakov, S., Smolin, D.: Integration platform for a learning environment. In: 2013 IEEE 13th International Conference on Advanced Learning Technologies (ICALT). IEEE July 2013
7. Bokhari, M.U., Ahmad, S.: Detailed analysis of existing multi-agent based e-learning systems. In: 2014 International Conference on Computing for Sustainable Global Development (INDIACom). IEEE March 2014
8. Bhaskaran, S., Swaminathan, P.: Intelligent adaptive e-learning model for learning management system. Int. J. Technol. Policy Manag **14**, 99–109 (2014)
9. Chen, Z.-H., Chen, S.Y.: When educational agents meet surrogate competition: impacts of competitive educational agents on students' motivation and performance. Comput. Educ. **75**, 274–281 (2014)

Multi-agent System for Knowledge-Based Recommendation of Learning Objects Using Metadata Clustering

Paula Rodríguez[1(✉)], Néstor Duque[2], and Demetrio A. Ovalle[1]

[1] Universidad Nacional de Colombia Sede Medellín, Medellín, Colombia
{parodriguezma,dovalle}@unal.edu.co
[2] Universidad Nacional de Colombia Sede Manizales, Manizales, Colombia
ndduqueme@unal.edu.co

Abstract. Learning Object (LO) is a content unit being used within virtual learning environments, which -once found and retrieved- may assist students in the learning process. Such LO search and retrieval are recently supported and enhanced by data mining techniques. In this sense, clustering can be used to find groups holding similar LOs so that from obtained groups, knowledge-based recommender systems (KRS) can recommend more adapted and relevant LOs. In particular, prior knowledge come from LOs previously selected, liked and ranked by the student to whom the recommendation will be performed. In this paper, we present a KRS for LOs, which uses a conventional clustering technique, namely K-means, aimed at finding similar LOs and delivering resources adapted to a specific student. Obtained promising results show that proposed KRS is able to both retrieve relevant LO and improve the recommendation precision.

Keywords: Clustering techniques · Learning objects · Metadata · Multi-agent systems · Recommendation systems

1 Introduction

The Learning Objects (LOs) differ from the traditional learning resources because of its immediate availability at Web-based repositories. LO can be located and accessed through their own metadata for educational purposes on virtual learning [1]. Generally, LO are stored on Learning Objects Repositories (LOR), which in turn are joined to form a repository federation for sharing and accessing the resources from each other [2]. Likewise, a Recommendation System (RS) is defined as a piece of software that facilitates users to discern more relevant and interesting learning information from LORs [3]. Multi-agent Systems (MAS)-being emergent computing approaches-are widely spread in several e-learning areas providing solutions for complex and restrictive systems. In contrast with conventional computing approaches, MAS has special features such as customization, intelligence, accessibility, safety, task distribution, decision making, among others [4].

Currently, data mining techniques classifying or clustering data have shown to be useful for the process of retrieving high-quality information that is delivering relevant

J. Bajo et al. (Eds.): PAAMS 2015 Workshops, CCIS 524, pp. 356–364, 2015.
DOI: 10.1007/978-3-319-19033-4_31

items to a specific user [5]. In particular, clustering aims to divide data into subsets of similar instances [6], having the advantage of not requiring a prior supervised knowledge on the underlying classes or groups to carry out the clustering or classification task. Instead, only the number of resultant groups and few initial parameters are required. Formally, clustering is the process is grouping homogeneous patterns using no any information about the nature of clusters contained in the data set [7]. Within the recommendation systems (RS) context, clustering can be used to find similar learning objects so that RS delivers learning-supporting and high-quality educational material to users.

Recent works [8, 9], introduced a model of a hybrid recommendation system for LO, which is based on a MAS having 8 agents, namely three of them are responsible for individually running a recommendation technique (Content-based, Collaboration-based and knowledge-based recommendation).The fourth agent is deliberative that is in charge of applying the hybridization technique. The fifth one is an ontologic agent that infers knowledge from the ontology. Other three agents are employed for communication purposes regarding user and federation of LO repository as well as a web service bridging between MAS and web application. Within this framework, this work proposes an improvement of the behavior of the knowledge-based recommendation agent incorporating the k-means algorithm as a clustering technique aimed at finding subsets of similar LOs previously ranked by students. To do so, a new clustering agent is introduced. Such an agent performs the clustering process over the LO metadata when adding a new LO to the LOR federation. Then, this work constitutes a first model approach for a MAS for knowledge-based recommendation agent using data clustering. Experiments are done using Repository Federation of Learning Objects Colombia-FROAC (available at: http://froac.manizales.unal.edu.co/froac/). For quantifying the retrieval quality, a precision metric is used.

The rest of the paper is organized as follows: Sect. 2 presents the conceptual framework of this research. Section 3 reviews some related works analysis. Section 4 describes the proposed model integrating the clustering techniques and the proposed MAS. Section 5 explains the model validation and the results of the proposed model, through a case study. Finally, the main conclusions and future research directions are shown in Sect. 6.

2 Basic Concepts

Following are the main concepts related to the LO recommendation using clustering techniques for knowledge-based recommendation.

According to the IEEE, a LO can be defined as a digital entity involving educational design characteristics. Each LO can be used, reused or referenced during e-learning processes with the purpose of generating knowledge and competences based on student's needs. In addition, LO have metadata that describe the educational resources involved and facilitate their searching and retrieval. LOR (LO repositories) are specialized digital libraries for storing LO, i.e., several kinds of heterogeneous educational resources and their metadata. A federation of LOR allows the access of available educational contents from one access point [10].

Recommendation Systems (RS) are a tool aims at providing users with useful information results searched and recovered according to their needs, making predictions about matching them to their preferences and delivering those items that could be closer than expected [11]. In the case of LO, the system should be able to recommend LO adapted to one or more user's profile characteristics using metadata [2].

Knowledge-based recommendation (KRS) attempts to suggest objects based on inferences about a user's needs and preferences. In some sense, all recommendation techniques could be described as doing some kind of inference. Knowledge-based approaches are distinguished in that they have functional knowledge: they have knowledge about how a particular item meets a particular user need, and can therefore reason about the relationship between a need and a possible recommendation. KRS is based on navigation history of a user and in previous elections [12].

Within the context of data mining, clustering techniques are part of the unsupervised methods aimed at data exploring, classifying and hierarchically ordering. These techniques are characterized by requiring no prior information on clusters contained into the data set, that is, they are discriminative type. By contrast, clustering only requires setting some initial parameters or any hint about the nature of data such as the sought number of groups. That said, the main purpose of clustering techniques is grouping homogeneous patterns from a clustering criterion, which is typically based on distances, dissimilarities or densities. Such grouping process is performed using no any supervised information about the underlying clusters [6, 7]. Probably, the most popular clustering algorithm is the so-called *K-means*, which works as follows: Data are considered as geometrical points, which are grouped according to minimal distance between data points and some representative pre-established points named as centroids or centers. The geometrical location of centroids is iteratively updated and refined in such a way that an optimization criterion is fulfilled. For instance, in case of minimum-squares-based clustering, centroids are moved according to a mean square error cost function. Doing so, objects within a cluster are similar to each other, but different from the objects belonging to other groups. Mathematically, a cluster centroid is a central point whose calculation can be done by the arithmetic average as the simplest form. In this work, we use the standard K-means algorithm [6].

3   Related Works

Currently, there are studies on data mining techniques to support adaptive recommendations, although generally used for collaborative filtering-based recommendation and these studies do not use knowledge-based recommendation. Here are some work that are related to the proposal presented in this article.

The work of Park, 2013, aims to reduce error rates of recommendation when a large list of items and some have low scores, but are good elements to the user, are located in a very low place in the list of results; recommendation are applied in a pool of qualified items (popularities) are the scores that are given to items previously by users. To apply the clustering take the items with lower grades and joining elements with higher scores, calling adaptive clustering, in order to give the user elements with low scores [13]. In this paper used a clustering technique to items by popularities, however do not work in a virtual learning environment to deliver educational materials to support student learning based on its previous history. Sabitha et al., used quality metrics to retrieve LO through clustering techniques on student preferences and user profile. This study presents the indicators which measure the LO metadata to perform clustering, in order to recover the fittest through search similar LO groups. So, efficient and relevant provision of LO using data mining techniques can be achieved. Perform user grouping [5]. The research of Anido et al., 2002 the authors say that to make an efficient search we need an efficient description of those resources to be located. This work show GESTALT the broker receives student queries, and tries to find the corresponding resources in other modules. When resources are located, the broker returns them to the user who made the query. The main limitation of this research is that not considered the user profile, therefore no recommendation system [14].

4 Proposed Model

This work proposes a multi-agent system for adaptive LO recommendation as a hybrid recommendation. The search LO result are recommended according to learning style, evaluation by other users and students prior knowledge. Prior knowledge are LO evaluated by students in the past. The LO is retrieved from LOR accessible via web and have descriptive metadata of these objects.

Figure 1 shows the process for generating recommendations based on knowledge, which are the focus of this article.

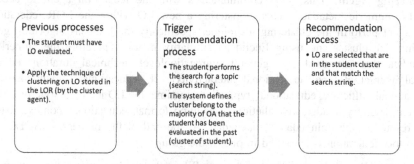

Fig. 1. Knowledge-based recommendation process

The system was built under the MAS paradigm in order to exploit its advantages: the *parallelism* to perform simultaneously recommendation processes, the ability of *deliberation* to decide on which LOs recommend; *cooperation, coordination,* and *distribution of tasks* to clearly identify the problems that must resolve each agent and define their boundaries. GAIA and more-CommonKADS methodologies were used for the analysis and design of MAS. The GAIA methodology used the model of roles, which are associated with responsibilities, permissions, activities and protocols, and the services model [15]. Of the methodology MAS-CommonKADS proposed by Iglesias in his doctoral thesis in 1998, used the seven proposed models [16].

Figure 2 presents the architecture of the MAS proposed, where there are agents presented in previous works and adds a new clustering agent, which is responsible for perform the k-means algorithm, and in this model improves the behavior of the Knowledge-based recommender agent, using the LOs cluster previously generated by the clustering agent.

Then explains the behavior of the agents that were modified in this work.

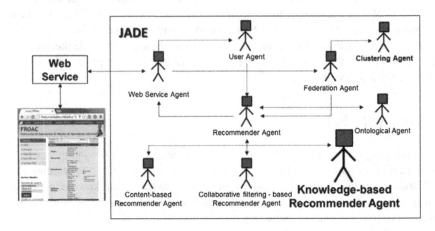

Fig. 2. Proposed architecture

Clustering Agent: This agent communicates with the federation agent to access the LO numeric metadata. When registering a new LO within the LOR federation, this agent perform the clustering technique, specifically the k-means algorithm generating five cluster and using Euclidean similarity metric. Therefore the numerical metadata that are used are: general_aggregationlevel, technical_duration, educational_interactivitytype, educational_interactivitylevel, educational_semanticdensity, educational_difficulty, educational_typicallearningtime, the LO learning style provides (Visual, auditory, reader, kinesthetic), In addition format, educational_context, learning_resource_type, min_edad y max_edad. At the end of the process, each LOs of repository federation is classified in one of the groups.

Knowledge-Based Recommender Agent: When the student enters the system to search resource, this agent located LO ranked in the past with a score equal or greater than 4, scale of 1 to 5, where 5 indicates that LO like the student. Accordingly, LOs belonging to found clusters, which in turn satisfy the searching criteria is the result of the recommendation. Finally this result comes to the process of making hybrid recommendation in the deliberative recommendation agent to be delivered to the user.

The JADE (Java Agent Development Environment) framework was used to perform the prototype implementation that offers a suite of resources to supply the development and implementation of MAS [17]. For this work, we have chosen JADE-LEAP (http://jade.tilab.com/), a FIPA-compliant agent platform that follows international agent communication standards.

5 Case Study

For the case of study to the model proposed knowledge-based recommendation, we extract 10 % of LO metadata from FROAC [10], which constitute the input of the MAS model. In addition students of Computer/Management Information Systems, Universidad Nacional de Colombia, Manizales, belonging to the research group on adapted and intelligent environment -GAIA, were selected to rank the relevance of the recommendation outcomes. The relevance is understood as the importance of LO delivered for carrying out a learning process. Formula 1 is the metric of precision that is commonly used to measure the quality of information retrieval.

$$Precision = \frac{Relevant\ LOs}{Relevant\ LOs + Retrieved\ LOs} \tag{1}$$

Only the result of Knowledge-based recommendation, which is the objective of this work, was taken for this article. Previously students LOs ranked and which constitute prior knowledge. Then delivered them LO results we ask to evaluate if those LO were relevant. Figure 3 shows the result of the clustering technique. Applied the k-means algorithm and selected a $K = 5$.

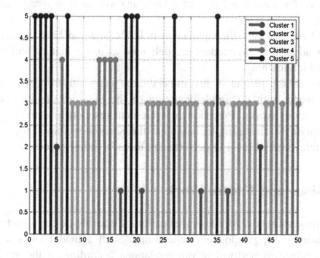

Fig. 3. Result of the clustering technique for each LO

Figure 4 shows the average of the results of the ranked. And Fig. 5 presents the comparison of precision metric using RS, against the choice the student delivered all the stored LO.

A precision metric was applied for performing the LO relevance evaluation. On average, Knowledge-based recommendation recovered around five LO for each student and on average three were relevant, therefore the result of precision was 0.54. If this result is compared, if delivered to the student all LO; i.e. 50 LO are recovered, on

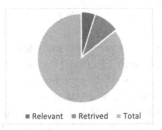

Fig. 4. Average of the LO recovered and LO relevant.

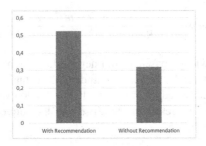

Fig. 5. Precision to use recommendation and without recommendation.

average 16 LO are relevant, then precision is 0.32., and can be concluded that recommendations adapted to the student are delivered as usage history and supports the process of teaching/learning.

Also compared the results of recommendation using clustering techniques, proposed in this work, with the implementation of the measure of similarity overlap, proposed in previous works. Precision measurement resulted in zero. It can be concluded that applying a clustering technique to the Knowledge-based recommendation improves the relevance of the LO delivered in the adaptation process.

6   Conclusions and Future Work

This paper proposes a model for recommendation of learning object, which is based on the MAS paradigm using repository federations. Such a model takes advantage of clustering techniques to perform recommendations according to the student's prior knowledge.

Broadly speaking, the proposed model works as follows: Once grouped all available LOs regarding similar numerical metadata, we seek for the clusters that match to those LOs previously ranked by a student. Accordingly, LOs belonging to found clusters, which in turn satisfy the searching criteria, are delivered. This is done at the moment when a student fills a query form provided by the LOR federation. More specifically, when registering a new LO within the LOR federation, the clustering agent performs its behavior being the k-means procedure. It is important to mention that we use the conventional K-means algorithm, which employs the Euclidean distance as a metric. Experiments are carried out over Repository Federation of Learning Objects Colombia - FROAC (http://froac.manizales.unal.edu.co/froac/). Our model not only slightly improves the precision rate but optimizes the amount and quality of delivered LOs.

As a future work, we are aiming at exploring and incorporating more data mining techniques within MAS, also expand the validation of the system. As well, the model performance is to be improved from an adequate agent behavior configuration.

Acknowledgments. The research presented in this paper was partially funded by the COL-CIENCIAS project entitled: "RAIM: Implementación de un framework apoyado en tecnologías móviles y de realidad aumentada para entornos educativos ubicuos, adaptativos, accesibles e interactivos para todos" of the Universidad Nacional de Colombia, with code 1119-569-34172. It was also developed with the support of the grant from "Programa Nacional de Formación de Investigadores – COLCIENCIAS". Authors thank to Prof. Diego H. Peluffo-Ordóñez as well as PhD. student Juan C. Alvarado-Pérez from Universidad Cooperativa de Colombia-Pasto for provided discussion and contributions on data mining.

References

1. Gil, A., García, F.: Un Sistema Multiagente de Recuperación de Objetos de Aprendizaje con Atributos de Contexto. In: ZOCO 2007/CAEPIA, pp. 1–10 (2007)
2. Li, J.Z.: Quality, evaluation and recommendation for learning object. In: International Conference on Educational and Information Technology (ICEIT 2010), pp. 533–537 (2010)
3. Sikka, R., Dhankhar, A., Rana, C.: A survey paper on e-learning recommender system. Int. J. Comput. Appl. **47**, 27–30 (2012)
4. Ahmad, S., Bokhari, M.: A new approach to multi agent based architecture for secure and effective e-learning. Int. J. Comput. Appl. **46**, 26–29 (2012)
5. Sabitha, A.S., Mehrotra, D., Bansal, A.: Quality metrics a quanta for retrieving learning object by clustering techniques. In: 2012 Second International Conference on Digital Information and Communication Technology and it's Applications (DICTAP) pp. 428–433. IEEE (2012)
6. Jain, A.K.: Data clustering: 50 years beyond K-means. Pattern Recognit. Lett. **31**, 651–666 (2010)
7. Peluffo Ordóñez, D.H.: Estudio comparativo de métodos de agrupamiento no supervisado de latidos de señales ECG (2009)
8. Rodríguez, P.A., Duque, N.D., Ovalle, D.A.: Modelo Integrado de Recomendación de Objetos de Aprendizaje. In: CAVA 2013 – V Congreso Internacional de Ambientes Virtuales de Aprendizaje Adaptativos y Accesibles, pp. 1–6 (2013)
9. Rodríguez M, P.A., Salazar, O., Duque, N.D., Ovalle, D., Moreno, J.: Using ontological modeling for multi-agent recommendation of learning objects. In: Multiagent system based learning environments (MASLE) (2014)
10. Tabares, V., Rodríguez, P., Duque, N., Moreno, J.: Modelo Integral de Federación de Objetos de Aprendizaje en Colombia-más que búsquedas centralizadas. In: Séptima Conf. Latinoam. Objetos y Tecnol. Aprendiz. 3, pp. 410–418 (2012)
11. Mizhquero, K., Barrera, J.: Análisis, Diseño e Implementación de un Sistema Adaptivo de Recomendación de Información Basado en Mashups. Rev. Tecnológica ESPOL-RTE (2009)

12. Vekariya, V., Kulkarni, G.R.: Hybrid recommender systems: survey and experiments. In: 2012 Second International Conference on Digital Information and Communication Technology and it's Applications (DICTAP), pp. 469–473. IEEE (2012)
13. Park, Y.: The adaptive clustering method for the long tail problem of recommender systems. IEEE Trans. Knowl. Data Eng. **25**, 1904–1915 (2013)
14. Anido, L., Fernández, M., Caeiro, M.: Educational metadata and brokerage for learning resources. Comput. Educ. **38**, 351–374 (2002)
15. Wooldridge, M., Jennings, N.R., Kinny, D.: A methodology for agent-oriented analysis and design. In: Proceedings of third Annual Conference Autonomous Agents - AGENTS 1999, Vol. 27, pp. 69–76 (1999)
16. Iglesias Fernández, C.Á.: Definición de una Metodología para el Desarrollo de Sistemas Multiagentes (1998)
17. Bellifemine, F., Poggi, A., Rimassa, G.: JADE – a FIPA-compliant agent framework. In: Proceedings of PAAM 1999 (1999)

Workshop in Intelligent
Human-Agent Societies

Revisiting the Delphi Method for Agents

Jorge J. Gomez-Sanz$^{(\boxtimes)}$ and Ruben Fuentes Fernandez

Universidad Complutense de Madrid, Madrid, Spain
{jjgomez,ruben}@fdi.ucm.es

Abstract. Research on agent interaction has attracted the attention of agent researchers for a long time. This paper revisits an old work to find uses of an argumentation protocol which borrows from social sciences to raise agreements among several agents. In this protocol, several agents discuss and provide a conclusion after some rounds of mutual information exchange. The work is reusing INGENIAS methodology to model and deploy the examples and illustrate benefits of this protocol proposal. It also analyses the requirements of this protocol for its application.

Keywords: Agent interaction · Agent protocol · Delphi method · INGENIAS

1 Introduction

Argumentation among agents [11] is a process intimately related with deliberation. How this argumentation takes place is still a matter of research. Previous work [3,4] studied actual automatic argumentation among experts for producing inter-agent discussion that lead to conclusions. The solution was based on the Delphi method, which was created in the fifties by the by the RAND corporation in Santa Monica (California).

Delphi method has several uses, from forecasting long-term decisions that guide the policy of a country or a company, to consensus reaching among a community of experts [2]. It is the later use what this paper focuses on. By using the Delphi method, individual experts are forced to look at the reasons of other experts. This extra information can force experts to reconsider their opinions and reach agreements. The method assumes there are experts that are consulted and one mediator that produces the consult to be answered. The moderator runs a finite number of rounds. Experts in each round answer a questionnaire the moderator has compiled. After each round, the moderator decides if received answers constitute an agreement. If there is not, the answers from the experts are used to compile a new questionnaire that each expert, again, answer. The hypothesis is that, by collecting information from each expert and reformulating questions, eventually, other experts will considerate arguments and modify their answers too. As a result, an agreement may arise.

The Delphi Process in general can be adapted to the situation. This paper follows the steps and guidelines stated in [1]. The automation of Delphi is considered first as a set of computers and software assisting human experts in the

© Springer International Publishing Switzerland 2015
J. Bajo et al. (Eds.): PAAMS 2015 Workshops, CCIS 524, pp. 367–376, 2015.
DOI: 10.1007/978-3-319-19033-4_32

process. In this line, literature mentions DEMOS [10], which is an on-line discussion system based on Delphi, and Turoff [17], who presents a Delphi method with computer assistance. Holsapple [7] provided a framework based on Delphi methodology. Within this framework the processors (human and/or computer-based) manipulate knowledge resources. This framework is descriptive, but considers and encourages the possibility of computer-based processors integrated in a delphi organisation.

Delphi process has not been applied widely to Multi-Agent Systems (MAS). Previous work [3] proved it benefits plain text document classification. It is our working hypothesis other problems are suitable for this method to be applied. A first step in this direction is identifying requirements for the application of the Delphi method. Another step is the reformulation of the Delphi method with state of the art technologies. The initial work was made with INGENIAS methodology [14] and many improvements have been made since then [5]. Both elements constitute the original contributions of this paper. The Delphi method essence remains, though.

The paper is organized as follows. Section 2 includes some thoughts about the Delphi method itself and why it makes sense for some situations. Section 3 introduces some primitives from the INGENIAS modeling language which may not be known to all readers. They are applied in the Sect. 4 for revisiting the Delphi method definition from [3]. Section 6 contains the conclusions.

2   A Brief Analysis of the Delphi Protocol

The Delphi protocol suites situations where there are questions that may have different valid answer. Though an individual may discover one answer, the Delphi proposes to let experts discuss alternatives and deliver an already discussed answer. Standard protocols do involve a few stages of interaction. Delphi has an inherent loop. It is related to the centralized information exchange to the different experts that the moderator performs.

In this protocol, a client requires an answer to some question. This question has to be one that has possible answers. Examples of questions can be "how can I travel from Madrid to Edinburgh?", "do you recommend to take an airplane from Madrid to Edinburgh?", or "is it expensive to travel from Madrid to Edinburgh?". The question is evaluated by a panel of experts, each one does issue a possible answer. A moderator distributes the question among the experts and collects the answers. A consultation round will be finished either when all experts have delivered an answer or when a timeout is triggered. At the end of each round, the moderator decides whether to stop (pre-arranged number of iterations has been reached without agreement or an agreement has been found before that deadline), or to continue. In the later case, a new questionnaire is elaborated that combines information from experts' answers with the current questionnaire. As a result, the question changes each round; it evolves towards something that experts can agree upon.

In order for Delphi to work as expected, some conditions have to hold:

- The question has to be expressed in a way the experts can analyse and issue an answer.
- It must be possible to issue a different answer to the question.
- Given one valid answer, it must be possible to perform an automated information extraction and produce a new valid question that includes information from the analysed answer.

The experts' opinion convergence depends greatly on the quality of the experts' implementation. It will not be proven in this paper, but, informally speaking, the more they can appreciate subtleties in the question, the more likely to converge. For instance, one may ask "ought I eat cookies?"', and one expert think "you were supposed to be on diet, don't do it"; if the same question is altered after one round with the expert opinion, it could turn out "ought I eat cookies if they are diet ones?", the expert may answer positively.

The question and its answers must be expressed in a suitable formalism that allows their proper analysis. In [3], the experts' panel had as goal to determine if a document was relevant with respect to a particular topic. The question was expressed as a set of words that made up the document whose relevance was going to be evaluated. The answers were a relevance evaluation plus the words that had been found as more significant. The question was modified from round to round by adding those keywords each individual expert highlighted. That way, each round the question was more precise until most of the experts agreed on the evaluation.

3   Introducing the Notation and Expected Semantics

The INGENIAS notation used in this Delphi protocol modeling includes traditional concepts from INGENIAS, but also new ones which have been incorporated in recent contributions. In particular, some elements declaration has been enhanced to suit frequent combination of elements. One example is the combination of task declaration and its responsible role, see Fig. 1(d), which usually was expressed separately.

The semantic from the elements are explained following. Figure 1(a) represent an agent, which is the entity which will be instantiated in runtime to perform actions. The agent will play roles, Fig. 1(f), and acquire the responsibilities associated to it. Agents and roles will be declared within organizations, Fig. 1(c). The organization will be made up of groups, Fig. 1(b), whose members are the agents and roles previously mentioned. The organization is instantiated as information belonging to the agents being part of it. There are further explanations in the Sect. 4, but the key idea is that each agent belonging to an organization knows which other agents belong too to it.

Agents and roles in the organization engage into workflows, see Fig. 1(f). The workflow involves tasks executed by at least two roles. Tasks are connected by

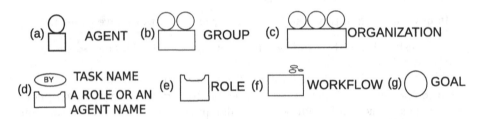

Fig. 1. Summary of INGENIAS modeling notation

either *feeds* or *precedes* relationships. In the first case, it means something created by the first task is used by the second task. In the second case, it implies that the second task will require the first to be executed before. In both cases, the relationship contains the information produced by the first task which is meaningful for the second. The information usually appear with the "++/−" symbol, meaning the first task creates the information, the "++" part, and the second consumes the information, the "−". Tasks and workflows are pursuing goals. Sometimes, a task produces something called *alternative*. This *alternative* represents a possible postcondition of the task. A task can produce always the same elements or declare there are possible sets of elements to be created, the alternatives. A goal, Fig. 1(g), represents a requirement to be satisfied in the system or a state to be achieved. It is used to control the behaviour of the agents.

This notation will be further explained during Sect. 4 using the Delphi specification problem.

4   Simplified Delphi Definition

Our initial work on Delphi method computerisation [3] was using a notation that was too complex. As an example, the *expert* to *monitor* information exchange required a diagram to represent the information exchange, another one to relate the information exchange to expected task execution sequence, and then several more to define individual tasks. With current INGENIAS, the Delphi definition takes less effort and additional issues can be expressed.

Figure 2 introduces the Delphi organisation. A Delphi organisation divides the agents belonging to it into two groups: *experts* and *moderators*. An *expert* role represents an agent capable of issuing opinions about one statement. A *moderator* is a role in charge of interacting with experts and driving the discussion towards specific conclusions. The *client* is a third party, agent belonging perhaps to another organization. The agent playing that role will participate in the workflow *delphi services provider* that regulates a request for a Delphi service. The request will be handled within the organization by the a *moderator*. This *moderator* will receive the request and will enact another workflow to consult the *experts*, the *consulting round* workflow. When the second workflow finishes, its result will be forwarded to the first workflow, but that will be described into Fig. 3.

The request workflow is represented in Fig. 3. The request starts with a *require delphi services* task executed by the *client*. This will provide the *initial*

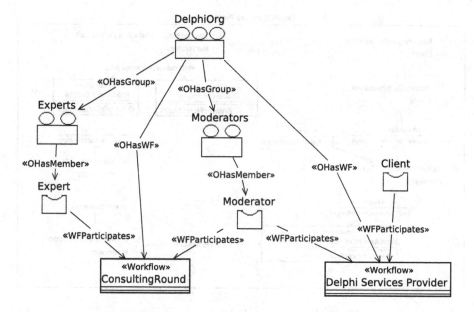

Fig. 2. The Delphi service provider organisation

question to the *moderator*. An *initial question* is a statement, represented by a string, which the client wants an opinion about.

The *moderator* then will decide whether the request is accepted or rejected. The *discard request* alternative contains an *answer from delphi* entity which is forwarded to the client by *deliver answer to client* so that it can be processed by task *process delphi answer*. As an alternative, the same entity *answer from delphi* may come from the result of a successful execution of the delphi consult. This second case is a consequence of the alternative *produce a delphi* produced by *evaluate and produce delphi call* task. The *moderator* produces in this case an *initial question* which triggers the second workflow by means of task *survey experts*. The end of the second workflow is processed by task *end of round decision*.

The *consulting round* workflow, see Fig. 4, has a different cardinality from the one appearing in Fig. 3. The cardinality of this workflow describes there will be one *moderator* and at least one *expert*. Hence, in this workflow, it may be the case that some tasks are executed several times, one per participant. The workflow starts with a *deliver questionnaire* tasks which sends a questionnaire to the different experts. These experts provide with individual answers to the original question, which are collected, by *processQanswer* task, and evaluated, by *end of round decision* task. The later performs analysis of the compatibility of the answers, looking for similarities. This is done with the aid of the helper app *DelphiHelper*. If there is no agreement and the number of rounds has not been supered, a new round is planned, alternative *another round is necessary*.

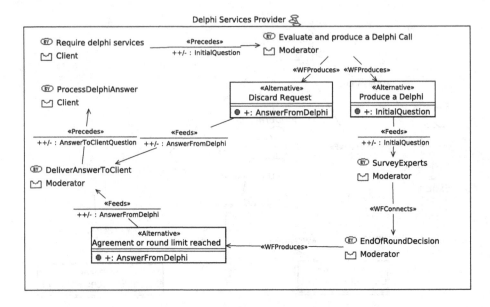

Fig. 3. Requesting a Delphi service execution

The new round uses as starting point another different question that combines previous ones together with experts' feedback.

The roles from Fig. 2 are played by agents which may provide specific implementations for tasks from Fig. 3 or 4. In this case, sample agents are created that play the default roles and, consequently, acquire the capabilities associated to the role. There can be several agent types playing the same role. Their instantiation will be explained later on in Figs. 5 and 6.

The deployment of the agents focus on declaring how are agents instantiated and how many instances per agent type there will be, see Fig. 6. A developer can define several deployments depending on the needs. In this case, the needs are determined by the testing that will check if everything works as expected. The deployment distinguishes between the organization and its members. There is a group instance per group identified in Fig. 2. The group *experts* groups together expert instances. There are four agents playing the *expert* role and two agent types, *expert1* and *expert2*. The group *moderators* include two instances of the *moderator1* agent. There are three additional *clients* that will perform the requests. The association of agent instances to the deployment package is labelled with a name which will be relevant during testing. The important names are *expert*, to designate any expert, *moderator* and *client*, which represents any moderator or client, respectively. These labels will be referred to in Fig. 7 and mean that any agent created will labelled accordingly.

The execution of the protocol may be easier to understand with the aid of workflow tests defined in Fig. 7. The labels cited in Fig. 6 are used to tell which execution sequences are expected. The test *client receives some answer* states

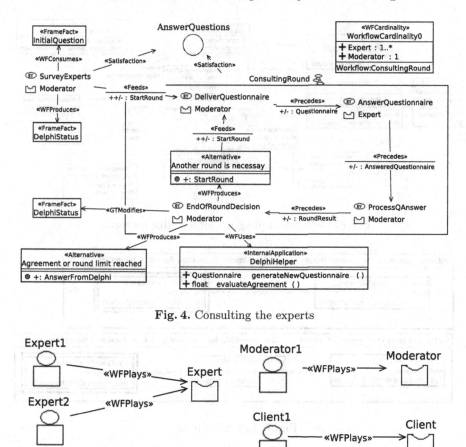

Fig. 4. Consulting the experts

Fig. 5. Agents playing defined roles

that the *client* will first execute *require delphi services* and that the information it provides will be processed further until it leads to *process delphi answer* execution by the *client*. The second test *there is basic involvement of moderator* means that between the *require delphi services* and *process delphi answer* executions, at least, the moderator will execute once the task *end of round decision*. As in the previous case, the task execution will be made using information generated initially by the task *require delphi services*. This time, the *process delphi answer*, will process information that will require to have been previously processed by *end of round decision* and *require delphi services*.

5   Related Work

The work is situated into the domain of argumentative systems but also into agreement technologies.

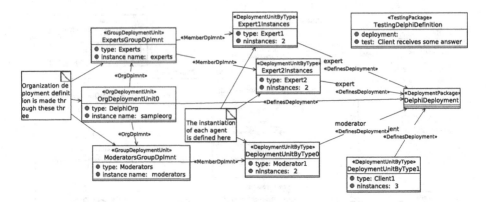

Fig. 6. Deployment of agents for a testing scenario

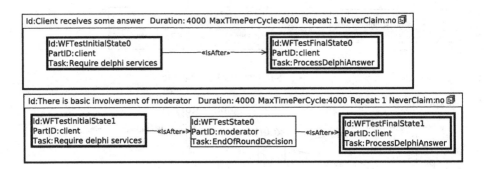

Fig. 7. Execution tests

Original work was compared [3] with consensus reaching algorithms [15] through game theory, the *Byzantine Generals problem* [8] through voting algorithms, or choosing the most frequent answer [6], or using trust and reputation models [16]. The solution from this work requires agents processing questions and producing answers.

Some of the requirements stated in Sect. 2 are similar to those enumerated in the proposal from [12]. Agents in this Delphi method are expected to change their believes along the process. Nevertheless, there is no really any dialogue among experts. There is no question/answer challenge, but a process of enriching the question until some expected outcome, like an agreement, is obtained. Nevertheless, there are elements that can be brought to this Delphi method and improve its understanding, such as stating the dialogue purpose and enabling the self-transformation of the participants.

Agreement technologies [9,13] designates the combination of negotiation, choreography of business processes, trust models, and norms for the purpose of reaching agreements among several agents. In the Delphi method, there is a protocol, but the essence of this method is about information exchange, its evaluation, and intelligent combination.

6   Conclusion

This paper has introduced a revisit of the Delphi protocol introduced in a previous work [3]. The modeling has been remade using current INGENIAS notation and testing services, which enables a simpler, yet richer, description of the problem. The specification is not complete in this problem, but provides essential details to reproduce the protocol elsewhere. Also, as a difference with the initial work, a new analysis has been included about how Delphi method works and what is required to be applied to a different domain.

The advantages of the protocol have been discussed as well. Its applicability to different problems is still a matter of discussion. As starting point, the paper has introduced requirements to be met for using this protocol, as well as some short examples of relevant questions related to the recommendation and decision making situations. Further work is needed to elaborate more specific examples that prove the benefits of this protocol. With one precedent on document classification [3], other domains ought to be studied.

A major issue in this protocol is the formalism used to express the queries to the system and the experts' answers. This formalisms can be an obstacle for some domains if there was none or it did not not suit the purpose of Delphi. It just may not be possible, or too expensive, to combine answers from the experts. For instance, if agents communicate using natural language, there is an implicit language understanding problem which is not solved yet. For Delphi to work, agents need to be able to process the question, elaborate an answer, and the answer cannot be just any. There has to be an algorithm for combining different answers and one question to produce a brand new question. This algorithm depends strongly on the the the nature of the answer.

Despite this limitation, there is still originality in the proposal and domains where it could be applied. This is a work in progress, so it should be expected advances in this line and further evaluation.

Acknowledgement. We acknowledge support from the project "SOCIAL AMBIENT ASSISTING LIVING - METHODS (SociAAL)", supported by Spanish Ministry for Economy and Competitiveness, with grant TIN2011-28335-C02-01 and by the Programa de Creación y Consolidación de Grupos de Investigación UCM-Banco Santander, call GR3/14, for the group number 921354 (GRASIA group).

References

1. Cuhls, K.: Delphi method. Technical report, Fraunhofer Institute for Systems and Innovation Research (2003)
2. Dalkey, N., Helmer, O.: An experimental application of the Delphi method to the use of experts. Manag. Sci. 9(3), 458–467 (1963)
3. García-Magariño, I., Gómez-Sanz, J.J., Pérez-Agüera, J.R.: A complete-computerised Delphi process with a multi-agent system. In: Programming Multi-Agent Systems, 6th International Workshop, ProMAS 2008, Estoril, Portugal, 13 May 2008. Revised Invited and Selected Papers, pp. 120–135 (2008)

4. García-Magariño, I., Gómez-Sanz, J.J., Pérez-Agüera, J.R.: A multi-agent based implementation of a Delphi process. In: 7th International Joint Conference on Autonomous Agents and Multiagent Systems (AAMAS 2008), Estoril, Portugal, 12–16 May 2008, vol. 3, pp. 1543–1546 (2008)
5. Gomez-Sanz, J.J.: Ten years of the INGENIAS methodology. In: Shehory, O., Sturm, A. (eds.) Agent-Oriented Software Engineering, pp. 193–209. Springer, Heidelberg (2014)
6. Hannebauer, M.: Multi-phase consensus communication in collaborative problem solving. In: Proceedings of the Third Workshop on Communication-Based Systems, pp. 131–146. Kluwer (2000)
7. Holsapple, C.W., Joshi, K.D.: Knowledge manipulation activities: results of a Delphi study. Inf. Manag. **39**, 477–490 (2002)
8. Lamport, L., Shostak, R., Pease, M.: The byzantine generals problem. ACM Trans. Program. Lang. Syst. **4**(3), 382–401 (1982)
9. Luck, M., McBurney, P.: Computing as Interaction: Agent and Agreement Technologies, pp. 1–6. Unknown Publisher (2008)
10. Luehrs, R., Pavón, J., Schneider, M.: DEMOS tools for online discussion and decision making. In: ICWE, pp. 525–528 (2003)
11. Maudet, N., Parsons, S., Rahwan, I.: Argumentation in multi-agent systems: context and recent developments. In: Maudet, N., Parsons, S., Rahwan, I. (eds.) ArgMAS 2006. LNCS (LNAI), vol. 4766, pp. 1–16. Springer, Heidelberg (2007)
12. McBurney, P., Parsons, S., Wooldridge, M.: Desiderata for agent argumentation protocols. In: Proceedings of the First International Joint Conference on Autonomous Agents and Multiagent Systems: Part 1, AAMAS 2002, pp. 402–409. ACM, New York (2002)
13. Ossowski, S.: Agreement Technologies, vol. 8. Springer Science & Business Media, Netherlands (2012)
14. Pavón, J., Gómez-Sanz, J.J.: Agent oriented software engineering with INGENIAS. In: Mařík, V., Müller, J.P., Pěchouček, M. (eds.) CEEMAS 2003. LNCS (LNAI), vol. 2691, pp. 394–403. Springer, Heidelberg (2003)
15. Rosenschein, J.S., Zlotkin, G.: Rules of Encounter: Designing Conventions for Automated Negotiation Among Computers. MIT Press (1994)
16. Sabater, J., Sierra, C.: Reputation and social network analysis in multi-agent systems. In: Proceedings of the First International Joint Conference on Autonomous Agents and Multiagent Systems: Part 1, pp. 475–482 (2002)
17. Turoff, M., Hiltz, S.R.: Computer based Delphi processes. In: Gazing into the Oracle. The Delphi Method and Its Application to Social Policy and Public Health, pp. 56–85. Jessica Kingsley Publishers, London (1996)

Applying a Social Emotional Model in Human-Agent Societies

J. A. Rincon[✉], V. Julian, and C. Carrascosa

Departamento de Sistemas Informáticos y Computación (DSIC),
Universitat Politècnica de València, Camino de Vera s/n, Valencia, Spain
{jrincon,vinglada,carrasco}@dsic.upv.es

Abstract. The purpose of this paper is to present the applicability of the *JaCalIVE* framework for developing human-agent societies. This kind of applications are those where virtual agents and humans coexist and interact transparently into a fully integrated environment. Specifically, the paper presents an ambient intelligence application where humans are immersed into a system that extracts and analyzes the emotional state of a human group. This social emotion is employed in order to try to maximize the welfare of that humans by playing the most appropriate music in every moment.

1 Introduction

Over the last few years trends in Ambient Intelligence (AmI) based on intelligent systems, have not had much success. There are two main reasons as the cause of this problem. First, intelligent systems have not reached the maturity level of other information technologies, and for a long time, they have forgotten traditional industry [1]. On the other hand, it is required an interdisciplinary perspective, which is hard to achieve, since a considerable amount of available resources (scientific, economic and human) would be required.

Agent technology, although still immature in some ways, allows the development of systems that support the requirements of AmI applications. Specifically it allows the formation and management of systems where the main components can be humans and software agents providing services to humans or other agents in an environment of whole integration. This kind of applications are what we call a *Human-Agent Society* [2], which can be defined as a computing paradigm in which the traditional notion of application disappears. Rather than developing software applications that accomplish computational tasks for specific purposes, this paradigm is based on an immersion of the users in a complex environment that enables computation. Nevertheless, working with humans is complex, they use emotions in their decision making. Human beings manage themselves in different environments, either in the working place, at home or in public places. At each one of these places we perceive a wide range of stimuli, that interfere in our commodity levels modifying our emotional levels. These variations in our emotional states could be used as information useful for machines. Nevertheless,

© Springer International Publishing Switzerland 2015
J. Bajo et al. (Eds.): PAAMS 2015 Workshops, CCIS 524, pp. 377–388, 2015.
DOI: 10.1007/978-3-319-19033-4_33

it is needed that the machines will have the capability of interpreting or recognizing such variations. This is the reason for implementing emotional models that interpret or represent the different emotions.

Our proposal is to employ the emotional state of a group of agents (humans or not) in an AmI application. Concretely, we propose in this paper a system for controlling automatically the music which is playing in a bar. The main goal of the DJ is to play music making that all individuals within the bar are mostly as happy as possible. Each of the individuals will be represented by an agent, which has an emotional response according to his musical taste. That is, depending on the musical genre of the song agents will respond varying their emotional state. Moreover, varying emotions of each agent will modify the social emotion of the group. The application has been developed using *JaCalIVE* framework [3], which is a framework for the design and simulation of intelligent virtual environments (IVEs). This framework differs from other works in the sense that it integrates the concepts of agents, humans, artifacts and physical simulation. Besides, IVEs developed using the *JaCalIVE* framework can be easily modified thanks to the XML modellation and the automatic code generation. The main reason to employ *JaCalIVE* is that allows an easy integration of human beings in the system. This framework can be downloaded from this url: http://jacalive. gti-ia.dsic.upv.es.

The rest of the paper is organized as follows. Section 2 presents the related work which motivates this proposal. Section 3 shows the main characteristics of the *JaCalIVE* framework. Section 4 explains the proposed AmI application. Finally, some conclusions are presented in Sect. 5.

2   Related Work

Ubiquitous computing and ambient intelligence [4,5] changed the concept of smart home, introducing new devices that help to improve the quality of life of people. Devices that learn our tastes, smart homes that help reducing energy consumption [6], safer homes for elderly [7,8], among other applications. To achieve this, ambient intelligence and ubiquitous computing employ different artificial intelligence tools, sensor networks, mobile internet connections and new and sophisticated embedded devices. Ambient Intelligence (AmI) imagines a future where technology surrounds users [9], and helps them in their daily lives. The AmI scenarios described by the Information Society Technologies Advisory Group (ISTAG) exhibit intelligent environments capable of recognizing and responding to the presence of different individuals in a simple, non-intrusive and often unseen way [10]. AmI is heavily based on the concept of Ubiquitous Computing (UC), introduced by Weiss in the 90s, which describes a world where a multitude of computational objects communicate and interact in order to help humans in daily activities [11]. The main aim of AmI systems is to be invisible, but very useful. This raises three requirements for AmI based systems [8]: (i) the technology should be transparent to users, (ii) the services must be adapted to the context and user preferences, (iii) applications must provide intuitive and user-friendly interfaces. Those kind of systems represent an immense and ever-growing multi-disciplinary area of research and development. It brings a huge technological innovation and impact for the citizens and society as a whole. Because it is integrative, the SE technology has recently grown along with various disciplines including sensing technologies, wireless networking, software products and platforms, artificial intelligence, data analytics, human-computer interfaces, etc. We can detect a lack of research on how to use the existing technology to the best possible effect. The automatic recognition of human activities (i.e. emotions), as well as abnormal behaviours, is an obvious prerequisite for new AmI applications, and requires novel methods to improve recognition rates, enhance user acceptance, and preserve the privacy of monitored individuals. These are challenging issues, which must be addressed.

Similar to ambient intelligence and ubiquitous computing, the main challenge to achieve real human-agent societies lies in the design and construction of intelligent environments, in which humans interact with autonomous, intelligent entities, through different input and output devices. This means that there are two layers in which humans interact within the environmental and ubiquitous computing intelligence. The first layer is the real world where the human being interacts with other humans and with real objects. The second layer is a virtual layer in which humans interact with virtual entities and objects. This latter layer will be inhabited by intelligent entities (agents), which must be able to perform the different human orders. These virtual environments where agents are involved, are known as intelligent virtual environments or *IVE*.

An IVE [12], is a 3D space that provides the user with a collaboration, simulation and interaction with software entities, so he can experience a high immersion level. This immersion is achieved through detailed graphics, realistic physics, artificial intelligence (AI) techniques and a set of devices that obtain information from the real world. The *JaCalIVE* framework enables the design, programming and deployment of systems of this kind. In these *IVE's* exist different entities, which perform specific tasks. The framework facilitates to find agents in charge of accessing databases, agents which control some kind of complex object and agents which represent humans. These agents are in charge of serving as a wrapper between the real world and the virtual world. They help humans to interact with other virtual entities, which can be representations of other humans or entities performing some control in the real world. This allow humans a transparent interaction in both real and virtual environments. In order to allow agents to interact with the real world, it is necessary that these agents have access to specific devices which allow to collect real-world information. Devices such as cameras, Kinect, microphones allow agents to perceive the environment improving their interaction. Next section introduces how to use the proposed *JaCalIVE* framework.

3   JaCalIVE (Jason Cartago implemented Intelligent Virtual Environment)

In the last years, there have been different approaches for using MAS as a paradigm for modelling and engineering IVEs, but they have some open issues: low generality and then reusability; weak support for handling full open and dynamic environments where objects are dynamically created and destroyed.

As a way to tackle these open issues, and based on the MAM5 meta-model [13], the *JaCalIVE* framework was developed [14]. It provides a method to develop this kind of applications along with a supporting platform to execute them.

The presented work has extended both the MAM5 meta-model along with the *JaCalIVE* framework to develop Human-Agent Societies, that is, to include the human in the loop.

MAM5 allows to design an IVE as a set of entities that can be virtually situated or not. These entities are grouped inside Workspaces (*IVE Workspaces* in the case of virtually situated). Entities that are divided into Artifacts (*IVE Artifacts* if situated) and Agents (*Inhabitant Agents* if situated). One new type of situated agents, that is, of *Inhabitant Agents* are *Human-Inmersed Agents*, that model the human inside the system. Figure 1 presents the extended MAM5 meta-model.

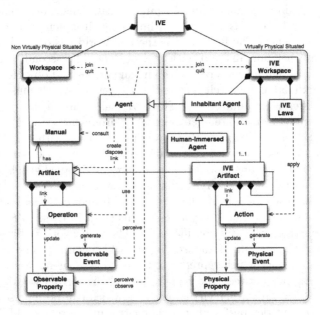

Fig. 1. Extended MAM5 to include Human-Inmersed agents.

Figure 2 shows the steps that should be followed in order to develop an IVE according to the *JaCalIVE* framework:

1. Model: The first step is to design the IVE. *JaCalIVE* provides an XSD based on MAM5 meta-model. According to it, an IVE can be composed of two different types of workspaces depending on whether they specify the location of its entities (IVE_Workspaces) or not (Workspaces). It also includes the specification of agents, artifacts and the norms that regulate the physical laws of the IVE Workspaces.

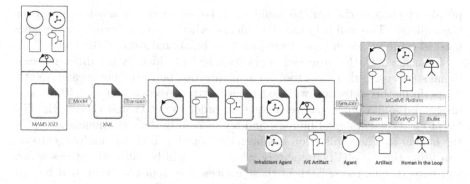

Fig. 2. General scheme, JaCalIVE

2. Translate: The second step is to automatically generate code templates from design. One file template is generated for each agent and artifact. $JaCalIVE$ agents are rational agents based on JASON. The artifacts representing the virtual environment are based on $CArtAgO$. The developer must complete these templates and then the IVE is ready to be executed.
3. Simulate: Finally the IVE is simulated. As is shown in Fig. 2, $JaCalIVE$ platform uses JASON[1], CArtAgO[2] and JBullet[3]. JASON offers support for BDI agents that can reason about their beliefs, desires and intentions. $CArtAgO$ offers support for the creation and management of artifacts. JBullet offers support for physical simulation. $JaCalIVE$ platform also includes internal agents (JASON based) to manage the virtual environment.

4   Case Study

4.1   Problem Description

The developed application is centered in the analysis of the emotional state of a group of people trying to improve their emotional state through the use of music as a way to influence in the human mood. Concretely the example has been developed in a bar, where there is a DJ in charge of playing music and a specific number of persons listening that music. The main goal of the DJ is to play music making that all the people within the bar are mostly as happy as possible.

In an specific moment, each one of the persons placed in the bar will have an emotional response according to his/her musical taste. That is, depending on the musical genre of the song, people will respond varying their emotional states. Moreover, varying emotions of each person will modify the social emotion of the group. If the DJ could have a way to evaluate the emotional state of the

---

[1] http://jason.sourceforge.net/wp/.
[2] http://cartago.sourceforge.net.
[3] http://jbullet.advel.cz.

people which is in the bar, he could know the effect that the songs have over the audience. This will help the DJ to decide whether to continue with the same musical genre or not in order to improve the emotional state of the group.

In such a way, the proposed application seeks to identify the different emotional states using them as a tool of communication between humans and agents. To perform this detection we need to use pattern recognition algorithms and image and audio processing techniques in order to detect and classify the different emotional states of humans and try to modify the environment in which the human is. The application has been developed as a virtual multi-agent system using the JaCalIVE framework where there will be different entities which will have specific roles. Each of these entities may represent from real human beings, agents that mimic humans and a DJ agent. The main characteristics of the proposed agents are defined in the following subsection.

4.2 Application Design

The application is composed of two types of entities, a DJ agent which is the responsible of playing the music and different agents that represent humans who are inside the bar (Fig. 3). The main tasks of these agents are:

- DJ agent: it is in charge of selecting and playing music in the bar. The main goal of this agent is to achieve a emotional state of happiness for all of the people which are in the bar. When the DJ agent plays a song, it must analyze the emotional state of people. According to this analysis it will select the most appropriated songs in order to improve, if possible, the current emotional state of the audience.
- Human-immersed agent: it is in charge of detecting and calculating the emotional state of an individual which is in the bar. This information will be sent to the DJ agent using a subscription protocol. In order to accomplish its tasks, this agent must have access to a variety of input/output information devices as cameras, microphones, ...

In order to facilitate the access to this kind of devices, they have been modeled as artifacts (as can be seen in Fig. 3)[4]. Concretely, there has been designed an artifact for managing each camera which allow the face detection; each microphone is managed by an artifact which captures the ambient sound in order to classify the music genre; the music DB has been designed as an artifact employed by the DJ agent (it stores around 1.000 songs classified by genres) and there is an artifact for controlling the multimedia player and the amplifiers for playing songs in the bar with the appropriated volume.

Within the environment there exist some agents that allow humans to be immersed in the *MAS* generating, what we call, a human-agent society (*HAS*).

---

[4] In this Figure and in the following ones, we are using data from a simple example with only 3 Human-Immersed Agents.

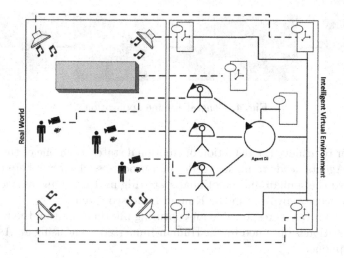

Fig. 3. General scheme of the application

There are also others agents within the environment that do not represent humans (*inhabitant agents*) and, also, there are artifacts (*IVE Artifacts*). On the other hand there are agents and artifacts that do not have a physical representation within the environment, as the music database and the DJ agent.

Each one of these entities has been designed using *JaCalIVE* through an XML file describing all its different properties (including physical ones). The XML file allows to describe if you need some kind of sensor to capture information, some type of actuator or simply an agent that does not need real-world information. It is also in this XML where humans are associated with each agent. These XML files are automatically translated into code templates using the *JaCalIVE* framework.

4.3   Implementation

The present application has two different type of agents, as commented above: DJ Agent and Human-Inmersed Agent. Due to space limitations, this section focuses in the Human-Immersed Agent details.

Regarding the DJ Agent, this agent uses the information sent by the Human-Immersed Agent to analyze the group's emotional state, using it to decide which is the following song to play. The goal of the DJ Agent is that all the humans feel as happy as possible. To achieve this, each of the agents representing humans will communicate their emotional state. It is necessary to provide each Human-Inmersed Agent with a series of tools so that the DJ agent would be able to know the emotional state of each human. Those tools will help Human-Immersed agents to perceive the real environment, to interpret human it has associated and be able to classify the different emotional states this human expresses. So, each one of these agents contains both audio processing and image recognition algorithms.

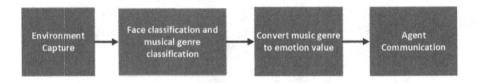

Fig. 4. General scheme application

In order to achieve the detection of emotional states, each one of the Human-Inmersed Agents needs to make a series of 4 processes which will help the agent to recognize the human and emotional state. Figure 4 gives an overview of the different processes involved in the Human-Inmersed Agent.

The first process is responsible for capturing information from the real world. This information is obtained by the Human-Immersed agent using an *Asus Xtion* and microphone.

The second process is responsible of extracting the most relevant information, using the different images and ambient sounds. This information allows us to make two steps, the first one is a face detection using the Viola Jones algorithm [15]. The Human-Immersed Agent uses these images to classify the different humans and so identify the human associated to him.

The images detected and extracted by the Viola Jones algorithm are resized to $92x112$. Each one of these matrices is transformed to a uni-dimensional vector. This vector is formed by concatenating the rows of the image matrix, so for a $92x112$ image it will have 10304 elements. All the image vectors are grouped forming a matrix (each vector is one row) of NxM, where N represent the number of images and M is the maximum amount of pixels of the initial images. Clearly this new matrix is very big and the number of values is more than is required (Fig. 5).

Once you have the NxM matrix with all the images of our data set, it is necessary to reduce dimensionality. The Principal Component Analysis algorithm (PCA) allows us to perform this task, reducing our dimensionality as can be checked in Table 1.

This new matrix is used with the K-Means algorithm to partition it into k groups (Fig. 6). This is a fast method to determine if the face seen by the agent is the same which has been associated to him. Nevertheless, this does not mean

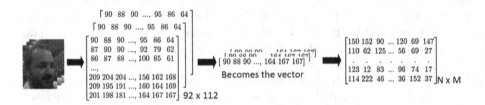

Fig. 5. Processed image

Table 1. Comparison between applying or not PCA to image processing.

	n-Image (N)	pixels (M)
Without PCA	30	10304
With PCA	30	2

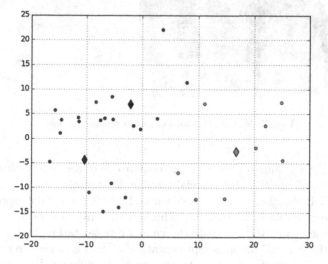

Fig. 6. Face clusters identified in the example of the application.

you can not use other more complex face recognition algorithms such as using support vector machines [16], or neural networks [17], among others.

The second step of the second process is to capture the ambient sound to classify the music genre. To make it possible the Human-Immersed Agent uses its microphone to capture the ambient sound. There are different possibilities in the literature to classify music [18,19]. The Human-Immersed Agents use an statistical classifier [20] to decide which musical genre fits with the input song from ten different genres: blues, country, electronic music, funky, heavy metal, pop music, rock, soul, and tropical music.

The third process uses the information obtained by the musical genre classifier to obtain the new emotional value. This emotional value is obtained using a fuzzy logic algorithm, which returns three values corresponding to the *PAD* model [21,22]. To obtain these values, it is necessary to know how the different musical genre influence on the human. This information allows to modify the membership function of the fuzzy logic algorithm. The variation of this membership function depends on the corresponding human musical preferences, e.g. a human can respond favorably to pop music but not to the blues music. This is the reason why it is needed that each human configure its Human-Immersed Agent before using the system, varying the membership function of the fuzzy logic module.

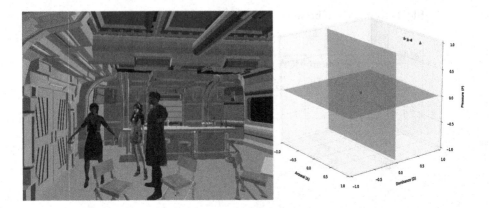

Fig. 7. Virtual Bar and emotion representation.

And finally, the fourth process is the responsible of communicating the emotional state to all entities and especially to the DJ agent.

Figure 7 left shows our bar distribution and how is the virtual representation of the different entities representing a human that lives in the real world. To build it we used Unity3D[5] to create the virtual representation, and used free 3D models for the bar and humans representation[6]. The Fig. 7 right represents the emotions value in the *PAD* space of each one of the different Human-Immersed Agents in the left image.

5   Conclusions and Future Work

Multi-agent systems allow the design and implementation of applications where the main components can be humans and software agents interact and communicate with humans in order to help them in their daily activities. In this sense, this paper presents an ambient intelligence application where humans and agents must coexist in a framework of maximum integration. The application has been developed over the *JaCalIVE* framework allowing an easy integration of the human in the multi-agent system and a visualization of the system in a virtual environment. The proposed system is able to extract (in a non-invasive way) and to analyze the social emotion of a group of persons and it can take decisions according to that emotional state. Future work in this research area will focus on developing a learning module which will allow the DJ agent to anticipate to future emotional states of the people. This module will improve the decision making of the DJ agent comparing current situation with similar previous situations.

---

[5] http://unity3d.com/.

[6] http://tf3dm.com/3d-model/vega-strike-starship-bar-economy-class-88446.html,
http://tf3dm.com/3d-model/alexia-89488.html, http://tf3dm.com/3d-model/dante-33087.html, http://tf3dm.com/3d-model/girl-44203.html.

References

1. Hendler, J.: Where are all the intelligent agents? IEEE Intell. Syst. **22**, 2–3 (2007)
2. Billhardt, H., Julián, V., Corchado, J.M., Fernández, A.: An architecture proposal for human-agent societies. In: Corchado, J.M., et al. (eds.) PAAMS 2014. CCIS, vol. 430, pp. 344–357. Springer, Heidelberg (2014)
3. Rincon, J.A., Garcia, E., Julian, V., Carrascosa, C.: Developing adaptive agents situated in intelligent virtual environments. In: Polycarpou, M., de Carvalho, A.C.P.L.F., Pan, J.-S., Woźniak, M., Quintian, H., Corchado, E. (eds.) HAIS 2014. LNCS, vol. 8480, pp. 98–109. Springer, Heidelberg (2014)
4. Satyanarayanan, M.: A catalyst for mobile and ubiquitous computing. IEEE Pervasive Comput. **1**(1), 2–5 (2002)
5. Mangina, E., Carbo, J., Molina, J.M.: Agent-Based Ubiquitous Computing. Atlantis Press, World Scientific, Amsterdam, Paris (2009)
6. Han, D.-M., Lim, J.-H.: Smart home energy management system using IEEE 802.15. 4 and zigbee. IEEE Trans. Consum. Electron. **56**(3), 1403–1410 (2010)
7. Intille, S.S.: Designing a home of the future. IEEE Pervasive Comput. **1**(2), 76–82 (2002)
8. Satyanarayanan, M.: Pervasive computing: vision and challenges. IEEE Pers. Commun. **8**(4), 10–17 (2001)
9. Augusto, J.C.: Ambient intelligence: the confluence of ubiquitous/pervasive computing and artificial intelligence. In: Schuster, A.J. (ed.) Intelligent Computing Everywhere, pp. 213–234. Springer, London (2007)
10. Ducatel, K., Bogdanowicz, M., Scapolo, F., Leijten, J., Burgelman, J.-C.: Scenarios for ambient intelligence in 2010. In: Office for Official Publications of the European Communities (2001)
11. Weiser, M.: The computer for the 21st century. Sci. Am. **265**(3), 94–104 (1991)
12. Hale, K.S., Stanney, K.M.: Handbook of virtual environments: design, implementation, and applications. In: Human Factors and Ergonomics. Taylor and Francis (2002)
13. Barella, A., Ricci, A., Boissier, O., Carrascosa, C.: MAM5: multi-agent model for intelligent virtual environments. In: 10th European Workshop on Multi-Agent Systems (EUMAS 2012), pp. 16–30 (2012)
14. Rincon, J.A., Garcia, E., Julian, V., Carrascosa, C.: Developing adaptive agents situated in intelligent virtual environments. In: Polycarpou, M., de Carvalho, A.C.P.L.F., Pan, J.-S., Woźniak, M., Quintian, H., Corchado, E. (eds.) HAIS 2014. LNCS, vol. 8480, pp. 98–109. Springer, Heidelberg (2014)
15. Viola, P., Jones, M.J.: Robust real-time face detection. Int. J. Comput. Vis. **57**(2), 137–154 (2004)
16. Osuna, E., Freund, R., Girosi, F.: Training support vector machines: an application to face detection. In: Proceedings of the 1997 IEEE Computer Society Conference on Computer Vision and Pattern Recognition, pp. 130–136. IEEE (1997)
17. Lawrence, S., Lee Giles, C., Tsoi, A.C., Back, A.D.: Face recognition: a convolutional neural-network approach. IEEE Trans. Neural Netw. **8**(1), 98–113 (1997)
18. Li, T., Ogihara, M., Li, Q.: A comparative study on content-based music genre classification. In: Proceedings of the 26th Annual International ACM SIGIR Conference on Research and Development in Informaion Retrieval, pp. 282–289. ACM (2003)
19. Talupur, M., Nath, S., Yan, H.: Classification of music genre. Project Report for, 15781 (2001)

20. Holzapfel, A., Stylianou, Y.: A statistical approach to musical genre classification using non-negative matrix factorization. In: IEEE International Conference on Acoustics, Speech and Signal Processing, ICASSP 2007, vol. 2, p. II-693. IEEE (2007)
21. Mehrabian, A.: Analysis of affiliation-related traits in terms of the PAD temperament model. J. Psychol. **131**(1), 101–117 (1997)
22. Nanty, A., Gelin, R.: Fuzzy controlled PAD emotional state of a NAO robot. In: 2013 Conference on Technologies and Applications of Artificial Intelligence (TAAI), pp. 90–96, December 2013

A Case-Based Multi-Agent
and Recommendation Environment
to Improve the E-Recruitment Process

Oscar M. Salazar, Juan C. Jaramillo, Demetrio A. Ovalle$^{(\boxtimes)}$,
and Jaime A. Guzmán

Universidad Nacional de Colombia, Sede Medellín, Medellín, Colombia
{omsalazaro,jcjaramilloa,dovalle,jaguzman}@unal.edu.co

Abstract. The current growth of information and communication technologies has promoted the development of tools in order to facilitate the process of e-recruitment; benefiting both recruiters as jobseekers. This paper presents a case-based Multi-Agent System which aims at integrating an ontology in order to select and to recommend adapted jobseekers to the recruiter job postings or vice versa. For this reason, the ontology considers the HR-XML standard for map-ping CVs in order to standardize the knowledge representation. The MAS was designed following the Prometheus Methodology and then a prototype has been implemented. A case study was performed within a testing phase in order to validate our work. As a result of this phase, we can prove the effectiveness of using this kind of technologies in the e-recruitment process.

Keywords: E-recruitment · Recommender systems · Ontologies · HR-XML standard · Case-based reasoning · Negotiation support systems

1 Introduction

The current growth of information and communication technologies has promoted the development of tools in order to facilitate the process of e-recruitment, benefiting both recruiters and jobseekers. The use of electronic means to identify, attract, and select potential candidates (jobseekers) for an employment is called e-recruitment process [1]. The e-recruitment process is a current trend in the Human Resource Management (HRM) field, which has led to a marked change from the traditional approach used by organizations that are characterized as a cyclical, slow, and expensive process [2].

A breakthrough in the e-recruitment process is the consolidation of websites that allows automating the publication of job offers and the postulation of jobseekers, however, although the use of these new technologies has brought benefits in terms of cost reduction related with paperwork, transport, communication, and dissemination of calls, there are still very manual tasks in this process. In addition to this problem, these sites collect a lot of information concerning jobseeker CVs and job offers, which are usually found in different formats. This is the reason why it is impossible to have a well-defined and standardized structure that allows the diffusion, migration and auto-matic analysis of the documents [2, 3].

© Springer International Publishing Switzerland 2015
J. Bajo et al. (Eds.): PAAMS 2015 Workshops, CCIS 524, pp. 389–397, 2015.
DOI: 10.1007/978-3-319-19033-4_34

"From an organization's viewpoint, a typical recruitment process can be divided into four main phases: describing the requirements of the job posting, publishing the job posting, receiving of applications, and final decision making" [4]. However, this is an expensive and slow process. The e-recruitment concept seeks to automate the process using the fast dissemination of electronic documents and information through technological tools like the internet [5]. The main issues associated with this process are related to: electronic CVs, online interviews, online ratings, recommendation and candidate ranking. Thus, e-recruitment becomes a valuable service where organizations can publish job postings and jobseekers can postulate their CVs; furthermore, the jobseekers recommendations should be focused on the organization's needs.

According to Tim Berners-Lee [6] "The Semantic Web is an extension of the current Web in which information has a well-defined meaning, it is understandable by computers and where people can work cooperatively and collaboratively". From this new paradigm, ontologies appear as the means to represent knowledge on the Web in a way that is made readable and usable by computers. "An ontology is the result of selecting a domain and apply the same method to obtain a formal representation containing the concepts and relationships that exist among them" [7]. A Recommender System is a tool aims at providing users with useful information results searched and recovered according to their needs, making predictions about matching them to their preferences and delivering those items that could be closer than expected. To do this, the user's information profile and preferences require to be stored [8].

The aim of this paper is to analyze the HR-XML [9] standard for representing CV through XML files, later propose an ontology that focuses on the design of a semantic description of the HR-XML components. This procedure must be done in order to consolidate a model that allows from inferences made in the ontology, selecting and recommending adapted jobseekers to the recruiter job postings or vice versa. Besides, we also consider the jobseeker profile which describes his/her preferences, needs and limitations. Subsequently, we decide to integrate the ontology with a case-based Multi-Agent System (MAS), due to the research problem is highly distributed, as well as the mobility, communication, and cooperation characteristics of the software agents play an important role for improving the precision and efficiency of the recommendations. The rest of the paper is organized as follows: Sect. 2 presents a brief a description of the concepts and thematic used throughout the article. Section 3 analyzes previous works in the research field and how they relate to our work. Section 4 describes the MAS design and development processes using the Prometheus methodology, whereas Sect. 5 shows the model implementation and validation through the integration of different techniques. Finally, last section presents the concluding remarks and future work.

2   Related Works

This section presents some related works with the research field, and compares them in order to identify their strengths and weaknesses. Several researches have been performed in the e-recruitment field, covering mainly two fronts. The first has focused on development of models to standardize the process of e-recruitment by means of knowledge representation. Whereas the second front, points rather to the development of architectures that attend to improve the automatic selection of jobseekers also known as jobseekers ranking.

In [10] the use of semantic web techniques is proposed in order to reduce to the recruiters, the generated high costs by publishing job postings. As a result, this research proposes an ontology to improve the selection of jobseekers and vacancies, using a semantic matching of a controlled vocabulary. However, this research does not consider important features related to the user's profile, which can be adapted in order to enhance the results for both recruiters and jobseekers.

Dorn et al. Propose in [11] an ontology for human resource management focused on two axes: first, it focuses in a meta-search engine for job postings on web portals. Instead, the second area focuses on the university competition management system, which describes functional and behavioral skills for job postings. However, this research aims to describe concepts related to the needed attitudes and skills to apply for a particular job, obviating the jobseeker requirements.

The research work presented in [12] enhanced the accuracy of the selection algorithm, through the adaptation of job postings to the user's interests and considering the past searches results. This model was developed from a recommendation MAS for search and selection of job postings on the Internet. Due to the model is integrated with several information systems, XML files are used for representation and information exchange. This system is based on an own representation of the contained CVs knowledge. Therefore, the system does not complaint to a information exchange standard, which leads to scalability problems in the integration of new repositories, web portals, and systems information.

E-Gen performs in [13] the classification and analysis of the job postings located in unstructured text (emails, documents, etc.), for the subsequent jobseekers analysis and selection. Machine learning is applied to the problem of ranking jobseekers in [13]. In this paper the problem of jobseekers selection becomes into a regression problem in which the system learns the scoring function in order to sort the selection results. This system is based on the representation structure used by LinkedIn website to extract features from jobseekers using linguistic analysis techniques. Nevertheless, using only one standard could generate scalability problems.

Our research work matches with some of the goals established by the researches presented above in this section. In contrast to them, we propose a new mechanism to represent information, in which user features are considered from jobseeker profiles. In addition, we propose recovery functionalities through software agents allowing to adapt the information, for both recruiters and jobseekers. Finally, we consider a case-based reasoning module to support the decision making process, i.e., the MAS takes into consideration previous experiences in order to deliver better results.

3   MAS Design

Prometheus methodology was chosen to design the MAS, since it supports the development of intelligent agents by non-expert users. It is a practical, complete and detailed methodology. In the same way, Prometheus methodology provides everything that is needed for defining and designing agents and it also consider goals and plans to develop robust and flexible agents [15]. Prometheus consists of three design phases that are developed further on: the system specification phase, the architectural design phase, and the detailed design phase.

System Specification Phase. This phase includes a system overview, specifying the objectives, actors, roles and, use case scenarios. Likewise, the system's interfaces are described based on actions, perceptions and, external data.

During this phase two scenarios were identified: the application for job postings scenario and the publishing job postings scenario: The first scenario's main goal is to postulate the jobseeker CV to the job posting published by the recruiters. Whilst the second seeks to adapt jobseekers CVs to the requirements of a specific job posting.

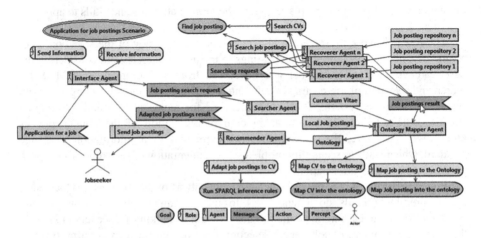

Fig. 1. Analysis overview diagram of job postings application scenario.

The actors are all the people or external systems associated with the MAS. In our system we identify two actors: the jobseeker and the recruiter. Also five types of agents have been identified, in order to achieve the system goals. The interface agent is responsible for managing the communication interfaces with previously identified roles, i.e., it receives the requests and then delivers the responses to these requests. The search agent receives the searching requests and readdresses it to the recoverer agents, who are responsible for performing the searches on the repositories associated to the MAS (there is a recoverer agent for each repository associated with the MAS). Likewise, there is an ontology mapper agent whose task is to map the searching request results within the system's ontology. This ontology will be used by the recommender agent in order to make inferences from SPARQL queries. Also, the ontology allows to standardize the information about the job postings and the CVs, by ensuring the same information transfer scheme, regardless of the formats used by each associated repository. The representation of knowledge by the system ontology is detailed further on. Figure 1 shows the analysis overview diagram of the application for job postings scenario and the goals associated to this scenario.

Finally, this phase includes the hierarchical definition of goals (see Fig. 2). From this specification, we define two high level goals related to the scenarios previously proposed. Lower level goals (related to specific tasks) are distributed among agents in order to achieve the high level goals.

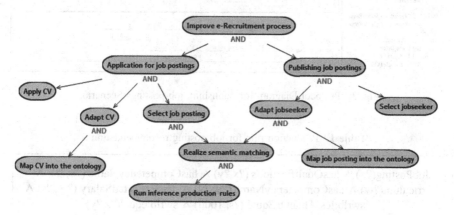

Fig. 2. MAS goal overview diagram

Architectural Design Phase. The purpose of this phase is to define the interactions among the system agents based on the roles defined in the previous phase. The relationship between agents and roles maintains the structure presented in Fig. 2. In addition, Fig. 3 shows the agents interactions protocol intended to perform the goals associated to the publishing job postings scenario and in this way, we must develop the protocol corresponding to all other scenarios.

Detailed Design Phase. During this phase the internal BDI structure of each of the agents is described. Each agent is depicted based on perceptions, actions, capabilities, plans, and information resources.As a result of applying the Prometheus methodology, a highly distributed topology through interconnected nodes was obtained. On the primary node the main platform of the system is located, in which reside the associated agents in charge of executing main system functionalities. Moreover, the connection with child nodes which are external repositories is established.

Recommendation process. The recommendation process consists of two different mechanisms, which are used to adapt the results to the jobseeker needs. As mentioned above, the inferences are performed from the internal structure of the Recommender Agent. The following describes each mechanism:

- **SPARQL Inference Rules.** The first mechanism considers performed inferences through the MAS ontology designed using Methontology methodology [16]. These inferences were developed using production rules that allow to adapt the jobseekers to the job postings and vice versa. Some production rules are presented in Table 1, a rule is composed of multiple matching axioms.

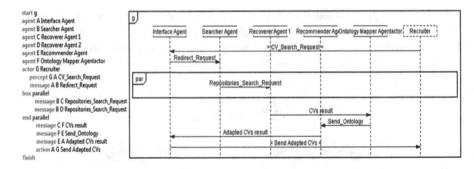

Fig. 3. Protocol Diagram for publishing job postings Scenario.

Table 1. Production rule for job posting recommendation

JobPosting(?x) ∧ hasQualifications (?x,?y) ∧ hasCompetencyName (?x,?z) ∧ Curriculum(?w) ∧ hasCompetencyName (?w,?y) ∧ hasExpectedSalary (?w, ?s) ∧ swrlb:lessThanOrEqual (?s, 1000) ∧ swrlb:equal(?z,?y) → ContenidoSeleccionado(?x)

– **Case-Based Reasoning.** This module comprises a database of previous successful cases in order to make recommendations. Then, each of the successful cases is stored as instances within the same ontology; thereafter, the recommender agent has the ability to infer similar cases based on the availability of vacancies, the availability of CVs and/or some features related to CVs.

– **Similarity percentage and recommendation ranking.** In order to measure the similarity percentage of each recommendation making by the MAS, we consider the Eq. 1. The recommendation ranking is based on the obtained results using the equation.

$$\text{Similarity percentage} : \frac{\text{successful matches}}{\text{possible matches}} \quad (1)$$

4 Model Implementation and Validation

The e-recruitment MAS was implemented using the FIPA complaint JADE Framework. This feature provides interoperability to the platform, what is needed for interconnect platforms and repositories. JADE was developed using JAVA language, this feature allows to integrate the ontology using the JENA framework. It is important to highlight that the ontology was mapped to OWL language by Protégé framework. As a result, SPARQL query language was used to perform inferences from the ontology. This language is supported by the W3C to perform queries on RDF and OWL graphs, thus enhancing the information search and selection on the semantic Web. The represented knowledge by the ontology includes the HR-XML standard for human resource management, the jobseekes profile that describes preferences and limitations, and a case-based reasoning module that will be explained next.

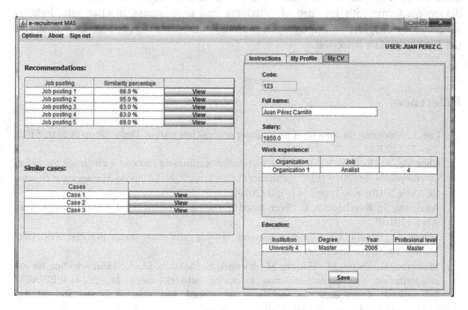

Fig. 4. Recommendation interface for e-recruitment study case

Figure 4 presents the recommendation interface concerning the study case model validation. This interface shows the recommendations made to a logged jobseeker, also it shows the similarity percentage of the CV and the jobseeker profile with the job posting requirements. Finally, the interface presents some successful cases thrown by the case-based reasoning module, which have some relationships with the jobseeker information. The information concerning to the jobseeker profile was previously entered into the MAS in order to set his/her preferences and limitations. Similarly, the jobseeker uploaded his/her CV with related information with the desired positions, expected salary, experience, degrees, among other information defined by the HR-XML standard.

5   Conclusions and Future Work

This research work has enabled the development of a case-based MAS customized recommendation model providing a considerable improvement to the e-recruitment process. As evidence of this, different techniques have been integrated in order to provide successful recommendations by using ontologies that allow to represent and standardize the application domain knowledge. The system validation results show that the use of this kind of techniques allows to adapt both job postings and CVs. Furthermore, the use of case-based reasoning efficiently supports the decision-making process by the organization recruiters.

As future work we pretend to consider more features of the HR-XML standard to make better recommendations. Moreover, we expect to migrate the MAS to a mobile device platform, with the aim of providing real-time access mechanisms. Finally, we attend to integrate an Expert System module that could be used in order to advise the final candidate selection.

References

1. Lee, I.: Modeling the benefit of e-recruiting process integration. Decis. Support Syst. **51**(1), 230–239 (2011)
2. Chounde, A., Keskar, S., Desai, A.: Web based recruitment process: a challenge for indian i.t. companies. In: 2010 IEEE International Conference on Advanced Management Science (ICAMS 2010), vol. 1, pp. 347–350 (2010)
3. Amdouni, S., Bouchoucha, C.: Web-based recruiting. IEEE/ACS Int. Conf. Comput. Syst. Appl. (2010)
4. Maniu, G., Maniu, I.: A human resource ontology for recruitment process. Rev. Gen. Manag. **10**(2), 12–18 (2009)
5. Malherbe, E., Diaby, M., Cataldi, M., Viennet, E., Aufaure, M.-A.: Field selection for job categorization and recommendation to social network users. In: 2014 IEEE/ACM International Conference on Advances in Social Networks Analysis and Mining (ASONAM 2014), pp. 588–595 (2014)
6. Berners-Lee, T., Hendler, J.: Publishing on the semantic web. Nature **410**(6832), 1023–1024 (2001)
7. Tramullas, J., Sánchez-Casabón, J., Garrido-Picazo, P.: An evaluation based on the digital library user: an experience with greenstone software. Procedia - Soc. Behav. Sci. **73**, 167–174 (2013)
8. Li, J.: Quality, evaluation and recommendation for learning object. Int. Conf. Educ. Inf. Technol., no. Iceit, pp. 533–537 (2010)
9. HR-XML Consortium - Leading the Development of HR Integration Standards. http://www.hr-xml.org/. Accessed 12-Dic-2014
10. Bizer, C., Heese, R., Mochol, M., Oldakowski, R., Tolksdorf, R.: The impact of semantic web technologies on job recruitment processes. In: Frestl, O.K., Sinz, E.J. (eds.) Wirtschaftsinformatik 2005, pp. 1367–1381. Physica-Verlag, Heidelberg (2005)
11. Dorn, J., Naz, T., Pichlmair, M.: Ontology development for human resource management. 4th Int. Conf. Knowl. Manag. (2007)
12. De Meo, P., Quattrone, G., Terracina, G., Ursino, D.: An XML-based multiagent system for supporting online recruitment services. IEEE Trans. Syst. Man, Cybern. - Part Syst. Hum. vol. **37**, no. 4, pp. 464–480 (2007)
13. Kessler, R., Torres-Moreno, J., El-Bèze, M.: E-Gen: automatic job offer processing system for human resources. In: MICAI 2007: Advances in Artificial Intelligence, vol. 4827, pp. 985–995. Springer, Berlin Heidelberg (2007)

14. Faliagka, E., Ramantas, K.: Application of machine learning algorithms to an online recruitment system, no. c, pp. 215–220 (2012)
15. Giorgini, P., Henderson-Sellers, B.: Agent-oriented methodologies, IGI Global (2005)
16. Holanda, O., Isotani, S., Bittencourt, I., Elias, T., Tenório, T.: JOINT: Java ontology integrated toolkit. Expert Syst. Appl. 40(16), 6469–6477 (2013)

Ethic Design for Robotics: Place Man and Cultural Context on the Center of the Project: Case Study on Robotics in Museums

Claudio Germak[(✉)], Luca Giuliano[(✉)], and Maria Luce Lupetti[(✉)]

Politecnico di Torino, Turin, Italy
{claudio.germak,luca.giuliano,
maria.lupetti}@polito.it

Abstract. A reflection about Roboethics and its declinations has been conducted starting from the analysis of the robot semantic and the cultural perception that has arisen towards these machines. The analysis faces also the meanings, the technological limits and the expectations about Robotics today, laying the foundations to define a design approach that put the man at the centre of the project, with its community and the context. As a case study is introduced Virgil, example of museum robotic activity carried out in the spirit of ethic design for a specific Cultural Heritage, which consist in the Savoia's Royal Residences, in Piedmont, Italy.

Keywords: Robo ethics · Ethic design · Rights · HRI

1 Evolution of the Idea of Robot: Between Science Fiction and Real Applications

The idea of robots conceived as mechanical replicas of man rooted in the collective imagination has recently celebrated its ninetieth birthday. It was, in fact, the 25th of January 1921 when the term "robot" was introduced for the first time into the theatrical drama "RUR" (Rossum's Universal Robots) by Karel Čapek. The Czech writer used the term robot for indicate independent artificial beings whose purpose was to do tasks that were considered too much tiring for men. Establishing a first but still valid today ethical principle.

Man's desire to replicate his physical and cognitive characteristics through robots goes much further back than Čapek's play, but it was in the 20th century, with the advent of the first computers, that the idea of a future collaboration between artificial intelligence and human nature began to take place.

These relationships are expressed in terms of cooperation and competition, generating in this way an oxymoron. On one side man accelerates the exploration on the mind uploading (transfer of consciousness in non biological artefact) [7], on the other side, man is frightened of the speed with which the robotics civilization is entering into the everyday life of people [8].

© Springer International Publishing Switzerland 2015
J. Bajo et al. (Eds.): PAAMS 2015 Workshops, CCIS 524, pp. 398–408, 2015.
DOI: 10.1007/978-3-319-19033-4_35

Before the fiction of Čapek this subject has been treated for several times, for example, in the works of Jules Verne (1870 ca), where is possible to find not only authentic androids, but also machines able to conduct actions dictated by a human-like consciousness. But, even before these, in 1818, the novel "Frankenstein" by Mery Shelley, highlighted the relationship between man and his invention. On the anthropological side the creature created by doctor Frankestein is a monster, or rather something supernatural created through electricity (the use of this physical phenomenon was not usual, in fact, a little later, electricity would have become very popular thanks to the born of the light bulb). On ethical side, contrariwise, Frankenstein's monster is a dangerous subversive, who represent the revolt of the artificial construct against mankind and nature, generating fear from the technological device that becomes indomitable and it is totally out of control. It has been necessary to wait Isaac Asimov's laws on robotics to change radically the perspective of cohabitation between man and robot.

With the progress of technological systems, the robot has become soon a friend and helper, namely a creature so evolved to has rights and duties in society. The science fiction in this way is anyway a training ground for thought.

On one hand, science fiction books often allow readers to transcend the limits of technological innovations, influencing and suggesting alternative possibilities of structuring reality (Cognitive estrangement) [12].

On the other, the products of this literature are focused on the critique investigation on the scientific evolution and its repercussion on society [17].

The robot, therefore, is not just the result of technological achievement, but also of the careful exam on the technological reflections about the cultural context on which it operates. Today the ambition of robotics is no longer only to perform androids who walk, who talk and who are indistinguishable from human being. The robots embody a new form of link between the physical world and the digital universe, allowing people to move very forward in the cognitive analysis. It is useful to understand not only how humans interact with the robot, but also how the robot perceives the world, assigning a value to what it has around in order to act to determinate a change. New generation robotics requires a high sense of ethical responsibility and critical evaluation from who design the activities (the planning of the service function that is offered by the robotic device). In addiction, the design of the robotic artefact plays a key role on the man perception of the service so, in this perspective, designers can be fundamental to the robotics development. Common interest is to design artefacts that could be recognizable by the society for a specific use in a given situation. To achieve this aim it is, then, necessary to involve the end user right from the start of the project (man on the centre of the project) [6], taking into account those generic needs that will become specific requirements for the project.

2   From Interaction to Ethics

The robots in the future will be more and more interactive with the man, with whom they will share spaces both physical and digital.

In the interaction between humans and robots it is important to refer the user's system of ethics, empathy and action and to the relations created between user and the device.

The current limited presence of robotic equipment in our everyday lives does not, however, favour certain forecasts on the possible forms of behaviour that people can implement in relation to robots. It is, therefore, necessary to explore different fields of research from those of robotics, for example computer science, to investigate these aspects of interaction.

It is on these assumptions that the TAM methods [2] are based, which summarise the relationship between man and technology in three factors:

- Perceived functionality;
- Form and appearance;
- Social ability;

Modelling robotic activities on these three factors, it is possible to achieve very high acceptance results (first phase of the interaction). We have to add the analysis of the user's cultural and territorial background to these so that a robot is not seen exclusively as a friendly identity but more as a really useful tool (second phase of the interaction). Breaking down the interaction into these three factors and comparing the robot to a highly evolved technological device is not the only way to investigate the interaction between man and robot. In sector-specific literature there are various others keys of reading. An interesting point of view in relation to the way in which mankind and its relationship with technology are progressing is offered by Hooker, according to whom the man-robot interaction can be compared to the master-slave relationship [13]. To better understand this claim, it is necessary to introduce the Human agency concept; which is the inalienable right to freely apply their own decision making capacity.

The Human agency concept is based, therefore, on 2 assumptions:

- The ability to make choices;
- The ability to make these choices executive in the world.

Depriving a slave of agency ability means depriving him of the ability to choose, to act, and to show intentionality in behaviour. Extending this concept on robotics, Hooker, suggest that, in the moment in which an agency ability is assigned to a robot, then, under an ethical point of view, it is also necessary to guarantee to that robot the same rights of the human beings. The idea of professor Hooker is not that robots and humans have to be considered equal, but, rather, that if the agency ability starts to be attributed to robotics beings then treating them unjustly, means acting in a way morally incoherent compared to the human ethics itself.

The issue is widely important and generates the following questions, to which, for now, is hard to give answers and are:

1- will affect the moral balance of the people by the way in which the robot will be treated?
2- is there the risk that social interactions of high level that people have with robots, could change the way in which social high-level interactions, between people themselves, are handled?

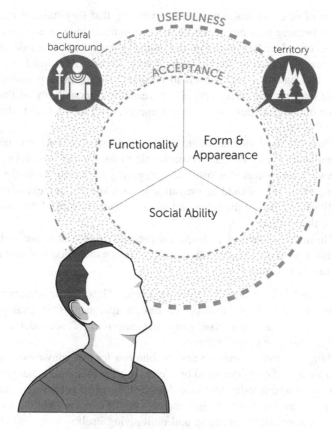

Scheme 1. Interaction factors

3 Roboethics and Ethic Design

Robotics is a rising science, born by the merging of many disciplines belongings to the humanities and natural ones. In 2003 GianMarco Veruggio conceived the concept and the world Roboethics [18], for indicate the positive relationship that should exist between robotics designer, manufacturer, users and intelligent autonomous devices, defining a complex relationship that links humans and robots. In according with Veruggio, before facing the problem of the artificial ethics, it needs to be increased the public awareness about the robotics issues; in order to allow the society to take an active part in the process of creation of a collective consciousness able to identify and prevent technological misuses. The ethical, social and legal questions established by robotics fall into the general framework about correct the use of the scientific and technological products, and are related to the responsibilities of designers and users in the application of use of these sophisticated technologies.

Following this line of thinking, concerning the ownership of responsibility the first question that arises is: if the machine causes damage, who is responsible?

In the case of machine learning devices, meaning that they have to exhibit intelligent behavior because they are operating in environments little or less structured, the answer is more complex. It is therefore necessary to think and act for degrees.

First condition of roboethics thinking: in order to discuss of artificial ethics must be developed a valid human ethics related to robotics. The main responsibility of this challenge falls onto robotic designers, as has been the responsibility of the physicist start the debate on the peaceful use of nuclear energy, or of the biologists deal with the many issues of bioethics.

Second condition of roboethics thinking (it comes from the first): it is necessary to structure a multidisciplinary design approach able to handle the complexity of a relational system very sophisticated (ethical design) giving responsibility to the designers. Rights and responsibilities should be measured in each specific context of use, in each specific functions assigned to the robot and in each characteristics of the user to which it is addressed the service.

The interdisciplinary team of each specific robotics project must ask itself over and over again what will be the impact of design decisions on the individual user and on the community. In other words:

- How the project will change the future scenario? How the development and dissemination of robots could change the design approach? One example are the everyday robots, machines, that carry out activities of secondary importance compared to the main ethical issues.

  One thing is to think about the design solutions for everyday robots, other thing is to consider how their widespread of use in the near future will change the beliefs and the ways in which today them are designed. Just like is also important that the project team is aware that a design choice with little reason behind today, could produce critical situation spreading and multiplying itself;
- Persons who work in the field of the interaction design knows that this being a cross-discipline, when we study applications for an ambit, such as the automotive ones, is of great help to see what happens in the home automation, robotics and vice versa.

However, in case of machine learning, the response is more complex.

To define accurately these ethical requirements is necessary to define a multidisciplinary design approach that allows to handle the complexity of a very sophisticated relational system (ethics design). Rules of cohabitation able to govern human robots interactions must be necessarily formulated. Rights and duties should be measured in each environment of the use context, of the specific function assigned to the robot and of the uses characteristic for which the service is addressed.

The interdisciplinary project team has to share these premises and constantly wonder about what will be the impacts of design choices on social system. To get into the critical dimension of the robotic project, looking only at the experts skills is limited. Others aspects on which it is required to refer are:

1- **predict future scenarios**: nowadays the everyday robots are involved in secondary importance actions compared to the main ethical issues; but one thing is to think about design solutions for today, other thing is to consider how the wide spread of use of robots in the near future is going to change the beliefs about how robotics design is done today. Multiplying low incentivized choices today can be devastating for the future.

2- **understating how society is using the technology** in general sense (ubiquitous computing) and analyse people behaviours in different fields other than robotics: who works in the field of interaction design knows that this is a cross discipline, car applications, for example are developed looking also to other area of scout like appliance or mobile phone market.

4 Ethics Design: An Approach

As described earlier, the concept of roboethics arises from the robot has cognitive system which makes it free to think and act within the sphere of use. But if the robot has no decisional power, who has to take care of the ethical aspects of its actions? In this case, during the design phase it is necessary to envisage the repercussions of use of robotic systems with regard to the analysed cultural context.

Therefore it means to adopt a methodological approach to the project that is able to ménage a scenario made by:

- Context of use
- User Typology and needs
- Technological benchmarking

During the first phase of project approach it is necessary to define the cultural weight of the operation that is going to be designed. All the skills useful for define the material aspects of the context of use, come from the architecture research field methodology. Through the cultural background of the architects it is possible to establish and build relationships between the robotic activities (both service and product) and the physics space [3]. Once defined the characteristics space context in which the robot is going to be used, it is necessary to define the needs of the potential user. Cognitive ergonomists, are able in this phase to predict and measure the user needs by the understanding of the man behaviour. The phase of transformation of the needs into physical or digital interface solutions has to be made by Designers. In the final step of the approach with a technological benchmarking it is possible to study and define: the strength points and the weak point of the concept, and even their physical realization.

After this analysis, the quality of the project is to be further evaluated according to the following ethical principles:

- Not to be into competition with human work and do not replace it
- Do not cause damage to the psycho-physical people using it
- Do not violate the privacy
- Do not interfer with the physical environment in which they operates.

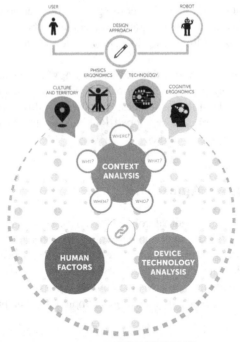

MULTIDISCIPLINARY APPROACH

Scheme 2. Methodology approach

5   Experimentation Scenario

The Virgil project [11] developed with the ethics design approach, born from the scope to not produce any one of the cases mentioned at the end of the previous paragraph.

It is the result of collaboration between experts from various disciplines (robotics, computer science, telecommunications, vision science, marketing, design) that have worked on the profile of the stakeholders and the cultural context /space.

Starting point was the benchmarking applications in robotics museum, which include two types of activities for the robot:

- Exploration;
- Museum guide support.

From the point of view of museum exploration, treated subjects include the remote exploration of the museum and the use of a robotics guide as a substitution of a Museum Guide. An example of this last case is the Robina [16] project (2007) at the Toyota Kaikan museum exhibition (Tokyo, Japan), which a robot valet it has been used for receive the visitors in the museum spaces.

The project, definitely audacious on the innovation side, however has not had so much success and it has been abandoned because of the difficulty of interaction between users and robots. The technological machine has been considered aseptic and empathy not comparable at the relationship with a human museum guide.

From the ethical point of view the idea to replace human labour with a techno-logical appliance that could decrease the cultural level of the experience and could become the museum visit more banal and repetitive, should be considered a mistake of approach to the problem.

Much more interesting in these terms is the Norio [15] project (2013) at the Orion Castle (Mont S. Michel, France). In this case the robot is used as an avatar to allow disabled people to visit places otherwise inaccessible because of their physical limit.

However, the robot structure and its movement limits have led to a hard infra-structuring of the museum with raised platforms, difficult to accept into a precious architecture museum. Also this design choice can be seen as an ethical error, because it would disfigure the artistic heritage of the museum.

After Dark [1] (2014), the project activated by the Tate Gallery in London offers new emotional experiences to the visit. Upon reservation, the "rover" is driven in the dark of night by the user remotely. The uniqueness of the night tour is beyond the ethical issues, because it permits to increase the attractiveness of the Museum: this is an ethical goal [5].

The other area of scouting found in the benchmarking analysis is the use of the robot as support at the Museum Guide. The use of robots in these terms is ethically acceptable because it does not remove away the job of the Guide; indeed, it provides a greater communication opportunity with the visitors.

An example is CSIRO [9] (2013), proposed by the National Museum in Acton (Australia): here the robot follows the Guide Museum as a valet, and thanks to a video device allows to present to the visitors a deepening multimedia content on museum's exhibited collections.

In compliance with the ethical guidelines mentioned in the previous paragraph, Virgil is a service robot designed to explore museum spaces temporarily not accessible (for security reasons, for restoration and cataloging of works in progress) and also to be a valet for the Museum Guide. This activity relates to the heritage of the Royal Residences of the Savoy family in Piedmont (Italy).

The project, not substitutive of human labour, provide a valuable support tool for the competence of the Museum Guide and also aims to connect the visitors in a cultural network that starts from the Castle of Racconigi and moves through other artistic /architectural sites with the support of the cloud technology.

The interdisciplinary working team has worked on different aspects of service robotics, with focus on telepresence, where aspects of the robot's hardware architecture blend with those of software digital information and with those of cognitive ergo-nomics, as the interaction man- machine - man, but first the service design and the machine then.

The activity began with work on the critical matters that the Cultural Association, which managed the experimentation venue, has identified:

- discontinuous affluence flows of visitors;
- lack of new attractions;
- not visitable spaces.

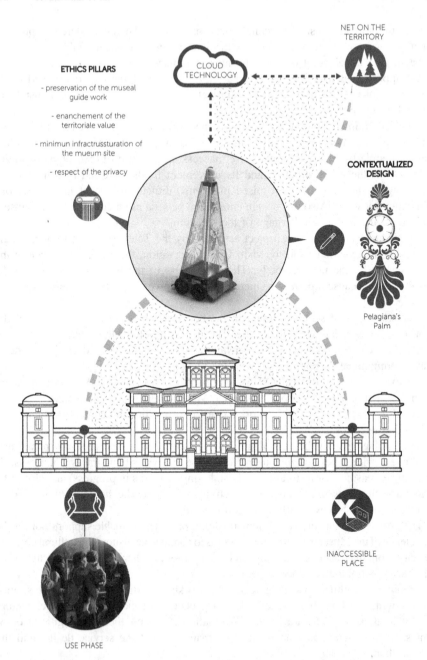

Scheme 3. Activity general scheme

The physical design of the product had its share in this trial: in addition to fulfilling requirements physical /mechanical (stability and lightness), Virgil seems to belong from ever to the museum: it integrates with the environment through transparent materials and dresses with decorations typical of this museum site.

Virgil is to be considered an ethical design project because:

- It respects the privacy of visitors (not detect the presence and does not disclose information about the person visiting);
- It safeguards the operator museum (indeed, is a new tool professional);
- It enhances the identity of the place through its design, wearing artistics decorations typical of the Castle);
- It doesn't need infrastructures because it has been equipped with advanced internal sensors.

Beyond that, it is thought about some possible upgrade using as term of comparison the virtual tour services with which Virgil could compete.

Considering the widespread of virtual tour unethical, because remote visit might weaken the physical attractiveness of the museum, it was thought a direct interaction between visitors and robots to enhance the attraction of the museum site. Therefore today the study about to use Virgil as a tool for cultural game (something close to a cultural treasure hunt) is in development.

Actually the Virgil robot is operative and in experimentation phase.

6 Conclusions

Consider the robotics science like a visionary field has played a key role for the society in terms of innovation. But we know that this is not equivalent to the progress and human development. They are different things, as we know that over time there have been innovations that may not have been positive for the progress of society.

However, we must not be afraid of technological innovation in an ethical sense; you just need to understand its true meaning. The innovation should be distinguished from the new. The novelty is the new vision in the short term and follows one another quickly. Innovation, the real one, is rather slow. In fact, one can speak of innovation when it has repercussions on the change of the system; in other words, when will be note its permanence in time and the repetition of its model.

So, push the research on the actions of the robot thinking is useful to society. But, to be considered an ethical process, it is necessary that the wins are subject to a process of discussion and sharing, in which two are the main players:

- The roboethic design team, which must be necessarily multidisciplinary character so that the achievements of a discipline are immediately and before being released publicly, subject to the judgment of other disciplines;
- The user man, that needs to be involved in cognitive tests and into user experiences in large numbers, because many times from these testing activities emerge unforeseeable behaviours that are able to direct the research in new directions.

References

1. After dark project website. http://www.tate.org.uk
2. Beer, J.M., Prakash, A., Mizner, T., Wendy, R.: Understanding robot acceptance. Technical report HFA- TR – 1103, Georgia Institute of Technology (2011)
3. Bistagnino, L.: Systemic design: designing the productive and environmental sustainability. Slow Food Editors, Bra (CN) (2011)
4. Breazeal, C.: Toward sociable robots. Robot. Auton. Syst. **42**, 167–175 (2003). Elsevier
5. Brown, M.: Robots to roam tate britain at night. The Guardian (2014)
6. Casiddu, N.: Human centered robotic design. Alinea Editrice, Firenze (2011)
7. Chiusi, F.: Trans umano, la trionferà, L'Espresso, 06 febbraio 2014
8. Gaggi, M.: E il robot prepara coktails e fa la guerra, Corriere della Sera, La lettura 26 gennaio 2014
9. Csiro robot project website. http://www.csiro.au
10. Germak, C.: Man at the center of the project. Design for a new humanism. Umberto. Allemandi & C, Torino (2008)
11. Germak C.: From the interview of Strappavecchia M.C., La Robotica nei Musei. L'Indro. http://www.lindro.it/0-cultura/2014-11-17/158271-robotica-musei. Accessed 17 Nov 2014
12. Harrison, B.: Inconvenient fiction. Yale University Press, New Haven and London (1991)
13. Hooker, J.: Busisness ethics and rational choice. Pearson Prentice Hall, Upper Saddle River (2010)
14. Nourbakhsh, I.: Robot futures. Massachusetts Institute of Technology press, Cambridge (2013)
15. Norio robot project website. http://www.oiron.fr
16. Robina project webssite. http://www.toyota-global.com/
17. Suvin, D.: Metamorphoses of science fiction. Yale University Press, New Haven (1979)
18. Veruggio, G.: The brith of roboethics. In: IEEE International Conference on Robotics and Automation Workshop on Robo-Ethics, Barcelona (2005)

An Approach for a Negotiation Model Inspired on Social Networks

João Carneiro[1(✉)], Goreti Marreiros[1], and Paulo Novais[2]

[1] GECAD – Knowledge Engineering and Decision Support Group,
Institute of Engineering – Polytechnic of Porto, Porto, Portugal
{jomrc,mgt}@isep.ipp.pt
[2] CCTC – Computer Science and Technology Center,
University of Minho, Braga, Portugal
pjon@di.uminho.pt

Abstract. Supporting group decision-making in ubiquitous contexts is a complex task that needs to deal with a large amount of factors to be successful. Here we propose an approach for a negotiation model to support the group decision-making process specially designed for ubiquitous contexts. We propose a new look into this problematic, considering and defining strategies to deal with important points such as the type of attributes in the multi-criteria problem and agents' reasoning. Our model uses a social networking logic due to the type of communication employed by the agents as well as to the type of relationships they build as the interactions occur. Our approach intends to support the ubiquitous group decision-making process in a similar way to the real process, which simultaneously preserves the amount and quality of intelligence generated in face-to-face meetings and is adapted to be used in a ubiquitous context.

Keywords: Group decision support systems · Ubiquitous computing · Automatic negotiation · Social networks · Multi-agent systems

1 Introduction

Many existing Group Decision Support Systems (GDSS) prototypes use automatic negotiation models as a strategy to support the decision [1–4]. Argumentation-based negotiation models are one of the most used and best suited automatic negotiation technics to support the decision-making [5, 6]. It is consensual that the possibility of justifying a request using an argument facilitates reaching an agreement or solution [6, 7]. Albeit all the recognized advantages in the use of argumentation models in decision-making, and the time necessary to study argumentative models in the area of computer science is traced back to a few decades, the truth is that such models have not yet been embraced by organizations. The existing models are barely adaptable to the business world reality, have difficulty in reflecting the decision-making natural process, and create a certain discomfort in their use by decision-makers. It is also important to note that the actual evaluation of the argumentation models is not the one an organization would want to use. The fact an argumentation model gives a solution in lesser rounds or in lesser seconds than another, are not the most relevant points for whom is concerned about using

© Springer International Publishing Switzerland 2015
J. Bajo et al. (Eds.): PAAMS 2015 Workshops, CCIS 524, pp. 409–420, 2015.
DOI: 10.1007/978-3-319-19033-4_36

a mechanism to potentiate the decision quality. Maybe because of that, business intelligence techniques have a much higher growth than GDSS.

In literature there are various negotiation models adapted to group decision-making [8–12]. However, the existing models are limited to very specific contexts and do not support the decision-maker in the smarter way. Looking for studies on argumentation-based negotiation models adapted to group decision support systems, the results are practically inexistent. The few existing results are old [11, 13] and if some seemed promising in the way they could be adapted to this area [14, 15], the works that came next followed most of the times another path (even with some of them remaining within decision support). Forgetting negotiation models for a moment, we find that even the existing argumentation approaches are not oriented to problems that include multiple agents simultaneously. It is even possible to verify that in the most recent argumentation studies, authors with more than a decade of work, point the inclusion of multiple agents as a future expansion for their work [16, 17]. When agents have "one-to-one" communication the process is simple. However, things become more difficult when an agent receives messages from multiple agents. Another important issue is how most authors test their argumentation models, the majority opt for the "seller-buyer", example [5, 6, 18–21], which has a type of dialogue much oriented to that kind of problem.

Defining a type of adaptable dialogue for use in an argumentation-based negotiation model which has the objective to support group decision-making is a complex task. Walton [22] believes that dialogues should be classified based in their primary objective, and presents six major dialogue classes for that: inquisition, persuasion, negotiation, deliberation, demand for information and eristic. However, what is the most adaptable dialogue for a group of people, employees of the same company, whose common objective is to solve a certain problem, but at the same time satisfy their own objectives? Maybe a mix of several types of dialogue could be the solution, or the creation of a new class. This makes it very complex to adapt an argumentation theory to this scenario.

We believe that part of the failure of group decision support systems developed until today is due to the perspective used to analyse the problem and how they have been evaluated.

Here we propose a theoretical negotiation model that intends to support the ubiquitous group decision making process similarly to a real process, which simultaneously preserves the amount and quality of intelligence generated in face-to-face meetings and is adapted to be used in a ubiquitous context. To achieve this, a model that uses a social networking logic is proposed. The model is based on the agents' type of communication and type of relationships that they build as the interactions occur.

With the inclusion of the work we have been developing [23, 24] in the model here presented we believe it will be possible to enhance the decision quality.

The rest of the paper is organized as follows: in the next section is presented our approach, where the theoretical ideas for the negotiation model are described, and the attribute types' definition and the agents' reasoning are presented. Finally, some conclusions are taken in Sect. 3, along with the work to be done hereafter.

2 Proposed Model

The model here proposed is theoretical and results from the study conducted by the authors in the last years in this area. It seems clear that despite decades of study in the GDSS area they have had acceptance difficulties by the firms. On the other hand, the business intelligence techniques that came from decision support systems have had a great acceptance in the last years. We believe our approach can eventually be a solution to the problems that are leading to the difficulty in accepting the GDSS. Thus, in this section we present our theoretical negotiation model, as well as we identify some of the points we consider as problematic, proposing solutions and explaining how our approach can solve those problems. Besides its clear objective, this proposal aims to be an incentive to reflection for the researchers working in this area.

Much of the existing literature that uses agents for negotiation purposes [25–27] mainly considers scenarios where the agents are fully competitive, in which each agent seeks to achieve its own goals [28, 29] or fully collaborative, where all seek to find a solution that is satisfactory to all [30–32]. In the case of a GDSS that aims to support an organization's decision group to make decisions, this issue should be viewed with other sensitivity. Considering a system will have agents, where each agent represents a decision-maker, they should be a mix of competition and collaboration. We could consider that as all the agents are part of the same organization, they should be collaborative in that all seek to achieve the best possible decision for the firm. However, for human nature reasons, that would lose certain existing advantages in the context of meeting. Although "all wear the same sweater", in a real context the decision-makers also seek to achieve their own goals. This happens for several reasons, but in this situation we are interested in highlighting that this happens for conviction reasons. The decision-maker considers in his logic that his preferred alternative is the best solution to solve the problem and will defend his alternative until arguments that make him consider a more benefic alternative are used. It is this behavior that enriches the meetings, introduces new knowledge and allows higher quality decisions to be attained. This is the behavior we intend to include in our negotiation model and that we consider to be important to introduce in this kind of systems.

The negotiation model here proposed is inspired by the communication logic used in social networks. The main idea follows two main types of communication: Public Communication (PC) in the form of public posts, and Private Communication (PrC) in the form of private chat. The visual idea of the communication form is much alike to the one used for instance in Facebook®. The fact of considering the way of communication used in social networks a good approach to serve as inspiration for this work topic is related to three main factors: the agents communicate in a context similar to the one practiced by the decision-makers in face-to-face meetings, the environment and the agents communication/interaction is easily understood by the participants (decision-makers), and the possibility to use the techniques already developed to study the relationships (in the social networks literature).

Figure 1 represents the two different types of communication. The agent is part of a single PC but can have several PrC simultaneously.

Public Conversation   **Private Conversations**

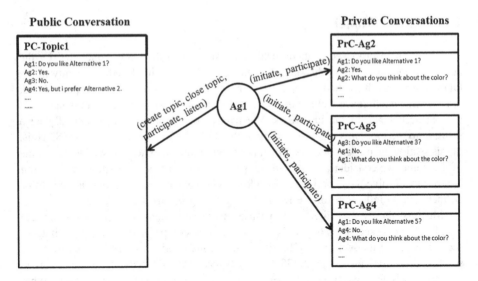

Fig. 1. The two different types of communication

A PC is an open conversation and its functioning reflects the type of dialogue practiced by the decision-makers in a real context. Sometimes public conversations or conversations between multiple agents are mentioned, but in practice what happens is that there is a group of agents that exchanges messages where each message has a single receptor. In the case of PC, messages are exchanged as happens in reality, where a group of people are seating at a table and even when a message has only one recipient it can be heard by all. This allows the agents to gather information and create relationships through the messages they listen, even when they are not directed to them. In PC agents can only address one topic at a time, i.e., there is any participant agent at a certain time when there is not an open topic that creates a topic about a certain theme. As mentioned, there can only be an open topic at a time. Any agent can propose the closure of a topic, which will be closed if no agent has anything else to say. Obviously all agents can participate in a PC and read all the messages.

PrC are all the private conversations of each participant agent, and as mentioned, an agent can keep several PrC simultaneously. At most, it can have a PrC with each of the other agents. An agent can initiate a PrC with any other agent provided it does not already exist. A PrC can stay open during the entire process without the need to be terminated. The existence of PrC are an advantage over the actual meetings that do not allow simultaneous private conversations during the process.

In literature (to the best of our knowledge) in the context of support for group decision-making the agents use requests and questions as a way of communication. The communication allows them to use strategies to persuade the other agents as well as to gather the necessary information to reason about the problem. In addition to questions and requests, in our approach we introduce the concept of statement. The statement is a way of communication that will be used by the agents to demonstrate their points of view. This means agents can share information or perform indirect persuasion through statements. For instance, Agent1 can say "to me consumption is the most important attribute". For example, this action can make Agent2, which considers Agent1 as the most expert in the issue that is being discussed, to redefine the importance he gives to the consumption attribute. Another situation that may occur with this statement is that other agents can create a relationship with a certain strength (see Sect. 2.2) with Agent1 because they identify themselves with his point of view. As mentioned earlier, it is essential to give prominence to the decision process since strategies that propose solutions based on the problem's initial settings lose the process's richness existent in real meetings. Negotiation automation should continue to allow the existence of two fundamental questions: change of opinion/problem reformulation by the decision-makers when they realize/agree with the arguments presented by other interveners, and learning with the assessment of the process by the decision-makers. Statements, requests and questions can be used with and without the inclusion of arguments and can be used in PC and PrC. Counter-arguments and acceptance or rejection responses are also made through those three types. A communication is defined as follows:

$$Type(Sender, Receiver, Message, Args, CC)$$

Where:

- *Type*: Is the type of message, which can be a statement, message or question. For example, a response to a request or question is always of the type statement;
- *Sender*: Is the agent that communicates/sends the message;
- *Receiver*: Is the agent or group of agents that receive the message. In the case of PC there can be an addressed agent although all agents can read the message. In PrC there is always just one recipient;
- *Message*: Is the message that is of type *Type*;
- *Args*: Are the set of arguments used to justify the message;
- *CC*: Is the conversation's identification code where the message will be read.

2.1 Attribute Types

Our model is specifically designed to handle with multi-criteria problems. It is not our goal to include any type of natural language mechanism in our prototype. However, we believe it is possible and essential that the agents understand what is happening in the "conversation". For that it is necessary to make a proper definition of type of attributes used.

Let us imagine that a group of decision-makers need to decide on a new car to add to the company's fleet. Considering one of the attributes as the car's consumption and that it was defined as a minimization numerical attribute, if Agent1 says "for me the most important decision factor is consumption" it will allow other agents to argue with Agent1 saying "accept alternative C because it has the lowest consumption". As it is possible to understand this strategy allows the agents to have the ability to perceive a lot of different information. Another major advantage of this approach is the easiness an agent has in generating perceptible reports for the real participant. Besides being able to present data that supports the decision (for instance, charts, tables, statistics, etc.) it also allows to present the argumentation between the agents and the motive that led the agents to propose a certain decision in a perceptible way.

The types of attributes considered can be visualized in Fig. 2. Two main types of attributes can be considered:

- Objective: objective attributes are comparable with each other. This means that in the case of the car consumption, if car1 has a lower consumption than car2 and the consumption is a minimization numerical attribute, car1's consumption is invariably better than car2's consumption. The values of the objective attributes are always absolutely true. For instance, if the air conditioning attribute of an alternative is true then the possibility of that car not to have air conditioning cannot be considered. There are three types of objective attributes:
  - Boolean: are used in situations where the attribute can be classified by only two values, e.g., on/off, yes/no, 0/1, true/false; in this case the most advantageous situation must be specified (true or false). However, this specification is not mandatory. The situation that offers a greater value is considered to be advantageous even if that value does not suits the problem to be solved. Considering the same car that with and without air conditioning costs exactly the same price, the fact of having air conditioning is an advantage, even assuming that for health reasons it will not be used;
  - Numerical: the numerical type attributes are used to define measurable attributes, for example: consumption, height, width and distance. This type of attribute is defined as maximization or minimization attribute. However, this specification is not mandatory. For instance, we "always" want to minimize costs, but on the other hand, we always want to maximize the profits. However, we may not be interested in minimizing or maximizing an employer's height.
  - Classificatory: this type of attribute is used to specify attributes with a defined and recognized classification. For instance, we can use this type of attribute to specify a car's safety. However, this classification should not be made by someone without credentials. An expert or a classification that has been published in a reference location can be used to make this classification. The classification will function as a scale.
- Subjective: subjective attributes allow agents to perceive what issues do not make sense to argue. For example, it will not make sense to argue a car is better than another because of the color. The fact an agent prefers a certain color (in a certain context) is considered by this type of attribute as a personal taste about which I cannot argue. Other examples of subjective attributes (always depends on the context) are: car design, food taste, beauty, sound quality, etc.

We believe this proposal on the types of attributes for the multi-criterion problem is simple but effective. This way it is possible to set a lot of problems with a strategy that allows agents to understand about what they are arguing. We believe this approach makes the agents as well as the dialogues more intelligent allowing richer and perceptible outputs.

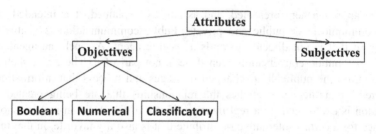

Fig. 2. Attributes' types

2.2 Agents' Reasoning

To Jennings and Wooldridge an intelligent agent is capable of flexible autonomous actions in order to meet its design objectives [33]. To them, an intelligent agent needs to be: responsive, proactive and social (for further information about these definitions see [33]). To Wooldridge what makes a rational agent is its autonomy [34]. In the last decades we have seen many examples in literature that address the topic of intelligent agents [35–37]. It is also known that there are agents that perform the same task more intelligent than others. However, if it is known that in the case of humans the reactive decision is processed by the brain in a different location of the proactive decision, in the case of agents or computational systems the proactive decision can exist but always in a simulated way.

On the subject of intelligent and rational agents, there is a relevant point that merits consideration regarding the group decision-making support systems. Let's suppose we have a system that rapidly can propose a solution to a certain problem according to the decision-makers preferences. It is obvious that this indicator is not enough to know whether the system is good or bad. The proposed solutions can always be unacceptable for the decision-makers making the system useless. However, let us consider the system can always propose acceptable solutions for the decision-makers ending up to have a great impact on a particular organization. Taking into account these data it would be hypothetically possible to say this system had quality. However, this may not be true. When someone wants to develop a negotiation model to adapt to a group decision-making support system there is an important factor that normally is forgotten. In the case of face-to-face meetings the decision-makers have time to think over the subject during the process, and often they start the meeting with certain beliefs which are then changed when they hear the others' opinion and argumentations. Sometimes our opinion changes when new knowledge is demonstrated to us or when the arguments used invalidate our logic. This fact is what makes face-to-face meetings the choice to make important decisions, and no system is still prepared to deal with this situation. The way models and systems are designed make this crucial part of a real meeting to be lost. This led us to think that research on negotiation models for group decision-making support systems needs to start concerning about that. It is important the agent has the capability to seek to understand why other agents have other preferences, and not only seek to achieve his goals forgetting that on the other side there may be an agent that can change of opinion without sharing the why of his initial convictions with the group.

In the approach here presented, and as already explained, it is intended that the agents communicate in public and private. Public communication is visible by all agents even if it is not directed towards a specific agent. As such, an agent will be listening to a public conversation even if he is not part of it. The agent shall gather information on the publically exchanged messages and process that information. The idea here is that the agent studies the relationships that are being created as the information is exchanged. In a real meeting, if one of the decision-makers shows his preference for a certain alternative or attribute that is also my favorite, in that instant a connection between us is created because we have that in common. Those created ties or relationships can be analyzed by social network algorithms in literature [38, 39]. The idea is to create a new link (or update it) in a directed weighted graph (Fig. 3) every time an agent reads a public message.

By creating the graph the agent can make several analyses depending on the algorithms used. The agent can create multiple graphs on different topics where the weight of the connection is related to the graph's topic. This will allow the agent to understand, even without interacting directly with every agent, which agents are the closest in certain ideas as well as the hypothetical groups that are in agreement. New arguments can be generated from the graph analysis, for instance, it is possible to understand if there is a majority towards an alternative, among other more complex analyses.

Another topic that also will be part of the agents' reasoning and whose advantages have already been previously addressed is the capability to seek to understand the why of the other agents' preferences. If we think clearly this approaches the agents' reasoning of what happens in reality: a decision-maker seeks to understand the why of the other decision-makers' opinion. Again, this will allow to generate a richer argumentation as well as to generate more useful and elaborated reports to be analyzed by the decision-maker. The agent will have the ability to understand why by analyzing and questioning the other agents on the evaluation and importance they give to the attributes. In the example of buying a car, if an agent gives much importance to the consumption and that agent has a preferred car which is the one with the lowest consumption, another agent can deduce that this is why he chooses that alternative. This will allow him to tell the agent to switch to his preference of another car which has a slightly higher consumption but is much cheaper, arguing that the difference he will spend on fuel is insignificant.

Finally, the agents will have the ability to analyze the prediction they make on their satisfaction, that is, the prediction on their perception of the decision quality at a given moment, taking into account the outcome they are predicting to happen. For that, they will use our model on satisfaction analysis previously published by us (for further information read [23, 24]). The fact they have the ability to analyze the final satisfaction of the decision-maker they represent makes them more intelligent. This allows them to know when they have to stop defending their favorite alternative to bet on another also favorite (although less) that will give them a greater final satisfaction than another they are predicting to be chosen. The model also allows to predict the group final satisfaction when their goal is a high satisfaction for all the elements. Satisfaction analysis will also be useful for blockage situations and will help the agents to better understand whether or not to accept requests from other agents.

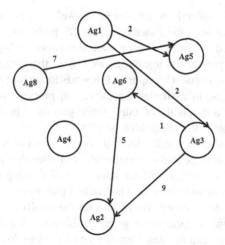

Fig. 3. Example of a directed weighted graph of relationships between agents regarding a subject

3 Conclusions and Future Work

The group decision support systems have been studied in the last three decades. However, after all this time, they are still facing problems in being accepted by the industry. Regardless the amount of artificial intelligence techniques applied, they still have too many limitations, especially in situations with time/space constraints. Furthermore, there are big challenges regarding the processes used to evaluate and validate these systems. The used evaluation processes allows to have good scientific results in certain cases but do not transmit enough confidence so the industry can understand all the potential of these systems.

In order to support the group decision-making in situations with time/space constraints, the GDSS evolved for the so-called Ubiquitous GDSS (UbiGDSS). They are the ultimate cleavage of GDSS. With the appearance of UbiGDSS some other problems appeared, for instance, how to: overcome the lack of human-interaction, understand the decision quality perception in the perspective of each decision-maker and overcome the communication issues.

One of the usual techniques in UbiGDSS is automated negotiation. The idea behind automated negotiation, as for instance argumentation, is allowing agents to find a solution through an intelligent dialogue. However, there are no specific defined dialogues for these situations, plus there are only a few argumentation-based negotiation models proposed in literature where the majority was defined before the appearance of UbiGDSS. Going deeply, we can also verify that even the argumentation theories have difficulty in adapting to this scenario.

Here we propose a theoretical negotiation model specifically planned for ubiquitous decision-making support systems. More particularly, we propose new approaches on topics such as the type of attributes in a multi-criteria problem and the agents' reasoning. In addition to these specific proposals, this topic is addressed under a new look and approach. Multiple reflections are shared, as well as analysed issues that in the opinion of authors have been the cause of the GDSS problems.

The model proposed in this paper uses a social networking logic due to the type of communication employed by the agents, as well as to the type of relationships they build as the interactions occur. Our approach intends to support the ubiquitous group decision-making process, in a similar way to a real process, which simultaneously preserves the quantity and quality of intelligence generated in face-to-face meetings and is adapted to be used in a ubiquitous context.

As for future work there are still a lot of things that need to be done. We will work on the creation of the argumentation framework, and after that we will define all the concepts behind the dialogues. At a later stage we will develop a new prototype that will include all the topics addressed here and others previously published. We believe that in the end we can draw strong conclusions on the results obtained from using this new look over automatic negotiation in group decision-making support systems.

As a final remark, we can say that there is a lot of work to do to adapt GDSS to this new Era. This is a very complex area and involves so many different other areas, but working in this field is so much exciting and can result in outstanding results.

Acknowledgements. This work is part-funded by ERDF - European Regional Development Fund through the COMPETE Programme (operational programme for competitiveness) and by National Funds through the FCT - Fundação para a Ciência e a Tecnologia (Portuguese Foundation for Science and Technology) within project FCOMP-01-0124-FEDER-028980 (PTDC/EEISII/1386/2012) and SFRH/BD/89697/2012.

References

1. Herrera, F., Herrera-Viedma, E., Verdegay, J.: A rational consensus model in group decision making using linguistic assessments. Fuzzy Sets Syst. **88**, 31–49 (1997)
2. Maznevski, M.L.: Understanding our differences: performance in decision-making groups with diverse members. Hum. Relat. **47**, 531–552 (1994)
3. Moreno-Jiménez, J., Aguarón, J., Escobar, M.: The core of consistency in AHP-group decision making. Group Decis. Negot. **17**, 249–265 (2008)
4. Xu, Z.: An automatic approach to reaching consensus in multiple attribute group decision making. Comput. Ind. Eng. **56**, 1369–1374 (2009)
5. Rahwan, I., Ramchurn, S.D., Jennings, N.R., Mcburney, P., Parsons, S., Sonenberg, L.: Argumentation-based negotiation. Knowl. Eng. Rev. **18**, 343–375 (2003)
6. Marey, O., Bentahar, J., Asl, E.K., Mbarki, M., Dssouli, R.: Agents' uncertainty in argumentation-based negotiation: classification and implementation. Proc. Comput. Sci. **32**, 61–68 (2014)
7. Bonzon, E., Dimopoulos, Y., Moraitis, P.: Knowing each other in argumentation-based negotiation. In: Proceedings of the 11th International Conference on Autonomous Agents and Multiagent Systems, vol. 3, pp. 1413–1414. International Foundation for Autonomous Agents and Multiagent Systems (2012)
8. Ito, T., Shintani, T.: Persuasion among agents: an approach to implementing a group decision support system based on multi-agent negotiation. In: Proceedings of the 5th International Joint Conference on Artificial Intelligence (IJCAI 1997), pp. 592–599. Citeseer (1997)

9. Kudenko, D., Bauer, M., Dengler, D.: Group decision making through mediated discussions. In: Brusilovsky, P., Corbett, A.T., de Rosis, F. (eds.) UM 2003. LNCS, vol. 2702, pp. 238–247. Springer, Heidelberg (2003)

10. Gordon, T.F., Karacapilidis, N.: The zeno argumentation framework. In: Proceedings of the 6th International Conference on Artificial Intelligence and Law (ICAIL 1997), pp. 10–18. ACM (1997)

11. Karacapilidis, N., Papadias, D.: Computer supported argumentation and collaborative decision making: the HERMES system. Inf. Syst. 26, 259–277 (2001)

12. Marreiros, G., Santos, R., Ramos, C., Neves, J.: Context aware emotional model for group decision making (2010)

13. Karacapilidis, N., Papadias, D.: A group decision and negotiation support system for argumentation based reasoning. In: Antoniou, G., Truszczyński, M., Ghose, A.K. (eds.) PRICAI-WS 1996. LNCS, vol. 1359, pp. 188–205. Springer, Heidelberg (1998)

14. Kraus, S., Sycara, K., Evenchik, A.: Reaching agreements through argumentation: a logical model and implementation. Artif. Intell. 104, 1–69 (1998)

15. Sierra, C., Jennings, N.R., Noriega, P., Parsons, S.: A framework for argumentation-based negotiation. In: Rao, A., Singh, M.P., Wooldridge, M.J. (eds.) ATAL 1997. LNCS, vol. 1365, pp. 177–192. Springer, Heidelberg (1998)

16. Fan, X., Toni, F.: Decision making with assumption-based argumentation. In: Black, E., Modgil, S., Oren, N. (eds.) TAFA 2013. LNCS, vol. 8306, pp. 127–142. Springer, Heidelberg (2014)

17. Fan, X., Toni, F., Mocanu, A., Williams, M.: Dialogical two-agent decision making with assumption-based argumentation. In: Proceedings of the 2014 International Conference on Autonomous Agents and Multi-Agent Systems, pp. 533–540. International Foundation for Autonomous Agents and Multiagent Systems (2014)

18. Karunatillake, N.C., Jennings, N.R.: Is it worth arguing? In: Rahwan, I., Moraitis, P., Reed, C. (eds.) ArgMAS 2004. LNCS (LNAI), vol. 3366, pp. 234–250. Springer, Heidelberg (2005)

19. Ramchurn, S.D., Sierra, C., Godo, L., Jennings, N.R.: Negotiating using rewards. Artif. Intell. 171, 805–837 (2007)

20. De Melo, C.M., Carnevale, P., Gratch, J.: The effect of expression of anger and happiness in computer agents on negotiations with humans. In: The 10th International Conference on Autonomous Agents and Multiagent Systems, vol. 3, pp. 937–944. International Foundation for Autonomous Agents and Multiagent Systems (2011)

21. El-Sisi, A.B., Mousa, H.M.: Argumentation based negotiation in multiagent system. In: 2012 Seventh International Conference on Computer Engineering & Systems (ICCES), pp. 261–266. IEEE (2012)

22. Walton, D.: Commitment in Dialogue: Basic Concepts of Interpersonal Reasoning. SUNY Press, Albany (1995)

23. Carneiro, J., Santos, R., Marreiros, G., Novais, P.: Overcoming the lack of human-interaction in ubiquitous group decision support systems, vol. 49, pp. 116-124 (2014)

24. Carneiro, J., Santos, R., Marreiros, G., Novais, P.: understanding decision quality through satisfaction. In: Corchado, J.M., Bajo, J., Kozlak, J., Pawlewski, P., Molina, J.M., Gaudou, B., Julian, V., Unland, R., Lopes, F., Hallenborg, K., Garcia Teodoro, P. (eds.) PAAMS 2014. CCIS, vol. 430, pp. 368–377. Springer, Heidelberg (2014)

25. Huang, P., Sycara, K.: A computational model for online agent negotiation. In: System Sciences 2002 Proceedings of the 35th Annual Hawaii International Conference on HICSS, pp. 438–444 IEEE (2002)

26. Kakas, A., Moraitis, P.: Adaptive agent negotiation via argumentation. In: Proceedings of the Fifth International Joint Conference on Autonomous Agents and Multiagent Systems, pp. 384–391. ACM (2006)

27. Rahwan, I., Sonenberg, L., Jennings, N.R., McBurney, P.: Stratum: a methodology for designing heuristic agent negotiation strategies. Appl. Artif. Intell. **21**, 489–527 (2007)
28. Santos, R., Marreiros, G., Ramos, C., Neves, J., Bulas-Cruz, J.: Using personality types to support argumentation. In: McBurney, P., Rahwan, I., Parsons, S., Maudet, N. (eds.) ArgMAS 2009. LNCS, vol. 6057, pp. 292–304. Springer, Heidelberg (2010)
29. Rosaci, D.: Trust measures for competitive agents. Knowl. Based Syst. **28**, 38–46 (2012)
30. Yen, J., Yin, J., Ioerger, T.R., Miller, M.S., Xu, D., Volz, R.A.: Cast: collaborative agents for simulating teamwork. In: International Joint Conference on Artificial Intelligence, pp. 1135–1144. Lawrence Erlbaum Associates Ltd (2001)
31. Reicher, S., Haslam, S.A., Hopkins, N.: Social identity and the dynamics of leadership: leaders and followers as collaborative agents in the transformation of social reality. Leadersh. Q. **16**, 547–568 (2005)
32. Allen, J., Blaylock, N., Ferguson, G.: A problem solving model for collaborative agents. In: Proceedings of the First International Joint Conference on Autonomous Agents and Multiagent Systems: Part 2, pp. 774–781. ACM (2002)
33. Wooldridge, M., Jennings, N.R.: Intelligent agents: Theory and practice. Knowl. Eng. Rev. **10**, 115–152 (1995)
34. Wooldridge, M.J.: Reasoning About Rational Agents. MIT Press, Cambridge (2000)
35. Müller, J.P.: The Design of Intelligent Agents: A Layered Approach. Springer, Heidelberg (1996)
36. Sycara, K., Pannu, A., Williamson, M., Zeng, D., Decker, K.: Distributed intelligent agents. IEEE Intell. Syst. **11**, 36–46 (1996)
37. Jennings, N.R., Wooldridge, M.: Applications of intelligent agents. In: Agent Technology, pp. 3–28. Springer, Heidelberg (1998)
38. Borgatti, S.P.: Identifying sets of key players in a social network. Comput. Math. Organ. Theory **12**, 21–34 (2006)
39. Varlamis, I., Eirinaki, M., Louta, M.: A study on social network metrics and their application in trust networks. In: Advances in Social Networks Analysis and Mining (ASONAM), 2010 International Conference, pp. 168–175. IEEE (2010)

Author Index

Printed in the United States
By Bookmasters